# THE SCOTTISH TRADITION

R.G. Cant

# THE SCOTTISH TRADITION

*Essays in honour of*

## RONALD GORDON CANT

*edited by*

### G. W. S. BARROW

SCOTTISH ACADEMIC PRESS

1974

Published by
Scottish Academic Press Ltd,
25 Perth Street, Edinburgh EH3 5DW

Distributed by
Chatto and Windus Ltd,
40 William IV Street
London WC2N 4DF

SBN 7011 2039 8

St Andrews University Publications
No. LX

Printed in Great Britain by
R. & R. Clark Ltd, Edinburgh

# Editor's Preface

This volume has been planned and prepared by an Executive Committee consisting of M. Ash (Secretary), G. W. S. Barrow, J. K. Cameron (Chairman), T. I. Rae and R. N. Smart. The essays have been contributed by former students and a few other scholars, and they have been chosen to represent Ronald Cant's long-standing interests in scholarship and to illustrate their variety. The Committee would like to thank the Earl of Crawford and Balcarres for his Foreword, the contributors for their papers, and the subscribers for making publication possible. Thanks are also due to Mr Douglas Grant of the Scottish Academic Press for his help and advice.

# Abbreviations

*Wherever possible and appropriate, abbreviations have been standard-ised to conform to the* List of Abbreviated Titles of the Printed Sources of Scottish History to 1560 *published as a supplement to the* Scottish Historical Review *(1963). In Chapter 3* Kinninmonths *refers to 'The early charters of the family of Kinninmonth of that ilk', in D. A. Bullough and R. L. Storey,* The Study of Medieval Records *(Oxford, Clarendon Press, 1971).*

# Contents

# Ronald Cant

## by the Earl of Crawford and Balcarres

A cross-section of the character, quality and personality of Scottish life from east to west and through the centuries laid the foundation on which Ronald Cant has built his interests and achievements.

His father was educated in St Andrews at the Madras College and at the University, which he entered at the age of 15 and where he graduated in Arts, Science and Divinity. After serving as assistant at the East Parish Church of Aberdeen, he joined the Indian Ecclesiastical Establishment, became chaplain at Karachi and elsewhere, returning to Scotland for periodic furloughs and permanently in 1920, after which he held ministries first in West Lothian, later in Fife at Newburn and St Andrews, and finally at Creich, which became the family home.

His family came from Angus and in particular from the parishes of Mains and Strathmartine on the southern slopes of the Sidlaws where the name, recorded before 1400, is still localised. His ancestors included country merchants, farmers, lairds and craftsmen. His wife came from the west, where her father, descended from shipmasters at Greenock, merchants in Glasgow and farmers in Renfrewshire, was a minister. Both parents, influenced no doubt by their prolonged absence in the East, developed an exceptionally strong affection for Scotland and everything connected with the country, its landscape, people and their way of life, buildings, and in particular ecclesiastical history and architecture.

Ronald Cant's own earliest memories are not of his native India but of Aberdeen and its neighbourhood which had become the base of a much travelled family, to which his paternal grandfather had retired at the end of a military career and where relatives of both parents had made their home. He had been given the north-eastern names, Ronald Gordon, and has always felt a special identification with this part of Scotland, though his schooling was mainly at the Edinburgh Academy and his holidays were spent in the East Neuk of Fife. Here his interest in the history and antiquities of Scotland developed, and the desire formed to get to know the country as completely as possible: an ambition largely fulfilled. He covered most of the north-west Highlands on foot and, in recent years, has developed a deep interest in Orkney and Shetland.

At the age of 16 he matriculated in St Andrews University, partly because of his father's connection, partly because the family had now moved to Creich in Fife. He specialised in history, graduating in 1928 and continuing at Oriel College, Oxford, where he took his B.A. in 1932. After research work in Edinburgh, where he formed a life-long friendship of shared interests with William Beattie, already an outstanding authority on Scottish bibliography, he returned in 1935 as the only Lecturer in Medieval History in the University, a post he held till 1948 when he transferred to Scottish History, first as sole Lecturer and later, since 1954, as Reader. It would be interesting to discover how many chairs in other universities on both sides of the Atlantic he has been offered and refused but, as only he can answer a question which no one will ask, we shall never know. Perhaps he may have found the temptation less difficult to resist than others might have done: but his decisions were undoubtedly wise and Scotland has every reason for gratitude that St Andrews has remained the centre of his life, his interests, his work, and his scholarship.

This is made clear by Mr MacArthur's Bibliography which shows that in the many contributions between Ronald Cant's first published writing (1938) on 'The future of St Andrews: what preservation means' and one of the most recent, 'The development of the Burgh of St Andrews in the Middle Ages' (1971), few aspects, past or present, of the city have escaped his notice.

Although he has done important work for other ancient towns, Elgin, Dunkeld, Stirling and Aberdeen, as well as on more general Scottish historical subjects, the main concentration, consistently from first to last, has been on St Andrews, the Churches, the University and the Colleges, her history, buildings, people and character, but always viewed in the wider context of world history.

A layman cannot assess the value of this academic contribution, but he can enjoy and profit from it, because Ronald Cant writes with him no less than with fellow scholars in mind. The characteristic fact that his writings have a general as well as a specialist interest is among their chief and most welcome features. Similarly, the Bibliography shows how much of his energies has been devoted to stones as well as to parchment, to the practical no less than the theoretical aspects of preservation and to the local societies dedicated to this task who have always relied on his knowledge and experience. When in 1937 he was instrumental in founding the pioneer St Andrews Preservation Trust, parent of many similar bodies, there seemed to be little urgency in the matter, largely because our native Improvers were, as yet, slower than their English colleagues to discover the glittering private profits to be made from public destruction. But, though no one could have foreseen the post-war role of universities and national and local authorities in such matters, his writings (many of the most influential hidden in the annual reports of societies) show how early he became aware of and how consistently he has warned us of the dangers facing the character of our towns and villages or the affront to their personality by the destruction, through ignorance or greed, of the living records of our history. They cannot show his brilliant work for the Scottish preservation societies nor his influence, with the technical and practical help originally of such men as James Richardson and Ian Lindsay and now of Murray Jack and Hew Lorimer, or public opinion. They cannot show where he has failed in a city which since the war has suffered cruelly between its mutilated eastern and western boundaries: but throughout the Burgh many buildings which without his influence would have disappeared, still stand as living witnesses to our past history and to his work.

Related to this work of saving, modernising and giving a new life and purpose to the old buildings of the Kingdom was his part in founding such bodies as the Fife Folk Museum in Ceres and the Scottish Fisheries Museum in Anstruther: both in buildings scheduled for destruction. On a more 'official' level, he has served on the Boards of two great National Institutions, the National Library of Scotland and the National Museum of Antiquities, of which he has been a Trustee since its independence. There can be no more useful Trustee, or member of the Scottish Country Life Museum Trust, of the Historic Buildings Council for Scotland, or of the Committee on Listed Buildings, for no one has a wider general knowledge of these things. Since 1972 he has been a Vice-President of the Society of Antiquaries of Scotland and a member of the Advisory Committee of the Scottish National Portrait Gallery. The list sounds solemn: but no solemnity, pomposity, pretentiousness, or humbug can long survive his shafts. No meeting enlivened and stimulated by Ronald Cant can ever be dull. His common sense is matched by his sense of humour. If there is an answer, it is he more often than not who will provide it.

In 1615 Sir John Scott of Scotstarvit, author of *The Staggering State of Scottish Statesmen* and founder of the Chair of Humanity in St Andrews University, sought the help of his neighbour, Lord Lindsay of Balcarres, in the task undertaken by 'our auld Minister', Mr John Rae, of 'collecting and getting togidder of our Scottish poetis'.

Today, under the editorship of Professor G. W. S. Barrow, his colleagues, including another Mr Rae, have collected and got together a series of 'Essays in honour of R. G. Cant' remarkable not only intrinsically but also as having been written for him by friends and former pupils, thus reflecting the wide range of his influence. All are relevant to, centre on and evolve from his interests, yet, in spite of the great variety of their subjects, their unity is ultimately founded, as he would have wished, on that microcosm of Scotland, St Andrews.

We all owe him different debts. This is not so much an attempt to repay any of these, as to express some of our gratitude and affection and to give him pleasure.

# I

## St Andrews before Alexander I

The old Gaelic name of St Andrews, *Cennrigmonaid*, was used by an Irish annalist in 747.[1] It is last found about 1120 in Eadmer's phrase *pontificatum Sancti Andreae apostoli Chenrimuntensis*[2] and in Florence of Worcester (*Cenrimunt*) and his derivatives, with one stray later instance of *Kin-* in a copy of a charter given 1202 × 1214.[3] *Cenn-* 'head' was replaced by *Chil-, Kil-* 'church' which I have first noted in a copy of a charter given by David I 1128 × 1136.[4] *Kil-* forms in various literary texts are to be attributed to scribes who wrote later than the 1130s.

No doubt in the eighth century the place had a Pictish name, perhaps with the same meaning as the Gaelic, 'head of king's mount'. The 'king' could have been an overking of all the Picts, as were nearly all the Pictish kings of whom we have knowledge. Or he could have been a king of Fife, or even of some smaller unit corresponding to an Irish *tuath*. There was an *aula regis* at St Andrews when the A version of the foundation legend was composed, but we have as yet no evidence of a royal dwelling as early as the eighth century.

The Kirkhill, the little headland above the harbour, has yielded what may be evidence of a small Christian community which had received its faith from south of the Forth as early as the sixth century. There is no evidence of a church or of monastic life at that time.[5] Ostensibly the earliest evidence of the latter would be a note on St Cainnech of Aghaboe at 11 October in the Martyrology of Oengus: 'he has a *reicles* in Cell Rigmonaig in Scotland'.[6] It occurs in only two manuscripts, neither of which is older than the twelfth century.[7] The twelfth-century *Cell* could, however, be due to a copyist. Churches in Scotland associated with Cainnech are nearly all in the west. (Kennoway in Fife and Cambuskenneth near Stirling are not now supposed to bear his name.[8]) He died about 600, but it seems probable that the *reicles* of the note belonged to a later time. The *céli dé* (culdees) held Cainnech in special honour about the year 800.[9]

[1] Anderson, *Early Sources* (*ES*), i, 238.

[2] Haddan and Stubbs, *Councils*, ii, 199.

[3] *St Andrews Liber* (*St A. Lib.*), 237; fo. 109vo. in the Panmure ms, SRO, GD 45/27/8.

[4] *St A.Lib.*, 180.

[5] R. B. K. Stevenson in *PSAS*, lxxxvi (1951–2), 109; C. A. Thomas in Barley and Hanson, *Christianity in Britain*, 107–8; Hay Fleming, *St Andrews Cathedral Museum* (1931), App. II, and Joseph B. Davis in *Edinburgh New Philosophical Journal*, xiv (1861), 191–200.

[6] *Félire Óengusso Céli Dé*, ed. Whitley Stokes (1905), 222; *ES*, i, 55.

[7] On the age of this part of Laud 610 see Myles Dillon in *Celtica* v (1960), 64 ff.

[8] W. J. Watson, *Celtic Place-Names of Scotland* (1926), 277.

[9] See E. J. Gwynn and W. J. Purton, *The Monastery of Tallaght* (*Proc. Royal Irish Acad.*, xxix, C 5 (1911)), §22. On various meanings of *reiclés* see R.I.A.'s *Contributions to a Dictionary of the Irish Language*.

There was a monastery at Cennrigmonaid before 747, for the annal of that year records the death of its abbot Tuathalán. Hardly any Pictish information was then reaching the Irish annals, so the entry suggests that the monastery, or Tuathalán himself, had some Irish connection, possibly with Bangor. There is no evidence of an Iona connection. Iona is not known to have re-established its influence in the Pictish kingdom after its monks had been expelled thence in 717; and the Iona source of the Irish annals seems to have dried up a few years before 747.

Further written evidence for the Pictish period in Cennrigmonaid is wanting, but material evidence of wealth and status, which may be of the period, is the great 'sarcophagus' found deeply buried near the small church now called St Rule's.[10] That name seems not to have been attached to the church in the earlier middle ages, so it lends no support to the suggestion that the sarcophagus held the body of St Regulus. Also perhaps of the period is the house-shaped solid 'shrine' found, with associated burials, about 130 metres south-west of the same church. It has been compared with a Peterborough monument of about 800.[11]

Many slabs decorated with crosses in relief have been found at St Andrews, a number of them in the same general area as the sarcophagus, near what is believed to be the site of the medieval parish church.[12] It seems doubtful whether any of them are of the Pictish period, and the same is true of the curious cross-shaft (no. 19) found built into the twelfth-century cathedral.[13]

A list of post-Pictish bishops of St Andrews was used by Wyntoun and Bower in the fifteenth century, though not by Fordun in the fourteenth. Its first bishop, Cellach, is named in the Scottish Chronicle, about 906, in a context which suggests that he was chief bishop of the whole nation. But we have only the late evidence of the list to show that he was in fact bishop of St Andrews and not, say, of Abernethy or Dunkeld.

Cellach's contemporary, the king Constantine son of Aed, at the end of a long reign withdrew into religion;[14] to Cennrigmonaid/St Andrews according to two apparently independent sources. The Middle-Irish 'Prophecy of Berchán' says of him, 'God has called him away, to the *reicles* on the brow of the wave. In the house of the apostle he will die'.[15] The tradition on which this stanza

---

[10] No. 1 in Hay Fleming. See Mrs Cecil L. Curle in *PSAS*, lxxiv (1940), 97ff., and (as Cecil Mowbray) in *Antiquity* x (1936), 428ff.; R. B. K. Stevenson in *The Problem of the Picts*, ed. F. T. Wainwright (1955), 117–19, 125; Isobel Henderson, *The Picts* (1967), 149ff. Mr Ralegh Radford thought the sarcophagus later than the Pictish period, in *Archaeological Journal*, cxii (1955), 52–5, and *Antiquity*, xvi (1942), 1–18.

[11] The St Andrews 'shrine' is in St Leonards School. See Hay Fleming, App. I; on the date, Ralegh Radford, *Arch. Jour.*, cxii, p. 57, and appendix by Stewart Cruden. Further burials were found in 1967.

[12] The cross-slabs and fragments are grouped roughly by age in the southern half of the cathedral museum. See Stevenson as above, 126.

[13] Mrs Curle in *PSAS*, lxxiv, 107 (for 'St Mary on the Rock' read 'Cathedral'); cf. xliii, 385ff.

[14] *The Scottish Chronicle* (from Paris, Bib. Nat., ms. latin 4126) in my *Kings and Kingship in Early Scotland*, p. 252; and in W. F. Skene, *Picts and Scots*, p. 9. Constantine entered monastic life some time between 940 and 947; *ES*, i, 446.

[15] See *ES*, i, 448, where *reicles* is translated 'abbey-church', one of its several meanings.

is based may have been in writing before 1093.[16] A note in a version of the Scottish regnal list says that Constantine became abbot of the culdees (*Keledei*) of St Andrews. It may have been written in the twelfth century, perhaps before 1165.[17]

The culdees had originated in Ireland towards the end of the eighth century as a monastic reform movement. There may well have been a community of culdees at St Andrews by 945, but it is a question whether Constantine may not rather have been abbot of the old monastery to which the culdees were attached. We have, however, no actual evidence of monastic life at Cennrigmonaid in the post-Pictish period, other than that of the culdees. The absence of any *ab* (abbot) or *abthaine* (abbey land etc.) from the twelfth-century St Andrews records suggests that the office of abbot may have disappeared there at an early date, or rather may have been absorbed in that of the bishop.[18] Constantine's son Indulf is said to have died 'in the house of the same holy apostle', and so did an Irishman of royal blood in 965.[19]

Early in the reign of Dub (962–6), Indulf's successor, the Scottish Chronicle notes the death of a bishop *Fothach*. In the episcopal list Fothad follows Cellach[20] and is said to have been expelled by Indulf (954–962) and to have died eight years later. The Annals of the Four Masters enter at [963] the death of 'Fothad, Bran's son, scribe, and bishop of the islands of Scotland'. Since the Scottish Chronicle belongs to the east its entry goes some way to confirm that Fothad was in fact bishop of St Andrews. Possibly he spent his exile in Iona.[21] A bishop of St Andrews with whom the culdees of Loch Leven in Fife entered into a relationship of *precarium* is identified as *Fothath filio Bren* by the rather doubtful evidence of a note copied into the St Andrews cartulary.[22] Here, and also in the case of the bishop who made a gospel-cover for the church, we cannot rule out the possibility of confusion between Fothad I and Fothad II who died in 1093.

The curious Life of St Catroe, written apparently on the continent in the second half of the tenth century, mentions Rigmonath as a place of major importance.[23] The Scottish Chronicle may have been written during the tenth century, and possibly at St Andrews, for it says that in the reign of Culen son of Indulf (966–71) a man was killed in the 'church of St Michael'. A church of St Michael Archangel is one of seven that are said to have been built at Cennrigmonaid in addition to the church of St Andrew.[24]

In 1055 the Irish 'Annals of Tigernach' note the death of Maelduin 'bishop of Scotland, the glory of the Gaels'.[25] He is the *Maldunus episcopus Sancti*

[16] M. O. Anderson, *Kings and Kingship*, 50.

[17] Ibid., 283.

[18] See Gordon Donaldson, 'Scottish bishops' sees before the reign of David I' in *PSAS*, lxxxvii (1952–3), 113.

[19] *ES*, i, 471, 472.

[20] On the original order of the list see Goodall's note on *Scotichronicon (Chron. Bower)*, i, 339.        [21] *ES*, i, 471.        [22] *St A. Lib.*, 113.

[23] Skene, *Picts and Scots*, 108; *ES*, i, p. lxxiii.

[24] Version B of the foundation legend (*Picts and Scots*, 187). The same version says that St Regulus came ashore with St Andrew's relics on St Michael's night. Bishop Fothad II was the son of a *Malmykel*, 'servant of Michael'.        [25] *ES*, i, 599.

*Andree* of a Loch Leven notitia. His successor in the episcopal list, Tuathal, was also remembered as a benefactor of the culdees of Loch Leven.[26]

The last bishop of St Andrews to bear a Gaelic name was Fothad II (ca. 1059 to 1093). In his obit in the Annals of Ulster the title 'chief bishop of Scotland' (*ardepscop Alban*) is used by a contemporary writer for the first time. An Augustinian canon who between 1144 and 1153 wrote an account of St Andrews was no doubt translating this Gaelic title when he said that bishops of St Andrews were called *Summi Archiepiscopi Scotorum* or *Summi Episcopi Scotorum* 'in ancient as well as modern writings'.[27]

Fothad II must be the *Modach filius Malmykel* who made a gift to the culdees of Loch Leven;[28] and either he or Fothad I was believed to have taken them under his protection. One of the two made a silver-plated cover or shrine for an ancient gospel book, still treasured at St Andrews in Wyntoun's time, bearing an inscription in verse which named him *Fothet qui Scotis summus episcopus est.* The Augustinian writer, quoting the verses, describes the maker as *Fothet episcopus maxime vir authoritatis.* Wyntoun[29] identified him as Fothad I, possibly influenced by his own reading of the verses with *primus* for *summus,* so that the maker's identity remains a little doubtful.[30]

The small church with high square romanesque tower, known as 'St Rule's' or 'St Regulus', is now believed to have been built in the time of bishop Fothad II or even a little earlier.[31] It was known in the middle ages as the old church of St Andrew,[32] to distinguish it from the great cathedral which replaced it in the late twelfth century. As far as I know, Boece in about 1526 was the first to suggest that it had ever been called 'St Rule's church'.[33] Its Saxon affinities could be a fruit of Malcolm III's early years at the English court. At his instance and that of Queen Margaret it is said that Fothad professed obedience to an archbishop of York; but our authority is an archdeacon of York who wrote a generation after Fothad's death.[34]

Fothad died in the same year (1093) as Malcolm and Margaret. For the next fourteen years the bishopric was left vacant, its revenues declined, and the service of the church was neglected. When King Alexander I undertook the work of reconstruction (an abortive undertaking eventually carried out by his brother David I) the sad state of affairs described by the Augustinian had apparently been reached.[35] There were then no resident clergy to serve the altar of St Andrew. Five laymen who possessed hereditary shares in the altar offerings may

[26] *St A. Lib.*, 116.

[27] *Picts and Scots*, 190. The early date and consequent historical value of this account were ost sight of until rediscovered by Prof. Barrow, *Jour. Ecclesiastical Hist.*, iii (1952), 30f.

[28] *St A. Lib.*, 117.

[29] Wyntoun VI 9 (ed. Amours, iv, 192).

[30] The ages of some Irish book-shrines are listed by Joseph Anderson in *Scotland in Early Christian Times* (1881), i, 146.

[31] H. M. and Joan Taylor, *Anglo-Saxon Architecture*, ii (1965), 711–13 (cf. 647–53); and in *Celt and Saxon*, ed. Nora K. Chadwick (1963), 216ff.

[32] Wyntoun, ed. Amours, iv, 426f., 430f.; v, 58f.

[33] Boece, *Historiae* VI 15.

[34] Anderson, *Scottish Annals*, 131.

[35] *Picts and Scots*, 189ff.

well have been descendants of married clergy who had served the altar in the eleventh century. They may have had monastic antecedents going back even to the time of the Pictish kingdom.

By Alexander I's time the St Andrews culdees had no church of their own. They had partially abandoned celibate life, and it is very possible that they had done so long before.[36] The *scholastici* who in 1120 welcomed Eadmer to St Andrews as bishop-elect,[37] and the *pauperes scolares* who in 1208 × 1222 claimed 'ancient cain' from certain lands near St Andrews,[38] no doubt represented an endowed body of students that had existed since the eleventh century or earlier.

In the time of Fothad II the relics of the apostle were attracting so many pilgrims from south of the Forth that the queen was moved to provide hostels on either shore of the firth, and a free ferry.[39] The life of St Cadog in the eleventh century[40] mentions the *basilica Sancti Andree Apostoli* in Scotland as a place of pilgrimage comparable with Jerusalem and Rome. A shrine in which the relics were carried had a Gaelic name *Morbrac* about the year 1200.[41] Provision for pilgrims in St Andrews itself was perhaps never large. The Augustinian says that the guest-house (*hospitale*) received a seventh share of the altar offerings, but at the time of which he wrote it had room for only six guests. The five laymen who had shares in the altar were obliged to accommodate any further guests *more suo*, perhaps 'as their custom had been'. All the record evidence of endowments for the *hospitale* relates to David I's reign and later.

There is no detailed information about the St Andrews revenues before the twelfth century. Cennrigmonaid itself, as defined by bishop Arnold (1160–2),[42] covered an area rather larger than the precinct of the medieval cathedral and priory. The Augustinian writer believed that the church had been endowed at its foundation with land known as the *Cursus Apri*, the 'boar's chase' or 'boar's raik'. The places said to be within it show that it was more or less co-extensive with the modern parishes of St Andrews and St Leonards, Dunino, Cameron, Ceres, and Kemback.[43]

In 1144, when David I finally arranged the endowment of an Augustinian house to serve the church of St Andrew, the Cursus Apri was treated as distinct from episcopal property: *de episcopatu non erat*, says the Augustinian. It is not clear whether the distinction stemmed from an abortive arrangement made by Alexander I, or was older. It may be that lands in the Cursus Apri which later belonged to the bishop were held by him as the representative of the old abbots.

The culdees almost certainly had land in the Cursus Apri in the eleventh

---

[36] Kathleen Hughes (*The Church in Early Irish Society*, 227f.) mentions a head of the culdees at Clonmacnoise in the eleventh century who was apparently married.

[37] Haddan and Stubbs, *Councils*, ii, 200.

[38] *St A. Lib.*, 316.

[39] *Life of Queen Margaret*, chap. 9; *ES*, ii, 77.

[40] *Vitae Sanctorum Britanniae*, ed. Wade-Evans, 80, 82.

[41] *St A. Lib.*, 329.

[42] *St A. Lib.*, 127. Arnold's charter does not name the place, but it is named (*Kilrimoneth*) in the confirmation by bishop Richard (143).

[43] See Pinkerton's *Enquiry* (2nd edn, 1814), 469–70; *St A.Lib.*, 122; *Picts and Scots*, 193.

century. Between 1156 and 1161 they gave to the canons in an exchange the land of *alia Stradkines* west of St Andrews.[44] This seems to be the *Strathkinness Melserog* of an early-thirteenth-century list,[45] and may well have been an old possession. The 'ancient cain' claimed by the *scolares* was also from lands in the Cursus Apri.

A much larger area is defined by the B version of the foundation legend as the original *parochia* of the church of St Andrew, consisting of the whole of Fife east of a line drawn from Largo on the firth of Forth through Ceres to Naughton on the firth of Tay. I have not been able to find the significance of this boundary in relation to the medieval diocese. The diocese was very extensive, and between Forth and Dee it was curiously intermingled with other dioceses. Its detached portions may have represented affiliated churches, or actual possessions, of the old monastery.[46]

Tithes paid to the church of St Andrew by kings and nobles of the Picts are a feature of the A version of the foundation legend.[47] In the B version members of the Pictish royal family grant tithes or lands to God and St Andrew, and the king builds churches, at three places far from St Andrews: Forteviot (on the Earn), *Monichi* or *Monithi*[48] (probably in Angus), and Kindrochet (in Braemar). The first and perhaps the second were in the medieval diocese of St Andrews; the church of Kindrochet, dedicated to St Andrew, was in the diocese of Aberdeen. The *vicus* of Monymusk, in the same diocese, was said to have been vowed to St Andrew by Malcolm III in 1078 in return for victory in battle.[49] Early in the thirteenth century a community of culdees there claimed to have been established by a bishop of St Andrews.[50] The sole contemporary document earlier than 1100 is Duncan II's original charter to Durham (1093 or 1094), granting 'the *servitium* which bishop Fodanus [Fothad II] used to receive from Broxmouth' in east Lothian.[51]

The name of St Andrew was no doubt associated with Cennrigmonaid long before the author of the Prophecy of Berchán, late in the eleventh century, wrote of the 'house of the apostle'. Skene had an attractive theory that the saint's relics were brought to Scotland by bishop Acca, exiled from St Andrew's church of Hexham in about 732 within the reign of Angus I (ca. 729 to 761).[52] Certainly the monastery existed in 747, and the legend attributes the foundation to a Pictish king Angus son of Fergus (to use modern English forms). In both

---

[44] *St A. Lib.*, 131, 203.

[45] The existing manuscript is of the eighteenth century; printed in Pinkerton as above. Prof. G. W. S. Barrow has suggested that the name was *Melsnog* = Maelsnecht.

[46] Gordon Donaldson as above. Cf. Christopher Brooke in *Celt and Saxon*, 318.

[47] On tithe in the reign of David I see *Regesta Regum Scottorum* (*RRS*) i, 65f.; in Ireland before the eighth century, K. Hughes as above, 140, 142.

[48] See below for the readings, and cf. Skene in *PSAS*, iv (1863), 306.

[49] Boece, *Historiae* XII 11. Cf. *Aberdeen-Banff Coll.*, 171.

[50] *St A. Lib.*, 370ff.

[51] See A. A. M. Duncan, 'The Earliest Scottish Charters' in *SHR*, xxxvii (1958), 119. Some traces of early possessions of St Andrews in later records are discussed by Marinell Ash in a Ph.D. thesis (University of Newcastle upon Tyne, 1972), especially in chap. viii, part 6 and ix, 3.

[52] *PSAS*, iv, 312ff.

versions the founder leads a victorious expedition against the south; and although chronicle evidence tallies with neither version in detail, it does leave room for possible Pictish raids into Northumbria between, say, 732 and 740. In the B version the founder makes another expedition against Argyll, which Angus I did, but it fits so awkwardly into the story that it must surely be a late intrusion. A note in one group (Q) of Pictish regnal lists[53] attributes the foundation to a later Angus son of Fergus (Angus II, 820–34) of whose reign we know virtually nothing. There is a dearth of Northumbrian chronicle evidence at this time.[54]

St Andrews may have honoured an 'Angus son of Fergus' as its founder. But Angus I was so renowned a character that the attribution of his exploits to the founder does not show which king the author of the original legend had in mind, if indeed he was able to distinguish between them.

The king's name in both versions is (H)ungus, a seemingly hybrid form which the Q group of regnal lists uses for Angus II. The king's father in the A version is Urguist, a Pictish form which is gaelicized in the extant Q lists. The B version of the legend also gaelicized it, probably as Forgus(s)o (see below for the readings). This genitive in -o should be not later than about 980.[55] The For- instead of Fer- should be even older,[56] but may result from a misread abbreviation sign. It is possible that the author of the original legend copied the names from an early list of Q type. If so, and if B's -o is not a scribal accident, we should have to infer that Q's foundation note on Angus II had already been entered some time before 980. Even then the question of the founder's identity would, I think, remain open.

It is difficult to find anything in the legends that can be treated as history, apart perhaps from the name of the founder and incidental information about the writers' own times. The two versions have a common outline but very little common detail. Relics of St Andrew are removed from Patras to Constantinople; in A they remain there for a century. Then (Tunc, an abrupt transition, one of the few points that suggest a common written version of the legend) the Pictish king wins a battle in the south by the help of St Andrew. Certain bones of the apostle are brought by Regulus from Patras (B) or Constantinople (A) to Cennrigmonaid (ad verticem montis regis, id est Rigmund in A). The king and Regulus meet and a church is founded in honour of St Andrew.

The Patras/Constantinople sections seem to be drawn independently by A and B from related, if not identical, sources. The chief sources to be looked for are perhaps an account of the Translation of St Andrew partly based on Jerome,[57] and a Life of St Regulus of Senlis (Silvanectis). Regulus of Senlis was said to have come from Greece to Gaul in the fourth century. There was a

---

[53] Kings and Kingship, 77ff.
[54] See F. M. Stenton, Anglo-Saxon England (2nd edn), 94f.
[55] Tomás O'Maille, The Language of the Annals of Ulster (1910), 62ff.
[56] Kings and Kingship, 97n.
[57] In B the emperor removes St Andrew's shrine first to Rome and thence to Constantinople; this seems to be suggested by Jerome's Constantio Romam ingresso ossa . . . a Constantinopolitanis miro favore suscepta (ed. Fotheringham, 322f.). A's miro favosoque ductu echoes the same passage of Jerome.

church of St Andrew at Senlis.[58] Late medieval calendars enter the Scottish Regulus on the day of Regulus of Senlis (30 March) and on that of an Irish saint Riaguil of Mucc-Inis (16 October).[59] It may be that Regulus the bringer of St Andrew's relics to Scotland was a fiction, but the fiction could have been grafted on to a real local cult. The late medieval cult of St Regulus, however, seems to stem from the written legend. The association of 'good St Rule' with a cave at St Andrews (see Scott's *Marmion*) seems to be no older than the eighteenth century when hermits were in fashion. It does not appear in Martine's *Reliquiae Divi Andreae* (1683).

In the A version of the St Andrews legend the Pictish army penetrates the southern part of Britain as far as *campus Merc* where it winters. From the context and spelling I think this is more likely to mean Mercia (*Myrce, Merce*, etc. in the Anglo-Saxon Chronicle) than, as Skene thought, the Merse (*Merskes*, etc.[60]), the low-lying country between Lammermuir and Tweed.

In B the enemy is a king of the Saxons called Adhelstan, who is beheaded after his defeat by the Picts. Fordun tried to identify him with an Athelstan who in fact outlived Angus II by several years.[61] I suspect that the author of B, oblivious of history and chronology, had in mind that famous enemy of the Scots (not the Picts), the king of Wessex who successfully invaded Scotland in 934. The Picts encamp *ad ostium fluminis Tyne* which Fordun understood as Tynemouth in Northumbria.[62] Bower's *Scotichronicon* places the battle at Athelstaneford near to Haddington and the Tyne of East Lothian. But in the twelfth century the first element of this place-name was 'Ælfstan' (*Alstane*, *Elstan(e)*, etc.), not 'Athelstan'.[63] Bower did not invent the false etymology or the link with the St Andrews legend, for Wyntoun also connects the Athelstan of the legend with Athelstaneford, though he spells the name correctly *Elstanfurd(e)*. But there is no reason to suppose that the train of ideas is older than the fifteenth century.

There seems to be nothing to show when the legend first took shape, apart from the flimsy argument that B's *For(gus)so* was in writing before 980. Nor is it easy to date either of the versions. Version A was certainly composed at St Andrews (*huc, hunc locum, hic requiescunt*), possibly by a culdee as Ussher says. It reads like a homily for the day of St Andrew or of his Translation, awkwardly condensed from an earlier version. Its 'palmer pilgrims from Jerusalem', an obvious dating point, comes in a passage that may be a later addition; in Add. ms. 25014 the passage (*Ad istam enim civitatem* to *non possunt scribi*) begins with an unusually ornamental A, and the text would run more smoothly without it.

[58] Skene in *PSAS*, iv, 319f. The monastery of St Andrew at Northampton was founded by Simon de Senlis in 1084.

[59] See Dowden in *PSAS*, xxvii (1892–3), 247–54. Compare the French 'St Rieul' for the Senlis saint with our 'St Rule'.

[60] *RRS*, ii, no. 380 ('1195?'); *Dryburgh Liber*, no. 230 (1220); *St A. Lib.*, 31.

[61] See *ES*, i, 266.

[62] Cf. Bede, *Historia Ecclesiastica*, V 6; Symeon of Durham (ed. Arnold, Rolls Series), ii, 54.

[63] E.g. Lawrie, *Charters*, no. 186; *Holyrood Liber*, no. 30 (= *RRS*, ii, no. 517); *St A. Lib.*, 30, 329. An Asulf son of Elfstan or Elstan witnessed *Melrose Liber*, no. 1, and *RRS*, i, no. 41; an Ethelstan was the father of another witness on the same occasion.

A's *ad verticem montis regis*, implying *Cennrigmonaid*, not *Cell-*, should be not later than about 1130. The A version may belong mainly to the eleventh or even the tenth century, but I do not think we should take literally the present tense in 'all the churches that are *in regno Pictorum*'.

Version B purports to have been written for a king who is evidently the *Ferath filius Bargoit* of Pictish regnal lists, who reigned about 840. It seems extremely doubtful whether any part of it is so old. Its 'royal witnesses' are almost certainly taken from a regnal list, badly corrupted.[64] The Augustinian, writing not later than 1153, says that he found the legend (B) *in veteribus Pictorum libris scripta*, which I suspect means that he found it along with a Pictish regnal list.

A gloss *nunc Kilrymont* in B is probably later than about 1130. *Portus reginae* (Queensferry) is not older than Queen Margaret's time. Formulae with which, in B, the endowments are supposed to be made would have been appropriate to the twelfth century, just possibly to the eleventh for which Scottish charter evidence is wanting. The fact that Fordun does not mention *portus reginae* or the formulae does not prove these to be additions to the original B text. More significant is his agreement with A in calling Regulus an abbot. B's insistence that Regulus was a bishop may reflect attempts made in the twelfth century to have St Andrews erected into an archbishopric.[65]

### The St Andrews foundation legends

#### Version A

(1) (Ad): British Museum Additional ms. 25014, fos. 118 verso, b, to 119 verso, b, following Bede's *Historia Ecclesiastica*, Cuthbert's letter on the death of Bede, and an article on the bishops of Candida Casa.[66] See Plummer's edition of *Hist. Eccl.*, i, p. cvii, and the edition by Colgrave and Mynors (1969), pp. xlix, 579. The manuscript was written in the late twelfth century and bears an erased *ex-libris* of the Cistercian abbey of Newminster in Northumberland. It was listed as a Newminster manuscript by John Boston of Bury (*floruit* 1410) in his *Catalogus scriptorum ecclesiae*, where he attributed the St Andrews legend to Bede, though with reservations (*dicitur*).[67] This false attribution was repeated by John Bale,[68] bishop of Ossory (died 1563) and others, as noted by Ussher. The manuscript contains a note in Bale's hand. Samuel Gale (died 1754) in a marginal note in a copy of Camden referred to what sounds like the same manuscript, which he said was then in the possession of the earl of Aylesbury.[69] Hearne (died 1735) also seems to have referred to it.[70] It belonged at one time to a

---

[64] *Kings and Kingship*, 99.          [65] See *ES*, ii, 212, under 1151.

[66] The Candida Casa article was printed in *SHR*, xxxii (1953), 146.

[67] See the abbreviated version of Boston's catalogue in the preface to Thomas Tanner's *Bibliotheca Britannico-Hibernica* (1748), pp. xxixf.

[68] Bale, *Scriptorum Illustrium Majoris Britanniae catalogus* (Basle, 1557), centuria 2, cap. 1.

[69] See Gough's edition of Camden's *Britannia* (1789), iii, 370, and i, p. vii.

[70] See Skene in *PSAS*, iv, 308.

Francis St John, 'hence' says Plummer, it was probably the 'Gosford ms.' noted in Hardy's *Catalogue* i, 438, note †. In 1862 it was acquired by the British Museum from the estate of Sir Francis Palgrave, but Skene did not see it.[71]

(2) (Pop): Paris, Bibliothèque Nationale, ms. latin 4126, fos. 31 recto, a, to 32 recto, a, among other pieces relating to early Scotland. The manuscript (the 'Poppleton ms.') was written at York about 1360. The legend is printed with the other Poppleton pieces in *Kings and Kingship*, and as no. XVIII in Skene's *Picts and Scots*. Cf. *SHR* xxviii, 41. Higden (*Polychronicon* (Rolls Series 41) i, 388 ff.) used a text closely related to the Poppleton pieces; but the end of his St Andrews legend resembles the text printed by Ussher. Ussher thought, mistakenly, that Higden took the legend from Giraldus Cambrensis. Higden seems to have been Camden's source for the legend.

(3) Archbishop James Ussher in *Britannicarum Ecclesiarum Antiquitates* (1639), cap. XV, (Collected Works, vi, 187–90) printed a text very like Ad and Pop; he says it was written by a St Andrews culdee. Ussher mistakenly identified Newminster as New Minster at Winchester.

A text of A was used by the Aberdeen Breviary for the Translation of St Andrew at 9 May (i, part 3, fo. 96). Fordun's 'tithe of the kingdom' (ed. Skene, i, 77, 156) could have been taken from A.

Ad and Ussher share over twenty correct readings where Pop is at fault, e.g. *coheres* (*choeres* Pop 8),[72] *Constantii* (*-ini* Pop 15 end), *locum* masculine (feminine in Pop 53, 59), *manifestissime* (*infestissime* Pop 72). Ad and Ussher share also two or three probable errors, e.g. 'thirteen' divisions of the Pictish army; Pop's *xii* is probably for an original *uii* (*septem* in the B version, and compare A's *septem comitibus*).

A different relationship is suggested by *precedat* in Ad and Pop (33), *praecedet* correctly in Ussher, but he may have emended silently.

In the heading Ad omits Pop's reference to the Picts, and the promise of a treatise on abbacies. Ussher gives no heading.

Pop's final paragraph after *hic requiescunt* is absent from Ad. In its place Ussher's text says that Regulus and his monks made vegetable gardens 'where is now the house of master Samuel, his predecessors and successors'; also a mill etc. Britain, it continues, was Christian before Picts and Scots arrived, but their faith was augmented by St Andrew in person.[73] The archbishopric of all Scotia ought to be in this *civitas*, etc. The text ends with a reference to 'archbishop' Giricius, Machethad, and Gregorius, and a prayer on behalf of the writer.

*Version B*

(1) (Harl): British Museum, Harleian ms. 4628, folios 224 verso to 238 recto. The manuscript is an early-eighteenth-century copy of material derived from

[71] Skene, *Picts and Scots* (1867), p. li.

[72] The numbers refer to lines of the text of Pop, beginning *Qualiter acciderit*, in my *Kings and Kingship*, pp. 258–60.

[73] The Augustinian writer (1144 × 1153) had not seen this text, for he had not found in writing that St Andrew visited Scotland in person (*Picts and Scots*, 188).

the lost St Andrews *registrum*.[74] The legend is prefaced to the Augustinian canon's treatise on St Andrews; the combined text is no. XXXI in Skene's *Picts and Scots*.

(2) There are two copies of the B version in a manuscript of the Herzog August Bibliothek, Wolfenbüttel (Cod. Guelf. 1108 Helmst) written in the fourteenth century. Both copies (folios 28 verso, line 8, to 30 verso (Wolf 1), and 32 verso to 35 recto (Wolf 2)) are closely similar to Harl.

Version B was used by Fordun (II, 46-48, IV, 13, 14; *Chron. Fordun*, i, 75-8, 156 f.; also in Bower's *Scotichronicon* (II, 58-60, IV, 13-14; *Chron. Bower*, 94-7, 190f.), and Wyntoun (ed. Amours, iv, 170-3). The Aberdeen Breviary used it, apparently through Fordun or *Scotichronicon*, in lessons for St Regulus at 30 March (i, part 3, fos. 82 to 83 recto).

The following is a selection of variant readings of the B texts, mostly of proper names. Other variants are comparatively few. I have used Skene's text of Harl which I have checked with the manuscript. The hand is very clear, and Skene's text is usually accurate. For the Wolf texts I have used microfilm, for which, and for permission to cite the texts, I am indebted to the kindness of Dr Milde of the Herzog August Bibliothek.

| *Picts and Scots,* p. 183, | Harl | Wolf 1 | Wolf 2 |
|---|---|---|---|
| line 2 | Constantinus | Constancius | Constantinus |
| 24 | Ferlon | Forso | Forso |
| 24-5 | | | (*Scotorum* added above pictorum)[75] |
| 28 | Hungo (dative) | Hungus | Hungus |
| p. 184, lines 27-8 | Ardchinnechun | ardchinnechenam | (omits all between *dicitur* and *ligno*) |
| p. 185, line 14 | Kylrimont | chilrimonith | chilrímoníth |
| 19 | curamentum | tutamentum | tutamentum |
| 21 | S. Samiano[76] | sancto damiano | sancto damíano |
| 24 | Hungi (genitive) | Hungus | hungus |
| 25 | Phinguineghert | phinguinegarfe (final *e* doubtful) | phinguinegraf |
| 31 | Moneclatu, qui | Monethatha que | monechacha qui |
| 33 | Kylrimont | chilrímoníth | chilrímonith |
| 36 | om. | Et ibi cruce quadam erecta, regine et loco illi benedixerunt | (as Wolf 1, but omits *illi*) |

---

[74] *Kings and Kingship*, p. 54ff.

[75] Wolf 2 reads *scoti* etc. for *picti* etc. several times below (p. 183, line 28; p. 184, lines 13, 16, 22).

[76] *Damiano* Skene. Harl's *S* has probably been misread from a round fourteenth-century *D*.

| Picts and Scots, | Harl | Wolf 1 | Wolf 2 |
|---|---|---|---|
| p. 185, | | | |
| 37 | lacum | locum | locum |
| 38 | Doldencha | Doldauha | doldahua |
| 38–9 | Chondrochedalvan | Chendrohedalian | chondrohedalian |
| p. 186, | | | |
| line    5 | Doldancha | Doldaucha | doldauha |
| 13 | partem . . . illam | situm . . . illum | situm . . . illum |
| 21 | comitibus | cantibus | cantibus |
| 32–3 | Ishundenema | ihwdenemur[77] | ihwdenem' |
| 33 | Sletheuma | slethemur | sletheum' |
| 35 | Sireis canum | sires | sereis canum |
| | Sireis | sireís | síres |
| 35–6 | Hyhatnouhten Machehirb, quae tellus nunc dicitur[78] | om. | hyhatnachten que nunc dicitur |
| 36 | Hadnachten | hadhnachten | hadhauchten |
| 37 | Chilrymonth | chilrímonith | chílrimoneth |
| 38 | pratu | cum pratis | cum pratis |
| p. 187, | | | |
| line   11 | Ythernbuthib | ytherubuthib | ycherubuthib |
| 12 | Garnach | Giartuath | kartnach |
| | Dosnach | difnach | dolnach |
| | Drusti | Drust | Druss |
| 13 | Wrthrosst | Wythrossi | Wrthrossi |
| | Nachtalich | Nacthaleth | Nachaleth |
| | Shinah | Shínach | shinach |
| | Lutheren | litheren | luthern |
| 14 | Forchete | foichele | forchete |
| | Pheradach | Pherathach | pherathach |
| | Finleich | Phinleich | phinlech |
| 14–15 | Phiachan sui filii, Bolge | Phihacnansin[79] filii bolg | om. |
| 15 | Glunmerach | Giluníneruh | om. |
| 16 | Aunganena | chinganena | om. |
| | Duptalaich | Duptalarch | om. |
| | Bergib | bargoth | om. |
| 17 | geniti | progeniti | progeniti |

[77] Apparently=Irish *muir n-Giudan*, the firth of Forth. See William Reeves, *The Culdees of the British Islands*, 124; cf. Bede, *Hist. Eccl.* I 12. *Slethemur* must from the context be the firth of Tay.

[78] Compare Melchrethre (*al.* Malchrethre, Malcrether, Melgrethre), the name of a ploughgate in 'Adnectan' (Naughton), *St Andrews Liber*, 274–5; *RRS*, i, 252; ii, 137. I owe these references to the editor.

[79] Perhaps for *Fiachna fin(n)* 'the White'; cf. *Fiachua albus*, eleventh in Pictish regnal lists of the Q version.

| Picts and Scots, p. 187, | Harl | Wolf 1 | Wolf 2 |
|---|---|---|---|
| 18 | Chilrymont | chilirimonith | chilrimonith |
| 20 | diaconi | om. | diaconi |
| 22 | om. | honorabilis senioris | honorabilis senioris |
| 24 | Muren | Mouren | muren |
| 28 | sanctorum | om. | [Wolf 2 omits from *haec sunt nomina* onwards] |
| 30 | ipse Mattheus[80] | episcopus Matheus | |
| 32 | Neruius | Nermus | |
| | Crisenius | Chusemus | |
| | Nola | Creta | |
| 33 | Thuluculus | Chubacl's | |
| | Nathabeus | Natchabeus | |
| | Silvius | Silicius | |
| 34 | Juranus | Saranus | |
| 35 | Philippus | Philipphus | |
| | Lunus | Lucíus | |
| 36 | Colossia | Collossia | |
| | Kiduana | Triduana | |
| | Cineria | Omeria[81] | |
| 37 | Anaglas | Anagles | |
| p. 188, line 1 | Thana | Chana | |
| | Dudabrach | Dubabrath | |
| | monumentum | monímentum [?] | |
| 2 | Bergeth | Bargoth | |

MARJORIE ANDERSON

[80] *Maltheus* Skene. In this list of Regulus's companions Harl's *S.* could sometimes be read as either *sanctus* or (as sometimes elsewhere) *scilicet*; but Wolf 1 reads *sanctus* etc. throughout the list.

[81] or *Emeria*. Fordun has *Emerea*.

# 2

## Peter's Pence in Scotland

Peter's Pence is one of the best-known of the payments made to the papacy in the middle ages. It was instituted by the old English kings, and was an annual payment, although when the original grant was made, by whom and the exact nature of it are all very uncertain questions.[1] A similar payment was made by other northern countries such as Sweden, Denmark, Norway, Poland, Hungary and parts of Russia, where it was instituted somewhat later.[2] But the Celtic countries of Britain do not appear to have paid Peter's Pence in any regular way, although there were attempts by the papacy to institute it at different times. As far as Scotland is concerned there has been no thorough investigation of the question, although Dowden implies that it was a customary payment when he says 'there are many notices of the appointment of agents, frequently foreigners, commissioned to collect Peter's pence in Scotland'.[3]

The first systematic papal taxation record, the *Liber Censuum* (c. 1188–9) includes the payments of Peter's Pence which came from England (and Denmark).[4] A list of the amounts to be paid by the English bishoprics is given. But from Wales, Scotland or Ireland no similar payment was exacted.[5] Nor, apparently, was the payment collected in the English bishoprics of Durham and Carlisle, which abutted on the Scottish border.[6] Just at the date, however, when the *Liber Censuum* was compiled there comes the first evidence that the papacy attempted to extend the due into the Celtic countries of Britain. Giraldus Cambrensis tells how at the close of the twelfth century there was a move to put the Welsh dioceses directly under the pope. If this favour was granted, the Welsh, it is said, were prepared to pay a penny to St Peter from each house, as was done in England.[7] Nothing, however, came of the suggestion and in 1316 the archbishop of Canterbury told the pope, in response to a later enquiry about Peter's Pence, 'in the dioceses of (Wales) nothing whatever is collected now,

---

[1] W. E. Lunt, *Financial Relations of the Papacy with England* (Cambridge, Mass., 1939), i, 4.

[2] W. Ullmann, *The Growth of Papal Government in the Middle Ages* (London, 1955), 335n. See below, p. 16–18, for Peter's Pence in Scandinavia.

[3] J. Dowden, *The Medieval Church in Scotland* (Glasgow, 1910), 321. As will be discussed below these entries in *CPL* provide no evidence that the agents ever collected Peter's Pence in Scotland.

[4] *Le Liber Censuum de L'Eglise Romaine*, edd. M. P. Fabre et L. Duchesne (Paris, 1905), i, 226–7. A similar payment is listed under Norway and Sweden also, although not called Peter's Pence; see below, p. 17.

[5] There is not a single reference to Peter's Pence in Scotland in either of Lunt's books on papal revenue. Ullmann also omits Scotland, Wales and Ireland when listing the important countries which paid the due (Ullmann, *Papal Government*, 335n.).

[6] *Cambridge Medieval History*, vi, 554.

[7] *Opera* (Rolls ser., 1861–91), iii, 55, 78, 175 (cited by Lunt, *Financial Relations*, i, 60).

nor was anything in the past . . . by . . . anyone so far as known'.[8] Nor does it appear that the payment was collected in Ireland either, for in Adrian IV's Bull of 1155 a condition of his suggested concession of Ireland to Henry II was that Peter's Pence would be imposed there.[9] Although Scotland was placed directly under the pope at about this date, there is absolutely no evidence that this move was accompanied by any offer of an annual payment like Peter's Pence or that such was demanded. If it had been instituted the fact would probably be apparent from the *Liber Censuum*, in which every Scottish diocese is described as 'qui est domini Pape'.[10]

The attempt to extend the exaction of Peter's Pence to Wales and Ireland in the late twelfth century was not successful, but there appears to have been another drive in the first half of the fourteenth century, and on this occasion Scotland was included. In 1316 an enquiry into the full payment of Peter's Pence was made by John XXII[11] and this enquiry may have covered Wales, for as has already been mentioned, it was reported at this time that the payment had never been made there. In the very next year a papal letter referred to the collection of Peter's Pence 'about which the pope has written to the archbishop of Canterbury and the other prelates of England and Scotland'.[12] This is the first hint that any attempt was being made to connect Scotland with the payment of this due. All earlier entries in the *Calendar of Papal Letters* concerning Peter's Pence – which Dowden appears to have taken as evidence that the payment was made in Scotland – only include the due *along with* cess, debts, tens, twentieths and all other papal payments which papal nuncios were to collect from England, Ireland, Scotland and Wales.[13] But, as has been seen, the payment of Peter's Pence was not made in Ireland or Wales, which shows that these entries cannot be taken as proof that it was made in Scotland. The 1317 entry, however, may indicate a first attempt to link Scotland with the payment of Peter's Pence. This is the year following the accession of John XXII, the pope who more than any other of the Avignon popes did all he could to increase the papal revenues and to ensure that all the amounts of papal taxes that were collected were actually received. He made a strenuous attempt in particular to collect the whole sum of Peter's Pence from England instead of the fixed traditional amount which left a surplus in the hands of the local collectors.[14] But if he was thinking of extending the due to Scotland the time was not propitious for such an attempt. The years after Bannockburn saw a state of lawlessness in the border areas

---

[8] W. E. Lunt, *Papal Revenues in the Middle Ages* (New York, 1934), ii, 67; although G. Williams, *The Welsh Church from Conquest to Reformation* (Cardiff, 1962), 370, says there is evidence that some monasteries paid small contributions in the later middle ages.

[9] R. Foreville, *L'Eglise et la royauté en Angleterre sous Henri II* (Paris, 1943), 85.

[10] *Liber Censuum*, i, 230–2.

[11] Lunt, *Papal Revenues*, ii, 66–7.

[12] *CPL*, ii, 430. In 1316 a mandate was addressed to archbishops, bishops and all prelates secular and regular of England, Ireland, Scotland and Wales warning them to carry out the orders contained in the letters from the Pope touching the collection of Peter's Pence (*CPL*, ii, 126–7).

[13] *Ibid.*, i, 423 (1266); 475 (1282); 564 (1296); 617 (1304); ii, 126 (1316).

[14] Lunt, *Papal Revenues*, i, 69. W. E. Lunt and E. B. Groves, *Accounts rendered by Papal Collectors in England, 1317–1378* (Philadelphia, 1968), p. xlii.

between England and Scotland, culminating in the attack on Cardinals Gaucelin and Luca Fieschi in 1317. Robert I had refused to admit the legates over the border, and was excommunicated as a result, while Scotland was laid under an interdict. (See additional note below, p. 22.)

This situation continued until the years 1328–9, and immediately after the resumption of relations between Robert I and John XXII in those years there comes the first direct evidence of the actual attempted imposition of the ancient due of Peter's Pence on Scotland. In 1329 Bertrand Cariti and Raymond de Quercu, papal nuncios, were granted faculty to exact Peter's Pence from ecclesiastics and seculars in Scotland, and from all persons in Scotland seculars and regulars, exempt and non-exempt.[15] This date was peculiarly appropriate for any papal attempt to impose the due. In October, 1328 Bruce had been released from the ban of excommunication and a bull of 13 June 1329 authorised him and his successors to be crowned and anointed kings of Scotland.[16] In return the papacy demanded full payment of all arrears of papal taxes, which appear to have been paid. The desire of the Scottish Crown to reach an agreement meant that the papacy was in a strong bargaining position. It is characteristic of the imposition of Peter's Pence for it to be paid by small countries in return for the support of papal authority in the secular sphere.[17] It was paid in Norway from 1152–3 when the province of Nidaros was created in which were included the dioceses of Orkney and the Isles, which was a boost to national prestige.[18] This aspect is also relevant in the cases of Denmark, Poland, Bohemia, Croatia, Aragon, Portugal and the two Sicilies. So, if Pope John had seized the propitious moment in 1328–9 to attempt once more to impose Peter's Pence on Scotland, the granting of faculty to the newly-appointed nuncios may reflect an agreement that was reached with the Bruce dynasty in return for acknowledgement of its position. The two letters granting faculty on the sole matter of Peter's Pence in Scotland are undoubtedly concerned to regulate its payment; and the wholesale imposition on all members of the secular and regular clergy – whether the order was normally exempt from papal taxation or not – gives the impression that it was a new tax which was being imposed on the Scottish Church.

Indeed, it would be surprising if Scotland, which, like most of the countries paying Peter's Pence, was small and close to an overmighty neighbour, had not paid the tax. But it may be doubted whether Pope John's attempt of 1328–9 was successful, for there is no record of any sum of money being accounted for which included the payment of Peter's Pence from Scotland, although a three years' tenth and the fruits of void benefices are accounted for at this time.[19] There are moreover many references in the *Calendar of Papal Letters* to the sum of Peter's Pence which had been collected from England. A few years later, in 1335, Master Bernard Sistre was appointed papal nuncio in England, Ireland,

---

[15] *CPL*, ii, 490.                [16] *Ibid.*, 489, 493.

[17] A. O. Johnsen, *Studier vedrørende Kardinal Nicolaus Brekespears Legasion til Norden* (Oslo, 1945), 256.

[18] *Ibid.*, 327–8.                [19] *CPL.*, ii, 502, 505, 507.

Scotland and Wales, and he was also given power to collect and compel the payment of Peter's Pence.[20] This is once more taken by Dowden to mean that he had the power to collect it in Scotland,[21] but this is not explicitly stated. The faculty for Bernard Sistre to exact and receive from all ecclesiastics the yearly cess is said to be specifically 'in the aforesaid parts' over which he was appointed, which points a contrast to the wording of the faculty concerning Peter's Pence where the area of collection is *not* specified.[22] On the evidence available therefore it would appear that the Avignon popes were not successful in their attempt to impose Peter's Pence on Scotland at this time, and that it never became a permanent papal due in this country. The records do not give one piece of information to show that the sum was ever collected from Scotland.

Such evidence as there is for the imposition of Peter's Pence in Scotland comes from the fourteenth century. It does not appear that the papacy attempted to impose it at an earlier date, even though there is evidence that its imposition in Ireland and Wales was under discussion in the late twelfth century. In this context it is of interest to mention a grant made by Harold Maddadson earl of Caithness and Orkney of one annual penny from every inhabited house in the earldom of Caithness during the pontificate of Alexander III (1159–81). This payment had been made, as stated in a letter of Innocent III in 1198, out of reverence for the blessed Peter and Paul and had been collected specifically for the needs of the Roman Church.[23] This sounds to be exactly the same as the payment of Peter's Pence as known in England and other northern European countries at this date, and is the first and only evidence that such a payment was made by any part of Scotland during the middle ages.[24] There seems little doubt that the inspiration for this imposition on his Scottish earldom came from the earl's knowledge of Peter's Pence in his Norwegian earldom of Orkney. The payment of Peter's Pence became customary in the three Scandinavian countries fairly early on, following the example of England and testifying to the close cultural relationship across the North Sea. King Cnut probably established it in Denmark after having been king of England, for it certainly existed there in 1104.[25] In Norway the English cardinal Nicholas Breakspear introduced the

---

[20] *Ibid.*, ii, 559.   [21] Dowden, *Medieval Church*, 322.
[22] *CPL*, ii, 559.
[23] *CPL*, i, 1; *Diplom. Norv.* vii, no. 2: 'denarium unum de qualibet domo in Comitatu Catenensi habitata annuatim pro elemosina colligendum et ob reverentiam beatorum apostolorum Petri et Pauli ad sedem apostolicam dirigere consuevit, quam visitationem nomine elemosine annuatim ad opus Romane ecclesie colligende'.
[24] C. Innes, 'Two Ancient Records of the Bishopric of Caithness' (*Bannatyne Misc.*, iii, 5, n. 2), called it 'an imitation of the hearth-tax, called Peter's pence or 'romfeoh', in Saxon England'. Dowden, *Medieval Church*, 320, also cited the grant as an example of Peter's pence in Scotland, although it was a completely unique example of the payment. In the *Liber Censuum* (i, 229), Peter's Pence in Norway and Sweden is not actually called 'denarius beati Petri' or 'census beati Petri', but 'quod singule domus .. singulos dant denarios monete ipsius terre'.
[25] Lunt, *Papal Revenues*, i, 67.

due when he was legate in 1152.[26] In 1188–9 the payment of Peter's Pence from Denmark was recorded in the *Liber Censuum*[27] and the payment of one penny from every house in Norway and Sweden was also mentioned which is apparently exactly the same papal due.[28] Peter's Pence would therefore have been known in the diocese of Orkney throughout most of Harold Maddadson's period as earl. The earliest direct evidence for payment being made in Orkney does not come until 1327 when it is recorded that £6 5s. had been paid by the bishop of Orkney for two years payment of Peter's Pence;[29] although in 1320 this same bishop had been suspended for having withheld payment during the previous fifteen years.[30] There is little doubt, however, that the due had been collected in Orkney long before this, for in 1206 the archbishop of Trondheim had been ordered to collect Peter's Pence throughout his province, in which the bishopric of Orkney lay[31]

The annual payment of one penny from each house in Caithness granted to the papacy by Earl Harold can therefore be regarded as a deliberate copy of the customary payment of Peter's Pence as he knew it from his Orkney earldom. It appears that it was fairly common for secular lords in Norway to obtain the protection of the Roman Church for themselves and their lands by paying a regular tax of this kind.[32] There are examples of similar grants also in Scotland; one is of a grant of two shillings made to the papacy at the same date as Earl Harold's grant by Earl Gilchrist of Mar.[33] Another is of a grant made to the monks of Paisley by Reginald, son of Somerled, 'dominus de Inchegal', of 'singulis annis unum denarium ex quolibet domo totius terre sue unde fumus exit', about the year 1180.[34] There is no evidence that either of these benefactors of the church received the same opposition to their grants as Earl Harold, which is the only reason why anything is known about the grant of an annual penny from Caithness. It had been made originally by the earl during the pontificate of Alexander III (1159–81), when the grant had been confirmed by the first known bishop of Caithness, Andrew, and 'other nobles of those parts'.[35] But Andrew's successor John had obstructed the payment,[36] and in 1198 Innocent

[26] E. Vandvik, *Latinske Dokument til Norsk Historie* (Oslo, 1959), 62. As Pope Adrian IV Nicholas Breakspear was responsible for suggesting that Peter's Pence be imposed on Ireland in return for its cession to Henry II (see above, p. 15).

[27] *Liber Censuum*, i, 226–7.          [28] *Ibid.*, 229.

[29] Lunt, *Papal Revenues*, ii, 74.

[30] *CPL*, ii, 484; *Diplom. Norveg.*, ix, no. 87.

[31] *Ibid.*, vii, no. 6.

[32] *Kultur-Historisk Leksikon for Nordisk Middelalder* (Copenhagen, 1960–), x, 257.

[33] *Liber Censuum*, i, 232. I am very grateful to the editor for pointing out this reference to me.

[34] *Paisley Reg.*, 125. This is the date given for the document in *SP*, under 'Lords of the Isles', and is of the same period as Earl Harold's grant. Reginald would also have been acquainted with the payment of Peter's Pence in the Western Isles which still lay under the Norwegian diocese of Nidaros and over which he had temporal rule. He made the grant to an important monastery which had links with the Scottish part of his lordship.

[35] *Diplom. Norveg.*, vii, no. 2.

[36] Bishop John had not allowed the payment to be made 'ab his qui sunt in diocesi constituti auctoritate propria' (*ibid.*), which appears to mean that the interdict was sent out on his authority to the people of his diocese.

III ordered the bishops of Orkney and Rosemarkie to restrain John from preventing its collection. It is the opposition of this bishop to the due which is really the most interesting thing about it; why did he attempt to prevent it, when this only brought the threat of papal censure upon him? His opposition cannot be seen as part of the Scottish Church's struggle with the papacy, for this had been settled previously, with the election of Roger to the see of St Andrews and with the bulls *Super Anxietatibus* of 1176 and *Cum Universi* of 1192. Rather it would appear to be a result of the turbulent history of the north at this period. The background to this incident will now be examined.

Harold Maddadson is one of the best-known of the earls of Orkney and Caithness, mainly because of the clashes which he had with both the king of Norway and the king of Scotland. He was unfortunate enough to live at a time when both kings were extending their authority over the remoter areas of their kingdoms. This process continued throughout his time as earl and reached a climax in the years 1195–8, during which years the earl was most hard-pressed. In 1193 he had been involved in the rising of the Eyskjeggar in Norway and by 1195 he had lost control over Shetland and some of his authority in Orkney as a result.[37] In the very next year he rose in revolt against William the Lion in Caithness which led to an expedition north by the Scottish king, the first known occasion when any king of Scotland entered Caithness.[38] As a result half of his earldom was taken from the old earl and given to a rival claimant, Harold Ungi; and when the former failed to bring some hostages to the king in the following year he lost the other half as well.[39] Although Harold Maddadson defeated and killed his rival at a battle near Wick in 1198,[40] he failed to regain possession of his former earldom which was given instead to Rognvald Gudrodson, king of the Hebrides.[41] Not until the year 1201 did the old earl do anything about getting his Caithness earldom back, when he organised the murder of one of Earl Rognvald's stewards and then embarked on a rash expedition against the bishop of Caithness which resulted in the maiming of the bishop which itself led to the final submission of Earl Harold to King William.[42] It was a fatal mistake to antagonise the church in this way, even though Harold appears to have been otherwise a generous benefactor of the Church.[43] But there is no doubt that the expedition across the Pentland Firth was organised for the sole purpose of attacking the bishop in his castle of Scrabster.[44] For present purposes the interest of this attack lies in the person of the bishop, for it was John, the same bishop who prior to 1198 had prevented the earl's payment of one penny from every

---

[37] *The Orkneyinga Saga*, trans. A. B. Taylor (Edinburgh, 1938), 348.

[38] *Chron. Fordun*, 270; *Chronica Magistri Rogeri de Houedene*, ed. W. Stubbs (Rolls series, 1871), iv, 10; cf. also *RRS*, ii, 15–16.

[39] *Chron. Houedene*, iv, 10.     [40] *ES*, ii, 350.

[41] *Orkneyinga Saga*, 345; *Chron. Houedene*, iv, 12 (where 'son of Somerled' is an error for 'son of Gudrod').     [42] *Orkneyinga Saga*, 346; *Chron. Fordun*, 271.

[43] He made a grant of an annual mark of silver to the canons of Scone (*Diplom. Norveg.*, ii, no. 2), put the convent of 'Bencoryn' under his protection (*APS*, i, 116), as well as granting the annual penny from Caithness to the papacy.

[44] The saga narrative tells how the earl's army 'rushed up from the ships to the (bishop's) fortress' (*Orkneyinga Saga*, 346).

household in his earldom. The immediate reason for the 1201 attack is not mentioned in the saga account. Fordun said that Earl Harold considered the bishop to be 'an informer and the instigator of the misunderstanding between him and the lord king'.[45] There is some evidence that Earl Harold may indeed have been involved in subversive activities at this time, for he was in contact with King John of England, an enemy of King William and a man not averse to building up alliances with another's vassals.[46] Whether this had been reported to King William is a matter of conjecture, but the deliberate mutilation of Bishop John's eyes and tongue would appear to be a symbolic punishment, typical of the age, for a crime involving spying and informing. In any case, the antagonism between earl and bishop went back before 1201 and before 1198 when the bishop had been forbidding the earl's papal grant. This antagonism was probably a result of the part played by the church in Caithness in the expansionist schemes of the Scottish kings, which posed such a threat to the earl's position in his earldom.

The church was an important factor in the process of establishing royal control over the northern mainland of Scotland in the twelfth century. In fact the imposition of an ecclesiastical organisation appears to have been the precursor of the establishment of royal authority. It was during Earl Harold's long period of rule in the north that this imposition of ecclesiastical organisation took place as well as the assertion of royal control over the independent earl. The bishopric of Caithness was founded by King David prior to 1147–51, before which it is assumed that Caithness had formed part of the ancient bishopric of Orkney.[47] The earl's secular control over Caithness implies that there would also have been ecclesiastical control over the area from Orkney, and this may not have ceased with the foundation of a Scottish bishopric of Caithness. In 1152 moreover the dioceses of Orkney and the Isles became part of the ecclesiastical organisation of Norway with the creation of the archbishopric of Nidaros and the incorporation of those bishoprics within it. Any attempt to continue to exercise authority over Caithness from Orkney thereafter would be done under the aegis of the Norwegian Church. On the other hand, the Scottish king's creation of a bishopric of Caithness and his encouragement of the activities of monks in Dornoch[48] can be regarded as part of a deliberate policy of detaching the area from the neighbouring Norse influence. The church was to prepare the ground for succeeding royal control. But the establishment of a

---

[45] Chron. Fordun, 271.

[46] In January 1202 King John issued safe-conducts for Harold earl of Orkney to come to him in England and confer (CDS, i, 324). In the Pipe Roll accounts for Northumberland in 1201 ten marks were allowed on the account to Adam, chaplain of Orkney and his 'socii', going to Orkney on the king's affairs (Pipe Roll Society, n.s., xiv, 244).

[47] Watt, Fasti, 62; for Andrew as first known bishop, cf. ibid., 58 and Traditio, xxvi (1970), 351.

[48] Lawrie, Charters, 132. It is probable that these monks were from the south, making a new establishment in Caithness (G. W. S. Barrow, 'Scottish Rulers and the Religious Orders', TRHS, 5th. ser., iii, 98) rather than an existing Culdee settlement. In the following reign, Malcolm earl of Ross was similarly ordered to protect the rights of the monks of Dunfermline, presumably in his earldom (RRS, i, 179).

Scottish bishop and new customs was resented by the earl and men of Caithness from the evidence of friction which followed. It is not known whether the first bishop Andrew (1147 × 1151–1184) ever visited the diocese but it was his successor John (1189 × 1199–1202) who was attacked at the episcopal castle of Scrabster in 1201 by a band under the leadership of Earl Harold.[49] Furthermore, the third bishop, Adam (1213–22) was burnt alive in his residence at Halkirk in 1222, and on that occasion the earl, the son of Earl Harold, was considered to have been a party to the crime.[50] The main cause of unrest on this occasion concerned the payment of teinds, which Bishop Adam had attempted to impose in accordance with the general law of the church. It appears that this was far in excess of what the farmers of Caithness were accustomed to pay – traditional amounts probably fixed when Caithness lay within the area of jurisdiction of the Orkney bishops.[51] Although there was general antagonism to the payment of teinds in Scotland and elsewhere in the twelfth and thirteenth centuries,[52] it looks as if the situation in Caithness was exacerbated by the changing of the old Norse custom to bring the northerly diocese into line with the rest of Scotland. The murder of the bishop by his own flock with the apparent connivance of the earl can only have been the culmination of a great deal of unrest. The maiming of Bishop John in 1201 is likewise evidence of disturbances which at this date appear to have arisen particularly out of a personal quarrel between the earl and the bishop.[53]

Bishop John's attempt in the years before 1198 to prevent the payment of Peter's Pence which had been granted by the earl to the papacy from his Scottish earldom is the first evidence of this quarrel. It also can be seen as an example of the clash of Scottish custom and personnel with local tradition. Peter's Pence had been introduced into Norway by Nicholas Breakspear in 1152–3 and sometime thereafter (during the pontificate of Alexander III, 1159–81) was imposed in Caithness, an area which until recently had probably been under the control of the bishop of Orkney. We do not know whether this was done by the earl with the deliberate intention of keeping Caithness in line with Norwegian developments, but the opposition of the second bishop of Caithness is only understandable as part of a determination to root out all Norwegian influence in an area which the Scottish kings were trying hard to incorporate within their kingdom.[54] This sole example of the payment of

---

[49] See above, p. 19.

[50] *Chron. Fordun*, 284–5; *The Orkneyingers Saga*, Icelandic Sagas III, trans. G. W. Dasent (Rolls Series, 1894), 232; *SAEC*, 337.

[51] The saga account of the murder gives details as to how much butter the bishop had been demanding above the 'old custom' that he should have a spann for every thirty cows (*Orkneyingers Saga*, Rolls ed., 232). A spann was a Norwegian measure.

[52] In particular in the Hebrides, where teinds of butter and cheese had been withheld at just the same time (*Diplom. Norveg.*, vii, no. 10).

[53] See above, p. 20.

[54] As there is no further record of the grant of one penny from every house in Caithness, and it does not appear in the *Liber Censuum*, the Scottish bishops must have been successful in preventing it from becoming a permanent due. The attempt to impose Peter's Pence in Caithness in the twelfth century was as unsuccessful therefore as the papal attempt to impose it throughout Scotland in the fourteenth.

Peter's Pence in Scotland provides us with further evidence therefore of the tension which existed in the far north when it was drawn away from the Norwegian sphere of influence and brought slowly under Scottish control during the twelfth and thirteenth centuries.

BARBARA CRAWFORD

*Additional Note.* After this chapter was in page-proof my attention was drawn to a document copied into a MS. at Córdoba (Biblioteca de la Mezquita MS. 40, ff.168–71) which is to be published by Dr. P. Linehan in the *Bulletin of the Institute of Historical Research.* In this document, evidently a draft prepared for the Scots in Anglo-Scottish negotiations of 1321, is the statement that whereas King Alfred of England granted the Roman Church as tribute one penny from every house emitting smoke in his dominions, this penny is not levied from Scotland (*qui tamen denarius a Scocia non percipitur*). I am grateful to Dr. Linehan for information about this source and for permission to publish the important passage relating to Peter's Pence in Scotland.

B.C.

# 3

## *Some East Fife Documents of the Twelfth and Thirteenth Centuries*

As a group the eleven documents edited here have little in common save that they relate to East Fife in the century from *c.* 1190 to *c.* 1290 and have not been printed previously. Nos. 3 and 4 both deal with the office of archdeacon of St Andrews in the days when it still lacked an adequate permanent endowment. Nos. 5, 8, 9 and 11 are concerned with the complex subinfeudation of the episcopal estate at Tarvit. The rest stand by themselves, although nos. 1 and 10 both have to do with the cathedral priory of St Andrews, while nos. 2, 6 and 7 are connected with places, persons and events as various as North Berwick nunnery, the shrine of St Thomas Becket at Canterbury and the seemingly inappropriate financial embarrassment of John Monypenny.

For the best part of forty years Ronald Cant has lived and worked among the community of East Fife, townspeople, gownspeople and the good folk of the landward parishes. I hope, therefore, that he will not think it out of place to be offered a handful of documents which, dry and formula-ridden though they may be, nevertheless take us for a brief spell into the richly varied company of East Fife worthies (and others) of an earlier century: Malpatric master of the schools and Hugh the bishop's butler, Master Ranulf the archdeacon, Cormac Luhoc suspended before our gaze in the moment of being evicted from his bondage holding near Earlsferry, that very early Canterbury pilgrim Michael Scot of Rumgally, ancestor of the Scotts of Balwearie and perhaps himself descended from the culdees of St Andrews, John Monypenny forebear of the lairds of Pitmilly, Sir Walter de Percehay murderer of the young Earl Duncan of Fife, and John Blair of Nydie, still under age, for whom his 'Tutor' acted in consultation with his mother and uncle.

Eight of the eleven documents are originals located at the Scottish Record Office (nos. 5, 8, 9, 11), the National Library of Scotland (nos. 3, 4, 10) and St Andrews University Library (no. 1). The three printed from later copies are derived from MSS in the National Library (nos. 2, 7) and among the archives of the Dean and Chapter of Canterbury Cathedral (no. 6). I am grateful to Dr Marinell Ash for drawing my attention to the charters concerning Tarvit, and I should like to thank Sir Donald Makgill of Makgill and Messrs Haldanes and McLaren, W.S. for kindly granting me permission to publish nos. 5, 8 and 11 and the Dean and Chapter of Canterbury for their kindness in permitting the publication of no. 6.

1  Walter the prior and the convent of St Andrews Cathedral Priory grant to Hugh the butler and his heirs the land (in St Andrews) which the priory bought from Master Malpatric, immediately east of the land belonging to the late Cuthbert dean (of Fife), for an annual rent of 3s., half at Easter and half at Michaelmas (1189 × 1198, probably 1189 × 1196).

Universis Sancte Matris Ecclesie filiis . Walterus dei gracia prior de Sancto Andrea . 7 Conuentus eiusdem loci . salutem. Sciant omnes tam futuri quam presentes . nos dedisse 7 Concessisse 7 hac nostra carta confirmasse Hugoni pincerne 7 heredibus suis terram nostram quam emimus a Magistro Malpatrico . proximam uidelicet terre illi que fuit quondam Cuthberti decani a parte orientali . Tenendam sibi 7 heredibus suis libere 7 quiete ab omni seruicio 7 exactione 7 Consuetudine . Reddendo nobis inde annuatim tres solidos . dimidium ad pasca 7 dimidium ad festum Sancti Michaelis . Testibus his . Willelmo capellano de Deruessyn . Radulfo 7 Johanne clericis domini electi . Germano . Roberto de Rokesburgia . Magistro Aiulfo . Alexandro Francigena . Ada fabro burgensibus Sancti Andree. Johanne de Berefordia . Willelmo de Ardift . Et aliis quampluribus;[a]

Endorsement: No early endorsement.

Description: Foot folded, with slits for seal-tag, which survives, 0·7″ wide, with well-preserved example of the seal of the cathedral priory bearing a representation of the south elevation of the 'old cathedral' (i.e. 'St Rule's'). Dimensions are 7·0″ (17·8 cm), top, 6·8″ (17·4 cm.), bottom × 4·7″ (12 cm.), L.H., R.H. Unruled. Hand an upright court hand with thin strokes, similar to but not identical with that of Kinninmonths, p. 122, no. 5.

Source: Original, St Andrews University Library, MS 30276.

Note: a us written as capitals to fill up line.

Comment: The beneficiary of this charter was butler to the bishops of St Andrews Richard (1165–78) and Roger (1189/98–1202); St And. Lib. 134–6, 138–41, 153. Master Malpatric was evidently master of the schools of St Andrews and occurs in documents of Bishop Richard's time (ibid. 133, 137, 259–60). He had a son Malcolm who granted part of Denork (an endowment of the schools) to Adam of Kinninmonth the priory's steward (Kinninmonths, 125–6). Master Patrick, master of the schools c. 1212 (St And. Lib., 316–18), was presumably another son of Malpatric. The property in question seems to have been in the burgh, for the toft of Cuthbert the dean is referred to in 1183 (ibid. 59); Cuthbert had been dean of Fife in the period 1165–72 (Watt, Fasti, 314). Two other features confirm the burghal location, first, the very unusual rent terms of Easter and Michaelmas, second, the attestation of five St Andrews burgesses (note the surnames 'of Roxburgh', 'Frenchman', 'wright'). William parochial chaplain of Dairsie witnessed acta of Bishops Richard (N. Berwick Carte, no. 4) and Roger (St And. Lib., 45) and perhaps witnesses no. 3 below. John of 'Berefordia' (Bearford in Haddington, E. Lothian?) witnessed acta of Bishop Roger before and after consecration (ibid., 153, 154; Kinninmonths, 122). 'Ardift' is Airdit in Leuchars. Date: Prior

Walter, after a lengthy rule, demitted office probably in 1196, and this seems to belong to the years when Roger was bishop-elect.

2   Waltheof son of Merleswein grants to North Berwick Priory common pasture in his land of Kincraig (in Elie and Earlsferry) for beasts belonging to the cell of North Berwick (i.e. Ardross hospital); saving the donor's meadows and crops. Waltheof also concedes the removal of Cormac Luhoc with his whole dwelling from the cell of North Berwick, so that neither he nor other tenants of the donor should ever dwell in the vicinity of that cell. (c. 1200–10).

Sciant omnes tam presentes quam futuri has literas visuri . Me Waldef filium Merlesuein dedisse etᵃ concessisse et hac presenti carta mea confirmasse Deo et monialibus de Norberwic . Communem pasturam terre mee de Kincrag propriis animalibus suis ad predictam cellam pertinentibus . tenendam sibi de me et heredibus meis in puram et perpetuam elemosinam . preter mea prata et segetes . libere et quiete ab omni servitio sicut elemosina liberius et quietius potest dari . et concedi. Concessi itaque ut Cormac Luhocᵇ removeatur a cella predictarum monialium . Scilicet . ab hospitali cum tota sua habitatione . ita ut nec predictus Cormac nec aliqui alii meorum amplius preter homines predictarum monialium habitent propinquius et vicinius terre predicte celle . quam in tempore patris mei et antecessorum meorum habitare solebant . his testibus . Nesso de Ramesey . Toma de Lundin . Willielmoᶜ persona de Kilconwat . Willelmo de Ramesey . et aliis multis.

Heading: Out of Grange Malcolm's papers, 10 May 1710.
Note at foot: (Ex originali. The seal in white waxe, of the bigness of a Crown, – Hath on it a Man upon horse-back.)
Source: National Library of Scotland, MS Adv. 34.6.24, p. 217.

Notes: a Here and almost throughout the transcriber has used an ampersand.
       b Lukoc might be read.
       c Sic.

Comment: Waltheof was son and heir of Merleswein whom William I had infeft in Ardross, Fife, for knight-service (RRS, ii, no. 137). Lord of Ardross and Kennoway, he appears in record of the late twelfth and opening years of the thirteenth century (e.g. St And. Lib., 272, 319, 381, 383; N. Berwick Carte, no. 7).
     This curious document was overlooked when Cosmo Innes produced his edition of the North Berwick charters for the Bannatyne Club in 1847. By gift of Earl Duncan II of Fife, the Cistercian nuns of North Berwick possessed a pilgrims' hospice or hospital near the north end of the 'earl's ferry' at Ardross, founded by Earl Duncan I (ibid., no. 2). This was the cella or hospitale referred to here. The concession that Cormac Luhoc and his habitatio (dwelling or household?) should be removed from its neighbourhood recalls the abbot of Holyrood's promise, c. 1141, that the toun of Pittendreich (in

Lasswade, Midlothian) should never be moved nearer to Newbattle Abbey (Lawrie, *Charters*, no. 151).

Ness of Ramsay occurs frequently in record of the earlier thirteenth century (e.g. *N. Berwick Carte*, nos. 7, 10; *St And. Lib.*, 107, 155, 245; *Dunfermline Reg.*, nos. 213, 214 – *socius* of the earl of Fife in 1227). It does not seem absolutely certain that he was the same as the Master Ness of Ramsay, royal physician and laird of Bamff, for whom evidence is plentiful in the 1230s; perhaps this Ness, father of Master Peter of Ramsay, Robert Grosseteste's successor as lecturer to the Oxford Franciscans and bishop of Aberdeen 1247–56, was the physician's father (cf. *N. Berwick Carte*, nos. 17, 28; *Ramsay, Bamff Charters*, nos. 1, 2). William of Ramsay witnessed charters of William I in the 1190s (*RRS*, ii, nos. 229, 292, 297, 368). For Thomas of Lundin of that ilk cf. *ibid.*, i, 31 and n. 8; he granted land at Aithernie to North Berwick more or less contemporaneously with this document (*N. Berwick Carte*, no. 10). 'Kilconwat' of which William was parson is Kilconquhar, i.e. '[Saint] Duncan's church'. It seems impossible to suggest any date for this more precise than *c.* 1204 or up to a few years later.


3    Patrick abbot of Dunfermline, Guy (Wido) abbot of Lindores and Hugh (de Mortemer) prior of May, acting as judges-delegate appointed by Pope Innocent III, pronounce a decision in the dispute between Ranulf archdeacon of St Andrews on one part and Hugh the steward and his nephew Jordan on the other part, anent the lands lying on the west of the 'new work' towards the houses of Lamburc. By agreement, Hugh and Jordan have resigned and quit-claimed the lands, together with the buildings which they have built upon them, to the archdeacon and his successors. In return, the archdeacon has given Hugh 15 merks and Jordan 10 merks and four perches of land, immediately east of the house of Simon the clerk, which he had received from Prior Thomas and the convent of St Andrews Cathedral Priory, for a rent of one pound of cumin. Seals placed by the three judges-delegate and the bishop of St Andrews. (20 September 1202 × 11 April 1206).


.P. et W. abbates de Dunfermelin et de Lundores . et .H. prior de Pethneweme . Omnibus ad quorum noticiam et intellectum tenor presentis scripti pervenerit . salutem in domino. Noverit fraternitas vestra mandato domini pape Innocentii suscepto nobis iniunctum fuisse . ut questionem quam Ranulfus archidiaconus de Sancto Andrea proponebat adversus Hugonem seneschaldum et Jordanum nepotem ipsius super terris ex occidentali parte novi operis existentibus versus domos Lamburc quas asserebat ad archidiaconatum suum spectare . convocatis partibus et auditis vel iudicio decideremus . vel compositione interveniente liti finem imponeremus. Convocatis igitur aliquociens partibus tandem mediante domino episcopo Sancti Andree Willelmo . et partes suas interponente nobis etiam auctoritatem prestantibus et operam et diligentiam adhibentibus. compositum est inter partes ita quod Hugo Senescaldus et Jordanus nepos eius resignaverunt et quietas inposterum clamaverunt terras illas cum edificiis in eis ab ipsis constructis .R. archidiacono et succesoribus*a* eius. Ipse vero .R. archidiaconus pro resignacione facienda et pro bono pacis dedit Hugoni senescaldo .xv. marcas . et Jordano .x. marcas . et quatuor perticatas terre quas a .T. priore et eius conventu . accepterat proximas domui Symonis clerici ex parte orientali tenendas de se et successoribus suis sibi et heredibus suis solvendo annuatim unam libram cimini . et ut hec compositio rata consistat et imperpetuum inconcussa permaneat inviolabiliter observanda . tam sigilli domini episcopi quam nostrorum appositione est corroborata et confirmata. His testibus . Domino .T. priore et eius conventu . Andrea de Moravia . Magistro Ada . Magistro Stephano . Magistro Ysaac . Magistro Symone . Willelmo de Karel decano . Willelmo capellano de Brechhin . Willelmo de Dervesin . Petro et Eadwardo capellanis domini episcopi . Johanne de Hautuisel . Willelmo de Golin . Johanne de Londoniis . Radulfo nigro . Johanne maraschaldo . Symone de Nuisi . Eutropio dispensatore . Petro et Hugone de Nidin et Roberto de Kalledouer pueris domini episcopi . Willelmo Lambin . Gileberto Britone. Symone clerico.

*Endorsement*: resignacio terre ex occidentali parte novi operis versus domum Lamburg' (xiii cent.)

*Description*: Foot originally folded, with slits for four seal-tags; no tags or seals remain. Dimensions are 8″ (20·3 cm.) × 4·2″ (10·1 cm.). The parchment is ruled, apparently in pencil. The hand is a neat charter hand, using a crossed form of tironian 'et'.

*Source*: Original, NLS, MS Adv. 15.1.18, no. 33.

*Note*: a Sic.

*Comment*: Patrick was elected abbot of Dunfermline in 1202 and was still abbot in 1217; Guy first abbot of Lindores ruled from *c.* 1191 to 1219; Hugh de Mortemer was prior of May *alias* Pittenweem from before 1198 till some date before 11 April, 1206. Thomas (a witness) was prior of St Andrews from *c.* 1199 to 1211. Ranulf was archdeacon of St Andrews from 1199 to 1209. He had evidently brought an action at the papal curia against Hugh the (bishop's) steward and his nephew Jordan anent the land west of the new cathedral (begun in 1162 and completed in 1318), where stood in later times the archdeacon's manse, succeeded *c.* 1570 by Dean's Court. The pope remitted the case to the customary trio of judges-delegate, whose settlement (reached after mediation by Bishop Malvoisin) was that Hugh and Jordan resigned the land and buildings as properly belonging to the archdeaconry, receiving compensation in money and a small plot of land. This property may be seen as the earliest permanent endowment of the archdeacon's office, to be augmented a few years later when Bishop Malvoisin granted it the modestly endowed parish kirk of Tarvit on the episcopal demesne (1209–12; NLS, MS Adv. 15.1.18, no. 14).

Among the witnesses, the three 'boys' of the bishop, presumably being brought up and educated in his household, are noteworthy. The steward Hugh was perhaps the bishop's tenant at Nydie, and it may be that the boy Hugh was the Hugh son of Hugh of Nydie who in the burgh court of St

Andrews sold a plot south-east of the castle to Prior John White between 1236 and 1253 (*St And. Lib.*, 284–5).

4  Walter of Roxburgh the younger quitclaims to Ranulf archdeacon of St Andrews Scoonie(hill) (in St Andrews and St Leonards) and Balkaithley (in Dunino) and the land on the south side of the city of St Andrews between the burns, all possessed by Walter (of Roxburgh) archdeacon of St Andrews, uncle of Walter the younger, for the term of his life. Walter the younger has resigned to Archdeacon Ranulf all the right which he might have had in these lands whether by gift or grant or confirmation of Bishop Hugh of St Andrews or of his uncle Archdeacon Walter, and has also restored to Archdeacon Ranulf the charters which he had concerning these lands, recognising them to belong to the archdeaconry. Seals placed by Walter the younger, Ralph bishop of Brechin and Henry abbot of Arbroath. (Arbroath or Montrose (?), July 1202 × April 1207).

Universis sancte matris ecclesie filiis Walterus iuvenis de Rokesburg' . salutem in domino. Noverit universitas vestra me concessisse et quietas clamasse Rannulfo archidiacono*a* de sancto Andrea*a* et successoribus eius in perpetuum . Sconin . et Balekathelin . et terram que iacet ex australi parte urbis sancti Andréé inter torrentes quas terras pie memorie Walterus archidiaconus eiusdem loci avunculus meus tenuit et possedit in vita sua . quas etiam post eius tempora ego ipse habui et possedi. Resignavi etiam predicto *Rannulfo* archidiacono totum ius quod in predictis terris habui . sive ex dono . sive ex concessione . sive ex confirmatione pie recordationis episcopi Hugonis . sive avunculi mei Walteri archidiaconi . et Cartas quas de terris illis habui . eidem prenominato *Rannulfo* reddidi cum scirem illas ad archidiaconatum sancti Andréé pertinere . et ut hec concessio et resignatio rata sit et inconcussa infuturum . illas corroboravi appositione sigillorum domini R[adulfi] Brethinensis episcopi . et H[enrici] abbatis de Aberbruthot . et mei . dependentium a presenti pagina. Volens tenori eius et continentie fidem haberi inposterum. His testibus . R[adulfo] episcopo Brethinensi . H[enrico] abbati de Aberbruthot . et conventu eiusdem loci . [      ]*b* archidiacono Brethinensi . Willelmo et Petro capellanis domini Brethinensis . Henrico capellano de Munros . Hervico persona de Insula Brioci . Alano clerico de Munros . Rogero de Inverkethin . Herberto de Munros . Willelmo filio Ede . Sthephano*c* le mare . Roberto de Hales . et multis aliis.

*Endorsement*: Resignacio terrarum de Sconyn et Balkathelyn et terrarum iacentium ex australi parte urbis inter torrentes et cartarum ad archidiacon-[at]um pertinentium (xiii cent.)

*Description*: Foot originally folded, with slits for three seal-tags; no tag or seal remains. Dimensions are 9·25″ (23·5 cm.) × 2·4″ (6·2 cm.). The parchment is ruled in pencil or faint ink. The hand is a neat charter hand of the turn of the twelfth and thirteenth centuries, using a crossed form of tironian 'et'.

*Source*: Original, NLS MS Adv. 15.1.18, no. 47.

*Notes*: *a Large minuscule initial* a.
   *b Space left for initial* (*Supply* G[regorio]*?*).
   *c Sic.*

*Comment*: Like the preceding document (which might be later in date) this quitclaim shews us a further instalment of the process by which the archdeaconry of St Andrews acquired a permanent endowment. Master Walter of Roxburgh had been archdeacon of St Andrews from *c.* 1172 to *c.* 1189. He and his nephew both witnessed an act of Bishop Richard (*Dunfermline Registrum*, no. 97). This nephew, Walter the younger of Roxburgh – possibly a burgess in the city – had on his uncle's death succeeded to the estates of Scoonie(hill) and Balkaithley, and to a piece of land on the southern edge of the burgh 'between the burns' – presumably between the Kinness Burn on the south and the 'Abbey Burn' on the north, to the east of the old hospital of St Leonard. Archdeacon Ranulf was evidently successful in reclaiming these estates as justly belonging to the archdeacon's office, and improperly alienated by his predecessor, abetted by the 'intruding' Bishop Hugh (1180–1188). The witnesses (among whom the absence of St Andrews names is striking) strongly suggest that the quitclaim was issued either at Montrose or Arbroath. Hervey is the earliest known parson of what later became Craig parish but had been known (after the little Rossie Island at the mouth of Montrose Basin and its patron saint) as Inchbrayock, that is the island of Saint Brioc or Brieuc. Date: determined by the consecration of Bishop Ralph of Brechin in 1202, before July, and the death of Abbot Henry of Arbroath about 20 March 1207.

5   John of Wilton grants to his sister Maud land worth a hundred shillings a year in the toun of Tarvit (formerly in Tarvit, now in Ceres), to be held heritably by herself and the heirs born to her. If she should not bear a child the land will revert to John and his heirs. The *reddendo* is a pair of silver-gilt spurs or 6d. at Whitsun, saving the forinsec service due to the king and the bishop of St Andrews. (*c.* 1228?).

Sciant presentes et futuri quod ego Johannes de Wilton' dedi et concessi et hac presenti carta mea confirmaui Matild*i* Sorori mee pro humagio et seruicio suo centum solidatos terre in villa de Teruet . Habendos et tenendos libere . et quiete . et honorifice . et integre . et Jurehereditario*a* cum omnibus libertatibus et aisiamentis ad dictam terram pertinentibus infra et extra . de me uel heredibus meis . sibi uel heredibus suis qui de se exibunt. Et si forte euenerit quod de se infantem non habuerit*b* . dicti c. solidati terre . predicto Johanni uel heredibus suis remanebunt. Reddendo inde prefato Johanni uel heredibus suis calcaria subaurata . uel sex denarios ad festum pentecosten . pro omni seruicio consuetudine et exactione . saluo forinseco seruicio domini mei Regis et domini Episcopi Sancti Andree. Hiis testibus Domino Willelmo episcopo Sancti Andree . Douenaldo de Mar Willelmo Auenel . Waltero fili*o* Alani . Hugone de Mortemer . Willelmo de Diue . Gilberto Auenel . Waltero de Wdeford . et multis aliis*c*

*Endorsement*: Carta de Terwet (xiv cent., same hand as endorsements of nos. 8 and 11).

*Description*: Foot folded, with slits for seal-tag which remains, 0·4″ wide. Seal (obverse only) in greenish wax, diam. 1½″, a triple plant device, legend ( + ?) . . GILL' IOH͞ES*a* DE WIL[   ]VN Dimensions are 7″ (17·8 cm.), top, 7·1″ (18 cm.), bottom × 3·8″ (9·7 cm.), L.H., 3·9″ (10 cm.), R.H. Unruled. Hand a very neat pleasing business hand, using crossed form of tironian 'et'.

*Source*: Original, SRO, GD 82/1 (Makgill of Makgill charters).

*Notes: a* Sic.

   *b* rt *originally followed* habue *to complete a line, but has been erased and replaced by a hyphen, with* rit *beginning the next line.*

   *c* Final s *extended into a long flourish to complete the bottom line.*

*Comment*: This simple example of a tailzie or conditional estate introduces us to a brief series of documents (the rest are nos. 8, 9 and 11) relating to a feudal estate created in that part of Tarvit (evidently the eastern half of the old parish which is now merged in Ceres) which belonged to the bishops of St Andrews. The granter was John of Wilton the younger, son of a previous John. It seems that he (or one of his recent ancestors) had been infeft in Tarvit by a bishop of St Andrews or perhaps by the crown during a vacancy. The Roxburghshire parish of Wilton beside Hawick formed a small barony held in chief of the crown before the end of William I's reign, probably from the middle years of the twelfth century. John younger of Wilton proved his right to the patronage of Wilton kirk *c.* 1225–7 (*Glasgow Reg.*, i, no. 100). Here we see him acting as lord of Tarvit and making provision for his sister Maud, apparently on the occasion of her marriage to Gilbert Avenel (son of William?), one of the witnesses, although this deed is not formally worded as a grant in marriage or free marriage. As in the case of Blebo (no. 7 below), forinsec service is reserved both to the bishop of St Andrews and to the king; we know that the bishop was entitled to cain from Bleboshire (*St And. Lib.*, 123, 145) and from Glaidney in Tarvit (nos. 8, 11 below).

   It is hard to date this document precisely, but Donald of Mar (son of Morgund earl of Mar?) witnessed a royal act of 12 April 1228 (*ibid.*, 237), while Bishop Malvoisin died on 9 July 1238.

6   Michael Scot 'of the realm of Scotland' grants to God and the Blessed Thomas the Martyr of Canterbury, for the purpose of providing lights before the martyr's shrine, an annual rent of 20s. sterling, payable from his feu of Rumgally (in Kemback) in two instalments, at Whitsun and Martinmas; for himself and his wife and their children and for the souls of their fathers and mothers and other ancestors and of all faithful Christians. (1238 × 1240).

Universis Christi fidelibus hanc cartam inspecturis vel audituris Michael Scotus de regno Scocie in domino salutem. Universitati vestre significo me divine pietatis instinctu concessisse et hac carta mea confirmasse Deo et beato Thome martiris Cantuar' ad luminare ante feretrum eiusdem martiris annuum censum viginti solidorum sterlingorum perpetuo percipiendum in feodo de Radmagalli ad duos terminos, scilicet ad Pentecosten et ad festum Sancti Martini, tenendum et habendum de me et heredibus meis pro me et uxore mea et liberis meis et animabus patrum et matrum et antecessorum nostrorum et pro animabus omnium fidelium Christianorum liberum et quietum in puram et perpetuam elemosinam ab omni servicio, exactione, consuetudine uel demanda. Testibus Domino Galfrido de Dunfermelin abbate, Domino Thoma de Kil-maronᵃ, Domino Bernardo de Beckery,ᵇ Philippo de Lophor, Patricio de Perglassi,ᶜ Dunchano Scoto, Johanne de Bladboch, Adaᵈ de Kenbach et multis aliis.

*Rubric*: Carta Michaelis Scottiᵉ de viginti solidis redditus (in red, *A* and *E*).
*Source*: Dean and Chapter, Canterbury, MS Register A, fo. 451ʳ (=*A*); MS Register E, fo. 143ʳ (=*E*).
Printed here from *A* with *E*'s variants noted.

*Notes*: *a* Kylmaron, *E*.
    *b* Sic, *A* and *E*. Read Petkery?
    *c* Sic, *A* and *E*. Read Petglassi.
    *d* Ada *in full*, *E*.
    *e* Scoti, *E*.
*Comment*: The cult of Saint Thomas the Martyr of Canterbury spread to Scotland very rapidly, perhaps stimulated by the overlordship which Henry II of England imposed on the Scottish realm from 1174 to 1189. Scots kings such as William I and Alexander III and nobles such as the hereditary Stewart and Robert Bruce (1220) responded to the appeal exerted by the murdered archbishop by founding abbeys, making pilgrimages to his shrine, or offering him gifts from their material possessions (*SHR*, xxxi, 16–17; *The Stewarts*, ix, no. 3, 230–33). The interest of this particular charter lies partly in the way in which it shews a member of the middling Scots gentry being caught up in the same fervour of martyrolatry. Indeed, because of the description of the donor as 'of the realm of Scotland', it is tempting to suggest that his charter was issued at Canterbury and to see the testing clause as a list of Fife notables all visiting Canterbury on a single excursion the holy blissful martyr for to seek. A less fascinating but perhaps safer surmise is that the charter was given at Dunfermline Abbey, whose convent would still be mindful of the historic links between their house and Christ Church, Canterbury.

    The value of this charter, however, is by no means confined to its bearing on the cult of Becket in Scotland. The donor, Michael Scot, is a figure of much interest both in his descent and in his descendants. His father was Duncan son of Michael son of Malotheny, who held the estate of Cairns (in Cameron, south of St Andrews), as well as – by gift of Earl Malcolm I of Fife – the lands of Rumgally ('Ratmagallyn'), Pitlour (formerly in Aber-nethy detached, now in Strathmiglo) and 'Eglismarten' (in Strathmiglo). About 1240 Duncan gave Cairns with its mill to St Andrews Cathedral Priory (*St And. Lib.*, 309–10). The priory's terrier of *c*. 1222 (surviving only in the rather poor copy in BM, MS Harl. 4628, ff. 240ff.) includes Rumgally ('Rathmergullum') and Cairns among the lands which the culdees (*célidé*) of

St Andrews possess. Their holding of Cairns is confirmed by *St And. Lib.*, 318–19, *c.* 1198–99. There seem to be three possible inferences from the foregoing facts. Duncan's father Michael or grandfather Malotheny may have been a member of the old unreformed community of culdees, who are known to have held their better property individually, not in common. Or Duncan (or his ancestors) may have been infeft in Cairns by the culdees, whose 'reformed' successors, the collegiate kirk of St Mary of the Rock, evidently recovered Cairns from the priory (G. Martine, *Reliquiae Divi Andreae*, 217). Or, finally, the earls of Fife may have possessed an interest in the culdees and their estates – suggested by Earl Duncan II and three of his sons witnessing the important agreement of 1198–99, *St. And. Lib.*, 319 – and have granted some of their lands to trusted dependents. The high status of Duncan son of Michael son of Malotheny and his family's close links with the earls is shewn by the fact that Duncan's son Michael married Margaret, daughter of Duncan of Ceres son of Adam of Ceres, a younger brother of Earl Duncan II (*Dunfermline Registrum*, nos. 174–6). Duncan's father Michael son of Malotheny ('Maliton') witnessed charters of Earl Malcolm I (*SHS Miscellany*, iv, 311; *Morton Reg.*, i, Appendix, no. 1) and occurs as Sir Michael son of Malloch in a charter of John lord of Wemyss, *St And. Lib.*, 269. Malotheny was not a rare name in twelfth-century Fife: the bishop's thane of Dairsie *c.* 1160–2 was Ewen MacMallotheni (*ibid.*, 128), while a marischal called Malotheni appears at Kilrymont before 1152 (*ibid.*, 193), although he was probably a royal household servant not specially connected with St Andrews (*RRS*, i, 35).

The son and heir of Michael Scot and Margaret of Ceres was the Duncan Scot who witnesses this charter. He must have married the daughter and heir of Sir Richard of Balwearie, knight, son of that important royal servant and sometime sheriff of Fife Geoffrey son of Richard steward of Kinghorn, for whom cf. *RRS*, ii, 41, 419, 434–5. Duncan's son inherited the lands both of his father and of his maternal grandfather and is famous in history as Sir Michael Scot of Balwearie who with Sir Michael Wemyss of that ilk was despatched to Bergen in 1290 to arrange for the little Maid of Norway to be brought to her kingdom (*Chron. Fordun*, i, 311; cf. Rymer, *Foedera* (orig. edn), ii, 533). Sir Patrick Spens of the ballad might almost be a conflation of these two doughty knights of Fife, who both witness no. 9 below.

Geoffrey III was abbot of Dunfermline only from 1238 to 5 October 1240. Sir Thomas of Kilmaron was a prominent vassal of the earls of Fife (*SHS Miscellany*, iv, 311, 339–40). A John of Petkery occurs *c.* 1206–09 and 1212 × 1225 (*St And. Lib.*, 397, also 381; 40, better 322), while a Sir Richard of Pethkery was a canon of St Andrews Priory in 1264 (*ibid.*, 349). Pitkerry is in Leslie, Pitkierie in Kilrenny; a 'Pethkeryn' is listed among the culdees' lands in the terrier already cited. Philip of Lochore witnessed *Dunfermline Reg.*, no. 176 with his son Constantine. Patrick of Pitglassie witnessed *ibid.*, no. 192 (1231). John of Blebo ('Bladboch', 'Blabolcd') witnessed *Balmerino Liber*, no. 46 (1240–8). 'Kenbach' is Kemback, immediately east of Rumgally.

7   John Monypenny, son and heir of the late Richard Monypenny, grants to Nicholas of Milton clerk of the king's chamber and his heirs and assigns,

his whole land of Morton in the tenement of Blebo, within the marches: as far as the burn of 'Inchelman', as far as St Andrews Wells, to the marches of Magask opposite to 'Glasencur', by the ditch made as a boundary when the land was sold to the donor's father Richard Monypenny; with half the meadow to the east of Blebo. The *reddendo* is one pair of white gloves or 1d.; paying to the heritor of Blebo 10s., 5 at Whitsun and 5 at Martinmas; rendering as much aid of the king and of the bishop (of St Andrews) as belongs to the third of a davoch; and finding food for one man in the king's army. Nicholas and his tenants must grind their corn at Blebo Mill, up to 20 vessels at a time and taking precedence of everyone save the heritor of Kinninmonth. The grant is made in return for a certain sum of money which Nicholas has paid the donor to save his inheritance in his urgent necessity and to purchase another estate. (25 March 1263 × 17 March 1264).

Omnibus hoc scriptum visuris vel audituris Johannes Monipeni filius et*a* heres quondam Ricardi Monipeni – Confirmasse Nicholao de Miltoun tunc clerico de Camera Domini Regis et heredibus suis vel suis Assignatis et eorum heredibus pro quadam summa pecunie quam dictus Nicholaus mihi in maxima necessitate mea ad hereditatem meam salvandam et quandam aliam terram emendam prae manibus totaliter pacavit, totam terram meam de Mirton in tenemento de Blathbolg sine aliquo retinemento, per istas scilicet divisas – *b* – usque rivulum de Inchelman – usque ad fontem Sancti Andree ad divisam de Malgasc – in opposito de Glasencur' – fossa que facta fuit pro divisa quando terra illa vendebatur Ricardo Monipeni – patri meo – Tenend' et habend' dicto Nicholas et heredibus suis – De me et heredibus meis in perpetuum, cum dimidietate prati quod jacet versus orientem de Blathbolg, et cum omnibus rectitudinibus, reddendo inde annuatim michi et heredibus meis ad Pentechosten unum par albarum cirotecarum vel unum denarium, et heredi de Blathbolg annuatim decem solidos, scilicet – quinque solidos ad pentechostem et quinque solidos ad festum Sancti Martini, et auxilium Domini Regis et Episcopi quantum pertinet ad tertiam partem unius Davach. Et inveniendo in exercitu Domini Regis cibum unius hominis. Predictus vero Nicholaus et heredes – hominesque sui in terra illa manentes molent ad molendinum de Blathbolg ad vicesimum vas et an*te* omnes homines excepto herede de Kininemund. Et – contra omnes homines et feminas warrantizabimus. Ad omnia /vero/*c* premissa fideliter et sine dolo observanda in perpetuum obligo me et heredes meos sub pena Centum librarum dicto Nicholas et heredibus – solvendarum quocunque quotienscunque et quandocunque contigerit me vel – contra prescripta – *d*. Subiciendo nos jurisdictioni ac potestati Domini Episcopi Sancti Andree et ejus officialium qui nunc sunt vel pro tempore fuerint, quod ipsi vel eorum aliquis sine cause cognitione vel strepitu judiciali possint vel possit nos compellere per sententiam excommunicationis vel interdicti tam ad predictam pene solutionem si commissa fuerit quam ad omnium prescriptorum fidelem et perpetuam observationem. Renuntiata autem pro me et pro heredibus meis omni exceptione, cavillatione et contradictione et omni juris remedio ecclesiastico et civili, et omnibus scriptis munimentis et literis papalibus, regiis seu episcopalibus, et omnibus privilegiis crucesignatis indultis et indulgendis impetratis et impetrandis per quo contra prescripta vel eorum aliquem articulum in parte vel in toto possit prejudicium generari. In cujus rei testimonium huic scripto sigillum meum feci apponi. Hijs testibus Venerabili patre Gamel*ino* Sancti Andree Episcopo, Domino Gilberto priore Sancti Andree, Domino Hugone de Abirnithi, Domino Willelmo de Montealto, & Bernardo fratre ejus, Domino Willelmo de Hauden', Ranulfo de Pethscoty, Petro de Balfur, Ricardo de Stikelaw, Elya de Kyninemund, Michaele de Strivilyn burgensi de Sancto Andrea, Radulpho de Strivilyn clerico, et aliis. Acta anno gratie Millesimo ducentesimo sexagesimo tertio.

*Heading*: At Cambo. Out of Cambo papers. 15 June 1710.
*Note at foot*: Ex autographo.
*Source*: National Library of Scotland, MS Adv. 34.6.24, pp. 248–9.

*Notes*: *a Here and frequently the transcriber uses an ampersand.*
　　　 *b Here and elsewhere spaces are left indicating omitted matter.*
　　　 *c Added above the line.*
　　　 *d* P. 249.

*Comment*: Richard Monypenny (Manipeny) is the first recorded member of this famous East Fife family, for many centuries lairds of Pitmilly in Kingsbarns, which they originally held of the priory of St Andrews (*St And. Lib.*, 269, 285). It seems that his son John borrowed from Peter of Balfour (a witness to this deed) and in order to repay the debt persuaded Nicholas of Milton (an otherwise unknown royal clerk) to lend him the necessary money, receiving as security the tenancy of Morton in Blebo for a nominal rent – a very early example of a wadset. Walter Macfarlane of Macfarlane (*Gen. Coll.*, i, 47) reports the existence in the early eighteenth century not only of this document (unfortunately surviving only in this hasty and careless copy) but also of a licence (1263) from Peter of Balfour to John to give this wadset and of a confirmation of the transaction by Bishop Gamelin of St Andrews (Cambuskenneth, 18 May 1264). A little earlier (Thursday, April 24 1264) Richard of Sticklaw, another witness (for whom see no. 9 below), styled 'lord of Blebo', set to Nicholas of Milton in feu ferme 'Upper and Nether Reskes etc.' (unidentified).

It is noteworthy that despite his nominal rent to John Monypenny Nicholas of Milton was obliged to meet fairly heavy outgoings from this small estate – 10s. to the heritor of Blebo (presumably Richard of Sticklaw), aid as assessed on $\frac{1}{3}$ of a davoch to both the king and the bishop of St Andrews and food for one man in the king's army (apparently a form of the well-known 'Scottish service' or 'common army'). On the credit side he enjoyed certain privileges in the use of Blebo Mill, yielding only to the heritor of Kinninmonth – suggesting, incidentally, that the mill had anciently been common to the shires of Blebo and Kinninmonth. For Elias of Kinninmonth cf. *Kinninmonths*, 115, 130–1.

Two points of legal terminology worth noting are the early occurrence of adding the word *assignati*, 'assigns', to the usual 'heirs' (note also its use in the charter of 1260 embodied in no. 9 below), and the equally early use of *heres* apparently in the sense of 'heritor', proprietor of a heritable estate.

The earliest explicit example of a wadset (*impignoratio*) known to the editor is the Lease of Coille Bhrochain (in Blair Atholl) by Eugenius (Ewen) son of Coning to Coupar Angus abbey (9 October 1282; *Fraser Papers* (SHS, 1924), 217–19). But the twenty-year lease granted to Newbattle abbey by Robert de Quinci in 1170 (*SHR*, xxx, 42–4) may be regarded as a form of wadset, and the same may be true of the pledge of land at Ecclefechan of the later years of the twelfth century (*Dumfriesshire Trans.*, 3rd ser., xxxiii, 84–90).

8   Walter de Pershay son and heir of the lady Jean of Wilton grants to Thomas Wallace all his land of 'Tarvetandane' (Nether Tarvit?) and all his land of Glaidney (formerly in Tarvit, now in Ceres) and an annualrent of 2s. payable from the 2s. 6d. due to Walter from Gilbert of Balass. The *reddendo* is 3d. at Whitsun for all services etc., saving the donor's right to ward and relief. Thomas must pay to the bishop of St Andrews 11s. from 'Tarvetandane' and 15s. from Glaidney, and perform forinsec service due to the king. He must perform suit of court to the bishop for Glaidney, but will be exempt from suit to the donor's court. Walter grants warrandice against all men and women. (*c.* 1280?).

Omnibus Christi[a] fidelibus presens scriptum visuris vel audituris Walterus de Pershay filius et[b] heres domine Johanne de Wilton salutem in domino. Nouerit uniuersitas vestra me dedisse concessisse et hac presenti carta confirmasse Thome Walensi et heredibus suis pro homagio et seruicio suo totam terram meam de Taruetandane et totam meam partem terre mee de Gledyny et duos solidos de Balhas annuatim recipiendos de illis triginta denariis in quibus Gilbertus de Balhas annuatim michi tenetur. Tenend' et habend' dicto Thome et heredibus suis de me et heredibus meis libere et quiete et pacifice in terris et aquis . in pratis et pascuis in moris et mareseis[c] . in viis et semitis in molendinis et omnimodis aliis libertatibus et aysiamentis ad dictas terras pertinentibus uel aliquo tempore pertinere ualentibus. Reddendo inde annuatim dictus Thomas et heredes sui michi et heredibus meis tres denarios ad pentechosten pro omni seruicio consuetudine exactione et demanda saluis michi Wardo et releuio. Et reddendo domino Episcopo Sancti Andree undecim solidos de terra de Taruetandane et quindecim solidos de terra de Glediny . et faciendo forinsecum seruicium domini regis . et sectam ad curiam domini episcopi Sancti Andree . pro parte sua terre de Gledyny. Set dictus Thomas et heredes sui erunt quieti de secta ad curiam meam. Et hoc faciendo volo quod dictus Thomas et heredes sui sint liberi et quieti omnimodis peticionibus et consuetudinibus et exactionibus que a me et heredibus meis aliquibus temporibus exigi possunt uel poterunt saluo seruicio prenominato. Ego uero Walterus et heredes mei hanc donacionem meam dicto Thome et heredibus suis contra omnes homines et feminas in perpetuum warantizabimus adquietabimus et defendemus. Et ut ista donacio sit stabilis et inconcussa presens scriptum inpressione sigilli mei roboraui. Hiis

testibus . Domino Nich*olao* de Haya . Jamis'*c* de Ramisay . Willelmo de Ramisay . Alexandro de Gruddin' Willelmo fratre meo et aliis.

*Endorsement*: Carta de terwet (xiv cent., same hand as endorsements of nos. 5
 and 11).

*Description*: Foot folded, with slits for seal-tag, which remains, 0·4" wide.
 Seal (obverse only) in white wax, diam. 1", device a shield bearing a cross
 pattée fitched at the foot, legend +S' DOMINI WALTERI [DE?] . .ERS . .
 Dimensions are 9·2" (23·4 cm.), top, 9·3" (23·7 cm.), bottom × 5·45" (13·9
 cm.), L.H., 5·4" (13·7 cm.), R.H. Ruled in ink, with double ruled margins.
 Business hand of last quarter of thirteenth century, which nevertheless em-
 ploys an uncrossed tironian 'et'.

*Source*: Original, SRO, GD 82/2 (Makgill of Makgill charters).

*Notes*: *a Written* x¹.
  *b Uncrossed tironian sign throughout.*
  *c Sic.*
*Comment*: See below, p. 37.

9   Walter Percehay knight, son and heir of the lady Jean of Wilton, issues an
*inspeximus* of a charter by which William Avenel, son and heir of Gilbert
Avenel and his wife Maud (of Wilton), quitclaimed to Thomas Wallace son of
Adam Wallace his whole land of 'Tarvet In dan' (Nether Tarvit?), to be held
of the heirs of the late Sir John of Wilton who had infeft William Avenel in
that land; the *reddendo* being one pair of gilt spurs or 6d., saving the forinsec
service of the king and the bishop of St Andrews. William's charter is dated at
Berwick on Tweed, 29 May 1260. (1283 × 1285).

Omnibus Christi fidelibus hoc scriptum visuris vel audituris Walterus Percehay
miles filius et*a* heres domine Johanne de Wilton' salutem in domino. Noveritis
me cartam Willelmi Avenel filii et heredis Gilberti Avenel et Matildis sponse
sue in hec verba inspexisse. Omnibus Christi fidelibus hoc scriptum visuris
vel audituris Willelmus Avenel filius et heres Gilberti Avenel et Matildis
sponse sue salutem in domino. Sciant presentes et futuri me dedisse concessisse
et quietum clamasse pro me et heredibus meis Thome Walensi filio A*de*
Walensis totam terram meam de Tarveht In dan cum omnibus pertinen*tiis*
suis sine aliquo retenemento et totum jus et clamium quod ego vel heredes mei
habuimus vel habere potuimus vel poterimus ad eandem terram Tenendam et
habendam eidem Thome et heredibus suis vel suis assingnatis*b* de heredibus
quondam domini Johannis de Wilton' in feodatoris*c* mei in feodo et hereditate
Ita libere et quiete plenarie et honorifice . sicut ego aut antecessores mei eam
liberius quietius plenius et honorificentius de eis aliquo tempore tenuimus aut
tenuisse debuimus Reddendo eis annatim*d* unum par Calcarium deauratorum
vel sex denariorum ad Pentechosten pro omni servicio consuetudine et exactione
salvo forinseco servicio domini Regis et domini Episcopi Sancti Andree. In
cuius rei testimonium sigillum meum apposui huic scripto. Hiis testibus.

Domino Gamelo Episcopo Sancti Andree . Magistro Ada de Malcaruiston'
tunc officiali suo . domino David de Louchor . Domino Thoma de Brade .
Domino Rogero de Walucohp.[b] Magistro Thoma de Carnoto Gilberto de
Heriz et Thoma de Lastalric . domino Willelmo de Dalgernok persona de
Ratheu . domino Ada de Anand' Ricardo de Styklaw . Willelmo de Curmanoc.
Johanne de Cunyngham . et aliis apud Berwic tercio kalendas Junii Anno gratie
mo cc. sexagesimo. Ego vero Walterus predictam donacionem dicti Willelmi
Avenel filii et heredis Gilberti Avenel et Matildis sponse sue ratam habens
firmam et stabilem salvis michi humagio et serviciis que Johannes de Willton'
feodator Willelmi Avenel et antecessor meus sibi salvavit In carta feofamenti
quam inde fecit Willelmo Avenel et Matildi sponse[d] sue. In cuius rei testimonium presenti scripto sigillo meo signato dictam collacionem confirmo.
Testibus . Domino Johanne de Moravia . Domino Michaele de Wemes .
Domino Michaele Scoto militibus . Hugoni de Louchor . Constantino de
Louchor' . Moricio de Menetheth . Marcho de Clapham . et multis aliis[e]

*Endorsement*: Tarwetht (xiv cent.?)
*Description*: Foot folded, with double slits for seal-tag, which survives, but
    without any seal. Dimensions are 9·9″ (25·2 cm.) × 4·4″ (11·3 cm.). Unruled.
    Hand a small rather 'English' looking business hand.
*Source*: Original, SRO, GD 241/381/1.

*Notes*: a *A rectangular piece of parchment 0.3″ long has been cut out here.*
    b *Sic.*
    c *Written as two words.*
    d *Sic. Read* matri?
    e *Line filled up by four horizontal strokes, increasing in length from left to right.*
*Comment on nos. 8, 9 and 11*: These three documents almost complete the series
    begun with no. 5 – a final *inspeximus* (1312) of a confirmation by Bishop
    Gamelin (?Tyninghame, 9 January 1262) is unfortunately too imperfect to be
    included here. It will be best to comment on all three together. Nos. 8 and
    9 are very closely related but seem from the witnesses and the fact that the
    donor is not styled a knight in no. 8 to belong to different dates.
    Sir Walter de Pershay or Percehay is, at least as far as Scottish record goes,
    an obscure figure. It seems that the senior line of the barons of Wilton had
    devolved upon coheiresses (daughters of John of Wilton, donor of no. 5?).
    One of these, Johanna or Jean, had married a de Percehay, while another
    seems to have married a Charteris. This may be inferred from these two
    charters together with one of Robert I (*RMS*, i, no. 17) referring to half
    the barony of Wilton having once been held by the late William de Charter(i)s
    and Walter de 'Pertehay' (read Percehay). A small niche in Scottish history,
    however, is secured for Sir Walter by the fact, recorded by John Fordun who
    calls him 'Sir Walter de Percy knight' (*Chron. Fordun*, i, 320; *Chron. Bower*,
    ii, 138) that he, along with Sir Patrick of Abernethy, ambushed and murdered
    the young earl of Fife, Duncan III, one of the Guardians of Scotland, at
    Pitpollok, west of Brechin, early in September 1289 (Barrow, *Robert Bruce*,
    38 and n. 3). The real instigator of the crime seems to have been Hugh (whom
    Fordun wrongly calls William), lord of Abernethy. Having been imprisoned

in Douglas Castle, Hugh is last heard of trying to make his peace with the pope through the intercession of the bishop of Brechin and King Edward I of England (*Rot. Scot.*, i, 2a–b; Stevenson, *Documents*, i, 69). Of the actual murderers, Patrick of Abernethy fled to France where he died, while Sir Walter de Percehay and two esquires, overtaken in their flight at Covington in Lanarkshire, were executed on the spot by Sir Andrew Murray of Petty, who was perhaps already justiciar of Scotland north of Forth.

What quarrel lay between the Abernethys or Sir Walter de Percehay and the earl is not known. The Abernethys were of course his rather distant kinsmen, their twelfth-century ancestor Orm being a son of Hugh younger son of Gillemichel earl of Fife, while the earls were descended from Gillemichel's eldest son Duncan. The Abernethys were perhaps the largest lay landowners in Fife after the earls, and a property dispute may have lain behind the Lanercost Chronicle's sententious verdict on young Earl Duncan III that he was 'cruel and greedy above the average' (*Chron. Lanercost*, 127). Conflict over property might conceivably have been Sir Walter's motive for joining the plot, for his estate in Tarvit was surrounded on three sides by earldom lands in Cupar, west Tarvit and Ceres.

Earl Malcolm I of Fife (1204–28) created a knight's fee for Richard son of Andrew of Linton out of his 'three Tarvits (Tarvez)', 'Findakech' (Findas west of Tarvit?) and half of Balbirnie (in Markinch); *SHR*, viii, 222. Save for Balbirnie, these lands were evidently in the western part of Tarvit and would have included Tarvit Mill, Scotstarvit and perhaps 'Inglistarvit'. The eastern part of Tarvit, however, where the parish church of St Michael was situated not far from the River Eden, and including the present Hilltarvit and Tarvit House, belonged from early times to the bishop of St Andrews, and Bishop Malvoisin, as we have seen (above, comment on no. 3), gave the church to the archdeaconry. The land known as Tarvet In dan, Tarvetandane or Tarvetadan has not been found elsewhere under these names. Professor Kenneth Jackson, in a letter, has made the very helpful and interesting suggestion that these forms might stand for Tarvet *an t'abha(i)nn* or (with *t* voiced to *d* after *an*) *an d'abha(i)nn*, i.e. 'Tarvet of (= by) the river'. This might very well have been pronounced *an d'a'an*. Thus, quite independently, there is support for the view that these names may have corresponded to Nether Tarvett listed in the 'Golden Charter' of 1479–80 (Martine, *Rel. Divi Andreae*, 115), and to the modern Tarvit House estate. This seems to be confirmed by the probability that 'Tarvetanard' (no. 11), i.e. Tarvet *an aird*, 'Tarvit of the height', would correspond to Hilltarvit (rising to 692', the highest point of this small but hilly parish). Balass is in the north-east corner of the parish, and on 8 September, 1288 Gilbert of Balass gave St Andrews Priory leave to make a mill-dam for Dairsie Mill on his land of Balass, on the far (i.e. north) side of the Eden (*St And. Lib.*, 339–40). Glaidney is in what used to be the southeast corner of the parish, just west of Bridgend of Ceres. The unidentified 'Westfield' of no. 11 is more likely to have been part of Tarvit than the Westfield of Cupar still in use as a name today.

All three charters shew that forinsec service was due to the bishop of St Andrews, and nos. 8 and 11 shew this to have been fairly large sums due as cain, 11s. from 'Tarvetandane' and 15s. from Glaidney; and in addition suit of court was owed to the bishop from Glaidney. As in the case of Blebo (no. 7 above), forinsec service was also due to the king, but we are not told what form it took. A complex tenurial situation is posited by the charters but unhappily not fully revealed. The bishop held Tarvit of the crown, evidently by the most full and privileged kind of tenure since he was entitled to cain, a regalian right. The barons of Wilton held of the bishop. The Avenels held of the Wiltons, for silver-gilt spurs or 6d. The Wallaces – Thomas son of Adam and after him his son John – held of the Avenels at the same rent for 'Tarvetandane', and of a Wilton (descendant of a younger branch of the family?) at the unusual rent of a merlin or 1d. for Glaidney (a play on the word *gled*, a kite?). Another free tenant was settled at Balass. None of the documents mentions the half-free or unfree population, bonders, cottars and gresmen, who presumably lived and worked at the little 'ferm touns' of which Tarvit was composed.

Of the witnesses to no. 8, Sir Nicholas de la Hay lord of Errol is well known. He and James Ramsay (I have not come across elsewhere this interest- ingly vernacular spelling of his Christian name) witnessed a royal act of 1284 along with Patrick of Abernethy, Sir Walter's fellow-murderer (*Highland Papers*, ii, 124), by which time James was a knight. William Ramsay was perhaps the royal household officer occurring in 1278 (*Dunfermline Reg.*, no. 86). Alexander of Gruddin (Gruddy) was a witness at the justiciary court at Perth in 1260 (*St And. Lib.*, 346). Sir Walter's brother William does not seem to be recorded elsewhere – perhaps he was one of the unnamed esquires executed summarily in 1289.

No. 9 gives a double set of witnesses, those of the 'inspected' charter dated at Berwick in 1260 being typical of the entourage of Bishop Gamelin of St Andrews who himself heads the list. David of Lochore was sheriff of Fife in 1253 (SRO, GD 254/1) and in 1264-5 (*Exch. Rolls*, i, 4, 34); Sir Roger of Wauchope was perhaps a dependant of Alexander Comyn earl of Buchan (a suggestion I owe to Mr Alan Young). Richard of Sticklaw took his name from a place now called Stickley in south-east Northumberland, one mile north east of Cramlington. His presumed kinsman (son?) Master Weland was afterwards to become prominent first in Scottish and later in Norwegian royal service, being chamberlain of Scotland in 1284 and in later years gover- nor of Orkney (cf. B. Crawford, *Historisk Tidskrift* (Norsk), lii, 4, 1973). Of the witnesses to Sir Walter's *inspeximus*, Sir John Murray was presumably the John son of Malcolm of Murray (knight) who granted Aldie (in Fossoway parish) and land in Strathbogie to his brother William Murray first of Tulli- bardine, *c*. 1284 (Raine, *North Durham*, no. 144; *Moray Reg.*, Appendix, Carte Originales, no. 8); Sir John's homage to Edward I is recorded in 1291 and 1296 (*Instrumenta Publica*, 16, 88, 157). The lairds of Wemyss and Bal- wearie are well-recorded (above, comment on no. 6). Hugh of Lochore and his brother Constantine, sons of David of Lochore, each (like his father) served as sheriff of Fife, in 1293 and 1290-1 respectively (*Highland Papers*, ii, 128 and cf. *Spalding Miscellany*, ii, 312, no. xv; *Exch. Rolls*, i, 50; *Instru- menta Publica*, 15). In the period 1285-9 Hugh acted as special attorney for Earl Duncan III of Fife (Earl of Moray's Muniments, Darnaway, Gray of Kinfauns Papers, Bdle. 84, no. 2, box 5), and both brothers witnessed this unpublished deed of the young earl.

The next witness, who also witnesses no. 11 where he takes precedence of

Sheriff Constantine, was Maurice (=Murdoch) of Menteith, in whom we may see another link with the earls of Fife. He was apparently one of the younger sons of Alexander earl of Menteith and actually became earl himself in 1320, dying some twelve years later, perhaps killed at the battle of Dupplin. He appears as witness to several connected deeds of 1293 (*Panmure Reg.*, ii, 152–5). Since in 1315 the then earl of Menteith (Alan son of Alan) was agreed to be heir presumptive to the earldom of Fife (Barrow, *Robert Bruce*, 391), it seems that Earl Alexander must have married a daughter of Malcolm II earl of Fife (1228–66). It is certainly hard to explain the Menteith claim in any other way. If this suggestion is correct, Murdoch and his brothers (Alan, Peter and Alexander) would have been first cousins of the young earl who was Earl Malcolm II's grandson. The last witness, Mark of Clapham (i.e. Clephane), presumably of the family who became well-known as lairds of Carslogie, was listed as a tenant in Fife of the bishop of St Andrews in 1296 (*Instrumenta Publica*, 147) and was possibly the episcopal steward.

Of the persons figuring in no. 11, the homage of John son of Thomas Wallace of Fife was recorded in 1296 (*ibid.*, 145), as was that of Sir Henry of Dundemor (in Abdie), evidently the son of Sir John and grandson of an earlier Sir Henry (for whom see *Lindores Chartulary passim*). John of Haddington became prior of St Andrews in 1264 and ruled for forty years. Maurice or Murdoch of Menteith and Constantine of Lochore have been noticed already. A second John of Haddington (otherwise seemingly unknown) was a member of the collegiate kirk of St Mary of the Rock, by now no doubt a chapel-royal (cf. *Laing Chrs.*, no. 15). The fact that of the last six witnesses no fewer than five were burgesses of Perth, while the sixth, Michael of Stirling, may well have been one also, not only suggests strongly that the charter was issued at Perth. It raises also the interesting question of whether it was granted about the time (24 July 1291) when King Edward I was at Perth to receive the homage of the alderman, John of Perth, and burgesses and community of the burgh (*Instrumenta Publica*, 17). On the 17th he had been at Dunfermline where the sheriff of Fife had done his homage; on the 22nd at St Andrews, where he had received that of Prior John; conceivably, these two had gone on to Perth in the English king's company. On the other hand, in the period 1290–1 there may have been one or two occasions when this otherwise rather odd-seeming mixture of personages were present at Perth together – a Scone parliament, for example, or a session of the justiciary court. For mention of John Aylbot, Christinus de Insula, John of Perth, Gilbert Cokyn and Adam of Letham see *Instrumenta Publica*, 17, 121; *SHS Miscellany* iv, 319, 349–50.

10    Agreement between the prior and convent of St Andrews Cathedral Priory on the one part and Constantine of Lochore, guardian or tutor of John, son and heir of Sir Alexander of Blair knight, on the other part, in the following terms: Constantine, with the consent of John's mother Helen and of his uncle William Ramsay, has conceded to the prior and convent the site of their mill of Nydie on the River Eden, downstream towards the east, until John comes of age, in return for a payment to Constantine of one pound of pepper at St Andrews Fair. Should John when he comes of age not wish to continue this

agreement he may compel the prior and convent to remove their mill to its original site, and they may so remove it, or to any other site outwith John's land, together with the stone and timber buildings erected at the mill. The prior and convent's right to their old mill is reserved to them and they are to be freed from the payment of the pepper if they are required to move the mill to its original site. (11 November 1286).

C IROGARPAHUW[a]

Anno gratie millesimo ducentesimo octogesimo sexto ad festum Sancti Martini. Facta est hec convencio inter priorem et conventum Sancti Andree ex parte una et Constantinum de Louchor custodem seu tutorem :[b] Johannis filii et heredis domini Alexandri de Blar' militis ex altera . videlicet quod dictus Constantinus de voluntate et consensu domine Elene matris eiusdem *Johannis* ac Willelmi de Ramesay avunculi eiusdem concessit predictis priori et conventui situm molendini sui de Nidyn inferius super aquam versus orientem in tenemento ipsius *Johannis* de Nidyn usque ad legitimam etatem eiusdem *Johannis* et ob hoc dicti prior et conventus solvent annuatim dicto Constantino racione custodie ipsius *Johannis* unam libram piperis in nundinis Sancti Andree. Si vero dictus *Johannes* cum ad legitimam etatem suam pervenerit dictam convencionem ulterius observare noluerit . liceat dicto *Johanni* dictos priorem et conventum per bona sua mobilia et immobilia ubicumque fuerint inventa . sive in terris ecclesiasticis vel elemosinatis vel extra . sine aliquo inpedimento vel contradiccione compellere ad dictum molendinum removendum . ad situm et locum pristinum . non obstante aliquo iure privilegio ecclesiastico vel civili et liceat dictis priori et conventui dictum molendinum cum fabrica lapidea et lignea ibidem constructa libere et sine contradiccione dicti *Johannis* seu alicuius alterius domineum[e] dicti tenementi habentis vel custodientis ad pristinum situm vel ubicumque melius extra terram prefati Johannis potuerunt absque inpedimento removere . salvo dictis priori et conventui in omnibus et per omnia iure molendini antiqui et cum contingat dictum molendinum ad pristinum situm revertere quieti sint dicti prior et conventus a prestacione piperis supradicti . salvo iure utriusque partis quod antiquitus habere debuerunt. In Cuius rei testimonium parti huius convencionis penes dictum Constantinum residenti sigillum commune predictorum prioris et conventus est appensum . parti vero penes dictos priorem et conventum residenti :[b] sigillum dicti Constantini una cum sigillo magistri Gregorii Archidiaconi Sancti And*ree* ad instanciam utriusque partis est appositum. Subicientes se ex utraque parte iurisdiccioni eiusdem arch*idiaconi* ad observacionem omnium premissorum.

*Endorsement*: Composicio Inter Nos et Joha*nn*em de Blare de situ molendini de Nydin (xiii cent.)

1266[c] [        ][d] of the Regne of Alex. 3 (xvii cent.)

*Description*: Foot originally folded, with slits for one seal-tag; neither tag nor seal remains. Dimensions are 10·4″ (26·5 cm.) × 5·5″ (14 cm.). The hand is a cursive business hand with no special characteristics save for the colon-like *punctus elevatus* and an excessive use of the full point which has been mini-mised editorially. The second endorsement may be in the hand of Sir James Balfour of Denmylne.

*Source*: Original, N.L.S., MS Adv. 15.1.18, no. 52.

*Notes*: *a Large capitals cut through with thirteen indentations.*
    *b* Punctus elevatus *indistinguishable from a modern colon.*
    *c Sic.*
    *d Almost illegible words, perhaps* the fifteenth *?*

*Comment*: A family using the surname 'de Blar' etc., perhaps from Blair in Wemyss, were prominent in the entourage of the earls of Fife during the thirteenth century. Their descendants are said to have been the Blairs of Balthayock (in Kinfauns). Alexander (son of William?) of Blair was a promi-nent witness of acts issued by Earl Malcolm I (*SHR*, viii, 222; *St And. Lib.*, 345; *N. Berwick Carte*, no. 7; *SHS Miscellany*, iv, 312). His son William served as steward of the earldom under Earl Malcolm II (*Dunfermline Reg.*, no. 179). Evidently his son was Sir Alexander of Blair, knight (*ibid.*, no. 315), whose son John is the central figure of this agreement. John's widowed mother Helen (Elena) is listed as doing homage to Edward I in 1296, and is said to have been the daughter of Sir William Ramsay of Dalhousie (A. Jervise, *Memorials of Angus and the Mearns* (1861), 453). Constantine of Lochore, sheriff of Fife, 1290–1, belonged to a remarkably tenacious native family of West Fife whose use of the Christian name Constantine over many genera-tions seems to be the hallmark of their familial conservatism. The first re-corded Constantine of Lochore appears as early as 1160–62 (*St And. Lib.*, 128); this later namesake witnessed a deed of 1282 (*ibid.*, 342), and his appear-ance in nos. 9 and 11 of this collection has been noticed above. Here he acts as 'guardian or tutor' of the minor John of Blair – a fairly early occurrence of *tutor* in that sense in a Scots secular legal document. John's possession of Nydie and power to permit St Andrews Priory to alter the site of their mill at Nydie downstream from its old site would seem to have derived from the marriage before 1228 of Alexander of Blair, John's great-grandfather, to Ela daughter of Hugh of Nydie, for which there is evidence in a surviving marriage grant dealing with 'Konakin' (Knock Hill in Nydie?); *SHS Miscellany*, iv, 312.

The canons of St Andrews had been granted the 'old mill' of Nydie, as one of their earliest endowments, in or before 1144 by Bishop Robert (*St And. Lib.*, 123). The reference to the mill structures of stone and timber is interesting in view of the general presumption in favour of merely timber buildings in this period for all purposes save castles, churches and the homes of the well-to-do.

Gregory is known to have been archdeacon of St Andrews from 1279 to 1295 (Watt, *Fasti*, 305).

11    Robert of Wilton grants to John, son and heir of Thomas Wallace, his whole land of Glaidney and the homage, service and rent which Thomas used to render to the donor for 'Tarvetadan' (Nether Tarvit?) and 'Westfield', and the service which used to be owed for 'Tarvetanard' (Hilltarvit?) and the homage, service and rent which were owed for the tenement of Balass. The *reddendo* is one merlin or 1d. on Saint Mary Magdalene's Day (22 July); John

paying 15s. to the bishop of St Andrews as cain for Glaidney. Robert grants warrandice to John against all men and women. (At Perth (?), c. 1290–91).

Omnibus hoc scriptum uisuris uel audituris Robertus de Wyltona salutem eternam in domino. Nouerit universitas uestra me pro me et heredibus meis dedisse . concessisse et hac presenti carta mea confirmasse Johanni filio et heredi Thome Walays totam partem meam terre mee de Gledeney cum omnibus pertinenciis . libertatibus et aysiamentis ad dictam terram spectantibus uel spectare ualentibus. Tenend*am* et habend*am* sibi et heredibus suis et assignatis de me et heredibus meis in feodo et hereditate adeo libere . quiete . pacifice et honorifice sicut ego et antecessores mei dictam terram aliquo modo uel tempore tenuimus. Preterea dedi et concessi dicto Johanni et heredibus suis et assignatis totum homagium seruicium et redditum quod Thomas Wallays michi soluere consueuit de Taruetadan' et de Westfeld cum pertinenc*iis* suis et totum seruitium quod michi et heredibus meis debebatur de Taruetanard' cum pertinenciis et eciam totum homagium seruicium et redditum cum pertinenc*iis* que michi debebatur de tenemento de Balhas Ita quod nullum ius uel clameum ego aut heredes mei imposterum in predictis ualeamus exigere. Reddendo inde annuatim michi et heredibus meis tantum unum meruelun' uel unum denarium in festo beate Marie Magdalene . et Domino Episcopo Sancti Andree quindecim solidos sterlingorum pro Can dicte terre de Gledeney . pro omnibus seruiciis secularibus . consuetudinibus . exactionibus et demandis quas ego aut heredes mei a predicto Johanne uel heredibus suis seu assignatis de cetero vendicare poterimus. Ego uero Robertus et heredes mei predictam terram de Gledeney cum prenominatis homagio seruicio et redditu dicto Johanni et heredibus suis et assignatis contra omnes homines et feminas Warantizabimus . acquietabimus et imperpetuum defendemus sine aliquo retinemento. In Cuius rei testimonium presenti scripto meo pro me et heredibus meis sigillum meum apposui. Hiis testibus domino Henrico de Dundmur' milite . Domino Johanne priore de Sancto Andre*a* . Mauricio de Meneteth . Constantino de Lochor' tunc vicecomite de Fyf' . Johanne de Hadigton' canonico ecclesie Sancte Marie de Sancto Andrea . Cristino de Insula . J. Aylbot . J. de Perth . Gilberto Cokyn' . Michaele de Striuelyn . Ad*a* de Letham et aliis.

*Endorsement*: Carta de terwet (xiv cent., same hand as endorsements of nos. 5 and 8).

*Description*: Foot folded, with double slits for seal-tag, which remains, 0·4″ wide. Seal missing. Dimensions are 8·8″ (22·4 cm.), top, 9·3″ (23·7 cm.), bottom × 6·1″ (15·5 cm.), L.H., R.H. Ruled in pencil (?). Hand a large upright business hand with quill spread on many downstrokes.

*Source*: Original, SRO, GD 82/3 (Makgill of Makgill charters).

*Comment*: See above, p. 37. Since this paper was written no. 11 has been published, with facsimile and translation, by G. G. Simpson, *Scottish Handwriting, 1150–1650* (Edinburgh, 1973), no. 5 and p. 119.

G. W. S. BARROW

# 4

## William Lamberton, Bishop of St Andrews, 1297 - 1328

The role of the higher clergy in the Scottish war of independence is one of the major themes in any study of the struggle with England. Modern historians of the period have tended to focus their attention on the educational and family background of the members of this ecclesiastical caste, stressing the hierarchy's essential identification with the aristocratic and popular support given to the early fourteenth-century struggle for independence. Bishop Robert Wishart of Glasgow is the outstanding example of the patriot prelate with aristocratic connections who gave consistent support to the Scottish cause. His brother bishop at St Andrews William Lamberton, is a more ambiguous figure and because of his waverings and changes is the more fascinating personality. Furthermore he was the representative of an ancient see, whose centre was the cathedral church of the national saint. The bishops of St Andrews gave up the alternative title of Bishop of the Scots late in the thirteenth century, but still retained a hegemony of prestige over all the other bishops in the Scottish province. In concert with the king, the bishops of St Andrews represented an ancient national identity.

The Lambertons had settled originally in the parish of that name in Berwickshire, but by the end of the twelfth century the family held lands at Bourtie in Aberdeenshire and Linlathen in Angus, the last being held for knight service of the crown by Alexander Lamberton.[1]

By this social inheritance William Lamberton was disposed towards the 'patriotic' side. He was the nephew or cousin of the Sir Alexander Lamberton who was an English prisoner in Edinburgh castle in 1304 and the younger brother to that Sir Alexander Lamberton who witnessed an episcopal charter in 1327.[2] These family propensities were reinforced by the circumstances of Lamberton's early training and career. He was university trained, probably in law, and owed his early advancement to the patronage of Bishop Wishart of Glasgow. Lamberton became chancellor of Glasgow Cathedral by the time he made his first recorded appearance in Scone at the time of King John's first parliament in February 1293, where he acted as a proctor for his corporation in their dispute with William Moray over the church of Smailholm.[3] It was from among the circle of men who served the bishop and church of Glasgow in this period that the future bishop would draw many of his own future servants and administrators, among whom were his brother Robert Lamberton who became

---

[1] *St Andrews Liber*, 235, 266–8; *Regesta Regum Scottorum*, ii, no. 564.
[2] G. W. S. Barrow, 'The Scottish Clergy and the War of Independence', *SHR*, xxxxi (1962), 6 and n. 2; *Holyrood Liber*, no. 90.    [3] *Glasgow Registrum*, i, no. 238.

archdeacon of St Andrews by 1319, and William of Eaglesham who became Official of St Andrews by 1310 and archdeacon of Lothian by 1317.[4]

Lamberton was a supporter of King John, and following Balliol's resignation in 1296 he swore fealty to Edward I.[5] Within a year of his oath, however, Lamberton was caught up in the revolt of William Wallace. The victory at Stirling Bridge coincided with the death in Paris of Bishop William Fraser of St Andrews and it thus became necessary to fill the vacant see with another loyal bishop. Wallace was instrumental in gaining Lamberton's election *per viam compromissi* on 5 November 1297.[6]

The provost of the Collegiate Church of St Mary of the Rock, Mr William Comyn, a younger son of the earl of Buchan (who had recently joined Wallace), raised a complaint about the election from which he as the representative of the 'Culdees' had been excluded.[7] This complaint was expanded into a claim to have been himself elected and superseded by Lamberton 'par force et par destresce.'[8] Although so far as is known this claim to have been elected was first raised on Comyn's behalf by Edward I in 1306 it is probable that Comyn had raised some sort of claim or questions at the time of the election, for the Lost Great Register of St Andrews priory contained an entry 'relatio quid acciderit de controversia post mortem Willielmi Phraser Episcopi et instrumentum de eo, 1209 (*sic*).'[9] This scrap may mean that whatever claims Comyn had raised he had been prevailed upon to withdraw or settle them in 1297. It was only nine years later when Scotland was again subject to English rule and the earl of Buchan had gone over to the English side that Comyn raised his claim to have actually been elected in 1297.

After his election Lamberton journeyed to the papal court with three members of the chapter and was consecrated there by Matthew bishop of Porto at some time before 17 June 1298.[10] Within a few weeks of his consecration Wallace had been defeated at Falkirk and the new bishop remained abroad. About the time of his consecration Lamberton may have taken part in the representations at the papal court which resulted in the bull *Scimus Fili* issued on 29 June 1299.[11] He certainly was involved in negotiations with King Philip of France and was considered dangerous enough by the English to have orders made for his capture following his return to Scotland in the summer of 1299.[12]

[4] *Ibid.*, and *Fasti Ecclesiae Scoticanae Medii Aevi*, ed. D. E. R. Watt (St. Andrews, 1969), (=Watt *Fasti*) 305, 310, 323.

[5] *Cal. Docs. Scot.* (=CDS), ii, no. 823 (p. 212).

[6] CPL, i, 576, printed in full in Theiner, *Vet. Mon.*, no. 362. The electors were John Fraser archdeacon of St Andrews, William Frere archdeacon of Lothian, the prior and subprior and four canons.

[7] Stevenson, *Documents*, ii, no. 512. For the 'Culdees'' claims in episcopal elections see G. W. S. Barrow, 'The Cathedral Chapter of St Andrews and the Culdees in the Twelfth and Thirteenth Centuries', *Journal of Ecclesiastical History*, iii (1952).

[8] Palgrave, *Docs. Hist. Scot.*, i, no. 149 (p. 332).

[9] *St Andrews Liber*, p. xxv, no. 4.                [10] *Vet. Mon.*, no. 362.

[11] *Anglo-Scottish Relations 1174–1328*, ed. E. L. G. Stones (=Stones, *Relations*) (London, 1965), no. 28.

[12] CDS, ii, no. 1071 and G. W. S. Barrow, *Robert Bruce* (London, 1965) (=Barrow, *Bruce*), 135.

Upon his return to Scotland the bishop was caught up in the growing tensions between the guardians and was present at the explosive scene between Sir David Graham and Malcolm Wallace at Peebles on 12 August. At the same meeting Lamberton was given custody of 'all the castles in his hands as principal captain.'[13] Lamberton's position as an essentially uncommitted figure in the factions surrounding the guardianship led to his being chosen to act as the mediator in a triumvirate guardianship composed of himself, the earl of Carrick, and John Comyn. It may be due to the bishop's ability as a neutralising force that this unsatisfactory tripartite guardianship lasted as long as it did. Lamberton joined Bruce and Comyn on a raid into the English held territory south of the Forth. The campaign of 1299 culminated in the capture of Stirling castle. By the winter of 1299–1300 the guardians were in the Torwood and were offering to cease hostilities with Edward I on the mediation of the king of France.[14]

This appearance of unity on the part of the guardians was soon broken for at some time between November 1299 and May 1300 Bruce resigned and the long-standing divisions between himself and Comyn became manifest at the Rutherglen parliament of 1300. Comyn initially refused to serve with Lamberton, but a compromise was eventually arranged by which Comyn and Lamberton were joined by Sir Ingram de Umfraville.[15] The summer's campaign was indecisive and a truce was agreed with the English in October 1300. At the end of the year Lamberton, Comyn and Umfraville resigned and were replaced by Sir John de Soules: the 'last experiment in multiple or joint guardianship' was ended.[16]

For Lamberton this change in guardianship meant that at last he could turn his attention to his diocese. On 12 December 1300 he was at Dunfermline Abbey, apparently on his way to spend Christmas in his cathedral city.[17] Early in February he confirmed the advowson of the church of Dairsie to his cathedral chapter, thus ending nearly a century and a half of controversy over the respective rights of the bishop and chapter in this capitular church situated in episcopal lands.[18] From the text of this charter it is clear that Lamberton was preparing to go abroad, for the terms included provision that if the bishop were absent when the present vicar resigned the bishop's representatives were to admit the chapter's nominee to the benefice.

Lamberton's embassy to France occupied most of 1301. Little is known of the outcome of the journey beyond the anonymous report of an English spy to Edward I which stated that following his return the bishop went about 'showing the people a letter under the king of France's seal . . . asserting that there will be no peace between him and the king of England unless the Scots are included.'[19] This letter was only part of a propaganda offensive which both sides had mounted in the course of 1301. By 23 February 1302 a parliament at Scone issued a letter to the French king about maintaining the common truce with England. Behind

---

[13] Barrow, *Bruce*, 152.
[14] *CDS*, ii, no. 1109.
[15] Barrow, *Bruce*, 156–8.
[16] *Ibid.*, 161.
[17] *Dunfermline Registrum*, no. 121; *Cambuskenneth Registrum*, no. 116.
[18] *St Andrews Liber*, 120.
[19] *CDS*, ii, no. 1431.

this action was the well-justified fear that a separate peace treaty might be made between the English and the French which would leave the Scots to face the undivided attentions of Edward I; a fear which was shortly fulfilled as a result of the French defeat at Courtrai by the Flemish citizen army.

The Scots attempted to forestall the inevitable by sending Lamberton to Paris at the head of an impressive embassy in the autumn of 1302.[20] The gesture was a vain one, for on 20 May 1303 an Anglo-French treaty was signed and the Scottish envoys in Paris found themselves virtual prisoners in enemy territory. Five days later they wrote what comfort they could to the 'faithful of the community of the realm' urging that if

> the said king of England be so obdurate . . . that he will not consent to truce but continue the war with you, by the mercy of Jesus Christ manfully and as one man defend yourselves . . .[21]

It may be that this letter never reached Scotland. In a private letter to Wallace written under his own seal, Lamberton urged him to continue the fight and promised him support.[22]

The advice and promised help were ineffectual and the English invasion of 1303–4 was soon under way. Lamberton and the other ambassadors to France were allowed to return to Scotland by way of England early in 1304.[23] By early May the bishop had sworn fealty to Edward at Stirling and had been restored to his temporalities, which he was henceforward to hold of the English crown. He further undertook to be responsible for any issues previously drawn from them without the king's leave, a clear reference to his attempted support of Wallace.[24]

Lamberton's submission was irksome and degrading, for it placed the premier Scottish bishop and his see in an unprecedented state of subservience. The conditions imposed by the English king went beyond anything claimed by the Scottish Crown in similar circumstances, yet submission was the only reasonable course of action open to the bishop for it allowed him at least to resume control of the administration of his neglected diocese. His action was prompted by other considerations as well, for just over a month after taking his oath to the English king the bishop and Robert Bruce entered into a secret league of friendship and alliance while both were in the king's army at the siege of Stirling.[25] Lamberton had clearly reached a turning point in his career, for his early patron Wallace was a hunted man and the bishop must look elsewhere for support.

The following year was an active one. Towards its end Lamberton met his first mentor, Bishop Wishart, at Melrose abbey where the two bishops issued a confirmation of the bulls of Boniface VIII which absolved the abbey from paying teinds from their lands.[26] The two men must have discussed the state of

---

[20] Barrow, *Bruce*, 177.

[21] *A Source Book of Scottish History*, edd. W. C. Dickinson and others (second edn, Edinburgh, 1958), i, 139, translating *APS*, i, 454–5.

[22] Palgrave, *Docs. Hist. Scot.*, i, no. 149 (p. 333).

[23] *CDS*, ii, nos. 1455, 1574.    [24] *Ibid.*, nos. 1529, 1531.

[25] Palgrave, *Docs. Hist. Scot.*, i, no. 146 (p. 323–4).

[26] *Melrose Liber*, i, no. 349.

Scotland for Edward I's plans for the future governance of Scotland were becoming increasingly clear. The country was to be merged into a greater kingdom of Britain, ruled by the English king and his heirs. The threat posed by this political arrangement to the ecclesiastical integrity of Scotland was obvious. One straw in the wind had been the attempted unilateral presentation by Bishop Antony Bek of Durham of his suffragan, the refugee bishop of Byblos, to the priorate of Coldingham.[27] The case had been discussed at Edward I's Lenten parliament of 1305, of which Lamberton may have had direct knowledge from the Scottish representatives who were in London at the time.[28] Lamberton himself had been present at the second parliament of the year, held at Westminster a few weeks after Wallace's trial and execution.[29] He was thus able to report to both Bruce and Wishart on the English king's plans for the future government of Scotland.[30] It seems likely therefore that the two bishops also discussed Robert Bruce's plans to take the crown of Scotland.

It is clear that Bruce planned to seize the throne, even if he could not have foreseen the event which would precipitate his coup. At the time of the murder of Comyn at Dumfries on 10 February 1306 both bishops were ready, although their actions immediately following the murder display a curious mixture of half-confused and half-planned action. Of the two prelates it was Lamberton who seems to have been caught more off-guard, for he was at Berwick at the time of the killing. He managed to reach Scone by the preordained date of 25 March, the feast of the Annunciation, where he carried out his traditional role in the enthronement ceremony of the new king of Scots. The ceremony was repeated two days later on Palm Sunday, with the countess of Buchan as representative of the Clan MacDuff placing the new king on his throne.[31] Lamberton then celebrated mass for his new king: a service which must have made use of the obvious parallel between Bruce's entry into his rightful kingdom and Christ's entry into Jerusalem.

The parallel with events in Holy Week can be taken further to the apparent total defeat of King Robert at Methven and his subsequent gradual winning of his kingdom. By the beginning of April 1306 Bruce's revolt was known to Edward I who ordered his Scottish deputy Aymer de Valence to suppress it and to capture those involved in Comyn's murder.[32] At the same time Lamberton was attempting to enforce obedience to the new king among his subordinates and to deprive those clergy of questionable loyalty, such as Mr William Comyn.[33] The bishop sent his tenants to fight for Bruce, but by the time of Methven on 19 June Lamberton was making peaceful overtures to the English.[34] For the first time in his career, however, Lamberton's foresight failed him and before his letter offering peace could reach Edward's representatives King Robert

[27] C. Fraser, *A History of Antony Bek, Bishop of Durham, 1283–1311* (Oxford, 1957) (=Fraser, *Bek*), 163, 194.

[28] *Memoranda de Parliamento, 1305*, ed. F. W. Maitland (London, 1893), p. xx.

[29] *Parliamentary Writs and Writs of Military Summons*, ed. F. Palgrave (Record Commission, 1827), no. 59 (p. 161).

[30] Barrow, *Bruce*, 190 and n. 3.

[31] Barrow, *Bruce*, 210ff.

[32] *CDS*, ii, nos. 1754–5.

[33] Palgrave, *Docs. Hist. Scot.*, i, no. 147.

[34] *Ibid.*, no. 145; *CDS*, ii, no. 1781.

had become a hunted man. Since May the English king had been demanding the bishop's capture.[35] By June the bishop of Glasgow had been apprehended and although Lamberton was still at large Edward's government was already making arrangements for the administration of his diocese during his inevitable absence.[36] This time there was to be no moderation: anything and anyone connected with Bruce and his revolt were to be destroyed and punished.

Lamberton was captured by the end of June and on 19 August at Newcastle upon Tyne he was presented with the captured documentary proof of his alliance with Bruce and his oath of allegiance to Edward.[37] There would be no trial, for in the eyes of the English king Lamberton was an erring feudatory who must 'come to his faith and receive his due.'[38] From the account of the proceedings at Newcastle it is clear that Lamberton shared this view of his position. When asked why he had not told Edward of his confederacy with Bruce the bishop replied:

> that on the occasion (of meeting with the English king) he had utterly forgotten the confederacy and therefore made no mention of it there.[39]

When asked why he had secretly stolen away from Berwick to take part in the enthronement of Bruce, Lamberton claimed that:

> he crossed the Scottish sea . . . only to have speech with him (Bruce), adding that because of Robert's severe threat made against him . . . he went to him to mollify his will and his command, for which he declared that he was now very sorry . . .[40]

The bishop was also charged with failing to deliver up Andrew the son of the Steward of Scotland, whom he had as ward, to the English king when asked to do so. Instead, he had handed Andrew over to Bruce. He was also accused of celebrating mass for the newly enthroned king. The bishop acknowledged these charges, because 'he was unwilling to tell falsehoods.' No defence was offered and the penalty was inescapable: two days before the bishop's confession was drawn up the king, at Durham, laid down the conditions for Lamberton's imprisonment.[41]

For the rest of Edward I's reign these conditions were severe, and the death of the old king on 1 July 1307 brought no immediate alleviation. Yet life in irons in a dungeon was better than the hanging to which the king had only been prevented from condemning Lamberton and Wishart because of their orders.[42] By 1308 the papacy demanded that Lamberton be released.[43] In May of that year Edward II ordered that the bishop to be set free from Winchester gaol to remain within the county of Northampton.[44] By 11 August Lamberton had sworn fealty to the English king and was permitted to move to Durham

[35] *Ibid.*, no. 1777.   [36] *CDS*, ii, nos. 1780, 1786, 1788.
[37] Stones, *Relations*, no. 35; *CDS*, ii, no. 1818.
[38] *Ibid.*, no. 1777.   [39] Stones, *Relations*, no. 35 (p. 136).
[40] *Ibid.* (p. 137).   [41] *CDS*, ii, nos. 1812–14.
[42] *Ibid.*, no. 1786; Barrow, *Bruce*, 216.
[43] Public Record Office (London), Papal Bulls 11(16), 12(16).
[44] *CDS*, iii, no. 44.

diocese where his custody was entrusted to Bishop Bek and his loyalty secured by a bond for six thousand marks.[45]

Edward hoped for Lamberton's support in his new offensive in Scotland and for several years after his release the bishop was able to play a double role, dealing with both sides in conditions of trust. By the early part of 1309 the bishop had returned to Scotland for a brief visit, perhaps as a negotiator for a proposed truce between the English, French and Scots.[46] Shortly thereafter he was summoned by Edward II to attend a parliament at Stamford in Lincolnshire, beginning on 25 July.[47]

It seems to have been intended that Lamberton accompany the English invasion of Scotland planned for the autumn of 1309. The campaign was delayed and instead the bishop returned to Scotland as an agent of Bishop Bek, who had been put in charge of enquiries into the Templars of the British Isles.[48] Shortly after the Stamford parliament both bishops began to make preparations for their inquests. Bek moved south to London where he met papal representatives who were to help carry out enquiries.[49] At this London meeting letters were issued to the dean of Dunblane cathedral, the archdeacon of Brechin and John de Solario, canon of St Radegund at Poitiers, ordering one or two of this number to assist Lamberton in his enquiries.[50]

Lamberton left Durham and by 17 November was at Holyrood abbey where, acting with John de Solario, he held an enquiry into the affairs of the Templars in Scotland.[51] The evidence which was obtained at this inquest was not acted upon in Scotland 'propter hostium incursus et guerrae continuam expectationem.'[52] In fact there were only two full members of the order remaining in Scotland at the time of the inquest and both were eventually tried and sentenced by the archbishop of York in 1311.[53]

Lamberton turned shortly thereafter to the resettlement of his diocese. The period of his absence had been a time of considerable disruption, although arrangements had been made for administration of what Edward I clearly regarded as a vacant see. In fact the diocese had effectively been without resident episcopal authority for nearly fifteen years. The first concern of the bishop coincided with that of King Robert, to determine and restore his temporal jurisdiction. Thus at some time in 1308 Thomas Randolph, guardian north of the Forth, carried out an inquest into the respective jurisdictions of the bishop, the Augustinian chapter and the Culdean collegiate church of St Mary of the Rock within the *Cursus Apri*, the lands immediately about the cathedral city.[54]

[45] *Ibid.*, no. 50; Fraser, *Bek*, 222–3.  [46] Barrow, *Bruce*, 373–4 and n.
[47] *CDS*, iii, no. 94.  [48] Fraser, *Bek*, 219.
[49] *Records of Antony Bek*, ed. C. M. Fraser (Surtees Society, 1953), no. 128.
[50] *Ibid.*, no. 144.
[51] 'Processus factus contra Templarios in Scotia, 1309', *Spottiswoode Miscellany*, ii (Edinburgh, 1845), 3–16.  [52] *Ibid.*, 16.
[53] *Register of William Greenfield* (= *Reg. Greenfield*), edd. William Brown and A. Hamilton Thompson (Surtees Society, 1937–40), iv, 336 and n. 2.
[54] *St A. Lib.*, pp. xxxi–ii, from Scottish Record Office (Edinburgh), 'Black Book of St. Andrews', B65/1/1 fo. xxxiv. For the extent of the *Cursus Apri* see M. O. Anderson's chapter in this volume.

It seems that Lamberton had as the model for this inquest the dispute he must have witnessed at Durham between the bishop and his chapter over a number of jurisdictional rights which had ended in 1308 in an episcopal victory. Antony Bek had thereby obtained recognition 'that the bishop's court had a jurisdiction concurrent with and equal to that of the King's Bench.'[55] Thomas Randolph's enquiry determined that the bishop's jurisdiction within the *Cursus Apri* was superior to that of the two corporations and included the right to hear all pleas of the crown except treason. Bek's triumph had been sealed by the English king issuing commissions of *oyer et terminer* to settle questions arising from the invasion of episcopal possessions and jurisdiction. The definition of the bishop of St Andrews' regalian jurisdiction was followed by the bishop and various of his officials acting in concert with royal agents to settle a number of outstanding jurisdictional disputes. Thus in the winter of 1309–10 Lamberton and his Official witnessed the inquest held by Sir Robert Keith, justiciar north of the Forth, into payments due to Lindores abbey from the men of Newburgh.[56]

Despite the apparent concern for the resettlement of his diocese, a process which involved a close working relationship with Scottish royal government, the bishop retained English trust for another year. He was allowed to remain in Scotland after Edward II returned south in 1311 and when Lamberton was summoned to the council of Vienne the English king asked that he be excused from attending 'to avoid the danger of souls which might chance in his absence.[57] The most striking evidence of Lamberton's working relationship with the English during this period concerns his contacts with various members of the English ecclesiastical hierarchy. Some time in the autumn of 1311 he ordained two priests of Durham diocese, who were accepted by the new bishop Richard Kellawe.[58] In the previous year Archbishop Greenfield of York had written to Lamberton asking him to make enquiries into the position of an Englishwoman, Beatrice of Hodsoch, who had been a nun at Coldstream before leaving that house due to the threat of war. She was now living as an anchoress near Doncaster.[59] Again Greenfield, writing from the council of Vienne,[60] delegated to Lamberton, along with the prior of Hexham and the archdeacon of Cleveland, the case between Mr William Comyn and Sir Henry Beaumont which doubtless concerned Comyn's attempt to claim the earldom of Buchan.[60a] Lamberton's appointment seems a curious choice for he was being asked to judge a case between the man who had claimed to be elected bishop in his stead and the man who had been given charge of the temporalities of St Andrews during his captivity. It is not known if he was ever called upon to execute this commission.

By 1311 the bishop's position of mutual trust was becoming increasingly difficult to maintain. It may be that it was during this period that Lamberton was threatened by the garrison of English-occupied Berwick when he attempted

[55] Fraser, *Bek*, 220.
[56] *Lindores Liber*, no. 10.
[57] *CDS*, iii, no. 223.
[58] *Registrum Palatinum Dunelmense*, i, ed. T. Duffus Hardy (Rolls Series, 1873), (=*Reg. Pal. Dun.*), 95, 102–3.
[59] *Letters from North Registers*, ed. J. Raine (Rolls Series, 1872), no. 123 and n.
[60] *Reg. Greenfield*, v, no. 2635.
[60a] *CDS*, ii, no. 1785.

to go there on the king of England's business.[61] Early in the following year the bishop entered Bruce's camp at Dundee and ended his period of equivocation.[62]

It was clear by 1312 that the initiative had passed to the Scots. Bruce's campaign in the north of England had brought the horrors of the war to the enemy. Bishop Kellawe had written to his former associate asking for his help to bring about peace and the reception of ambassadors from the pope and the king of France.[63] The tone of the letter, in which Lamberton is pointedly reminded of his past kindnesses and efforts for peace, indicates the change which had taken place in the relationship between the two dioceses and their governors.

The years immediately before and after 1314 were active ones for Lamberton. He had been an envoy to France in 1313.[64] He may have gone abroad again on an embassy after the battle of Bannockburn, at which he was not present.[65] There were to be further English invasions of his diocese in 1319 and 1322, but the dominant theme of the remaining years of the bishop's life after 1314 was reconstruction. Many of the surviving episcopal charters from this period are terminations of long-standing disputes and problems, and often contain references to the effects of the war.[66]

The association between king and bishop in the years of reconstruction was a close one, which reached a climax in the dedication of the completed and restored cathedral of St Andrews on 5 July 1318. Both the king and the bishop recognised the event as a symbolic occasion of the highest national importance. King Robert was the undisputed master of the realm, following the capture of Berwick early in the year. His brother, Edward Bruce, was king of Ireland. For Robert I the dedication of the cathedral set the seal on the restored prestige of his kingdom and the dynasty he hoped to found. For Lamberton the dedication of the cathedral symbolised the restored position of his diocese and the Scottish church. The cult centre of Scotland's patron saint was complete after a century and half of building. The dedication was attended by seven bishops, fifteen abbots and a large group of nobility.[67] In the winter parliament of 1318 at Scone the rights and freedoms of the Scottish church were confirmed, setting a political seal on the summer's ceremony.[68]

The decade of life which remained to Lamberton and his king following the dedication of the cathedral was in many ways anticlimactic. Never again would the situation seem so assured as it had seemed in the summer of 1318. The first blow was the death of Edward Bruce in the autumn of that year. The integrity of the church was threatened in a less direct way by continued English attempts to interfere with its personnel,[69] and to reassert influence over English cells in

[61] CDS, iii, no. 337.

[62] Barrow, Bruce, 374 and n. 5 (citing material collected by Professor A. A. M. Duncan for his forthcoming edition of the Acts of Robert I).

[63] Reg. Pal. Dun., 339–40.

[64] CDS, iii, no. 346.

[65] Ibid., no. 390.

[66] See for example, Newbattle Registrum, no. 161 and Kelso Liber, nos. 311–14.

[67] Chron. Bower, ii, 271–2. There is no surviving account of the ceremony, although the lost St Andrews Register contained such an entry. St Andrews Liber, p. xxvi.

[68] APS, i, 107.                          [69] CDS, iii, no. 653.

Scotland.[70] These random actions did not pose serious jurisdictional threats. Indeed, the poverty of English policy in this respect may be seen in the half-hearted attempt to unseat Lamberton by advancing the claims of yet another putative bishop. The pope was requested to depose Lamberton and 'restore' an English candidate to the see. By the autumn of 1318 the pope replied that there was no record of Thomas de Rivers' provision to St Andrews and no further action was taken on the claim.[71]

If this frivolous claim had any significance it was as a harbinger of a more vitriolic phase in relations between Scotland and the papacy. Pope John XXII was not prepared to allow secular rulers to act in areas which were conceived of as pertaining to papal authority and interest. Increasingly the Avignon popes attempted to gather such rights as provision to episcopal office into their own hands. An English Franciscan, John de Egglescliffe, was provided by the papacy to succeed Bishop Wishart of Glasgow after the chapter had elected two successive domestic candidates.[72] The Scottish response to this action was to regard Glasgow as effectively vacant until Egglescliffe was translated to the see of Connor in 1323.

In 1317 Edward II had taken crusading vows and the financial collection carried out by popes Nicholas IV, Boniface VII and Clement V was revived. Such a collection became for the Scots a matter which touched on a number of political points, including the specific one of the independence of the nation and its church from collections in support of English interest. The papal collector appointed to England, Rigaud d'Assier, was in one instance used as an envoy to arrange a truce with King Robert and was also empowered to collect in Scotland although he made no attempt to do so.[73]

All these random events serve to emphasise the anomalous position of the Scottish church as a national but acephalous church in a country ruled by an excommunicate king. A decade of papal hostility to Bruce's cause, however, had produced modifications in the peculiar and close relationship of the Scottish church with the papacy. Scottish churchmen could no longer look for papal support in defence against English encroachments and interference as they had been able to do in the previous century and a half. Thus in the remaining years of Lamberton's life the church began to work out a new relationship with the papacy in accord with a new set of political realities.

In the year following the dedication of St Andrews cathedral the pope cited the king and the bishops of St Andrews, Dunkeld, Aberdeen and Moray to appear before him by 1 May 1320.[74] The summons came at the end of the abortive two-year truce which the papacy had attempted to bring about between England and Scotland. During its term the Scots had recaptured Berwick, and Bruce had refused to receive papal envoys unless they addressed him as king of

---

[70] Durham Dean and Chapter Muniments, Miscellaneous Charter no. 5990, for example, is a reissue by Edward II of Edward I's confirmation of Coldingham priory's possessions.
[71] Public Record Office, Papal Bull 56(2).
[72] Watt, *Fasti*, 146–7.
[73] W. E. Lunt and E. B. Graves, *Accounts Rendered by Papal Collectors in England, 1317–1378* (Philadelphia, 1968), xxii.      [74] *CPL*, ii, 191.

Scots.[75] At the end of 1319 a sentence of excommunication was issued against King Robert and his supporters, and the king's subjects were absolved from their allegiance to him.[76]

The immediate result of this offensive was the drawing up of the declaration of Arbroath in April 1320 and the sending of a delegation to the papal court to deal with Bruce's title as king of Scots.[77] Before the embassy reached the papal court the papal chancery had issued letters of excommunication against the king and the bishops who had failed to appear before Pope John.[78] When Lamberton wrote to John XXII after his excommunication the papal response, in distinction to the evasive reply to the Arbroath letter, was direct and unambiguous. The bishop and his fellow prelates were said to have ignored papal demands for too long and were to be compelled to return to obedience by proceedings at the Curia.[79]

Like other unacceptable papal orders the excommunications were ignored. In the midst of an acrimonious paper war between Scotland and the papacy Lamberton continued his extremely active career as a national figure and diocesan bishop. Political and ecclesiastical integrity were seen as but two aspects of the overriding question of Scotland's national independence. This fact is reflected in the coincidental holding of parliaments and national church councils in July 1321 and March 1325,[80] and in a more general way in the close working relationship which existed between the king and Lamberton.[81]

The bishop continued to be an active diplomat on behalf of his king. In the spring and early summer of 1322 he was on an embassy to England.[82] Despite dangers on the journey, which included an assault on the bishop's servants, the mission was successful and a truce was drawn up at Berwick in June.[83] In 1324 Thomas Randolph, earl of Moray, and Lamberton formed an embassy to York to arrange for a final peace between English and Scots, but the negotiations were abortive and the bishop's last diplomatic journey ended in failure.[84]

It was probably in this last decade of life that the bishop was most fully involved in the physical rebuilding of his diocese. He is known to have built or restored a number of his residences throughout the diocese including St Andrews castle, Monimail, Torry, Dairsie, Inchmurdo, Muckhart, Kettins, Liston, Monymusk and Stow in Wedale.[85] This reconstruction was but part of a general reorganization of the bishop's temporal demesne and administration. Lamberton may have been the first of his line to employ local families to oversee the running of certain of his scattered estates. In 1316 the bishop

---

[75] Barrow, *Bruce*, 349–51.

[76] *CPL*, ii, 191.

[77] Barrow, *Bruce*, 426 and n. 1.

[78] *CPL*, ii, 199.

[79] *CPL*, ii, 428, printed in full in *Vet. Mon.*, no. 432.

[80] *Concilia Scotie*, ed. J. Robertson (Bannatyne Club, 1866), i, lxxii–lxxvi.

[81] The bishop was a frequent witness to royal charters. For example, Scottish Record Office, Register House Charters, 6/68, 6/68c, 6/85; National Library of Scotland (Edinburgh), MS. Adv. 34/6/24, fo. 250; *Aberdeen–Banff Illustrations*, iii, 211–12; *Scone Liber*, no. 129, *Reg. Mag. Sig.*, i, nos. 84, 331, 485–7, 805, 839, Appendix One, nos. 19, 27, 31–2, 35, 92–4.

[82] *CDS*, iii, nos. 809–10.

[83] *APS*, i, 119–21.

[84] *CDS*, iii, no. 851.

[85] G. Martine, *Reliquiae Divi Andreae* (St Andrews, 1797), 228.

granted Robert Lauder his lands on the Bass Rock for a *reddendo* of a pound of wax, thereby establishing the family of Lauder of the Bass as hereditary baillies of the estate of Tyninghame.[86] This infeftment may have been one of the first steps in the career of a man who rose from obscurity to become one of the trusted agents of Robert I, being created justiciar of Lothian in 1321 and sole guarantor on behalf of his king of the treaty of Edinburgh-Northampton in 1328.[87]

It is the consistent and tireless activities of Lamberton in the reconstruction of the state, his diocese and its administration which allow us to come closest to the essential character of the man. He was certainly no saint, but his times demanded attributes other than sanctity. He was, however, a man of ability and ambition, and also a man of fears. Unlike Bishop Wishart of Glasgow he was prepared to trim his sails to suit the political and military wind, yet in the end his practical achievement was probably greater than that of his more inflexible episcopal colleague. In thirty years as a bishop and forty years as a public figure he achieved what he did by actions which were the expression of strong character, practicality and intelligence. George Martine the seventeenth-century St Andrews historian says of him that 'erat vir incredibili prudentia, genere autem illustris, sed doctrinae, virtutis et eruditionis nomine illustrior.'[88]

In his episcopate Lamberton not only rebuilt on the past but for the future. Within a few years of his death the diocese was again to experience armed invasion. His successor, James Ben, died in exile in 1332 and the see was not effectively filled again for ten years.[89] If proof were needed of the ultimate success of Bishop Lamberton it must be sought in the subsequent history of his diocese.

In a sense Lamberton's death well became the time at which it occurred. He had lived to see the fruits of his labour and the labours of the king he served begin to take root. Two months before he died he was present at the signing of the final peace with England.[90] He died on 20 May 1328 in the prior's chamber at St Andrews, a fitting end for a man who had achieved a particularly close and harmonious relationship with his cathedral chapter and who had done so much to improve the priory, building a new chapter house, and endowing the canons with new vestments and books for their library.[91] On 7 July, William Lamberton was buried on the north side of the altar in the cathedral church which he brought to completion.[92]

MARINELL ASH

---

[86] The original charter is now lost. It was printed in T. M'Crie, *The Bass Rock, Its Civil and Ecclesiastical History* (Edinburgh, 1848), 41–2, and in English translation in T. Dick Lauder, *Scottish Rivers* (Edinburgh, 1890), 306–7.

[87] Barrow, *Bruce*, 399, 401.                    [88] Martine, *Reliquiae*, 229.

[89] Watt, *Fasti*, 293–4.                          [90] *APS*, i, 124–7.

[91] *Chron. Bower*, i, 361.

[92] J. Dowden, *The Bishops of Scotland* (Glasgow, 1912), 21–3.

# 5

## The Architecture of Scottish Collegiate Churches

### General

The collegiate church was an important feature of the medieval ecclesiastical system. It was organised as a college of secular canons or chaplains, known also as prebendaries from their prebends or endowments, presided over by a provost or dean. Members resided in their own manses but were required to live a common life and carry out prescribed duties. Constitutions varied but the principal obligation was the rendering of the daily Divine Office and stipulated masses. Individual duties were assigned to each prebendary and other responsibilities might be the oversight of a parish, a hospital or almshouse, or the organisation of an educational establishment. Prebends were generally provided from the annexed teinds of some parish or from rents of lands or town tenements donated for the purpose.

### Scottish Developments

In earlier times the benefactions of wealthy Scots donors had been made to monasteries but in the later Middle Ages they were directed towards secular churches. This reorientation coincided with a great expansion of the chantry movement. A chantry was a mass said for the welfare of a patron during life and for the repose of his soul after death and it was customary for an individual donor, or a confraternity, to endow a chaplaincy for this purpose. A wealthy donor or corporation might erect a special chapel at the parish church or found a collegiate church, in effect an enlarged chantry chapel.

The majority of Scottish collegiate churches were chantry establishments and there were some forty whose foundation is authenticated.[1] Of these the following buildings survive in whole or in part: St Mary of the Rock, St Andrews (c. 1250), Maybole (1383–4), Lincluden (1389), Bothwell (1397), Dalkeith (1406), Yester (1421), Carnwath (1424), Corstorphine (1429), Methven (1433), Kilmun (1441), Dunglass (1443–4), Crichton (1449), St Salvator's, St Andrews (1450), Trinity College, Edinburgh (1460), St Giles', Edinburgh (1466), Guthrie (c. 1479), Restalrig (1487), Tain (1487), Seton (1492), King's College, Aberdeen (1500), Castle Semple (1504), Innerpeffray (1506), Crail (1517), Roslin (c. 1521), Foulis Easter (1538), Aberdeen (1540), Haddington (c. 1540), Cullen (1543), Peebles (1543), Biggar (1545–6) and Stirling (1546).

[1] Easson, *Religious Houses*, 173–86.

The Architecture of Scottish Collegiate Churches

PLATES

PLATE I. Crichton, Midlothian

PLATE 2. Corstorphine in 1817 (after an etching by Skene)

PLATE 3. Roslin, Midlothian

PLATE 4. King's College Chapel, Aberdeen

PLATE 5. St Giles, Edinburgh: Steeple, *c.* 1500

PLATE 6. Lincluden, Dumfries

These collegiate churches are notable exemplars of the last phases of Scottish Gothic architecture. As in other European countries this has a distinctive national character and in it French, Flemish and occasional English influences are skilfully naturalised. Plan forms vary. Small churches like Foulis Easter, Inner-peffray and Maybole are long gabled rectangles. Others like Castle Semple, King's College and St Salvator's have apsidal east ends. Transepts are sometimes secondary as at Dunglass, Seton and probably Crichton (Pl. 1), but larger churches are generally cruciform. Corstorphine, which was not parochial, comprised sanctuary and sacristy, choir, ante-chapel and west tower (Pl. 2). Roslin, also extra-parochial, has an aisled choir with eastern chapels and was intended to have transepts and a wide nave comprehending choir and aisles. Its exotic plan and architecture suggest Iberian or southern French origins (Pl. 3).

Ribbed groined vaults are general in the larger churches though seldom over the whole building but a common feature is the pointed tunnel vault, with or without ribs and covered externally with stone flags. The earliest is probably at Bothwell (c. 1400) and this construction was also employed at Corstorphine, Crichton, Dalkeith, Dunglass, St Salvator's and Seton. Lincluden had a ribbed vault with an orthodox groined vault below it and at Stirling a segmental ribbed vault is awkwardly contrived within the apse. A coved boarded ceiling with decorative ribs and bosses took the place of the masonry vault at Aberdeen over the choir of St Nicholas, which no longer exists and later at King's College which does (Pl. 4). The first was the work of John Fendour who may also have done the other. Similar ceilings were used at Guthrie, Hamilton and Foulis Easter.

## TYPES OF FOUNDATIONS

As earlier indicated, constitutions and buildings varied considerably but the following main types of foundations emerge:

(a) Parochial foundations:
    Rural churches
    Town churches
(b) Educational foundations
(c) i. Private foundations (extra-parochial)
    ii. Royal foundations

### Parish Churches, Rural

More than half of the collegiate foundations were set up in parish churches and the new establishment was generally marked by additions or extensive rebuilding. In the rural parishes of Bothwell, Guthrie and Seton new choirs were constructed, while at Biggar and Crichton total rebuilding took place.

Seton represents the typical development. Here an earlier rectangular church with a *c.* 1435 chantry aisle at its south-east corner was enlarged by the addition of a three-bay apsidal choir with sacristy and this was the full intention of the founder. Following the death of the fifth Lord Seton at Flodden, however, his widow Lady Janet Hepburn added first a north transept and then, in order 'to

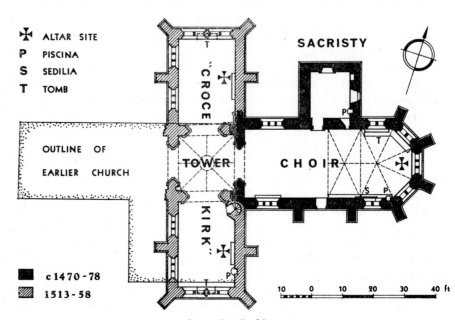

Seton, East Lothian

mak it ane perfyt and proportionat croce kirk',[2] demolished the old church and erected a south transept and crossing, capped by a broach spire which was never completed. Thus what started as a new choir became a total reconstruction. As at Crichton, the nave was never built but this was no great disadvantage for the college functioned in the choir and the parish altar was doubtless set up in the 'croce kirk'. The broach spire is an unusual feature but the remainder a typical essay of the period and akin to Dalkeith.

*Parish Churches, Burgh*

From early times Scottish burghs constituted single parishes. By the mid-fifteenth century their churches were quite imposing structures, enlargement having been encouraged by improved economic conditions and the chantry foundations of rich burghers, confraternities and guilds. The quaint asymmetrical bulk of Edinburgh's Hie Kirk is largely the result of such chantry expansions. It attained collegiate status as did Crail, Aberdeen, Haddington and Stirling but this was little more than a formal incorporation of their numerous chaplains, virtually collegiate in all but name.

Crail comprises a thirteenth-century aisled nave, choir and west tower but

---

[2] R. Maitland, *History of the House of Seytoun* (Glasgow, 1892), 39.

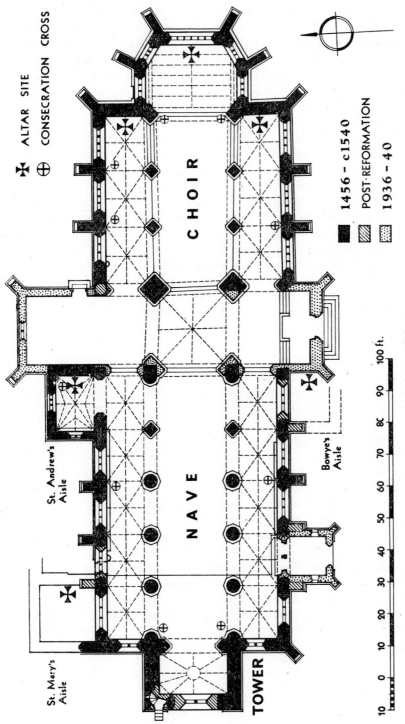

ALTAR SITE

CONSECRATION CROSS

1456 – c1540

POST-REFORMATION

1936 – 40

CHOIR

NAVE

TOWER

St. Andrew's Aisle

St. Mary's Aisle

Bowye's Aisle

Holy Rude, Stirling

the others were designed as aisled cruciform structures, vaulted in whole or in part. At Edinburgh and Haddington all save the nave was vaulted, both had central towers and crown spires (Pl. 5), but while the former attained an extreme in irregular development the latter is symmetrical apart from a sacristy projection. Probably the most interesting in respect of plan and architectural form is Holy Rude, Stirling.

The rebuilding of Stirling's parish kirk was initiated by erection of a five-bay aisled nave, west tower and south porch completed about 1470, to which three chantry aisles were soon added. 'Ane gud and sufficient queyr', transepts and central tower were started in 1507 and about 1540 work ceased with the completion of the three-bay choir and apse, the transepts and crossing being left in embryo to be completed in a somewhat dominating form in 1936–40.[3] The nave, which was intended to be higher, has a fine oak roof and cylindrical piers like those at Aberdeen and Dunkeld cathedrals; the loftier choir has clustered piers, while the apse with its tall windows and spreading buttresses towers in splendid composition above the sloping streets to the east. The main altar sites are clear but the liturgical arrangements for the parish altar and unfinished crossing are obscure. A small door and turnpike stair in the north wall of the choir led to an apartment over the crossing with a window into the choir, known as the King's Room, but this was removed about 1869.

*Educational Foundations*

The churches of St Salvator at St Andrews and King's College, Aberdeen were basic elements of two universities, but were more than college chapels. They were corporate chantries and collegiate churches, whose members performed educational and religious functions, and public buildings in which the services of the medieval church were performed with splendour.

St Salvator's, which was ready for consecration about 1460, is a dignified building of seven bays with a tall steeple at its west end, whose ample windows, apse and founder's tomb are evocative of France but whose original tunnel vault and slabbed roof were sternly native.[4] Nothing of its cloister, sacristy or fittings remains but its splendid Parisian mace of 1461 and a surviving *Inventory* indicate the richness of its plenishings.[5]

King's College is fortunate in having its screen and stalls, an original oak ceiling and a medieval pulpit from the nearby cathedral (Pl. 4), as well as foundation documents and an *Inventory* recording its equipment, layout and ceremonial.[6] Of similar width but slightly longer than St Salvator's, it is divided into six bays and has an apsidal end and to the south-west a buttressed tower with a crown spire (rebuilt in 1634 after destruction by storm). The shallow coved ceiling permitted of large traceried windows filling every bay save four on the south, where formerly stood the sacristy annexe built by Bishop Stewart

---

[3] RCAM, *Inventory* for *Stirlingshire* (1963), i, 129–38.
[4] Demolished 1773 and replaced by timber and slate.
[5] R. G. Cant, *The College of St Salvator* (Edinburgh, 1950).
[6] F. C. Eeles, *King's College Chapel Aberdeen* (Edinburgh, 1956).

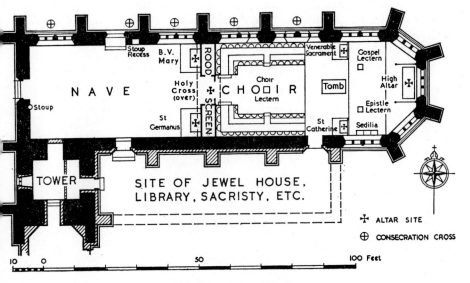

King's College Chapel, Aberdeen

(1532–46). When finished about 1510 the walls had crenellated parapets and the buttresses crocketted pinnacles. The stalls are now one bay west of their original site, the rood, the altars and retables and most of the tomb of Bishop Elphinstone, have gone, but this interesting building preserves much of the character of an authentic Scots collegiate church.

### Private Foundations (Extra-parochial)

Several private foundations were extra-parochial. They vary between simple rectangular structures like Innerpeffray, Maybole and Tain and more elaborate compositions such as Corstorphine (Pl. 2), Roslin and Lincluden. Midway between these extremes are Castle Semple, with an apsidal east end and a gabled west tower and Dunglass, designed as a nave and choir, which developed transepts and a central tower before its completion.

Related to these are the royal foundations only one of which was attached to a parish church.

### Royal Foundations

Four foundations constituted the Chapel Royal organisation. The earliest, the church of St Mary of the Rock at St Andrews, originated in a Culdee community and was reconstituted about 1250 as a college for a provost and five prebendaries. By 1290 it was a Chapel Royal designated *capella domini regis Scotorum*. It now consists of the foundations of a modest cruciform structure with twelfth-century nave and the remainder of thirteenth-century date.

From an early date there was a Chapel Royal at Stirling Castle dedicated to the Virgin Mary and St Michael. It was largely if not totally rebuilt about 1412 and was made collegiate in 1501.[7] Its foundation and equipment are well documented but little is known of the building itself. Its site lay somewhat athwart that of the present 1594 chapel and is marked on the paving. It seems to have been a rectangular building with some ancillary structures.

Trinity College, Edinburgh (Gordon of Rothiemay, 1647)

[7] C. Rogers, *History of the Chapel Royal of Scotland* (Edinburgh, 1882), p. xxxi.

The collegiate church of Restalrig had its origin in a *capella regis* built by James III adjacent to the parish church. In this chapel, a remarkable two-storey structure of hexagonal plan, the king endowed a chaplaincy in the upper chapel in 1477 and the church was erected into a college in 1487.[8] This new foundation initiated an ambitious reconstruction which proceeded no great length before it was abandoned, either on the death of the king in 1488 or after Flodden. The architectural evidences suggest an intended nave with aisles and an aisleless choir with the King's Chapel intruding rather clumsily into the south aisle. The lower storey of the chapel with a fine vaulted ceiling survives.

Though not one stone stands upon the original site, the most impressive and fully recorded of the royal foundations was Trinity College, Edinburgh. Founded in 1460 by Mary of Gueldres, widow of James II, and dedicated to the Holy Trinity, the Virgin Mary, St Ninian and all Saints, it had a provost, eight prebendaries and two singing boys. Attached to it was Trinity Hospital for the support of thirteen bedesmen. The church stood to the west of Leith Port, the north-east gate of the city, the manses of provost and prebendaries south of it and the hospital on the opposite side of Leith Wynd. The manses were destroyed during English attack in 1558 and the hospital was removed to their site in 1585. Gordon of Rothiemay's view of 1647 records the group at that date.

Though designed as a cruciform church, work ceased about 1531 and until its demolition in 1848 it consisted of a three-bay aisled choir with apse, sacristy, south porch and transepts, with a squat gabled tower over the crossing. French and Flemish influences are evident in this sophisticated job which was fully groin vaulted, with flying buttresses to the choir. Its master of works was John Halkerstone and the details are akin to contemporary work at St Giles' and Holyrood Abbey.

Records indicate that Trinity College was well equipped and there are references to images of the Virgin Mary and St Margaret, bells and an organ.[9] A pictorial allusion to the last occurs in one of the altarpiece panels now preserved in the National Gallery of Scotland. It depicts Edward Boncle, first provost, kneeling by an organ played by an angel.

All that survives of the building is the rebuilt choir without aisles, erected in 1872 as an annexe to a new church which has since been demolished.

*Architectural Features*

THE CHOIR

*The Altar*

No medieval altar remains *in situ* though a mensa is preserved at King's College and another in the sacristy at Corstorphine. According to the inventories, the high altars at St Salvator's and King's College had four brass pillars round

---

[8] I. MacIvor, 'The King's Chapel at Restalrig', *PSAS*, xcvi (1962–3), 247–63.
[9] *Midlothian Chrs.*, p. xxi.

them, supporting curtain rods and terminating in angel figures bearing the instruments of the Passion. The altars themselves had embroidered frontals and the usual ornaments, but at King's College there was in addition to the riddel curtains a large decorated retable (*una tabula magna, arte pictoria miro ingenio confecta*).[10]

The 'tabula' or flat retable was normally an alternative to the riddel curtain arrangement. It consisted of a number of panels within an architectural setting, carved in freestone, alabaster or timber, always highly coloured and gilded. Another type known as a 'tabernaculum' was much imported from Flanders and the Baltic. It had a carved oak centre piece and one or more pairs of hinged shutters painted with appropriate subjects. The well-known panel paintings of Hugo van der Goes from Trinity College formed the wings of such a retable, probably at the high altar.[11] The blank east walls behind altar sites in many Scottish churches testify to the use of such altarpieces.

### Sacrament House

The Sacrament was normally reserved in a hanging pyx over the high altar but during later medieval times there developed the custom of reservation in an elaborate wall aumbry or tower structure on the north side of the altar. Scotland followed this European vogue and in many of its churches the sacrament house became a prominent feature. It occurs in the east wall north of the high altar or the north wall.

There are good examples at Crichton, Cullen, Foulis Easter, St Salvator's and Tain. The St Salvator's example rests on a corbel in the form of two angels bearing a monstrance and the aumbry proper is surmounted by three shields. The centre, which has been erased, probably bore the Five Wounds, with the Royal Arms on the dexter and those of Kennedy on the sinister. The Foulis Easter sacrament house is an ogival headed aumbry flanked by pinnacles and over it a bust of the Saviour bearing an orb with smaller attendant figures holding respectively the cross and the pillar. The coved cornice has a rendering of the Annunciation and the projecting sill a narrow panel intended for an inscription. At Cullen, the sacrament house is in the elaborate style of the north east. The locker is enclosed by a crocketted ogival arch and above it a tall panel has the usual angels bearing the monstrance. An outer moulding frames the whole composition and above this is a Latin rendering of John vi, 55–56, capped by a cornice.

### Sedilia

For the celebrant, deacon and subdeacon sedilia were provided on the south side of the high altar. Sometimes, as in the case of an aisled choir, they were timber structures but more commonly were in the form of arched and recessed mural benches. Examples exist at Bothwell, Corstorphine, Crichton, Dunglass, Lincluden, Maybole, Seton and Tain. At Maybole a rudimentary lintolled

---

[10] Eeles, *op. cit.*, 14.
[11] RCAM, *Inventory for Edinburgh* (1951), 38–40.

recess seems to have sufficed. The Seton example has moulded jambs and an elliptical arch but all the others are triple sedilia. Bothwell, Corstorphine, Dunglass and Lincluden have canopies of ornamental tabernacle work, while at Crichton three very shallow recesses have moulded shafts and ogival arched heads.

## Piscina

It is usual to find a piscina south of an altar site, either in the same wall or in an adjacent south one. It is also to be found in some sacristies, usually towards the south-east corner. Its function is to dispose of water used at mass and it is usually in the form of an arched or canopied niche with a corbelled basin from which a small drain conveys the water to the consecrated ground below. At Corstorphine, a credence shelf is combined, upon which the cruets can be laid.

In addition to that mentioned, typical examples survive at Bothwell, Crichton (south transept), Lincluden, Maybole (nave and choir), Roslin (several), Seton (choir and south transept), and Tain (choir). The Crichton and Tain piscinas have trefoil heads, the Bothwell and Lincluden ones are enriched to match the sedilia and the levels of those at Maybole indicate that the choir floor was lower than the nave, following the site contours.

## Stalls

The western part of the choir was normally occupied by the stalls ranging along the side walls and flanking the doorway of the screen, with the choir lectern standing in the centre. It is often assumed that such work was wholly imported and while there are records of the purchase of altarpieces and other items from the Low Countries, there is equal evidence that much was made in Scotland, either by naturalised Frenchmen or Flemings or by native Scots. For example, for St Nicholas, Aberdeen, the provost, baillies and council contracted with John Fendour, wright, on 26 December 1507 to 'big oupmak and finely end and complet the xxxiiij Stallis in thar queir with the spiris and chanslar dur and ale uthir thingis according tharto . . .'.[12] Whether Fendour was an *émigré* craftsman or a native is not known. Similarly on 3 November 1552, the town council of Edinburgh for the choir of St Giles' 'haiffand respect to the grete expens maid upon the bigging of the north syde of thair stallis of the queir' appointed Andro Mansioun, wright, to make up the south range. It is thought that the north range may have been imported.

Nothing of the Edinburgh stalls survives and of Fendour's thirty-four at Aberdeen, little more remains than a range of four traceried canopy frontals. The panels which are of uniform design, competently carved in characteristic Flemish style, are now in the National Museum of Antiquities, Edinburgh. In the same place are preserved two stalls of mid-fifteenth-century date from Lincluden. They came from either the north return range or the east end of the south one and have carved haffits, misericords and pinnacled back posts, while the surviving piece of a back panel bears traces of a painted female figure amply

---

[12] *Aberdeen St Nicholas Cartularium*, ii, 346.

robed and crowned. This is a reminder that such furnishings were once bright with gilding and colour.

King's College Chapel, Aberdeen, alone retains its stalls and screen, albeit with some modification, and set one bay west of the original site. There are north and south ranges of twelve, two return sets of three and desks and subsellia, all amounting to fifty-two places. (Pl. 4.) There was depth enough in the screen to allow of a stair to the loft but access appears to have been by a doorway in the south wall from the upper storey of the jewel-house annexe. The altars of the Blessed Virgin and of St Germain stood against the west face of the screen, whose parapet was adorned with statues of the Saviour and the twelve apostles, while above the rood altar on the loft was the rood itself flanked by the figures of the Virgin and St John the Evangelist. (*Altare solii crucifixi, supra quod est crucifixus, et statue dive Virginis et Joannis apostoli et evangeliste*).[13] A small organ also stood on the loft having upon its upper part a panel painting of the Virgin.

The whole ensemble, apart from the modern stall backs, is enriched with elaborate vine ornament and tracery-work of Flemish type and several of the seats retain their original misericords. Some of the traceried canopy frontals are made up of diverse fragments and nine consist of two shallower panels. As the college was founded for thirty-six persons, the stalls were probably fewer in number originally and it is possible that the shallow frontals may belong to that arrangement. Though more varied in detail, the work resembles that from St Nicholas and as both works were done in Bishop Elphinstone's time it is possible that the King's College stalls came from the hands of Fendour.

## Nave and Transepts

The enclosed choir and the screen with its rood and rood altar was an invariable feature. At Lincluden the stone screen has an ornate corbel course displaying scenes from the life of Christ and adoring angels which supported the breast upon which were carved the twelve apostles, each within a narrow panel. The west wall at Roslin encloses the choir apart from three straight arched openings to choir and aisles and, at loft level, a tall enriched archway.

Like the King's College screen, those of Foulis Easter and Guthrie were of timber.[14] At the former the carved oak doors and some painted boarding survive. Here a painted Crucifixion on a boarded tympanum enclosed the space between the loft and the ceiling and the loft front displayed pictures of Our Lord, the apostles and martyrs. Painted fragments of similar late fifteenth-century date at Guthrie made up a Crucifixion and a 'Doom' or Last Judgment. The former doubtless occupied the corresponding position to the Foulis Easter one, with the 'Doom' on the choir side.

Screen sites are indicated by wall corbels at Castle Semple and Innerpeffray and by loft doorways at Biggar and Dunglass.

In parochial establishments the nave was the parish kirk with mass said at one

[13] Eeles, *op. cit.*, 16.
[14] M. R. Apted and W. Norman Robertson, 'Late Fifteenth-Century Paintings from Guthrie and Foulis Easter', *PSAS*, xcv (1961–2), 262–79.

of the altars before the screen. Apart from possible side altars the only other objects in it would be a pulpit half-way down its length and a font near the west door where there would be a holy water stoup. Medieval fonts, somewhat damaged, survive at Foulis Easter and Seton (2) and at King's College Chapel is Bishop Stewart's pulpit which came from the nave of St Machar's.

Transepts provided space for additional altars and their sites are indicated by piscinas, aumbries and corbels, usually against the east wall as at Crichton, Roslin and Seton. The gable walls were commonly the place for mural tombs as at Aberdeen, Dunglass and Seton.

It is difficult to visualise the original colourfulness of such interiors. As a background to the furnishings, walls were limewashed and painted with decorative and didactic subjects, as was the case at Foulis Easter and at Innerpeffray where surviving fragments of plaster bear consecration crosses and other motifs.

### SACRISTY AND TREASURY

The nature of the sacristy depended upon the size of the church and the extent of its equipment. Smaller churches, like Foulis Easter and Tain, had none. In such cases minimum provisions were probably made within the structure of the screen or behind the high altar. The normal site, however, is the north side of the choir from which it entered and it consisted often of a single vaulted apartment, as at Bothwell, Lincluden and Maybole. At Dunglass it is an aisle, opening from the choir through a wide arch which was closed by a timber screen. The desirable standard, however, was a two-storey tower-like annexe with a roof 'theikit in stane' over a masonry vault and an upper floor of timber supported on corbels. The lower chamber, which served as vestry – or *revestrie* – often had a piscina and one or more wall aumbries and the upper floor as the treasury in which valuable articles were kept. Such was the arrangement at Corstorphine (Pl. 2), Dalkeith, Haddington, Seton and Trinity College. The Seton vestry has a fireplace and a squint commanding a view of the high altar and here it is recorded that Lady Janet Hepburn 'loftit the revestrie, and maid grit lokit almeries thairin'.[15] Trinity College also had a fireplace and squint and a stone turnpike stair between the two floors. Elsewhere the stair was of more utilitarian timber type.

A doorway and a squint at Innerpeffray indicates the sacristy site as does the doorway at Castle Semple. The present vestries at Biggar and Crichton are late nineteenth-century structures upon the original sites. At Roslin the sacristy is to the east and by reason of the falling ground is set lower than the church. It is entered by a stair descending from the south-east chapel and is a rectangular chamber with a barrel vault, several wall aumbries and an altar and piscina at the east end. To the north is a windowless chamber, possibly a treasury, and in the south wall a fireplace and a doorway intended to enter another chamber but now leading outside.

The inventories of St Salvator's and King's College indicate that both were

[15] Maitland, *op. cit.*, 39.

richly endowed with altar goods and vestments and that ample sacristy and storage space was necessary. At the former a two-storey building on the north side contained an upper and lower sacristy and possibly the chapels of the Virgin Mary and St Katherine. At King's College a two-storey annexe, extending along the south side for four bays, was built by Bishop Stewart (1532–46) to accommodate sacristy, jewel-house and library. It was demolished about 1725 and its detailed arrangements are unknown, though its external appearance about 1660 is preserved in Gordon's view.

## FOUNDER'S TOMB

It was customary for patrons and founders during their lifetime to make arrangements for their tombs and monuments. This was so especially in the case of wholly new buildings or where a new choir was erected.

The siting of such tombs varied. In a church with a spacious choir a common site for the founder's tomb was a central position between the high altar and the liturgical choir. Such was the arrangement at King's College, Aberdeen and Dalkeith. An alternative position, and the one most frequently adopted in Scotland, was against the north wall of the sanctuary, as at Cullen, Lincluden, Castle Semple, Seton and St Salvator's, St Andrews. At Corstorphine two Forrester monuments flank the sacristy door and with it fill the north wall of the mid-fifteenth-century sanctuary. In smaller collegiate churches and those founded within pre-existing buildings, a common expedient was the addition of a transeptal aisle or chantry chapel, as at Carnwath, Guthrie and Methven. These aisles have survived their churches.

The simplest form of monument is the low relief ledger slab. Such recumbent slabs in Tournai marble were imported having effigies and other features in brass and coloured enamels, like the now denuded example at Seton. Bishop Elphinstone's free-standing altar tomb at King's College is now represented by its moulded marble base. It originally had a recumbent effigy of the bishop and attendant figures of angels and bedesmen, as well as others symbolising the cardinal and theological virtues and contemplation. The reassembled Douglas tomb, now by the north wall of the roofless choir at Dalkeith, consists of the figures of James Douglas, 1st earl of Morton and his wife Johanna, third daughter of James I and the sides of the chest.

Probably the finest of the wall tombs is that of Bishop Kennedy (d. 1465) at St Salvator's. It is a tall apsidal recess with flanking shafts and an elaborate cresting of traceried tabernacle work typifying the Celestial City. There was a figure of the bishop, probably kneeling, upon the Tournai marble tomb chest and the fine detail at the return ends suggests that the monument may have been intended to stand under the choir arcade at the cathedral.

A cresting of tabernacle work, of more homely type, also crowns the arched monument of Alexander Ogilvie at Cullen. Next to the Kennedy tomb, the Lincluden monument to Margaret, daughter of Robert III and wife of Archibald, 4th earl of Douglas, who died c. 1440, is probably the finest (Pl. 6). The elaborate arched recess contains an effigy and the arcaded front of the tomb chest nine heraldic shields. In the corresponding position at Seton, a late fifteenth-century monument with flanking buttresses and an enriched segmental arch enclosing an armour-clad effigy commemorates the founder.

There is a third Forrester tomb at Corstorphine in what was an ante-chapel west of the choir, while at Castle Semple is the elaborate arched and cusped monument to John, lord Semple who died at Flodden.

It should be understood that such monuments were once bright with colour, their heraldry in correct tinctures and their effigies as brilliant and lifelike as art could make them.

## ANCILLARY BUILDINGS

Little remains of the manses of collegiate church prebendaries. At Seton they stood to the south-west of the church but are now represented by a few walls, fireplaces and an oven, while at Roslin some dubious foundations between the church and the castle, known locally as 'the provost's house' are all that remain. The manses of Trinity College were destroyed by English action in 1558 and those of Restalrig were 'burned and largely destroyed' by the same agency. The buildings of Kirk of Field, Edinburgh, met the same fate. A mansion for the Duke of Châtelherault was built on the site of the hospital but the manses seem to have been rehabilitated. The murder of Darnley in 1567 took place in the provost's house, which was blown up, but the contemporary drawing of that event depicts the other dwellings in fair order, some of them labelled 'Ye Preistis Chalmers'.[16] At Lincluden the manses and hospital appear to have been disposed around a cloister court north of the church. Some early sixteenth-century remains on the east side in the form of a series of vaults and parts of a stair turret and tower house probably represents a common hall and the provost's lodging. They are generally ascribed to Provost William Stewart. The prebendaries' and bedesmen's quarters probably ranged around the remaining north and west sides.

In addition to these formal dwellings, chambers sometimes occur at the churches. At Kilmun certain rooms in the west tower, including one with a fireplace, formed a provost's lodging, while at Innerpeffray a room over the narthex was specifically reserved for the provost according to a confirming charter of 1581. At Biggar there is a room with a fireplace in the tower reached by the turnpike stair which gave access to the rood loft.

Hospitals for the poor, the sick or travellers were attached to several of the collegiate churches but almost nothing of them remains. The Kirk of Field hospital has been referred to, the post-Reformation successor to the original Trinity Hospital is illustrated in Gordon's view and at Soutra are some scanty remains of the travellers' hospital which was attached to the same church.

GEORGE HAY

[16] *Midlothian Chrs.*, p. xxxviii & pl. 5.

## *Acknowledgments*

The plan of King's College Chapel, Aberdeen, is reproduced from F. C. Eeles, *King's College Chapel, Aberdeen*, by courtesy of Aberdeen University Press and the photograph of the Chapel by courtesy of the Chapel Committee of the University. The illustration of Trinity College Church is Crown Copyright, and is reproduced by kind permission ·of the Royal Commission on Ancient Monuments, Scotland.

# 6

## Linguistic Relationships in Medieval Scotland

A previous Historiographer-Royal for Scotland, Sir Robert Rait, in an article in the *Scottish Review* for 1914, in restating his opinion that the Scottish people were essentially Celtic, made a plea for further investigation into the fortunes of the Gaelic tongue as it slowly retreated before the lowland speech which had established itself in Lothian from Northern England in the seventh century. No study of this sort has ever, to my knowledge, been printed although there is an unpublished Cambridge doctoral thesis by the late Librarian of Edinburgh University, L. W. Sharp, which makes a considerable contribution to the subject, well worth printing, and to which the following remarks are not a little indebted.[1]

While the broad sequence of political events is well enough known, the details, especially the linguistic details, are scattered, scanty and hard to find, often equivocal and seldom completely conclusive, and only the fringe of the most instructive source of all, personal- and place-names, has been touched. That the struggles between Northumbria and the Celtic kings of Scotland ended in a Scottish victory at Carham in 1016 or 1018 and the establishment of the Scottish nation as we still know it, and that the Anglian culture nevertheless prevailed in Lowland Scotland, is plain history. It is the purpose of this essay to trace, albeit sketchily, the progress of the second, and for that we can best begin on the day King Malcolm III, with the Gaelic nickname of Ceann mor, welcomed the refugee Prince Edgar of England and his sister Margaret at his court in English for, as Fordun tells us,[2] he had learned English as well as French, having lived in England for fourteen years after his father's death, an experience he prescribed also for his eldest son Duncan by sending him as a hostage to William the Conqueror at Westminster.

After her marriage Queen Margaret got to work on the unorthodox Scottish church with her confessor Turgot, an Englishman who became in 1107, amid Scottish protests, the first English bishop of St Andrews. In her arguments with the Celtic clergy Malcolm acted as interpreter as she never learned the language of the majority of her husband's subjects. But she knew English, of course, and French, and Barbour reminds us of her motto, somewhat ironical we feel, in Edinburgh Castle, 'Gardiss wouss de francoiss'.[3] To help her in her church reforms she applied to the archbishop of Canterbury who sent another English-man, Goldwin, to expedite the take-over. It is significant that the capital was

---

[1] L. W. Sharp, *The Expansion of the English Language in Scotland* (Cambridge Univ. Thesis 1927, unpublished).     [2] Fordun, *Scotichronicon* V, 14 (*Chron. Fordun*, i, 212).
[3] Barbour, *Bruce*, X, 746.

transferred to Edinburgh in English-speaking Lothian and that none of Margaret's children had Celtic names, with the presumption that Malcolm and Margaret spoke English together.

The second great anglicising influence, that of the feudal system, makes itself felt under their sons Alexander and David both of whom had been brought up at the Norman court of William Rufus during the first Celtic reaction to the new regime, and in their reigns were continually fighting against the men of the Mearns and Moray and Galloway. To secure himself King David dispossessed the rebels of their lands and gave these to the Anglo-Norman soldiers of fortune who had come to the Scottish court. The royal charters by which donatees were confirmed in their estates were addressed under Edgar and Alexander 'Scotis et Anglis', to which under David, 'Francis' is added.

French has now obviously to be added to the languages of the kingdom. A sidelight on this is to be noted in Jocelin's report on St Waldeve, stepson of David I and abbot of Melrose, as 'eloquens et disertus Gallicae et Anglicae linguae'[4] and the Barnwell chronicler (early xiii cent.) says that the more recent kings of Scots might be taken for Frenchmen from their speech and manner.[5]

The great prop of the feudal system, the charter, marks in essence the beginning of our corpus of Scottish historical documents and at this period the personal names in these charters are instructive for our purpose.

One of the earliest is the grant of Swinton in Berwickshire to the monks of Coldingham *a.* 1100, where the names of witnesses are Anglo-Saxon, Celtic, and, perhaps most interesting, since this type of name disappears fairly quickly from the charters, Norse, like Thor, Osbern, Cnut, Swein Ulfkillson, and an Anglo-Norse hybrid, Uhtred Eilaveson, a testimony to the Scandinavians whose speech underlies the basic dialect cleavage in English between the dialects of the South and those of the North and Scotland.[6] With David Norman names enter into the attestations in increasing proportions. In the charters to St Cuthbert's church in Edinburgh in 1127 the witnesses are Prince Henry and William de Graham, with Norman names, Thor Swainson from Tranent, a Norseman from a place with a Welsh name, and Malbead of Liberton, a Gael from an Anglo-Saxon settlement.[7] We are now obviously in a linguistic internationale. In 1136 the important occasion of the granting of the lands of Partick to the church of Glasgow was witnessed by Herbert abbot of Roxburgh (i.e., Kelso), William Cumin (Comyn) the chancellor, Earls Malise and Duncan, Fergus of Galloway, Aad [Aodh] with the beard, two Malodenis, Radulf son of Dunegal, Uchtred son of Fergus, Hugo the Breton, Gilbert of Stirling.[8] This again is a mixture of Norman, Anglo-Saxon, and Celtic names, in which the Celtic predominates, naturally enough since the document was signed in Glasgow. But the question arises – what language or languages did this mixed company speak? No doubt each had his mother tongue, and the churchmen at least would also have Latin, but it is difficult not to imagine some kind of *lingua franca* already in existence

---

[4] Jocelin, *Vita Sancti Waldevi* in *Acta Sanctorum*, 3 August.
[5] Walter of Coventry, *Memoriale* (ed. Stubbs, Rolls Series, 18), ii, 206.
[6] Lawrie, *Charters*, no. 20.          [7] *Ibid.*, no. 72.          [8] *Ibid.*, no. 109.

after two generations of Anglo-Norman influence in the Scottish realm, and it can hardly have been Gaelic for reasons that may be more apparent later. Undoubtedly the magnates could and did speak French for another two centuries or possibly longer; the minor officials of the court based on Lothian were in the main speakers of 'Inglis'. A list of dwellers on Tweedside given in the charter to Melrose in c. 1136 contains Welsh and Anglian names only.[9] Again in 1150 various clerics in Lothian witnessing to a grant to Holyrood have Anglian or Norman names, though one Herbert is designated Scottus.[10] This may indicate a Celt with a non-Celtic name, and if so this would be a testimony to the spread of the Teutonic speech among Gaelic speakers. We may anticipate somewhat by saying that in general the tendency was for Gaels throughout our period to give Anglo-Norman names to their children. The reverse process of a non-Gael giving his son a Gaelic name is exceptional.

North of the Forth the evidence is somewhat different for a time, especially north of Dunfermline and outside the pale of the royal court. The old Celtic church was well entrenched at St Andrews and St Serfs where the monks had reason to complain in 1128 of an encroachment on their lands by the 'Norman' Sir Robert Bourguignon.[11] In their deed they called to witness various personages from Constantine earl of Fife, downwards, all with Gaelic names. Further north at Deer in Aberdeenshire the names of local notabilities in the 1130s are all Gaelic, some even Pictish, like the bishop of Aberdeen whose name was Nectan, but whose successor was called Edward.[12]

It was however in 1130 that the Celtic resistance to the Anglo-Norman regime in Moray and the North-East was broken at Stracathro and the pace of southern penetration seems to have accelerated, though the Celts were still maintaining their linguistic identity and raised their war-cry 'Albanaich' at the Battle of the Standard in 1138.[13] Ailred significantly suggests that the battle was lost through dissension between the Celts and the Normans in the Scottish army.

By the end of the century King William had his seal attested in Elgin by Roman bishops and feudal earls instead of Celtic abbots and mormaers and Philip de Valognes, William Freskin, Walter Murdoch are also witnesses.[14] About 1210 the local clergy about Elgin included an assorted Malcolm, Gregorius, Ranulph, Gillebride, Lambert, Walter and Hugo,[15] and David had already founded priories at Urquhart with Benedictines from Dunfermline and at Kinloss with Cistercians from Melrose.[16]

The establishment of burghs in the twelfth century, however, with their concentrations of population must have done more than anything to anglicise the Lowlands of Scotland. The Celts were slow to take kindly to urban or commercial life. William of Newburgh writing of 1174 when William the Lion was captured at Alnwick, points out that 'the fortified places and burghs of the Scottish realm are known to be inhabited by English' and that the Celts

9 Ibid., no. 141.                    10 Ibid., no. 92.
11 Ibid., no. 80.                    12 Ibid., nos. 97, 223, 224.
13 Henry of Huntingdon, Historia Anglorum (ed. Arnold, Rolls Series, 1879), 263.
14 Regesta Regum Scottorum, ii, 381.
15 Moray Registrum, 43.              16 Lawrie, Charters, no. 255.

took advantage of the confusion of the Scottish defeat to pick off their English comrades in arms;[17] the same thing happened among the men of Galloway and there were certainly further unsuccessful Celtic *émeutes* in Ross and Moray during William's reign.[18] Yet even in strongholds of Celticism like St Andrews with its Culdee Church and its school under a *ferleighinn*, there were burgesses in the middle of the twelfth century called Elfgar, Arnald and William.[19] Sharp notes one family in Dunfermline changing names from Gaelic to Norman in four generations, from Gilgrewer to Gilchristin, who had a Gaelic nickname Mantauch, the stammerer, to Richard to Maurice, all in the course of the thirteenth century.[20]

The vocabulary of the burgh is basically Anglian or Anglo-Scandinavian – *burgh* itself, *toft, croft, rig, rood, alderman, gild, soc* and *sac, toll, gait, raw, wynd*, with the addition of some French like *provost* and *bailie, vennel, port, ferme*. Law and administration was another vehicle of anglicisation. The old *brithemne* (*judices*) of Celtic times with names like Meldoinneth, Dufgal, Macungal, Malcolm, are gradually displaced by sheriffs whose jurisdictions Malcolm IV had already firmly established south of the Forth. One of the first sheriffs at Forfar for instance was the Norman William Cumin (Comyn) in William the Lion's reign, and the earldom of Angus itself passed into the hands of the de Umfravilles by the usual marriage with the Celtic heiress in 1242. The old *mormairne* or 'stewartry' of Buchan had already gone the same way in 1214 to the Comyns and there the new earl founded the new Cistercian Abbey to replace the old Celtic institution at Deer.

All this story of Anglian and Anglo-Norman penetration and Gaelic recession has been told often enough not to require further elaboration. But the linguistic side of the picture has still to be filled out. It could be argued *a priori* that when the legal system and administration of a country changes, involving new administrators with a different speech, those who have recourse to the law will endeavour in their own interests to acquire a modicum at least of the language of the new judges. Interpreters are an unsatisfactory makeshift for a litigant anxious not to miss anything that is being said in his case, though the English made do with these for about two centuries. The Gaelic-speaking tenant in the new baron's court or in the nearest burgh market would soon find it very much to his advantage to know what was being said by the authorities and it is beyond doubt that most of the latter spoke Northern English, though possibly some attained to a smattering of Gaelic to help matters in difficult cases. Whether the baron himself spoke English or French or both – and the presumption is that they spoke French among themselves and English to their subordinates – it is quite certain that the subordinates themselves, their bailiffs, stewards and so on who were much more numerous, used English to one another and very likely to their masters, who after all in the end of the day came to speak English as their mother tongue themselves.

[17] *Chronicles of the reigns of Stephen, etc.* (ed. Howlett, Rolls Ser., 1884-9), i, 186.
[18] Anderson, *Scottish Annals*, 256.
[19] *St Andrews Liber*, 317, 124.          [20] *Dunfermline Registrum*, 221.

The argument rests chiefly on the *new* place-names. The bulk of the old place-names, the chief geographical features, the hills, rivers and lochs, the woods and plains, wells and bogs, cliffs, isthmuses and ferries, fords, hill- and river-crossings, sites of standing stones and stone-circles, religious buildings, lands especially good for growing certain crops, subdivisions of arable, pasture or moor land had nearly all been given by the Gaels or their predecessors and these were taken over by the new speakers almost in their entirety, subject only to the phonetic changes that the new languages involved. This had happened already in Strathclyde and South Scotland when English and Gaelic speakers alike had adopted the old British names like Tweed, Teviot, Nith, Niddrie, Glasgow, Linlithgow, Leith, Tranent and Traquair, Yester, Peebles and so on. So more than seventy per cent of Scottish place-names are Celtic, or a much higher proportion, if one thinks of north of the Forth only. Yet even there by the early thirteenth century new names begin to appear. We find Reidfurde in Angus in 1214,[21] in Strathisla in 1219 Strype, Staneycroft, Muirford, Corncairn, Stobstane, all in out-of-the-way spots;[22] in Aberdeenshire at the same date boundary marks are given the names of Byermoss, Gledcairn, Crawcairn, showing that the word *cairn* had already been adopted into the Anglic vocabulary[23]; in 1292 we have the names Bradwell and Harstanes at Coupar Angus.[24] These names could only have been given by people who could speak English, that is, by land-stewards of the barons, ground-officers or the like, or by incoming tenants. In 1206 the last Celtic earl of Buchan arranged an excambion which brought a small proprietor, John son of Uhtred (an Anglo-Saxon name if not an Anglo-Saxon owner), into lands adjoining a Celtic sheepfarmer, Ruadhri MacOan.[25] In the interests of good neighbourhood presumably they conversed in some mutually intelligible tongue which simply means that one or other or both were bilingual. It is especially instructive to note linguistic awareness in the entries in a Crail charter of 1205 'fontem illum qui Scottice Tolari nuncupatur'[26] and in the Arbroath Register of 1256, 'Hachethunethoner (*read* -methone) quod Anglice dicitur Midefeld ... Marresiam quamdam quae Scotice dicitur Moynebuche'. By the mid-fifteenth century in Kingoldrum at the foothills of the Mounth, many places seem to have had two names, one Gaelic and the other its Scots equivalent, as Myllaschangly (Scottismill), Athyncroith (Gallow Burne), Tybyrnoquhyg (Blind Well), Monboy (Yellow Pule), Carnofotyr (Punderis Carne) and these are set out as alternatives in a perambulation of the period, suggesting that both languages were still being spoken in the area and that some at least of the population were bilingual.[27] Undoubtedly there must have been a great deal more bilingualism, and even, among the higher social ranks, trilingualism, than is now normal in our strongly monolingual British society, of a kind which is of course still a regular feature of the smaller European nations.

The old tongue however did not die without traces in the vocabulary of the

[21] *Coupar Angus Chrs*, i, 51.  
[22] *Aberdeen–Banff Illustrations*, ii, 426–7.  
[23] *Ibid.*  
[24] *Coupar Angus Chrs.*, i, 136.  
[25] *Aberdeen–Banff Coll.*, 407.  
[26] *RRS*, ii, 433.  
[27] *Arbroath Liber*, i, 228, 103.

new. Celtic legal enactments and institutions survived, especially in the periphery in Galloway and Moray, and Gaelic terms lingered on often for two or three centuries and in the case of *cain* until living memory, e.g. *conveth, cuddeich, culrach, cateran, enach, cro* ('quod anglice dicitur grant before the king'),[28] *cro* (a fish-weir), *colpindach, cane, cumerlach, ferleighinn, scolog, toschodereth*. Much of Sir John Skene's commentary on the *Regiam Majestatem*, his *De Significatione Verborum* of 1597, is a treatise on this Gaelic vocabulary. The high honour accorded to poetry by the Celts is continued in the word *bard*, but it is geographical nomenclature that has lasted longest through place-names in words like *bog, cairn, craig, glen, loch, strath*; and so also *airt*, a point of the compass, and *peat*, which may indeed be the one Pictish survival in the common Scots vocabulary.

All this may be summarised by saying that Gaelic reached its maximum area of currency in the early twelfth century but almost immediately thereafter fell back under the impact of centralised feudalism until the plain-land of Scotland which had come under the control of Anglo-Norman nobles and prelates and their subordinates had gone over to the use of the Northumbrian tongue especially in the courts and in the municipalities. The classic statement is that of Fordun in the later fourteenth century, 'The manners and customs of the Scots vary with the diversity of their speech, for two languages are spoken among them, the Scottish and the Teutonic, the latter of which is the language of those who occupy the seaboard and plains, while the race of Scottish speech inhabits the highlands and outlying islands',[29] to which may be added Major's remark after making a similar statement in his *History* in 1521, 'but most of us spoke Irish a short time ago'.[30]

Two references to the diocese of Dunkeld throw an interesting light on the condition of and attitude to Gaelic there. Fordun (VI, xl) tells how the bishop of Dunkeld at the turn of the twelfth century asked that Argyll should be separated from Dunkeld because in Argyll the people knew only 'Scoticam et Hibernicam',[31] from which we infer that the people in Dunkeld knew English and that the Anglophile bishop did not want to be bothered with Gaelic-speaking clergy. But in the early sixteenth century we learn from the *Rentale Dunkeldense* how the much more sympathetic Bishop Brown was concerned in his clerical appointments that the higher parts of his diocese in Atholl, Dowally, Caputh, and Abernyte should be served by Gaelic speakers.[32] Incidentally we get an idea of where the Highland Line ran at the time.

Before discussing the evidence for the use of French in Scotland, it is worthwhile to summarise the corresponding state of affairs in England from the Conquest onwards. Under the first Norman kings, English kept a reasonably firm foothold in the nation. The kings themselves were not brought up with English and their efforts to acquire it seem to have been unsuccessful. Norman French had no literature and only the sketchiest written form, and the courts

[28] *Acts Parl. Scot.*, i, 276.
[29] Fordun, *Scotichronicon*, II, ix (*Chron. Fordun.*, i, 42).
[30] Major, *History*, I, iv.
[31] *Chron. Bower*, i, 356–7.
[32] *Dunkeld Rentale*, 304, 313, 330.

apparently were conducted in English, though their edicts and the state documents were, with insignificant English exceptions, in Latin. The king's own Council spoke French and French was the language of instruction in schools according to the often-quoted statement of Higden.[33] Anglo-Saxon law terms are peppered about in the Latin, *geld, Danegeld, scot, lot, sac, soc, team, hamsoc, infangthief*, and so on.[34] But with the coming of Henry II a new state of affairs sets in. Latin remains the language of the prime documents of Chancery but French is now employed for papers of the minor seal, royal letters, writs, wills and deeds of various kinds.[35] The language of the law was French from the reign of Henry III and the general court business, reports from and instructions to royal officials were also in French; throughout the next two centuries French dominated the scene, the lesser barons spoke it and literature began to be composed in it. It was the language both of culture and administration. The survival of English when it did ultimately triumph in the later fifteenth century is due to the fact that it persisted on the lips of the great majority of ordinary folk, in a literature of considerable bulk and quality and no doubt also because it was used in the sermons and homilies of the church. Becket for instance seems to have been fluent in all three tongues. But certainly when English re-emerges it is a very different language from that of 1066, full of French words and idioms, its accidence and syntax drastically altered and its spelling much modified by scribes who obviously knew French as their native tongue.

In contemporary Scotland things were different. The diplomatic documents of state were couched in Latin, the Scottish Chancery used Latin[36] with rare exceptions as in the dispute between Alexander III and Robert Bruce about lands in Annandale in which French is used.[37] But in the years after Alexander's death had precipitated Edward's interference in Scottish affairs, French documents proliferate. The Competitors at Norham submitted their claims, and most of the subsequent transactions were carried on, in French.[38] When a Scottish noble has anything to write to the King of England about, he uses French.[39] Baliol and the father of his successor were both testily reprimanded to their faces by King Edward in French[40]; the Bruces and Comyns both wrote letters to various correspondents in French.[41] Bruce's sworn enemy, MacDougall of Lorn, of ancient Celtic lineage, writes in French to Edward II whose admiral he was in the Western Isles where he would undoubtedly have had to use Gaelic also and he ended his days in London where his English, Northern though it was, would also have come in useful.[42]

[33] R. Higden, *Polychronicon* (Rolls Series, 18), ii, 159.
[34] P. Shelley, *English and French in England, 1066–1100* (Philadelphia, 1921), 85.
[35] M. D. Legge in *History*, xxvi (1941), 163–75.
[36] R. L. G. Ritchie, *The Normans in Scotland* (Edinburgh, 1954), 181.
[37] *Nat. MSS. Scot.*, i, no. xii.
[38] *Nat. MSS. Scot.*, i, no. LXXI, ii, nos. V, XV, XVI.
[39] *Cal. Docs. Scot.*, ii, nos. 216, 1541.
[40] *Chron. Wyntoun*, VIII, lines 1661, 1925, after Fordun.
[41] Francisque-Michel, *Les Écossais en France* (Paris, 1862), i, 53; F. J. Tanquerey, *Recueil de lettres anglo-françaises* (Paris, 1916), 41, 71, 85.
[42] J. Bain, *The Edwards in Scotland* (Edinburgh, 1901), 62.

There is evidence that some literature in French may have been written in Scotland, specifically the romance of Fergus of Galloway which Professor Legge argues was written about 1209 at the instance of Alan, lord of Galloway, by one of his secretaries,[43] and we are told by Barbour how Bruce whiled away the time with his men waiting to be ferried across Loch Lomond in pursuit of the above-mentioned John of Lorne by telling them stories from the romance of Sir Ferumbras, undoubtedly the French version, as an English version does not seem to have been current till the end of the fourteenth century.[44] On the other hand he cannot have told them in French to common soldiers, nor in Gaelic for his men were the remnants of Lowland barons' levies, including his own contingent from Annandale. Already some twenty years before we have the first surviving piece of folk-literature in what we now call Scots – the popular elegy 'Quhen Alisandre our kyng was dede,'[45] and Fabyan also quotes from two Scottish songs, one about the siege of Berwick in 1296 and the other about Bannockburn.[46]

The examination of our rather scattered and heterogeneous linguistic evidence leads unequivocally to support for the view already established by the purely historical facts. The feudal system of land tenure and dependent military obligations, the complex structure of law evolved to support this, the establishment of sheriff courts, a somewhat parallel organisation in the Church with the setting up of parishes and dioceses, and as a consequence the spread of popular education through church schools, and, probably the weightiest factor of all, the development of towns as the centres of trade and industry and the growth of burghal rights and privileges, these were all-important in the spread of the Lothian speech over the Lowlands from the Forth northwards and the Avon westwards. The Celtic system had little to match this close-knit highly centralised set-up or its languages, Latin for church and political diplomacy, French for the informal *causerie* of the ruling classes and the Northern Anglo-Saxon for the burghers and traders whose Teutonic speech was more akin to the tongues of the Low Countries and of Scandinavia with which they did business, and finally to that amalgam of French and Anglo-Saxon that was formed in the twelfth and thirteenth centuries and in a Scotland with recent memories of Gaelic speech and abundant reminders of it in its place-names, still sounded foreign enough to be called 'Inglis.'

The speech situation at the end of the thirteenth century is set forth in a classic passage in the *Wallace* VI, 131 sqq. which deserves closer examination, though it is not without its difficulties. We do not know the poet's source, if any, for the story; nor is it possible to be quite sure that he is not reading a situation much nearer his own time into an earlier period. The text itself is not absolutely certain and there are ironical overtones that make matters more confusing but it is still relevant to our subject. Wallace and his men had been to

---

[43] M. D. Legge in *Trans. Dumfries and Galloway Antiq. Soc.*, 3rd. ser., xxvii (1948–9), 163–72.

[44] Barbour, *Bruce*, III, 435–7.

[45] Some, however, suspect the song to be much nearer Wyntoun's own time (1420).

[46] R. Fabyan, *Cronycle*, ed. H. Ellis (London, 1811), 398, 420.

mass in their best clothes and an English champion 'salust thaim as it war bot in scorn; "Dewgar [Dieu garde], gud day, bone senzhour and gud morn"', pretending that he thought them envoys 'to bring an uncouth queyne', and therefore addressing them half in French as the spoken language of the diplomat. When Wallace answers him in English and the taunt misfires, the Englishman continues 'Sen ye are Scottish yeit salust sall ye be, "Gud deyn, dawch Lard, bach lowch, banyoch a de"' – 'Dawch lard' appears to be laird of a davoch, that is, bonnet laird or something even more insignificant; 'bach lowch' looks like Gaelic (the conjecture *balach* [i.e. bachlach, 'herdsman', 'rustic'], reported by M. P. McDiarmid in his S.T.S. *Wallace*, is plausible, as Professor Kenneth Jackson kindly assures me); 'banyoch a de' is modern Gaelic *beannachd Dhe*, God's blessing. The point of this somewhat macaronic line is not that Wallace spoke Gaelic, which is unlikely in the son of an Ayrshire laird of an estate with an English name, educated according to tradition by his priest uncle near Falkirk; and of course there would be nothing insulting in addressing a man in his own language, indeed quite the contrary. The gibe lay in using Gaelic at all and the inference is that already Gaelic was a source of ridicule to the speaker of Inglis, which would be even more true if, as seems probable, the passage reflects the state of thought of 1476 as the date of *Wallace* rather than 1297.

Gaelic was recognisable as such and probably still partially understood, and we can assume that tag-ends of it remained on the tongues of the people, pretty much in the same way that even the most anglicised Scot today can produce a word or two of 'the Doric' when he wants to be jocular. So this ironical use of *beannachd Dhe* seems to have been good for a laugh among the Lowlanders at this time to judge from other passages roughly contemporary. In the Auchinleck Chronicle we are told how one day in 1452 when the bishop of Argyll, a Lowlander called Lauder, was coming to his cathedral to investigate charges against two Highland clerics, the two accused caused a riot, reviled the bishop and 'for dispyte halsit him in errische, sayand *bannachadee*'. Apparently even in Lismore it was considered an insult to address one's bishop in Gaelic, instead, presumably, of Latin, and certainly to say *bannachadee* to him. Again in *The Buke of the Howlat*, the bird allegory written in honour of the Douglas family by Richard Holland, a priest of Elgin Cathedral about 1450, the Rook personifies 'a bard owt of Irland with *Bannachadee*', who bursts into a blatter of pidgin Gaelic, 'Gluntou, guk dynyd dach hala mischy doch . . .' and ends the verse in a kind of burlesque of the Highland seanachaidh's recital at a Scottish Coronation as reported by Fordun.[47]

The same implicit attitude towards Gaelic as a barbarous gibberish is shown by the poet Dunbar in his flyting with the Ayrshire poet Kennedy –

> I tak on me a pair of Lothian hippis
> Sall fairer Inglis mak, and mair parfyte
> Than thow can blabber with thy Carrick lippis
> Thou art but gluntoch.[48]

[47] *Sc. Alliterative Poems*, ed. F. J. Amours (S.T.S.), 74; *Chron. Bower*, X, ii.
[48] Dunbar, *Works* (S.T.S.), i, 14–15.

From which we can infer that Carrick was still associated with Gaelic speech, and that Kennedy, who was one of the Cassilis family, probably spoke it. He qualifies at least in Dunbar's view for the epithet *gluntoch*, also used by Holland in derision of the Highlanders. The word itself is of some interest. *Glundubh* is 'black (hairy) knee' in allusion of course to the Highlander's trouserlessness but it was also a nickname of Niall, high king of Ireland in the early tenth century, the supposed ancestor of several Argyllshire clans and it may be that the second allusion is meant to reinforce the first. To this Kennedy very properly retorts:

> Thow lufis nane Irische, elf, I understand,
> Bot it suld be all trew Scottish mennis lede,
> It was the gud langage of this land . . .
> Quhill Corpatrik, that we of tresoun rede,
> Throu his tresoun brought Inglis rumplis in.[49]

This is perhaps the first instance of linguistic nationalism to be found in Scottish literature. Kennedy is aware that Gaelic had been the speech of the greater part of the Scottish kingdom till the Norman Conquest of England, and though his historical allusions are blurred by an apparent confusion between the Gospatric of Northumberland of that period and Patrick earl of March, in the 1350s, it looks as if the traditions of the Celtic resistance in Galloway (and Moray) were still fresh after three and a half centuries.

In the meantime in the fourteenth century the linguistic situation in Scotland had been sorting itself out. By 1350 glosses in Inglis appear in Latin documents, deeds of various kinds exchanged between the landed gentry are engrossed in Scots,[50] the use of French becomes more and more exceptional though lords of parliament are still found occasionally writing it in instructions to their bailiffs.[51] But by the end of the century, we find King Henry IV receiving two noteworthy letters in the vernacular, one from Sir James Douglas and one from George Dunbar, who signs himself indeed 'Le Count de la Marche d'Escoce', but excuses himself for writing in Inglis because 'that is mare clere to myne understandyng than latyne or fraunche'. The swan song of French could hardly be more explicit.

It is quite obvious that Inglis is taking over by this time. *The Brus* had already been written, the feudal barons were now requiring that the old French romances should be translated into the vernacular for their easier comprehension as the surviving *Buke of Alexander* attests. The monopoly of Latin in Church and State was also invaded in popular versions of the Legends of Saints anglicised sometime before 1400 and in the Acts of Parliament in which the vernacular replaced Latin in the reign of Robert III, the first petition to Parliament in Scots dating from 1390, and from then on it can be said to be the official language of the kingdom except of course for Chancery purposes. French had become a foreign tongue, frequently enough acquired through the comings and goings under the Auld Alliance, and a source of quite a number of words still familiar in Scots,

---

[49] Dunbar, *Works* (S.T.S.), i, 22.  [50] Fraser, *Douglas*, iii, 28, 37.
[51] *Laing Chrs*, no. 32 (1324); Fraser, *Douglas*, iii, 21 (1360).

which are not part of the common French heritage of English and Scots, as for instance, in the earlier part of the period, *effeir, backet, disjune, purpie, rew, spairge, turcas, vaig, vennel* and *Bon-Accord,* the motto of Aberdeen; while the sixteenth century gives *aippleringie, fash, fiar, pand, visy, vivers, gardyloo, barley, hardheed, plack, turner, howtowdie, hogmanay, dams, bajan, caddie.*

The marked contrast between Highlands and Lowlands in social organisation as well as language is responsible for a new turn in Gaelic-Scots relations in the late Middle Ages, the fifteenth century. The Highlanders became relatively isolated from the rest of the kingdom and pursued their own way of life as independently as possible of the government in Edinburgh. The petty kingdom in the West under the hegemony of the Macdonalds, the Lordship of the Isles, came to an end in 1493 after having spent some considerable time in league with England against the king of Scots; and ironically enough where the English of Scotland had not reached, the English of England, and the reputedly best English at that, had access, for Donald, the eighth Lord of the Isles, was an Oxford man, having studied divinity (of all things) there about 1378.[52]

The results of all this we have seen in the satirical and generally hostile references to the Highlanders in Lowland literature. Dunbar keeps up his attack in his *Dance of the Seven Deidly Sins* on 'Ersche' and 'Erschemen'. Later in the sixteenth century the Laird of Hessilhead in Ayrshire, the poet Alexander Montgomerie, who spent some years in Argyll and must have learned some Gaelic there, replies in kind to *A Helandman's Invective* with a macaronic Scots-Gaelic squib recalling the verse in the *Howlat* and indeed containing one line exactly the same.[53]

The most significant development in our subject however is the change in nomenclature of the languages themselves. *Scotice, lingua Scotica* are the regular expressions in Latin documents for Gaelic till the end of the fourteenth century, *Anglice* for Northern English. By 1450 the Lowlanders were still calling their own speech *Inglis,* that of the Highlanders *Erse,* in Latin *Hibernica,*[54] with proper historical accuracy. By the end of the century consciousness of the distinctness from the King's English and of their own national independence had produced the adjective *Scottis* as applied to the Lowland tongue.[55] By ignoring the Highlands, state and speech after more than four hundred years had found unity, in the King's Scots, though the King in question, James IV, had the Gaelic too according to De Ayala.

For all the estrangement of Highlander and Lowlander, there was a further intake of Gaelic words into Scots, e.g. *coronach, clarsach, shenachie, banshee,* all in the *Howlat; clan, clachan, caber, fail* (sod), *connach, gob, crine, sons* and *sonsie, ingle, cranreuch, slogan, capercailzie, ptarmigan, tocher, corrie, partan, raith;* and, perhaps most significant of all, as a proof of the stability of Celtic folk-belief and tradition, the word *Beltane* for the Spring festival. The borrowing, of

[52] *Rotuli Scotiae,* ii, 11.
[53] Montgomerie, *Poems,* ed. Cranstoun (S.T.S.), 220; Montgomerie, *The Cherrie and the Slae,* ed. H. H. Wood (London, 1937), 87–9.
[54] Major, *History* I, iv.
[55] Caxton's *Book of the Order of Chivalry* (Early English Text Society, 1926), p. xxvii.

course, was not one-sided by any means. Gaelic must have taken over about this period or earlier a large number of words from Scots though in the absence of exact historical information it is difficult to be precise about dating. *Bonnach* must be a very early borrowing from Anglo-Saxon *bannuc*, a bannock; *bùrn*, in Gaelic always of running water, is from Scots *burn*; it is perhaps not surprising in view of the Highlander's nether garments, that he borrowed *briogais* and *truibhse*; other borrowings are *tasdan*, a shilling, via sixteenth-century Scots from French *teston*; *gartan* and *gairdean* (arm) are similarly through Scots *gartan*, *gardie* (arm) from French; *piob* was borrowed from Northern English (and its derivative *pìobaireachd* borrowed back in the eighteenth century as *pibroch*). Two further borrowings of greater significance are *cuidheall*, a spinning-wheel, and *breabadair*, a weaver, the implication being that skilled manufacture, especially cloth-making, was an importation from the Lowlands and ultimately from the Low Countries of Europe, *breabadair* deriving from *Brabander*, a native of Brabant, naturalised in Scotland in the surname Brebner.

Obviously, although there has always been a demarcation line between Gaelic- and Scots-speaking areas, one that receded westwards fairly quickly in the Middle Ages and more slowly thereafter till the eighteenth century, there must have been penetration in depth by Scots, through for instance the young Celtic bigwigs educated at the Scottish universities, like the Macdonald of Lochalsh who was surnamed *Gallda* because he had been educated in the Lowlands. This policy is indeed explicitly enunciated in the Papal Bull authorising the foundation of the University of Aberdeen 'quae insulis borealibus et montibus praedictis satis vicina est'.

It is worth noting that the great anthology of Gaelic heroic and medieval poetry, *The Book of the Dean of Lismore*, is written in a phonetic script based on the phonological system of Scots which the Dean must have spoken. An associated MS, *The Chronicle of Fortingall*, written about the same time, the first half of the sixteenth century, by one of the Macgregors of Glenstrae in Argyll, is partly in Latin and partly in Scots. A yet more notable later source is *The Black Book of Taymouth*, entirely in Scots by William Bowie, tutor to the grandsons of Sir Duncan Campbell of Glenorchy, a Gaelic poet of some distinction. An earlier Gaelic poet, the countess of Argyll, a Stewart by birth and a Campbell by marriage, writing love poetry in Gaelic, must have been equally at home in Scots. And while Donald, the lord of the Isles vanquished at Harlaw (1411), granted the only-surviving Gaelic charter in Islay in 1408, his wife, together with Lord Lovat, Macleod of Glenelg, Angus Gothrason of the Isles, and others were signatories to a deed of 1420 drawn up in Scots for the bishop of Ross in Inverness.[56]

No doubt the downfall of the lordship of the Isles which removed almost the only force which counteracted the centrifugal tendencies of Scottish Gaeldom was one serious blow to Gaelic. Another disintegrating factor was the Reformation of 1560 which divorced Protestant Scotland from Catholic Ireland and, linguistically speaking, broke the contact with the classical language of the

[56] *Moray Registrum*, 475.

West. We are now out of the Middle Ages and the period of our survey. Though there was a fresh literary outburst in Gaelic in the seventeenth century, it is, strictly speaking, a *dialect* literature which has continued to the present day. At the same time an almost exactly similar fate befell the Scots language. The same Reformation brought the English Bible into every lowland home; the Union of Crowns removed the focus of culture from the court and capital and the old national tongue fragmented into the dialects that are themselves breaking up under the impact of modern civilisation, if civilisation is the right word.

DAVID MURISON

# 7

## *The Illusory* Breve Testatum

The law of Scotland requires a high standard in the proving of facts. Hearsay evidence is generally rejected. Corroboration of a statement is necessary. Authority must be cited for a legal proposition. It is therefore surprising to find that amongst Scottish lawyers when they write on matters of legal history, there is a tendency to abandon the laws of evidence and indulge in the creation or perpetuation of what may, in a non-legal sense, be termed 'legal fictions'.

The *breve testatum* is an example of such a fiction. Over the past two centuries many writers learned in Scots law have suggested that in early Scottish feudal society there existed a writ known as the *breve testatum* out of which the charter developed. The most recent statement is by Professor D. M. Walker:

> A new feudal estate in lands was originally created by the Crown or a subject superior personally, on the lands and in presence of at least two vassals (*pares curiae*) delivering to the grantee a symbolical portion of the lands, earth and stone, as representing the whole, and the grantee thereupon swearing fealty to the superior. It subsequently became the practice to give a written testimony of the grant (*breve testatum*) sealed by granter and witness, or a certificate from a notary public, or of two witnesses to the investiture. This constituted proper investiture. . . . Subsequently a charter based on the *breve testatum* was introduced and since then writ has always been recognised as necessary for the constitution and not only for the proof of infeftment or of infeudation.[1]

This statement is clearly derived from earlier legal writings.[2] It would be tedious to cite these in full. The following are examples of the earlier references:

> Erskine: The ancient form of investiture in lands was extremely simple. . . . Their (i.e. *pares curiae*) presence was, by our ancient usage, so essential to a feudal grant, that it was void without it. . . . In the course of time, it was judged reasonable, for better preserving the memory of the grant, that the superior should on the ground of the lands give a declaration of it in writing; and in token of his consent, both he and the *pares curiae* appended their seals

[1] D. M. Walker, *Principles of Scottish Private Law* (Oxford, 1970), 1179.

[2] Similar references are to be found in the following works. The list is not exhaustive.

J. Erskine, *An Institute of the Law of Scotland* (Edinburgh, 1773), 2. 3. 17;

W. Ross, *Lectures on the History and Practice of the Law of Scotland relative to Conveyancing and Legal Diligence*, 2nd edn, 2 vols. (Edinburgh, 1822), ii, 120 *et seq*;

G. J. Bell, *Principles of the Law of Scotland* (Edinburgh, 1829), 2. 757;

A. Menzies, *Conveyancing according to the Law of Scotland*, 3rd edn (Edinburgh, 1863), 529; *Encyclopaedia of the Laws of Scotland*, iii (1927), 238;

H. H. Monteath, 'Heritable Rights from Early Times to the Twentieth Century', in *An Introduction to Scottish Legal History*, ed. G. Campbell H. Paton (Stair Soc., xx, 1958), 157.

to it. This declaration is called in the books of the feus, *breve testatum*, an attested brief, L. I. *Feud.* T. 2, 3, etc. and is of the same nature with a charter.[3]

Bell: Originally, a feudal vassal swore fealty on receiving a grant from his superior, and was thereupon invested in the land, by the hand of the superior himself, before the *Pares Curiae*. The written title was rather a record of what had already passed, than itself the grant; it was called *Breve Testatum*. The charter afterwards introduced expressed, in terms of conveyance, the superior's grant.[4]

Stair does not mention the *breve testatum*. He acknowledges the superior authority of Sir Thomas Craig on the origin of feus:

Our learned countryman, Craig of Riccarton, hath largely and learnedly handled the feudal rights and customs of this and other nations, in his book *de feudis*; and therefore we shall only follow closely what since his time by statute or custom hath been cleared or altered in our feudal rights ... he having written in the year 1600.[5]

Stair makes an important observation later in the same chapter:

He [Craig] hath indeed very well observed the origin and nature of feudal rights, and the customs of Italy where they began, and of France and England, whence they were derived to us.

On an examination of Craig's writings it becomes obvious that they are the source of all the later statements that the *breve testatum* was the forerunner of the charter in Scotland. He writes:

In former days no doubt it [proper investiture] was performed with more ceremony than is used now; for the compeers of the superior's court used to attend, which added much to the importance of the occasion. Later the superior became bound, if the vassal demanded it, to give him a *breve testatum* as a record of the investiture.[6]

He further writes:

It is certain that what we know as the charter was evolved from the *breve testatum*, the use of which in former days has already been referred to. .... If the charter-chests of any of our old families are examined, many of these charters in miniature will be discovered.[7]

Craig's purpose in the *Jus Feudale*, as observed by Stair, was twofold. Firstly, to examine the European origins of the feudal law and, secondly to give an account of the origins and development of Scottish feudal law. After graduating as a Master of Arts in the University of St Andrews, Craig studied law in Paris from 1555 to 1561.[8] At this time in France legal scholars were engaged in an extensive study of the origins of European feudal society. The *Libri Feudorum* produced by Lombardic judges and lawyers in the twelfth century particularly

---

[3] Erskine, *op. cit.*                [4] Bell, *op. cit.*
[5] Stair, *The Institutions of the Law of Scotland*, 2nd edn (Edinburgh, 1694), 2. 3. 3.
[6] T. Craig, *Jus Feudale*, trans. J. A. Clyde (Edinburgh, 1934), 2. 2. 13.
[7] Craig, *op. cit.*, 2. 2. 16.                [8] Craig, *op. cit.*, xx.

attracted the attention of these scholars. In the ranks of such scholars were François Baudouin, Jean Bodin, Jacques Cujas and François Hotman. It is possible that Baudouin was one of Craig's teachers.

In a recent study Dr J. G. A. Pocock has demonstrated the significance of the works of these French scholars in the rise of modern historiography.[9] He is also the first modern scholar to discourse at length on the influence of the French scholars on Craig and to recognise the importance of the *Jus Feudale* in modern historiography. It is worthwhile to illustrate from Dr Pocock's work the essential nature of the scholarship of the French lawyers of the sixteenth century:

> ... we shall remember the fact ... that non-narrative work of the highest originality and complexity was being carried on in the French universities of the sixteenth century ... and that this historical thought had developed in the faculty of law. ... The earlier scholars [the sixteenth century French lawyers] were more or less consciously engaged in returning facts to their historical context and interpreting them there, and it has already been suggested that this was bound to present complex problems for historical reflexion; problems concerning the relation of the past to the present, and its survival in the present. With the lawyers this was peculiarly the case, because the data they were assigning to a past context were simultaneously the principles on which present society was endeavouring to govern itself.[10]

This is the European background to Craig's writing. From his study of the origins of European feudal law and influenced by the teaching and writing of the most eminent French scholars of the time, Craig attempted to discover and trace the origins and development of Scottish feudal law. As an example of a new method in studying Scottish law Craig's work must be regarded as of prime importance. It must, however, be remembered that in his account of the origins of Scottish feudal law Craig tended to apply the patterns of development which were being postulated by the French scholars. As has already been stated the source of this study was the Lombardic *Libri Feudorum*. It must also be noted that the *Libri Feudorum* applied only to Lombardy and cannot be regarded as authoritative in describing the elements of feudal law and society in other parts of Europe.[11]

Important as his work is in attempting to describe and explain the origins of Scottish feudal law, Craig was in error in assuming that the prototypes of this law were necessarily to be found in Lombardic law. If the *breve testatum* existed in Lombardy it did not necessarily follow that it existed in Scotland. Craig made the assumption that it did. As far as can be ascertained there is no evidence that a writ known as a *breve testatum* ever existed in Scotland. It is true that many of the earliest Scottish writs of the twelfth century which relate to land transactions are very short documents. However, it cannot be maintained, as Craig

[9] J. G. A. Pocock, *The Ancient Constitution and the Feudal Law*, 2nd edn (New York, 1967), Ch. 1, 'Introductory: the French Prelude to Modern Historiography', Ch. 4, 'The Discovery of Feudalism: French and Scottish Historians'.

[10] Pocock, *op. cit.*, 8, 9.

[11] F. L. Ganshof, *Feudalism*, trans. P. Grierson (London, 1960), 60.

implied, that these 'charters in miniature' were writs known as *brevia testata*. The best modern comment on these early writs is by Professor G. W. S. Barrow:

> Before 1165 ... we are dealing with prototypes rather than actual examples of the Charter ... familiar to a later age. .... The 'writ-charter' form employed for the overwhelming majority of the acts of Alexander I, David I, Earl Henry and Malcolm IV was an extremely flexible instrument. Between 1153 and 1165, we are seeing it at the most protean stage of its development. In later years, it was to develop into several different types of document ranging from the short administrative or legal brieve or writ to the lengthy solemn charter.[12]

Although the terminology may be similar the *breve testatum* cannot be classified with either the administrative or the legal brieve. These in their various forms were essentially royal commands addressed to individuals or groups of individuals to enable administrative or judicial functions to be performed. The alleged function of the *breve testatum* was to provide evidence of a grant of land which had already taken place. It was clearly not a directive to an official to make a grant of land.

Craig's *Jus Feudale* soon came to be regarded as the fundamental text on Scottish feudal law. Stair accepted it as such, as also have subsequent institutional writers and authorities on Scots law. To this day no Scottish legal historian has attempted to assess the accuracy of Craig's account of the origins of Scottish feudal law. It may be unfair to suggest that this lack of critical assessment may be partly due to the fact that the first English translation of the *Jus Feudale* was published as recently as 1934. Since the *Jus Feudale* appears to have been accepted *pro veritate* by Scottish legal scholars, it is therefore perhaps not surprising that the existence in Scotland of such a trivial thing as the *breve testatum* has been accepted almost without question.

Only one man appears to have questioned the existence of the *breve testatum* in Scotland. This is William Rodger, writing in 1857.[13] There is much of value in Rodger's little book. He has attempted to make a serious historical examination of certain aspects of Scottish feudal law and practice. As a serious historical study, Rodger's work merits more consideration than it has received. Before commenting on the *breve testatum* Rodger notices that in Anderson's *Diplomata Scotiae* there is a reference in a 'charter' by David, Earl of Huntingdon dated *circa* 1110 concerning the land of Horverdean to 'the brief and gifts of my brother King Edgar'.[14] Rodger then continues:

> Here David calls his brother's charter of Horverdean, a *brief*. In like manner, Alexander and he made use of the same word, *breve*, when they had occasion to notice any of Edgar's other charters; but I have never seen any other ancient document in which a charter is termed a brief; nor can I believe, indeed, I deny most emphatically, that our ancestors, before they became acquainted with the charter, ever made use of a short certificate, called a

---

[12] *RRS*, i, 59.
[13] W. Rodger, *The Feudal Forms of Scotland viewed Historically* (Edinburgh, 1857).
[14] Anderson, *Diplomata*, Plate X (=Lawrie, *Charters*, no. 32).

*breve testatum.* In Scottish practice, the writ called a brief is or was a written order, issued from the Chancery-office . . . directing something or other to be done.[15]

Rodger was aware that the *Libri Feudorum* contained references to the *breve testatum* and that Craig was responsible for importing the term into Scottish feudal law. Although he misjudges the value of Craig's work, Rodger concludes that 'it is certain that our ancestors never adopted any of the *Consuetudines Feudorum* into their feudal system; neither could they know anything whatever about the infancy, the youth, and the manhood of Feus . . . so copiously and so learnedly descanted upon by Sir Thomas Craig, who was better acquainted with the laws and customs of France, where he received his legal education, than with the ancient history of Scotland.'[16]

Rodger discreetly draws a veil of anonymity over his references to the Scottish 'law-writers' prior to his time who were 'credulous respecting antiquities' in their uncritical acceptance of the existence of the *breve testatum* in Scotland.[17] It is unfortunate that 'law-writers' subsequent to Rodger appear to have been equally credulous and to have been unaware of Rodger's denial of the existence of the *breve testatum.*

The *breve testatum* in Scotland therefore seems to be an illusion sustained by credulity. Craig, however, was certain that it had existed in Europe. It may be of interest to consider more closely the continental authority from which the *Jus Feudale* in general and the *breve testatum* in particular are derived. Craig's authority for the existence of the *breve testatum,* as has been stated, was the *Libri Feudorum.* The *Libri Feudorum* were the fundamental texts commented upon by the French legal scholars in the sixteenth century. It may be possible to be more precise and to identify the specific source used by Craig.

In Du Cange there is this entry: '*Breve testatum, apud Otbertum lib. 1. Feud. tit. 4. est publicum instrumentum, uti interpretatur Eguinarius Baro lib. 4 de feudis cap. 7. . . .*'[18] Translated freely this states that the *breve testatum* according to Otbertus is a public instrument as explained by Eguinarius Baro in his work '*De Feudis*', Book 4, Chapter 7. 'Otbertus' is Obertus de Orto the renowned Milanese jurist who was created an Imperial magistrate sometime between 1133 and 1137 in the reign of the Emperor Lothair II. Obertus was the author of the earliest version of the *Libri Feudorum.*[19] The nucleus of this version, the so-called *Obertina,* consists of two letters written between 1137 and 1158 by Obertus to his son Anselmus who was studying law at Bologna. The letters discuss the sources of feudal law, the object of the feu, the rights and obligations between overlord and vassal, the modes of investiture and the transfer of feus.

Eguinarius Baro is the Latinized name of Eguiner-François Baron. Baron was a French jurist, born at Saint-Pol-de-Léon in Brittany about 1495 and dying at

[15] Rodger, *op. cit.,* 52, 53.          [16] Rodger, *op. cit.,* 53.
[17] Rodger, *op. cit.,* 53, 54.
[18] C. du F. du Cange, *Glossarium mediae et infimae Latinitatis,* ed. L. Favre, 10 vols. (Niort, 1883–7), ii, 745.
[19] E. Besta, *Storia del diritto italiano,* ed. P. Del Giudice (Milano, 1923), i, 441 *et seq*; E. Besta, *Il diritto pubblico italiano* (Padova, 1930), 171 *et seq.*

Bourges in 1550. He was an eminent teacher of law being successively a professor of law at Angers, Poitiers and Bourges. By his contemporaries he was regarded as being in the first rank of legal scholars. Noël du Fail referred to him as a veritable Scaevola and Cujas regarded him as the Varro of France.[20] The list of Baron's printed works is impressive. It includes the *Pandectarum Juris Civilis Oeconomia* (1535) dedicated to his friend Robert Irland,[21] *In Titulum De Servitutibus Libri VIII Pandectarum Notae* (1538), *De Beneficiis Commentarii* (1549) and *Ad Obertum Ortensium de Beneficiis Commentarii* (1549). This last work is of relevance in the present discussion. It is in all probability the particular work of Baron (and Obertus) referred to in Du Cange.

The treatise – the full title of which is *Ad Obertum Ortensium, de Beneficiis, Commentarii, Methodo in eundem subiecti* – was first published by Sebastianus Gryphius at Lyons in 1549. It is a commentary in two Books on the *Obertina*. The theme of the first Book is set in the opening words: '*Oberti Ortensii Consuetudines Feudorum. De iis qui feudum dare possunt, et qui non; a qualiter aquiratur, et retineatur.*' The two letters out of which the *Obertina* developed are found in the second Book. They are in Title 1, '*De feudi constitutione, Obertus de Orto, Anselmo filio suo dilecto salutem*', and Title 23, '*In quibus causis feudum amittatur. Obertus de Orto, Anselmo filio suo salutem.*'

The *breve testatum* is referred to in several titles in Books 1 and 2. The major references are in Book 1, Titles 2 and 4. In Title 2 Obertus states: '*Si vero castaldi aliquid nomine proprii feudi possederint non valebunt propterea possessionem sibi defendere, nisi per pares curiae vel breve testatum potuerint probare . . .*' This is followed by Baron's comment: '*Et ideo per pares curiae, id est alios eiusdem domini beneficiarios, vel per breve testatum, id est publicum instrumentum, parium subscriptione munitum, probare debet beneficiarius proprii beneficii investituram sibi a domino factum . . .*' This comment states that an investiture is to be proved either by the evidence of the *pares curiae* or by a *breve testatum* fortified by the written attestation of the *pares*. The *breve testatum* is similarly commented on by Baron in Title 4.

Baron's work was published before the publication of comparable works. Baudouin published *De institutione historiae et ejus cum jurisprudentia conjunctione* in 1561. Bodin's *Methodus ad facilem historiarum cognitionem* and Cujas' edition of the *Libri Feudorum* both appeared in 1566 and Hotman's *De feudis commentatio tripertita* in 1573.[22] Cujas and Hotman were, like Baron, professors of law at Bourges.

Craig, as has been stated, studied law in Paris from 1555 to 1561. Baron's writings would therefore have been immediately accessible to him. Although

[20] M. de Kerdanet, *Notices chronologiques sur les théologiens, jurisconsultes, philosophes . . . de la Bretagne* (Brest, 1818), 81 *et seq*; N. du Fail, *Contes et discours d'Eutrapel*, ed. C. Hippeau (Paris, 1875), Ch. 4; *Dictionnaire de Biographie Française*, ed. M. Prévost and R. d'Amat (Paris, 1951), v, 520.

[21] Irland (*d.* 1561) was born in Scotland but became a naturalised Frenchman in 1521. He was a professor of Law at Poitiers. He is referred to by Rabelais as 'that decretalipotent Scottish doctor'. See *Dictionary of National Biography*, ed. S. Lee (1908), x, 481.

[22] Pocock, *op. cit.*, 11, 13, 72.

the writings of the other scholars, apart from Baudouin, may not have been immediately accessible to Craig, it can hardly be doubted that while in France he was influenced by their teaching. It is evident from the text of the *Jus Feudale* that in its preparation, Craig referred to Baron, Bodin,[23] Cujas, and Hotman. Craig displays much critical ability when he considers that Cujas' views are to be preferred to Hotman's on the authorship and date of the *Libri Feudorum*.[24]

Baron is referred to by Craig as 'one of the greatest of modern commentators'.[25] Furthermore, in considering the arguments for identifying investiture with possession, Craig cites Baron – 'whose name carries much weight' – in the ensuing discussion of Book 2, Title 2 of the *Obertina*.[26] This Title refers to a '*publicum instrumentum*'. Baron's comment on this, with a reference to Book 1, Titles 2 and 4, is '*breve testatum alibi vocat quod hic publicum instrumentum*'. That is, 'He (Obertus) names it elsewhere a *breve testatum* which here is termed a public instrument.' Craig's discussion of the introduction of the *breve testatum* into Scotland closely follows[27] this section. From the close juxtaposition of Craig's reference to Baron – where Baron has discussed the *breve testatum* – to his own discussion of the *breve testatum*, it is possible to suggest that Craig, who clearly held Baron in high esteem, based his discussion on Baron's definition of the *breve testatum*. It may not be too fanciful to speculate whether the copy of the first edition of Baron's *Ad Obertum Ortensium, de Beneficiis, Commentarii, Methodo in eundem subiecti*, which is in the National Library of Scotland,[28] and without any marks of ownership, could possibly have been owned by or available to Sir Thomas Craig.

Even although Baron may not have been Craig's source for his comments on the *breve testatum*, it is certain that his general source was the writings of the French jurists. Through them he found the Lombardic *breve testatum* which he in error transferred to Scotland. In itself the *breve testatum* may not be a thing of great importance. As an earlier Scottish writer on feudal matters has observed, 'speculations . . . either from their apparent minuteness, or from their seeming insignificance, carry an unpromising and barren air'.[29] This present speculation on the existence in Scotland of the *breve testatum* may indeed be insignificant, unpromising and barren. What is of importance is the recognition of the fact that the existence of a thing for so long accepted by Scottish law-writers must now be doubted. This, in turn, leads to the question of how many other things written in the name of Scottish legal history could survive serious enquiry.

J. J. ROBERTSON

[23] Craig, *op. cit.*, 1. 1. 8 for a brief reference to Bodin.
[24] Craig, *op. cit.*, 1. 6. 3.
[25] Craig, *op. cit.*, 2. 2. 5.
[26] Craig, *op. cit.*, 2. 2. 11.
[27] Craig, *op. cit.*, 2. 2. 16 discussed above.
[28] NLS, Law Room, Shelf Mark 8. 2. 7, E. 181. 2.
[29] G. Wallace, *Thoughts on the origins of Feudal Tenures* (Edinburgh, 1783), 1.

# 8

## Some Observations on the Provinces of the Scottish Universities, 1560 - 1850

Whatever hardships expatriation imposed on Scots seeking a university education before 1411, it soon became clear that these were not entirely removed by the foundation of the University of St Andrews as the names of graduates in the first half century of the University show a clear bias towards names associated with the area of the diocese of St Andrews.[1] And although the foundation of Glasgow University and King's College, Aberdeen are often explained as moves in the game of episcopal one-upmanship,[2] the motive, explicit in the case of Aberdeen[3] to provide university education in a part of the country remote from St Andrews must have been a real factor in its creation, and the geographical argument probably also furnished just as valid an excuse for Bishop Turnbull's foundation at Glasgow. This is the situation as seen by John Major in his *History of greater Britain* . . .[4] where the richer and more populous area of the east coast is seen as the St Andrews province: 'Saint Andrews the seat of the primate of Scotland, possesses the first university; Aberdeen is serviceable to the northern inhabitants, and Glasgow to those of the west and south'. Again this view appears in the scheme relating to the universities in the *First book of discipline*,[5] where the plan to establish the principal university at St Andrews and two others at Aberdeen and Glasgow comes not so much from a preponderance of St Andrews interest on the drafting committee, but from the way in which the country, as Major forty years earlier, still regarded the existing institutions.

Supporting evidence comes from various sources. The nations into which the students at each of the universities were divided give a real indication of the relative importance of areas in providing the student body. Thus for St Andrews the nations were *Albany*, Fife and part of Perthshire, *Angus*, Scotland to the north of the Tay, *Lothian*, eastern Scotland south of the Forth, and *Britain*, south and west Scotland;[6] for Glasgow *Clydesdale* extended from the point where Dumfriesshire, Peeblesshire and Lanarkshire meet to Dumbarton and included the barony of Renfrew, *Teviotdale* comprised Lothian, Stirling and all

---

[1] J. M. Anderson, *Early records of the university of St Andrews* (Edinburgh, 1926), 1–38.
[2] P. H. Brown, *History of Scotland* (Cambridge, 1929), i, 245; J. D. Mackie, *The University of Glasgow, 1451–1951* . . . (Glasgow, 1954), 9.
[3] Bull of foundation as printed in *Evidence . . . taken and received by the commissioners . . . for visiting the universities of Scotland* (London, 1837), iv, 129–130.
[4] Major, *History*, 29.
[5] J. K. Cameron (ed.), *The first book of discipline* (Edinburgh, 1972), 137.
[6] R. G. Cant, *The University of St Andrews* (Edinburgh, 1970), 7–8.

to the east of the Urr Water in Dumfriesshire, *Rothesay* embraced the sheriffdom of Ayr, Galloway beyond the Urr Water, Argyll and the Islands, Lennox and Ireland, and everything north of the Forth was designated *Albany*[7]; and for Kings College there were *Mar* and *Buchan* both within the diocese of Aberdeen, *Moray* the rest of Scotland north of the Grampians and *Angus* the whole of Scotland south of that range.[8] Although there was some attempt to define and indeed to redefine these nations to give a rough equality between them this can only have been very approximate. Thus for the period 1492–1546 in St Andrews the actual identified numbers of students, and we should be safe to assume no bias in chance of identification, in each nation is Albany 394, Angus 254, Lothian 268 and Britain 170.[9] Or to look at Glasgow at a later period, 1750–1849, the ratios of student numbers in the four nations there, Clydesdale, Teviotdale, Rothesay and Albany if we divide the period into two half centuries are 4:1:2:1 and 3:1:2:1 respectively.

In the case of Glasgow University we find that the incomplete incorporations over the first century of the University's existence average ten a year[10] though with occasional peaks and this agrees with the statement of Major[11] that it was a University not rich in scholars. For King's College no record of incorporations survives for its first century and although there is evidence for an early period of intellectual distinction[12] there is none for a large body of students and we cannot be far wrong in accepting Randolph's statement in a letter to Cecil[13] that 'Aberdeen is a university of one college with 15 or 16 scholars'. At St Andrews for the period 1500–59, though again the record is by no means complete, the names of 2,096 students are recorded and matriculations from year to year vary except for completely blank years from two to eighty-six. The distribution of these matriculations, however, is such that the university in this period probably never had fewer than 100 or more than 250 students at any one time.[14]

Amongst the Scottish student body of this time foreigners appear rarely, but we do find a handful of Englishmen, and perhaps there were more than can easily be identified. There were rather more Irishmen, particularly friars in the reign of James IV. However it must be remembered also that throughout the sixteenth century a significant number of Scots are going abroad for their first university. A good illustration of this can be seen in the Scottish entries in the *Acta Rectoria Universitatis Parisiensis*[15]: out of 149 students recorded from St

[7] Mackie, *op. cit.*, 14.

[8] R. S. Rait, *The universities of Aberdeen: a history* (Aberdeen, 1895), 116.

[9] Anderson, *op. cit.*, xi.          [10] Mackie, *op. cit.*, 55.          [11] Major, *op. cit.*, 28.

[12] J. F. K. Johnstone and A. W. Robertson, *Bibliographia Aberdonensis . . . 1472–1640* (Aberdeen, 1929).          [13] Randolph to Cecil, 31 August, 1562, Rait, *op. cit.*, 100.

[14] T. M'Crie, *The life of Andrew Melville* (Edinburgh, 1819), i, 250 argues that 200 at one time seems to have been the maximum at the University of St Andrews in the sixteenth century. A. Grant, *The story of the University of Edinburgh* (London, 1884), i, 18 in quoting M'Crie leaves out the important qualifying phrase 'at one time' and J. Scotland, *The history of Scottish education* (London, 1969), i, 28 turns this into 'only two hundred students in all enrolled during the first half of the sixteenth century'.

[15] W. A. McNeill, 'Scottish entries in the *Acta rectoria universitatis Parisiensis*, 1519 to *c.* 1633', *SHR*, xliii (1964), 66–86.

Andrews diocese only twenty-five can be identified with any confidence as having been students at St Andrews University.

So much for the period before the Reformation. Although only a great deal of biographical research will allow us to determine with precision the relationship between the universities and to define their provinces some evidence does exist. We have from the Reformation in the *Fasti* of the Established Church[16] a large body of biographical information which covers all the Scottish universities. This contains identification of the universities of about ten and a half thousand ministers. There are difficulties in using the university identifications in the *Fasti*. Some are incorrect and many are not made which could have been. But in using the *Fasti* identifications in the way which follows the fundamental assumption has been made that a student of any particular university stands an equal chance of identification with the students of any other. No corrections have been made to the information presented in the second edition of the *Fasti* because in the present writer's hands these would have been totally biased in favour of St Andrews University. The *Fasti* material has been looked at to see how it would answer the question – where did the universities draw their students from? To do this we have to make the further assumptions that the place of origin of students who became ministers is a true reflection of the entire university population and that the arts education of the ministry, which is the normal university affiliation recorded by the *Fasti*, would be no different for students who became ministers than for others. In fact local variations of various sorts will have to be taken into account in any definitive attempt to discuss this problem. For example, a much smaller proportion of the Gaelic-speaking population reaches the universities. For the period after 1811 until 1896, when the Gaelic speakers become clearly distinguishable at St Andrews, it is evident that a much higher proportion of those that do become students study for the ministry and a much higher proportion achieve a greater degree of scholastic success than the student population generally. Out of 297 Gaelic-speaking students, 111 can be identified as getting church charges and of forty-three others whose careers can be followed seven got university chairs and another became a university chancellor. We shall return to the matter of local variations later.

Before presenting the geographical results of the analysis it is well to consider that the material is presented against a background of national evolution, particularly movements of population, and though it may be idle in our present state of knowledge to speculate about the precise effects on the university population of variations in the birth rate, dearths, civil and external wars or the changes in ecclesiastical polity or any number of other factors, nevertheless if we present the *Fasti* material in another way to show the proportions of ministers educated at each of the universities we can see a picture which is partly a reflection of student numbers, but also a reflection, it is suggested, of the result of these other forces. For the period between the Reformation and 1600, where the sources are most defective, a weighting in favour of universities with the

[16] H. Scott, *Fasti ecclesiae Scoticanae* (Edinburgh, 1915–28).

fullest records might seem inevitable. Nevertheless the result seems likely to be a fair reflection of the relative size of the universities except for King's College. St Andrews educates 53% of the ministers, Glasgow 25%, King's College 3·5% and Edinburgh, founded only half way through this period, was responsible for an astonishing 17·5%. After 1600 we have a better survival of university records and from this much firmer ground the pattern to 1850 looks like this:

## UNIVERSITIES OF ESTABLISHED CHURCH MINISTERS
### 1601-1850

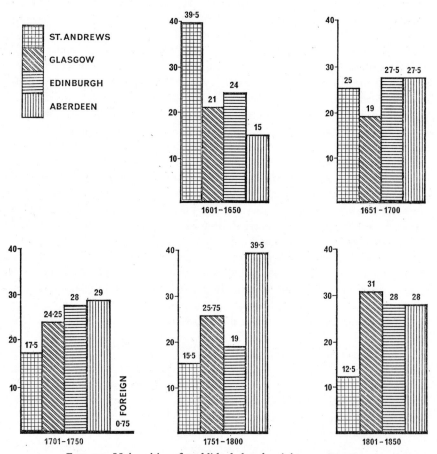

FIGURE I. Universities of established church ministers, 1601–1850

It is possible to demonstrate still further the way in which general forces affect the universities if we look at the matriculation patterns for 1728–1857.

The figures have been compiled in the case of Glasgow and Aberdeen from the published records of students. This has also been done in the case of St

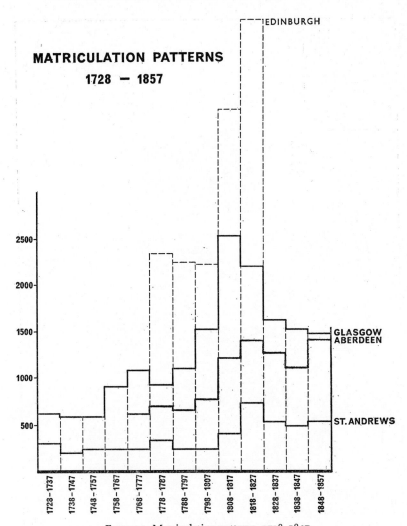

FIGURE 2. Matriculation patterns, 1728–1857

Andrews, except for the first two decades which are supplied from unpublished registers.[17] For Edinburgh we have only the highly suspect figures for arts students given in *Evidence*[18] and we represent the supposed Edinburgh figures by the dotted line. Although the particular shape of the graph is partly conditioned by the purely arbitrary decades chosen, the general trends can be seen to be affecting each of the universities. It is therefore against the background of a changing relationship between the universities and also a common experience in relation to more general social change that we must view the maps which follow.

[17] See references below, nn. 22–25, and St Andrews University Muniments UY305/3.
[18] *Evidence, Universities commissioners*, i, Appendix, 127–8.

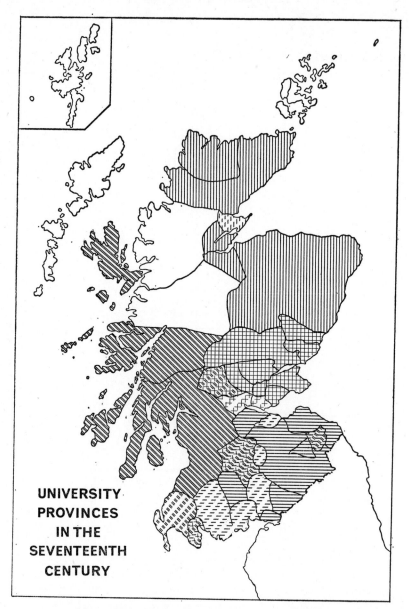

UNIVERSITY
PROVINCES
IN THE
SEVENTEENTH
CENTURY

MAP 1. University provinces in the seventeenth century

These maps, in which each university has been assigned its own form of
shading (corresponding to that used in Fig. 1), present crudely the provinces of
each of the universities in the seventeenth, eighteenth and nineteenth centuries.
The evidence has been analysed simply as presented by presbyteries. Each
presbytery with over half its students going to a particular university has been

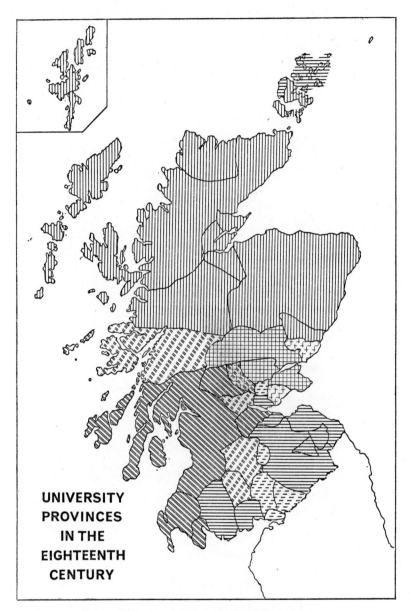

UNIVERSITY
PROVINCES
IN THE
EIGHTEENTH
CENTURY

MAP 2. University provinces in the eighteenth century

shaded completely; the percentage in fact in these areas is almost always in the
region of 70–80. In other presbyteries with a much greater share of students,
but less than half, going to one particular university oblique banding has been
used. Again usually there is no doubt, but in the few cases where two or more
universities have an equal hold this has been indicated by alternate bands of

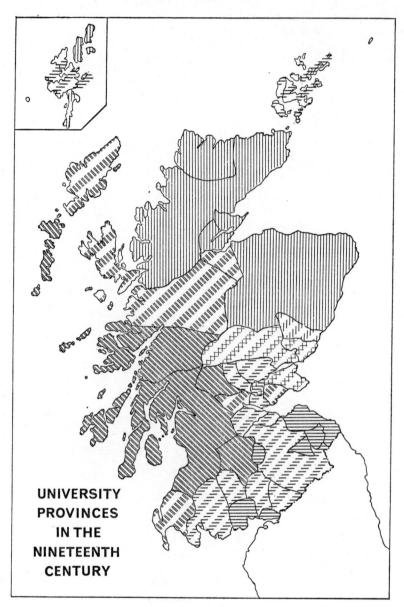

UNIVERSITY
PROVINCES
IN THE
NINETEENTH
CENTURY

MAP 3. University provinces in the nineteenth century

oblique shading. The white areas in the seventeenth century map are indeter-
minate – too few identified students for a meaningful result. In the first map we
have progressed from the situation at the Reformation where St Andrews
occupied the position of prime or national university, though this referred in
part to its size as it drew its students mainly from the immense area of the fertile

east and south, to a situation where, after the foundation of Edinburgh University directly and almost solely at the expense of the St Andrews province, St Andrews was to find its level, probably by the Restoration, certainly by the Revolution, with the rest of the Scottish universities. As far as providing arts education for Scotland was concerned they had all become mainly local universities. The general pattern revealed by the map is quite clear and neat although some of the anomalies in the south of the country are difficult to explain. While defective data are the first possibility to keep in mind, it may be asked whether the proximity of the presbytery of Duns to a far flung part of the old diocese of Glasgow may be an explanation. A strong St Andrews connection in Lanark and Wigtown is supported by the evidence of a few other identified individuals from the area, though there is more support for a connection with Dumfriesshire which does not show up on the map. In the map for the eighteenth century we see a number of local changes in boundary, but in the main a consolidation of the local province pattern, with, however, inroads on all sides into the province of St Andrews which derive in the main from changes in transport patterns and in particular the growth of the turnpike road system and the later development of the stagecoach routes.[19] The nineteenth-century map reveals a very considerable and general breakdown in the local university system although Glasgow and Aberdeen still retain much of their hold over their provinces. Here again transport changes must be the root cause with the capture of the Western Isles by Glasgow coming from the developing steamer routes[20] and the capture of the Perth area by Edinburgh brought about by the coming of the railway.[21] Indeed the terrible shrinkage which has befallen the university of St Andrews is directly attributable to its geographical position and the way in which all through transport routes passed the town by. It is interesting to note that special bursaries or the local traditions that often exist of students being directed by schoolmasters and ministers to particular universities away from the local university make no impact on the map. Thus for St Andrews, the Grant bursary brought students regularly from Cromdale/Abernethy, the Bayne bursary from Ross-shire and the Mackay bursary from the far north, but the maps show no hint of this. King's College and Marischal College (Aberdeen) have been lumped together in the maps, but their respective provinces were in fact quite different, as will be shown.

It is possible over a certain period to test the conclusions of the evidence of the *Fasti* for a different, if not wholly independent source – the records of students held by the universities. These records are not wholly independent in that they were used by the compilers of the *Fasti* in writing the ministers' biographies. For the period 1750–1850 we have published records for King's College,[22]

[19] A. R. B. Haldane, *Three centuries of Scottish posts: an historical survey to 1836* (Edinburgh, 1971), 74–102.

[20] C. L. D. Duckworth and G. E. Langmuir, *West highland steamers* (Prescot, 1967), 1–21.

[21] H. A. Vallance, *The Highland Railway* (Dawlish, 1963), 12; J. W. F. Gardner, *London, Midland and Scottish railway* (n.p., 1934), 18–20.

[22] P. J. Anderson, *Roll of alumni in arts of the University and King's College of Aberdeen* (Aberdeen, 1900).

Marischal College,[23] St Andrews[24] and Glasgow[25] Universities. Edinburgh's position can only be assessed by implication though it would be possible from material in the university's possession to publish a similar record. These published records vary considerably in their nature. In the case of Marischal College the register provides few identifications of origin between 1750 and 1768-9 though about a third have been supplied by the editor; thereafter the parish of origin is stated in most cases and only about six per cent remain mysterious. That there should be any geographical bias in the identifications in this record or indeed in that of any other university seems most unlikely and there is every chance that the percentage distribution revealed in the imperfect record would still hold were the origins of every student recorded. Glasgow has the fullest record, requiring or at least customarily providing parish of origin as well as father's name and occupation and student's position within the family. For King's College, Aberdeen through most of the period except the last two decades it is the county rather than the parish of origin which is given, but students of unidentified origin fall from four per cent in the first half of the period to a negligible proportion in the second half. In the case of St Andrews the primary record is unfortunately a mere list of names, but the present writer has been able from other sources to determine place of origin in 42% of cases in the first decade of the chosen century, rising steadily to 80% in the last two decades.[26] From these records the tables on pp. 102-103 have been compiled.

The general import of the tables is to confirm the pattern revealed in the maps compiled from the *Fasti* evidence. It will, however, be seen how very different are the provinces of King's College and Marischal College. The latter has a virtual monopoly of students from the town of New Aberdeen, takes a majority from Kincardineshire, has an equal hold in rural Aberdeenshire, but draws fewer and fewer within the Aberdeen province from the further North and West. An exception is Orkney which sends its students to Marischal College while Shetland is in the province of King's College, though it must be remembered that the *Fasti* evidence showed an anomalous Edinburgh connection for these islands. In this case local tradition provides support for the Edinburgh link. The tables also provide evidence of a remarkable divergence throughout the country in chance of a university education, with Aberdeenshire and Banff-shire clear leaders in the league – a dramatic demonstration of the ability which has sprung from that soil to enrich Scottish life and endeavour since at least the sixteenth century. For Edinburgh's province we can only point to the very few students at the other universities from what (according to the *Fasti* evidence) is Edinburgh's province and rely for confirmation on statements like the evidence

[23] P. J. Anderson, *Fasti academiae Mariscallanae Aberdonensis*, ii (Aberdeen, 1898).
[24] J. M. Anderson, *The matriculation roll of the University of St Andrews, 1747–1897* (Edinburgh, 1905).
[25] W. I. Addison, *The matriculation albums of the university of Glasgow from 1728 to 1858* (Glasgow, 1913).
[26] These figures are based on the writer's unpublished collections towards a biographical register of St Andrews University alumni, graduates and officers.

of Professor James Hamilton in 1826: 'the literary students are natives of this place (Edinburgh) and the adjoining counties'.[27]

Since 1850 which has been adopted as a nominal date limit the dissolution of the provincial nature of the universities with regard to first degree students has proceeded apace, especially as the idea of a uniform and common basic arts degree has been abandoned, first by the establishment of first degrees in other faculties and more recently by the creation of degrees in 'new' subjects. Nevertheless the vestiges are still with us. From the middle of the nineteenth century a new self-consciousness in the universities themselves provides a more detailed record of the origin of their students. Analyses on this very point for internal consumption or external purposes have appeared from time to time and we have not thought it necessary to carry the story further.[28]

It is important to emphasise that what has been demonstrated to this point are the provinces of the Scottish universities for students in arts only, and that there are many other questions to be asked. Is there any evidence of social provinces? What of the respective places of the universities in the higher branches of learning? What of their position *vis-à-vis* students from outside Scotland?

It has already been noticed that in the sixteenth century a surprising number of Scots were going abroad for their first university and it is clear that this practice continued, defining itself more particularly as being restricted to the nobility and the wealthier lairds. An increasing number of them from the latter part of the seventeenth century find that first university in England – a natural development as these classes seek a social integration with their English counterparts. This process by the second half of the eighteenth century has also reached the lesser lairds and official classes. Nevertheless, where noble sons reach the Scottish universities their first university seems normally to be the one expected under the province system, but movement between the universities is common in this class. Of course movement between the Scottish universities is a subject which could also bear investigation. So far as arts students are concerned it seems to have been to some extent a reciprocal movement. For example, in the case of St Andrews three per cent of arts students in the period 1750–1849 were at more than one university, about equally divided between those at another university before coming to St Andrews and those at another university after studying at St Andrews.

It is likely that there were social provinces, but we can be sure of this only in so far as the student populations reflected the composition of the territorial provinces already demonstrated. Thus we may infer that Glasgow reflected the industrial and commercial nature of its province, that Edinburgh reflected the professional and legal nature of its province, while St Andrews and Aberdeen had a rural craft and landed interest, tempered (in the case of Marischal College)

[27] *Evidence, Universities commissioners*, i, 304.
[28] A. C. O'Dell and K. Walton, 'A note on the student population of Aberdeen University', *Aberdeen University Review*, xxxiii, 1949–50, 125–7; St Andrews University geography department, 'Domicile of St Andrews students', *St Andrews geographer*, i (1970), 22–6, ii (1971), 22–5.

| | 1750–99 | | | | | 1800–49 | | | | |
|---|---|---|---|---|---|---|---|---|---|---|
| | St Andrews | Glasgow | King's College | Marischal College | Total | St Andrews | Glasgow | King's College | Marischal College | Total |
| Aberdeen | 2 | 23 | 468 | 1,010 | 1,503 | 11 | 28 | 1,140 | 2,513 | 3,692 |
| Argyll | 14 | 175 | 19 | 2 | 210 | 19 | 411 | 22 | 3 | 455 |
| Ayr | 2 | 253 | — | — | 255 | 19 | 862 | 4 | — | 885 |
| Banff | 8 | 2 | 274 | 105 | 389 | 4 | 4 | 429 | 205 | 642 |
| Berwick | 8 | 19 | — | — | 27 | 8 | 29 | 2 | 3 | 42 |
| Bute | — | 13 | — | — | 13 | 2 | 85 | — | — | 87 |
| Caithness | 1 | 7 | 31 | 11 | 50 | 6 | 12 | 150 | 25 | 193 |
| Clackmannan | 1 | — | — | — | 1 | 19 | 21 | — | 1 | 40 |
| Dumbarton | 1 | 118 | — | — | 119 | — | 275 | 2 | 1 | 278 |
| Dumfries | 7 | 46 | 3 | 17 | 73 | 46 | 150 | 3 | 3 | 202 |
| Edinburgh | 7 | 63 | 12 | 3 | 85 | 37 | 160 | 13 | 14 | 224 |
| Elgin | — | 3 | 134 | 62 | 199 | — | 3 | 321 | 69 | 393 |
| Fife | 289 | 41 | 5 | 4 | 339 | 527 | 61 | 5 | 19 | 612 |
| Forfar | 88 | 13 | 92 | 69 | 262 | 250 | 52 | 170 | 110 | 582 |
| Haddington | 10 | 5 | — | — | 15 | 6 | 26 | 3 | 2 | 37 |
| Inverness | 7 | 10 | 223 | 30 | 270 | 11 | 31 | 487 | 38 | 567 |
| Islands | — | 6 | 43 | 4 | 53 | — | 25 | 28 | 4 | 57 |
| Kincardine | 5 | 4 | 46 | 108 | 163 | 9 | 10 | 86 | 213 | 318 |
| Kinross | 2 | 12 | — | — | 14 | 20 | 5 | — | — | 25 |
| Kirkcudbright | 1 | 25 | — | — | 26 | 2 | 31 | 2 | 2 | 37 |
| Lanark | 5 | 1,778 | — | 1 | 1,784 | 24 | 2,606 | 0 | 0 | 2,728 |

| | | | | | Total | | | | | Total |
|---|---|---|---|---|---|---|---|---|---|---|
| Orkney | 2 | — | 1 | 8 | 11 | 1 | 2 | 5 | 22 | 30 |
| Peebles | — | 8 | — | — | 8 | — | 6 | — | — | 6 |
| Perth | 123 | 245 | 10 | 5 | 383 | 379 | 361 | 23 | 27 | 790 |
| Renfrew | 2 | 271 | — | — | 273 | 15 | 747 | 2 | 2 | 766 |
| Ross | 4 | 6 | 142 | 34 | 186 | 7 | 17 | 419 | 58 | 501 |
| Roxburgh | 2 | 10 | 1 | 4 | 17 | 7 | 30 | 1 | 3 | 41 |
| Selkirk | — | 2 | — | — | 2 | 1 | 8 | — | — | 9 |
| Shetland | — | — | 16 | 8 | 24 | — | 1 | 20 | 7 | 28 |
| Stirling | 6 | 286 | — | 4 | 296 | 15 | 551 | 3 | 4 | 573 |
| Sutherland | 1 | — | 28 | 14 | 43 | 4 | 14 | 127 | 13 | 158 |
| Wigtown | 1 | 55 | 2 | — | 58 | — | 119 | 2 | — | 121 |
| Ireland | 8 | 781 | — | 2 | 791 | 3 | 746 | 3 | 5 | 757 |
| England | 28 | 220 | 44 | 41 | 333 | 39 | 488 | 50 | 131 | 708 |
| Colonies | 8 | 144 | 18 | 62 | 232 | 25 | 221 | 25 | 208 | 479 |
| Foreign | 2 | 6 | 1 | 4 | 13 | 2 | 16 | 3 | 4 | 25 |
| Proportion of total arts students with county of origin identified | 46% | 100% | 96% | 79% | | 64% | 100% | 99½% | 93½% | |

FIGURE 3. Tables showing origin of students at the universities of St Andrews, Glasgow and Aberdeen, 1750–1849

by a reflection of the importance of New Aberdeen in providing its student body and (in the case of St Andrews) by a possible weighting as an attraction for the sons of the church. This seems as far as we can positively go.

An attempt to analyse the social structure of the Glasgow student body has been made.[29] These Glasgow figures relate to four selected decades and to use them with the knowledge of the considerable fluctuations in student numbers over the period at all the universities would entail the unjustified assumption that whatever forces were responsible for these operated uniformly for all occupations. It is also true that any such attempt based on the mere description of a father as for example 'merchant' or 'manufacturer' fails to take account of the extremes of social and economic power which may be comprehended by these terms. Nevertheless the figures given are an important first step in defining and elucidating the problem. We put them beside a similar set for St Andrews University for the period 1750–1849 where it has been possible to determine the occupations of the fathers of only a quarter of the students. The distortion in the St Andrews figures (where the information is not given in the registers) caused by the relative ease with which particular occupations of fathers may be determined as, for example, 'Established church', 'laird/ gentleman' or 'professor' is a further warning of the reserve with which the figures should be regarded, although there is a curious correspondence in the figures for such occupations as law, medicine and schoolmaster.

| *Glasgow University 1740–1839* (average of four selected decades) | % | *St Andrews University 1750–1849* | % |
|---|---|---|---|
| Administration | 1·6 | Army and navy | 5·0 |
| Army and navy | 0·7 | Established church | 26·0 |
| Church | 9·9 | Dissenting minister | 2·0 |
| Industry and commerce | 44·4 | Merchant | 6·0 |
| Law | 4·3 | Tradesman | 13·0 |
| Medicine | 3·2 | Law | 5·0 |
| Nobility and landed | 12·9 | Medicine | 3·0 |
| Teaching | 2·6 | Peer | 2·0 |
| Tenant farming | 16·9 | Laird/gentleman | 19·0 |
| Citizens | 1·6 | Schoolmaster | 3·0 |
| Miscellaneous | 2·0 | Professor | 6·0 |
| | | Farmer/tenant farmer | 12·0 |

That there is no evidence that the largest and lowest class of the new industrial society contributed many students is not to be wondered at. Recent studies[30] in our own age of 'equal opportunity' demonstrate that this class still provides a disproportionately low share of the student body. But the figures equally confirm our native traditions that from the rural areas a high proportion from

[29] W. M. Mathew, 'The origins and occupations of Glasgow students, 1740–1839', *Past and Present*, No. 33 (1966), 74–94.

[30] J. Abbot, 'Students' social class in three northern universities', *British Journal of Sociology*, xvi (1965), 206–20.

parents of low estate but justifiable pride in skill or function in society did reach the universities. As an example of the kind of local changes which were probably taking place on a much wider scale we demonstrate the trend in the case of Highland born students at Glasgow University:

| Date | Total students | Landed fathers | | Professional fathers | | Crofter/artisan fathers | |
|------|------|------|------|------|------|------|------|
| 1728–37 | 26 | 16 | 62% | 2 | 5% | 8 | 33% |
| 1788–97 | 44 | 13 | 30% | 4 | 9% | 27 | 61% |
| 1848–57 | 81 | 1 | 2% | 15 | 18% | 65 | 80% |

It we can only make tentative suggestions about the possibility of social provinces, the case with regard to the higher branches of learning is even more complex. Much of the training in law and medicine was done outside the universities (or even abroad), and few of the records of what was done within them are published. We are, for example, far from being able to assess properly the importance within the context of its own time of the 200 students from Europe studying theology at the Scottish universities in the early seventeenth century[31] compared with the as yet unknown number in the higher faculties in the eighteenth and nineteenth centuries. While we may acknowledge the special position of Edinburgh as the capital city and locus of the central law courts, the superefficiency of the Edinburgh University publicity service since the eighteenth century has done much to devalue the achievement of the other Scottish universities.[32] To take but one example, all the Scottish universities, as universities elsewhere, at some time or other conferred higher degrees on examination and/or testimonials only, but when St Andrews and Marischal College continued the practice after others had ceased, the calumny heaped on these institutions has prevented any rational assessment of the system. To examine and recognise knowledge however or wherever gained or to place part of the burden for doing so on individual members of a learned profession at large is not necessarily an educationally nefarious practice. In fact there is ample evidence that control was on the whole good and the results self-justifying. In the case of the 3,725 medical degrees conferred between 1747 and 1897 by St Andrews, of which 1,375 were granted on testimonials only, no less than twelve per cent of the holders have their achievements recognised by inclusion in the *Dictionary of National Biography* or, in the case of foreigners, in their own national biographical registers or in the standard dictionary of medical biography, *Biographisches Lexikon hervorragender Ärzte Zeiten und Völker* (A. Hirsch and others),

[31] M'Crie, *op. cit.*, ii, 490–6, prints an incomplete list of these.

[32] While it would be unfair to blame Edinburgh for the thin sound of the trumpets of the other universities, the way in which Grant, *op. cit.*, and D. B. Horn, *A short history of the University of Edinburgh, 1556–1889* (Edinburgh, 1967) both open with an emphasis on decay and decline in the other universities is the public face of an attitude in a long period of tacit inter-university competition. St Andrews University Library, MS. LFı111.P81.C99, 138, Letter of Francis Pringle to John Pringle, 18 February 1734, is the earliest example known to me. Francis Pringle, having been urged to forsake the decayed and dying university of St Andrews for a chair in Edinburgh, refuses.

not to mention the numbers in the higher ranks of the Army, Navy and Indian medical services. So it is not surprising to find Adam Smith defending the system as the only way in which merit could gain recognition against privilege.[33] The fact is, however, that between 1751 and 1850 Edinburgh University conferred 5,437 medical degrees and the other Scottish Universities together conferred 5,005. This question has been raised only to continue the plea which it is hoped has emerged from these notes and maps, that many of the problems in the history of the Scottish universities will only be dealt with satisfactorily when biographical registers at least as comprehensive as those provided for the Universities of Cambridge and Oxford exist for all the older universities of Scotland.

R. N. SMART

[33] J. Rae, *Life of Adam Smith* (London, 1895), 273–80. The Green referred to on p. 276 cannot be identified in the St Andrews records.

# 9

## *Some Early Scottish Books*

Ego uero 'in montis patrios et ad incunabula nostra' pergam.

Cicero, *Ad Atticum*

This paper is composed of notes made in the course of an attempt to describe yet again, in order of printers, some of the books that came from the Scottish press in the first century or so of its existence, the period covered by Robert Dickson and J. P. Edmond, Annals of Scottish printing (Cambridge, 1890).[1] While the notes themselves are by their very nature disparate, they have been arranged here in such a way as I hope may illustrate the kind of problem that appears to me to stand in urgent need of further study.

Today about 400 editions are known to have survived from the output of the Scottish printers in the sixteenth century. Many of them are mere proclamations or verse-broadsheets. The whole body is only a handful of what there must have been. About half of the editions are in Scottish libraries, 170 or so in the National Library of Scotland, most of them inherited from the Advocates but some acquired since 1925, and about 30 in Edinburgh University and elsewhere. Most of the remaining 200 are scattered between the British Museum and other collections in London, the Bodleian, Oxford and Cambridge colleges, and libraries in America, particularly Huntington, Harvard and Folger.

But the National Library of Scotland is rightly the best single place from which to survey the subject. That is because for fully forty years it has been able to spend time and money on systematically collecting photostats and microfilms of books that could no longer be acquired in original copies, and not only the books printed within Scotland but the books needed for the bibliographical study of them – those, for example, printed by Violette at Rouen and Van Doesborch at Antwerp, printers whose types, ornaments and illustrations we must make ourselves familiar with, if we are to understand their connections with our own printers. If we want to work on the proclamations and other broadsheets printed by Lekpreuik at Edinburgh, Stirling and St Andrews in the middle of the century, we have to travel in London between the Public Record Office, the Society of Antiquaries and the British Museum (and, within the Museum, between the North Library and the Department of Manuscripts). But in Edinburgh if we spread out the photostats, there may leap to the eye points that could hardly have failed to be lost from sight between Bloomsbury and Chancery Lane. The collection of facsimiles in the National Library of Scotland is accessible to anyone who may desire to pursue matters touched on here.

[1] In this chapter book-titles are not italicised.

The books, pamphlets and broadsheets known to have been printed in Scotland in the sixteenth century have been the subject of bibliographical study for more than two hundred years. In the first work on printing in Scotland, 'The Publisher's Preface' to The history of the art of printing issued by James Watson at Edinburgh in 1713, the writer confines himself on the whole to the seventeenth century. He mentions a few earlier books, and what he says about them deserves attention, but he has little material to go on. After all, he is not a bibliographer. His concern is with a decline in standards of printing, which he did much to remedy by precept and practice.

In Joseph Ames, Typographical antiquities (London, 1749) some twenty out of 600 pages or so are devoted to an attempt to list the books printed in Scotland up to 1600. This is done year by year, beginning with the Aberdeen Breviary of 1510, described from the copy in the Advocates' Library, the first part by Charles Mackie, Professor of History at Edinburgh, the second by Thomas Ruddiman himself, 'no small encourager of this undertaking, by his many searches for me at Edinburgh, and elsewhere'. Ames notes also that writers in Scotland made use quite early of foreign printers, such as Badius Ascensius, who printed Hector Boece, Scotorum historiae [Paris, 1527]. In the third volume (1790) of William Herbert's revision of Ames, the Scottish section has grown to over fifty pages. Attention is drawn to the resemblance between Chepman's device in the Aberdeen Breviary and that of Philippe Pigouchet in books of hours: 'This would seem to prove that the art of printing was first introduced into Scotland from France, and probably the types &c. came from thence'. Here is a hint of the truth that was to be revealed by the efforts of Claudin and others in the nineteenth century. Even more interesting is the description (among the corrections and additions) by George Paton of the volume containing Edinburgh tracts of 1508 lately presented to the Advocates' Library and commonly known today as the Chepman and Myllar Prints – a description that still deserves careful study, for it deals with the contents of the book as they were just after it reached the Library, some time before it passed through the hands of that infamous binder Charles Hering. Of the eleventh piece, Robyn Hode, now thought to have been printed by Van Doesborch, it is already noted: 'This woodcut is like that used by Pynson, in his first edition of the Canterbury tales [1492?], for the Squire's yeoman'. It is indeed a copy of Pynson's cut. Finally Paton makes a statement and shrewd conjectures that continue to tease his readers:

> If these were the earliest, Poesy was the first fruits of the Scottish press. It may however still be doubted that they were not the first poems printed in Edinburgh: some of Dunbar's latest pieces are here; but his Thristle and Rose composed in 1503, on queen Margaret's coming to Scotland, is not in this collection. King James I. was murthered in 1436; so his poetical compositions preceded the commencement of printing, and would probably have been among the first publications of that sort. There are people alive who remember to have seen the Kings Quair in a printed pamphlet long before Mr. Tytler's copy [1783], but now no where to be found.

A great advance in these studies was made soon after the appearance of Ames and Herbert, in a work that was never published. This is the collection of notes[2] by George Chalmers and his nephew James, who cover the sixteenth century much more fully than their predecessors and break fresh ground, right to the end of the seventeenth. The arrangement is chronological by printers and, within each press, by date of printing. It is the same as that used by Ames for England, except that Chalmers does not separate one printing town from another. It would be idle to think of either Ames or Chalmers as a scientific bibliographer, and yet each in his way uses a rudimentary form of the 'natural history method' familiar to students of fifteenth-century books, the method foreshadowed to a certain extent in Panzer, Annales typographici (1793–1803), applied in the mid-nineteenth century by Blades, Holtrop and Bradshaw to early printing in England and the Low Countries, and fully developed by Robert Proctor in his index of incunables in the British Museum and the Bodleian.

The books of one city were arranged in printer-order in the first work of scientific bibliography to appear in Scotland, J. P. Edmond's The Aberdeen printers, 1620–1736 (Aberdeen, 1884–6), supplemented by the privately-printed Last notes on the Aberdeen printers (1888). It is no surprise to find in the preface a warm acknowledgment to Bradshaw himself.[3] While Edmond's share in 'Dickson and Edmond', based partly on his colleague's notes and carried out with a certain measure of haste, is less good than either his earlier or his later work, yet that great book is so firmly rooted in use and affection and contains so much valuable information that I for one cannot think of it as ever likely to be wholly superseded. The authors used the Chalmers papers to advantage; and in its turn their work has been annotated in manuscript by, among others, F. S. Ferguson, from whose copy in the University of Bochum transcriptions and photographs have been kindly made available in the National Library of Scotland. Two facts should be stated about Robert Dickson and John Philip Edmond. That Dr Dickson, a medical practitioner in Carnoustie, should have been able at that time to describe almost unaided the Scottish output down to the death of Bassandyne is nothing short of miraculous and entitles him to a high place in the history of bibliography. Then, long before there was a national library in Scotland, these studies were fostered by two noble families: Dickson was in 1853[4] persuaded by Fox Maule, Lord Panmure afterwards Earl of Dalhousie, to come to Carnoustie, and Edmond was librarian to the Earl of Crawford at Haigh Hall, before being appointed to the Signet Library. In the same year (1890) as 'Dickson and Edmond' appeared, there was founded the first bibliographical society in these islands. The first volume of the Papers of the

---

[2] Most of them in Nat. Lib. of Scot. Adv. MSS. 16.2.21–2, 17.1.16 and 81.9.5–7 but some in Edin. Univ. Lib.

[3] 'To the late Mr. Henry Bradshaw, Librarian of the University of Cambridge, I owe more than I can find words to express. Encouragement at the commencement, direction while in progress, and commendation bestowed in unmeasured terms – all this I received from the friend whose opinion I valued above all others.'

[4] Obituary notice in Dundee Advertiser, 13 January 1893.

Edinburgh Bibliographical Society, completed in 1896, contained contributions to the study of early printing that were not only good in themselves but that laid down lines for future investigators – papers by Edmond himself, H. G. Aldis and, above all, the man who brought to his task the most acute mind yet displayed by a Scottish bibliographer, Edward Gordon Duff.

### The Two Books Printed for Myllar

It would appear to be in July 1893, on page 175 of his Early printed books, that Duff first published his important ascription to Pierre Violette's press at Rouen rather than to Hostingue's of the two books, Equiuoca and Expositio sequentiarum, printed for Andrew Myllar in 1505 and 1506. His evidence was that:

(1) Violette used, as far as could be seen, the same type;
(2) the cut of a man seated at a reading-desk, found on the title-page of Myllar's Equiuoca in 1505, was used by Violette in 1507 in the Expositio hymnorum et sequentiarum printed for Gerard Wansfort of York.

In a paper read to the Edinburgh Bibliographical Society in December 1892 but not issued until October 1893, Duff had added that

(3) the curious initial S, with two fishes in the bend of the letter, found in Myllar's Expositio in 1506, occurs also in the Sarum Missal printed by Violette in 1509 for Guillaume Candos.

So far as I know, nothing has been found to modify or supplement this evidence substantially. But there is something more to be said about the two books printed for Myllar.

The descriptions in Duff's Fifteenth century books (nos. 155–7) show that the phrase 'mira arte' in the colophon of the Equiuoca had occurred as early as Felix Baligault's edition of 7 August 1494 but that the fuller wording of Myllar's colophon reproduced in facsimile by Dickson and Edmond (page 35) is not found until Pynson's edition of 1496 and De Worde's of 1499. Myllar's edition has the same number of leaves (62) as De Worde's and, while it is not a paginary reprint, it was probably set up either from it or from a cognate edition. There is still a great deal of difficult work to be done on Myllar, and one subject that seems to be worth pursuing is his possible relation with De Worde, and with Pynson, who, like Violette, was a Norman.

In the second book, the Expositio sequentiarum according to the use of Sarum dated 10 June 1506, the additional sequences are introduced on leaf 54b with the words:

¶ Sequuntur expositiones Prosarum
seu. Sequentiarum in precedentibus
deficientium
¶ Et primo de hystoria Vistationis
beate marie virginis.

The arrangement follows line for line that in Pynson's edition of 1498 (Duff 141, part ii), where the only differences are the form 'Sequuntur', a full stop after 'deficientium', and the correct spelling 'Visitationis'. So with the colophon of Myllar's edition as reproduced in facsimile by Dickson and Edmond (page 41):

> ⸿Sequentiarum seu Prosarum secundum vsum
> Sarum in ecclesia Anglicana per totum
> annum cantandarum: diligen terque cor-
> rectarum finiunt feliciter. Anno domini Mil-
> lesimo quingentesimo sexto decima die. Iunii.

It follows Pynson's colophon line for line to 'Millesimo' except in two small points of punctuation. Without being a paginary reprint, Myllar's edition was set up either from Pynson's edition of 1498 or from one allied to it.

### Pierre Violette

Students of Scottish printing should know something of the career of Pierre Violette, who must not be thought of as exclusively a printer of modest service- and school-books in the early years of the sixteenth century. He first appears at Abbeville in 1487 at some time between 19 April and 20 May, when certain persons were condemned 'pour avoir navré maistre Pierre Violete, emprainteur de livres'. Between 1486 and the end of May 1487 the only press at Abbeville produced three books, of which the first and third were printed by Pierre Gérard alone, and the second (Augustine, La cité de dieu) by him in association with Jean Du Pré, who supplied the material for all three. The same type, Du Pré 113 (109) Bât., together with a woodcut from the Abbeville Augustine, is found in the first volume of Lancelot du lac completed at Rouen by Jean Le Bourgeois on 24 November 1488, of which the second volume had been printed by Du Pré in Paris on 16 September of the same year.

We owe most of our knowledge of the early Violette to the chapter on Du Pré in Claudin, who writes (I, 272–3):

> En relations avec les libraires de Rouen, pour lesquels, d'après Brunet [V, 940], il aurait imprimé le Coutumier de Normandie, ce fut lui [Du Pré] qui monta l'atelier que Jean Le Bourgeois établit à Rouen en 1488. Il est probable que notre imprimeur ne vint pas lui-même dans la capitale de la Normandie, mais qu'il y envoya un de ses meilleurs ouvriers, originaire du pays, et ayant déjà dirigé l'atelier créé par lui à Abbeville en société avec Pierre Gérard, en 1486–1487. Ce contre-maître [foreman], qui s'établit plus tard à Rouen, était un ancien étudiant de l'Université de Caen, du nom de Pierre Violete.

The fine folio York missal of about 1507 presented to Cambridge University Library by A. F. Scholfield in 1929 shows on what is left of the title Violette's large ornamental M embodying his name 'M. P. VIOLETTE' and a large lower-case l surmounted by a crown. The word 'Missale' with ornamented M

and l is printed from a block. It contains also two full-page cuts (of the Crucifixion and of God enthroned and surrounded by angels and the symbols of
the four evangelists) that had been used at Rouen in a Rouen missal completed by Martin Morin on 18 November 1495 and before that in a missal of
the use of Le Mans completed by Guillaume Le Talleur on 29 October 1489.
A similar but far from identical pair had appeared in Du Pré's Paris missal of
1481[5] and again in the missal of Séez printed by Le Talleur in 1488. Pierre
Violette is indeed of high descent in the line of French printers. This paragraph
could not have been written without the help of text and illustrations in the
eighth and ninth chapters of Pierre Le Verdier, L'Atelier de Guillaume Le
Talleur (Rouen, 1916).

Violette may also be pursued through the index to Léopold Delisle, Catalogue
des livres imprimés ou publiés à Caen avant le milieu du XVI<sup>e</sup> siècle (2 vol.,
Caen, 1903–4), in which he can be seen to have printed for Pierre Regnault at
least seven works: Missale Baiocense [1503?], Jacobus de Voragine, Legenda
aurea (1507), Angelus de Calvasio, Summa angelica (1511), Guido de Monte
Rocheri, Manipulus curatorum (1513) and the undated Tractatus de septem
peccatis mortalibus, Alexander de Villa Dei, Doctrinale and Marsilius Ficinus,
De triplici vita.


### Order of Printing of the 'Chepman and Myllar' Tracts

Leaving aside the eleventh tract Robyn Hode, probably printed by Van
Doesborch, let us consider the order of printing of the first ten tracts. To follow
the arguments, it is necessary to use the collotype facsimile issued by Edinburgh
Bibliographical Society in 1950. This conjectural arrangement modifies and
corrects the bibliographical note prefixed to that facsimile:

#### Printer of Dunbar, The Tua Mariit Wemen

| | |
|---|---|
| X (pages 177–96). Dunbar, The tua mariit wemen etc. | Undated |

#### Walter Chepman and Andrew Myllar

| | |
|---|---|
| VII (pages 137–48). Dunbar, The flyting etc. | [Before 4 April 1508] |
| VIII (pages 149–68). Henryson, Orpheus etc. | [Before 4 April 1508] |
| VI (pages 109–36). Lydgate, The maying etc. | 4 April 1508 |
| II (pages 7–52). Golagrus etc. | 8 April 1508 |
| I (pages 1–6). Chartier, The porteous. | 20 April 1508 |
| IV (pages 89–100). Dunbar, The golden targe. | [About 20 April 1508] |
| IX (pages 169–76). Dunbar, Barnard Stewart. | [About 9 May 1508] |
| III (pages 53–88). Eglamor etc. | Undated |
| V (pages 101–08). De regimine in Scots. | Undated. |

Several features distinguish the tenth tract. The type is different from that
used in the first nine, being the larger of the two types used in the two books

---

[5] Reproduced in Claudin I, 212–13.

printed for Myllar at Rouen. These and the first nine tracts are signed in the Norman way by the sheet, whereas The tua mariit wemen, which when complete would have run a⁶ b⁶, is signed on a3 and 4 and b1, 2 and 3. In it there is no leading between stanzas or poems, and there is no attempt in the lines about Kynd Kittok, as there will be in Chepman and Myllar's Golagrus (No. II) and in their Howlat,⁶ to establish a right-hand margin with the jutting final line of each stanza and the longest line on the same page. While the Equiuoca and the Expositio survive only in copies found in France, The tua mariit wemen survives only in Scotland and may have been printed there by Myllar, before he joined forces with Chepman, with type brought from Violette's office. So with the Donatus in Scots printed with a closely similar type and surviving only in a single leaf in King's College, Aberdeen. But this is mere surmise. We must be cautious and follow F. S. Isaac in distinguishing two eponymous presses 'The Printer of Donatus' and 'The Printer of Dunbar, The tua mariit wemen'. The first-named piece presents if anything a cruder appearance than the second, and neither is as well printed as the most primitive of the nine Chepman and Myllar prints.

This is Dunbar, The flyting etc. (No. VII), in which there occurs (on pages 142 and 145) an alternative form of B that is not found again, there is no leading between stanzas, there are two uncorrected faults of setting on the first surviving page, and the explicit comes as abruptly as that to The tua mariit wemen. That The flyting is the only one of the Prints to show Myllar's ladder intact as in the Expositio of 1506 would be overwhelming evidence of its earliness, were it not that the recto of the leaf containing the device is blank, and the mill is connected to the immediately preceding leaves not by print but only an inscription in a very early hand 'Heir endis the flytyn etc.' Altogether there is just enough evidence of one kind and another, I think, to justify placing The flytin as the earliest of the nine prints.

The beginning of the break in the third rung from the top of the ladder is found in Henryson's Orpheus etc. (No. VIII), in which there are other signs of early work – the failure ever to end the page with the end of a stanza, the bad setting of the last page, and the omission of any explicit or colophon.

The progressive deterioration of the rung is seen in the three dated books Nos. VI, II and I, The maying etc. (4 April), Golagrus etc. (8 April), and The porteous (20 April) in which the rung is split on both sides. At the same time one can observe a corresponding improvement in the standards of the printers' work. In the first book there is still no attempt to make the end of a page and the end of a stanza coincide, in the second the left-hand page ends with the end of a stanza, and in the third there is good leading between the sections of prose.

In Dunbar, The golden targe (No. IV) the rung is as in the Porteous. It is a well printed book, in which every third page ends with the end of a stanza. In the imperfect Dunbar, Barnard Stewart (No. IX), of which incidentally the

⁶ Reproduced in facsimile in Edinburgh Bibliographical Society Transactions II (1946), 393–7.

collation may have been [a⁶], an extension of the double split in the rung confirms the late date [about 9 May 1508] previously based only on the event described. But here again, as in The flytin, the leaf containing the device on the verso has a blank recto, which this time is connected with the immediately preceding leaves by nothing better than a rather late inscription.[7]

There is no evidence for the dating of either Eglamor etc. (No. III) or De Regimine (No. V). In each piece there is good leading. The first is the longest of the nine Prints except Golagrus etc. (No. II), and in the second every page ends with the end of a stanza. But in the absence of devices one cannot say more than that both pieces appear to be good, late work.

### Lost prints preserved in Manuscript

Dr Neil Ker has kindly given me prints of a manuscript poem of twenty-two eight-line stanzas in two columns in a sixteenth-century hand on flyleaves of the volume Cowie Collection no. 6 in the Mitchell Library, Glasgow. This is 'Ane ballat of the cuming of Crist and of the annunciatioun of our Ladye Compylit be maister Iohne Ballenden' and is the same poem as 'The benner of peete' by Bellenden, found twice in the Bannatyne MS. (Scottish Text Society edition I, 3 and II, 3) and beginning 'Quhen goldin Phebus mouit fra the Ram'. The Cowie MS. is of interest to students of Scottish printing, in as much as there are at the end in the same hand as that of the poem the words 'Imprentit be Iohne Scot' followed (in a larger, bolder, more formal hand) by 'Imprentit be me Iohne Scot'. Apart from this, there would appear to be no evidence that Scot printed the piece or intended to print it.

An item apparently unknown except in a transcript in a commonplace book of the Earl of Buchan acquired in 1934 by the National Library of Scotland (MS. 963, fol. 25–8), where it is said to have been printed by Waldegrave, is Archibald Napier. The new order of gooding and manuring field land with common salts (1595).

Later instances of the survival of one otherwise unknown and another almost unknown Scottish printed book are provided by a seventeenth-century MS. formerly at New Hailes and since 1937 in the National Library of Scotland (MS. 1806) which has aimed at reproducing title, ornament, signatures, page-divisions and catch-words of John Wreittoun's lost edition of George Lauder, The souldiers wishe (1628) and his edition of the same author's The Scottish souldier etc. (1629), of which a copy has survived in Huntington.[8]

---

[7] The four pieces, Nos. VIII, VI, IV and IX, show in enlargement a deterioration in Chepman's device which appears to correspond with that in Myllar's, except in the first two instances. In No. VI (The maying of 4 April) flowers and leaves on the left side look fresher than they do in No. VIII (the undated Orpheus). But Chepman's intricate device is less easy to work with in this way than Myllar's bold, simple one.

[8] For this MS. which contains also copies of little works by Lauder printed abroad but now hardly or at all known, see the list of contents in Nat. Lib. of Scot. Catalogue of MSS. II (1966), 2–3.

### The Final Cut in Rauf Coilyear

In the bibliographical note to the facsimile of The taill of Rauf Coilyear (Lekpreuik, St Andrews, 1572) issued in 1966, I foolishly neglected the warning of David Laing and wrote:

> The final cut, which has not been found elsewhere, appears to be related to the poem and to represent the King pointing a sceptre at Sir Rauf or offering him a baton, and, since it shows signs of worming, the block had perhaps been used already in an edition or editions now lost.

This blunder procured me a letter from Mr A. R. A. Hobson, in which he obligingly pointed out that I had ignored the harp on the king's sleeve and that the cut depicted David sending Uriah the husband of Bathsheba to the wars, as is narrated in II Samuel XI, 14–15:

> And it came to pass in the morning, that David wrote a letter to Joab, and sent it by the hand of Uriah. And he wrote in the letter, saying, Set ye Uriah in the forefront of the hottest battle, and retire ye from him, that he may be smitten, and die.

Mr Hobson added that the cut might have been associated with the Penitential Psalms; and in the Fairfax Murray Catalogue of French Books (I, 276–7) there are indeed shown a pair of splendidly elaborate cuts of David with Bathsheba and David with Uriah from Pigouchet's Horae of about 1502, the accompanying text being from Psalm VI, the first of the seven penitential psalms. It may be among humbler books of hours that the Rauf cut is to be traced to its origin.

### Types

The civilité type used by Bassandyne in Henryson's Fables (1571), in CL Psalmes (1575) and the letter of the Privy Council ordering every parish to advance £5 for printing the Bible (1575) and found again in, for example, Finlason's edition of The lawes and acts (1611) has been firmly established as the first civilité of all, founded by Robert Granjon at Lyons in 1557 (Carter and Vervliet[9] type A1).

A later script type has turned up in a book first given in J. P. Edmond, The Aberdeen printers (page 1) to Raban's St Andrews press. This is Andrew Melville, Viri clarissimi A. Melvini musae (1620), in which Greek words are printed with the script type of Hendrik van den Keere of Ghent of about 1570 (Carter and Vervliet type D1). Since Raban used Greek characters in Archibald Symson, Christes testament vnfolded (Edinburgh, 1620) and in his two St Andrews books of the same year, namely John Michaelson, The lawfulness of kneeling and Daniel Tilenus, Parænesis ad Scotos, he is unlikely to be the printer

[9] Harry Carter and H. D. L. Vervliet, Civilité types (Oxford Bibliographical Society, 1966).

of the little book by Andrew Melville, which was probably printed in Holland.

John Jonston, De cruenta morte Archibaldi Hunteri, a broadsheet in the National Library of Scotland printed by Waldegraue in 1590 shows the Canon (or 2-line Double-Pica) Roman attributed to François Guyot of Antwerp because it occurs with other letters of his in the anonymous specimen-sheet [about 1565] in Folger. The double serifs on both vertices of the M survive in the Edinburgh use, whereas they disappear from Antwerp printing soon after 1560. Another broadside printed by Waldegraue [1597], An epitaphe vpon Robert Bowes by William Fowler, surviving in copies in Edinburgh University Library and the Public Record Office, shows the Double-Pica Italic attributed to Guyot by its being in the Folger specimen and by a note of Christophe Plantin in his inventory of founts of 1575 where he wrote against a proof of this face 'Ascendonica Cursive de Guiot'. After having been used for the first time in Antwerp in 1557, the face was imported to England two years later by John Day.[10]

### Corrections of Titles and Authors

When the catalogue of a great library continues to miscall Lucan's poem 'Pharsalia', what hope is there of reforming the nomenclature of Middle Scots poems? 'Lament for the Makaris' has been hallowed by use and wont but must be recognized for what it is, an inspired improvement of David Laing in his edition of Dunbar, and we must firmly say of it as Betsey Prig said of Mrs Harris, 'I don't believe there's no sich a person.' Laing's title is shorter than Allan Ramsay's in The ever green, 'On the Uncertainty of Life and Fear of Death, or a Lament for the Loss of the Poets' or even the 'Lament for the Deth of the Makkaris' of Lord Hailes, R. Morison and James Sibbald. But the only authentic title is either 'I that in heill wes and gladnes' or else 'Quhen he wes sek'. Editors of Dunbar should notice such things, just as historians of mediaeval art should notice modern restorations. What is more to the point, the tenth piece in the 'Chepman and Myllar' volume containing 'I that in heill wes' is not known to have been printed by Chepman and Myllar in 1508 and so cannot be used as evidence on which to date the deaths of poets.

In my note to The maying or disport of Chaucer I wrote in 1950 that it was Lydgate,[11] 'The complaint of the black knight'; but that title appears to be the

---

[10] For discussion and illustration of the two Guyot types see H. D. L. Vervliet, Sixteenth-century printing types of the Low Countries (Amsterdam, 1968), pp. 228–9 and 286–7 and the Type Specimen Facsimiles issued under the general editorship of John Dreyfus (London. 1963), pp. 1–2 and plate 1.

Once more in 1597 the Double-Pica Italic is superbly displayed by Waldegrove in 'The Preface to the Reader' of King Jame's Daemonologie.

[11] The early inscription on the title of the Chepman and Myllar Print 'Liber probus atque amabilis atque pro auriculis audiendus [not 'arduus' as in Durkan and Ross, 136 under 'Pratt']' is someone's unconscious echo of Dunbar's tribute to Lydgate (and Gower) in another of the Prints:

Your sugurit lippis and tongis aureate
Bene to our eris cause of grete delyte.

invention of an eighteenth-century paraphrast Mr Dart. The true title is The complaynt of a louers lyfe, found in De Worde's edition of about 1525 in the British Museum (formerly Chatsworth).

Because it comes after Henryson's Orpheus in No. VIII of the Chepman and Myllar Prints, David Laing gave the poem 'Me ferlyis of this grete confusioun' to Henryson. If we were to apply this logic to the rest of the volume, we should find that (No. II) 'Thingis in kynde desyris thingis lyke' was by the author of Golagrus, (No. III) 'In all oure gardyn growis thare na flouris' was by the author of Eglamor, (No. VI) 'Qwhen þe dyvyne deliberatioun' was by Lydgate, and (No. VII) 'Devise, prowess and eke humility' was by either Dunbar or Henryson; and of course there in the tenth tract would be the evidence we have all been waiting for that Dunbar wrote the lines about Kynd Kittok! All this is great nonsense but it would be a quick and easy substitute for reasoning, and the effects would be every whit as good as those achieved by a recent process of northern wizardry. To return to Henryson, his next editor should, I think, either find a firmer ground than juxtaposition for the authorship of the lines 'Me ferlyis' or else place them among the doubtful and supposititious poems.

What are we to do when in 1603 Robert Charteris throws into Philotus as a make-weight the lovely lines

> What if a day or a month or a yeere
> Crown thy desire with a thousand wisched contentings,

and the latest American editor, whose commentary is sad stuff after Bullen and Vivian, tells us that the evidence for Campion's authorship is less certain than it was once thought to be? At such points as this, bibliography ends, and criticism begins.

## Originals of Edinburgh Translations

What originals were used in Scots translations printed in Edinburgh is a subject deserving closer attention than it has received. The porteous of noblenes of 20 April 1508 is a prose version of Alain Chartier's poem, Le bréviaire des nobles, of which (apart from texts in collected works) two editions are known to have been printed before, and one soon after, 1500. That printed at Lyons about 1498 (Pellechet-Polain 3524) is distinguished by having the following 'Rondel' at the end of the text, before the explicit:

> Vostre mestier recordez
> Nobles hommes en ce liure
> Quant vous serez discordez
> Vostre mestier recordez
> Vos faitz au nom accordez
> Se noblement voulez viure
> Vostre mestier recordez
> Nobles hommes en ce liure.

In the 1617 edition of Chartier the same lines are given within square brackets, with a note that they have been added from the manuscript.

On the other hand, in the 1484 edition of Le bréviaire there is a different poem running to 44 lines, and in the early sixteenth-century edition none.

In the Chepman and Myllar print, as in the Asloan MS., these verses inspired by though not closely translated from the 'Rondel' come immediately after the prose text:

> Nobles report your matynis in this buke
> And wysely luk ye be not contrefeit
> Nor to retrete sen leaute seikis na nuke
> And god forsuke breuily for to treit
> All that fals ar and noblis contrefeit.

It is then in the first group, the Lyons edition and any early printed and manuscript texts related to it, that editors should seek the source of The porteous.

Some other originals are easily identified. Ane breif gathering of the halie signes (Lekpreuik, 1565) derives from Sommaire recueil des signes sacrez first published in 1561. Bèze, Ane answer made the fourth [24th] day of septembre (Lekpreuik, 1562) must have been translated from the edition of the Response in which the same error 'quatrieme iour' for 'vingt quatrieme' occurs in the title. Propositions and principles of diuinitie (Waldegraue, 1591) was translated by John Penry from Theses theologicae (Geneva, 1586), just as the fuller edition from the same press (1594, reissued 1595) was based on the Genevan one of about 1591. And in a later period Phil. Nicolai, Chronologia sacra, shortly collected and augmented by Niels Michelsone (Wreittoun, 1630, reissued 1631) is a version of the work of Niels Mikkelsen Aalborg published at Copenhagen in 1628. In such cases clues can be found on the Edinburgh title-pages, and identities established with the help of, for example, Brunet, Ehrencron-Müller, or F. Gardy's bibliography of Bèze.

Problems of a more difficult nature are presented by Robert Noruell, The meroure of an Chrstiane, composed during his captiuitie at Paris (Lekpreuik, 1561), of which there are copies in Folger and Harvard and fragments in the university libraries of Cambridge and Edinburgh. Photostats of the Chalmers-Britwell-Folger copy are in the National Library of Scotland. Two of the pieces in the book are said to be translated from French by Noruell. The first, 'Death to All Humaines', is headed 'How death doeth answer maike and send: to them that do him vilipend.' It begins:

> Blindit people, fallin in fantaseis,
> Seduced & drouned, in doctrines humane,
> Why make ye me, suche pomp and obsiqueis?
> Sith that your mouthes, still exicrattes my name.
> Ye curse and warie when I your freindes clame:
> But when it commes, the diriges to sing,
> The pridfull papistes, they do me nothing blame,
> Cause gold and monie, to them I do inbring.

There follows 'The Iudgment of Minos. Vpon the preferment of Alexander the great Conquerour. Hanniball of Carthage, and Scipion the Romain, surnamed Affrican.' Here there is a hint, for this is the dialogue of Lucian that was translated by Clément Marot and published as 'Le Jugement de Minos' in L'Adolescence clémentine (Paris, 1532). The Scottish version begins:

> Alexandre.
> My vailyeant heart, full of honor & gloire
> May not suffre Hanniball to pas before
> Me, intill armes and dedes martiall:
> For suthe I thinke no man that is equall,
> Ought in dedes of armes, for to compair:
> There worthynes or actis vnto myne.

> Hanniball.
> I will defende, and manteyne the contrair, etc.

It is now possible to return to the first passage and identify it as 'La Mort à Tous Humains', part of Marot's 'Déploration de Florimond Robertet' first published about 1527 and beginning:

> Peuple seduict, endormy en tenebres
> Tant de longs iours par la doctrine d'homme,
> Pourquoy me fais tant de pompes funebres
> Puis que ta bouche inutile me nomme?
> Tu me mauldis quand tes Amys assomme,
> Mais quand ce uient qu'aux obseques on chante,
> Le Prebstre adonc, qui d'argent en a somme,
> Ne me dict pas mauldicte ne meschante.

These two lengthy pieces are the only avowed translations in the Meroure, but seven other short ones are also renderings of Marot. 'Minos' is followed by 'Psalm 5 | Werba mea auribus percipe | Psalmus 5', twelve stanzas of five lines, of which the first is:

> Vnto the wordes, that I shall say,
> If it may pleis the, len thy eare,
> To know the sore sighes and fear:
> Of my poore hart, boith nyght and day,
> Lord I the pray.

The French runs:

> Aux parolles que je veulx dire
> Plaise toy l'oreille prester,
> Et à congnoistre t'arrester
> Pourquoy mon cueur pense & souspire,
> Souverain Sire.

On earlier pages there is a group of ten 'Godlie Ballades', of which these six are translated from Marot:

'The Lords Prayer,' 14 lines beginning 'Oure Father God, which art in heauens gloir'.

'The 12. articles of our beleif,' 2 stanzas of 14 and 8 lines, beginning 'I Trow in God, the Father, Lord of all,' from 'Les articles de la Foy'.

'The ten Commandementes,' 9 stanzas of 4 lines, from 'Les Commandemens de Dieu'.

'Grace before dynner,' 8 lines beginning 'O Souerane, Lord, Pastour and heid' from 'Prière devant le repas'.

'Grace after dynner,' 8 lines beginning 'O Lord that gaue, vs in command', from 'Prière après le repas'.

'The Pellicane figuring Iesus Christ', 3 stanzas of 10 lines and a final one of 7, beginning 'The Pellicane, of the forest celest,' from 'De la Passion de Nostre Seigneur Jesuchrist', which like 'Minos' had appeared in L'Adolescence clémentine.[12]

Our translator is presumably the 'ro norvell' whose lines 'O most heich and eternall king' are in the Bannatyne Manuscript. Tedious rimester though he often is, the other facets of his Meroure may well repay inspection. So may such episodes in his life as his service with the archers of the Scottish guard, his captivity in the 'Bastillie' in 1555, and his later prosperity in Edinburgh. My present concern is merely with a link between an obscure Scots writer and the famous French one whose metrical Psalter with music adapted or composed by Louis Bourgeois gave a number of tunes to the Revised Church Hymnary of 1927. One of them, 'Les Commandemens de Dieu', originally meant for a poem that happens to be among those translated by Noruell, is used in the Church Hymnary, Third Edition, for Communion and funeral hymns, as well as being retained as the first tune for John Ellerton's evening hymn 'The day Thou gavest, Lord, is ended'.[13]

W. BEATTIE

[12] In the order in which the pieces are cited above, they are in Noruell on fol. 50, 53, 61 and 41–3. For the corresponding passages in Marot see the Guiffrey edition IV, 391, II, 29–44, V, 209, IV, 418–22 and V, 78. Alternatively the two pieces 'Minos' and 'De la Passion' included in L'Adolescence clémentine may be found on pages 43 and 136 of V. L. Saulnier's text of that collection (1958), and 'La Mort à Tous Humains' on page 152 of C. A. Mayer's edition of Marot's Œuvres lyriques (1964). Mr Mayer's bibliography (Geneva, 1954) and his other works on Marot should be consulted by anyone who may wonder which French texts Noruell might have seen.

[13] At the time of writing (January, 1973) I am indebted to the Revd Thomas H. Keir, D.D. for kindly answering my enquiry before the publication of the Hymnary.

# 10

# The Fair Isle Spanish Armada Shipwreck

## Introduction

In the summer of 1970 people in Shetland were startled by the news that a heavy bronze gun had been recovered from the underwater wreck of *El Gran Grifon* at the exact spot on the coast of Fair Isle where by tradition that Spanish Armada ship had been lost in 1588.

The present paper is an attempt to review the circumstances of this famous shipwreck and its aftermath. Except for one publication dated 1959 the written sources used have not been cited at first hand but through the relevant section of the huge manuscript record of Shetland wrecks compiled by the late R. Stuart Bruce, C.A., one of a family of landowners at Symbister, Whalsay, Shetland. Mr Bruce bequeathed this manuscript to Mr Thomas Henderson, now Curator of the Shetland County Museum, who kindly gave me access to it, added much helpful guidance and information and produced the photographs. In addition to his qualifications as an antiquarian Mr Henderson is a former seaman, and as a native of Dunrossness in Shetland is well acquainted with Fair Isle. All dates are here given in the New Style. I am much indebted to Mr Thomas Henry, Lerwick, for a brilliant interpretation of the route of *El Gran Grifon*, for superimposing that route on a map provided by the Shetland County Roads Department, and for drawing the maps of Fair Isle.

## Baptism of Fire

Mr Bruce says that *El Gran Grifon* was a ship of Rostock, 650 tons, an armed merchantman carrying thirty-eight guns mostly small iron pieces. She was the flagship of the urca or hulk squadron of twenty-three hired transports and store ships, mostly Dutch and German, and carried the squadron's admiral, Don Juan Gomez de Medina. He has been frequently confused with the Duke of Medina Sidonia, the commander-in-chief of the whole Armada, and traditions involving this error are accordingly suspect. His ship's company included forty-three mariners and 243 soldiers.

In *The Defeat of the Spanish Armada* published in 1959, the author, the late Garret Mattingly, professor of European history at Columbia University, gives a vivid account from Spanish sources of an event in the English Channel on 3 August 1588. This was *El Gran Grifon* straggling behind the seaward horn of the Armada crescent and being beset by a number of English ships which fired heavily on her. The foremost of these 'glided abreast of her, gave her a broadside, came about and gave her another, then crossed her stern and raked her at half-musket shot'. From circumstantial evidence Professor Mattingly identifies this English ship as Drake's *Revenge*. While the whole Spanish right rear became hotly engaged *El Gran Grifon* went out of control but was rescued by galleases sent by the Duke to take her in tow. Although this was a short action involving a minority of ships on either side '. . . Spanish casualties were officially reported as sixty killed and seventy wounded . . . the heaviest losses of any day in the Channel. Probably the terrible punishment taken by the *Gran Grifon* accounts for most of the casualties,'; Mr Bruce states that she had forty shot holes in her hull.

### Battling with the Sea

This severe mauling was a poor preparation on board *El Gran Grifon* for what was to come after the defeated Armada moved up into the North Sea and began to encounter the gales which ultimately destroyed exactly half the fleet of 130 ships. In volume XI of the New Series of the *Transactions of the Royal Historical Society*, p. 41 *et seq.*, Major Martin A. S. Hume makes extensive use of the diary of a man who was on board *El Gran Grifon*, printed in Spanish by Captain Fernandez Duro from the manuscript in the Royal Academy of History, Madrid. From this it appears that *El Gran Grifon* after losing sight of the main body through the night of 17-18 August when north of Orkney moved west between Orkney and Shetland in company with three other ships, the big Venetian *La Trinidad Valencera* and two hulks, the *Castillo Negro* and another known only as the 'bark of Hamburg'.

For twelve days they struggled slowly to the west against head winds making hardly any way. On 31 August the Hamburg bark signalled she was sinking. Her company of 250 men was quickly transferred to the other three ships but her stores went down with her in the rapid foundering. On the night of 2 September the *Castillo Negro* sank to be heard of no more and the same night the *Valencera* disappeared though actually she did not sink. *El Gran Grifon* struggled on alone against head wind, fog and sleet till 17 September, when in a great storm with the men at the pumps night and day unable to keep the water down it was decided to turn round and run before the wind for Norway. The diarist is now quoted verbatim:

'We ran back before the wind for three days when we sighted an island in Scotland in about 57½° north latitude[1] and after we had gone about ten leagues further we fell in with a north-west wind which invited us to turn our faces once more towards dear Spain, especially as the moon entered a new quarter and we thought the wind would hold. So we turned back and sailed for three days more to the latitude we had been in before. But when we got there we were

[1] Mr Henry suggests that this was Mormond Hill near Fraserburgh, which looks like an island from a short distance out to sea. This notion of a considerable southward reach, possible within the time stated, solves an otherwise inexplicable problem.

Bronze gun from *El Gran Grifón* in Shetland County Museum

*Obverse*

*Reverse*

Four-real coin of Philip II, minted in Toledo, recovered from wreck of *El Gran Grifón*

Suggested route of El
Gran Grifon

100    200    300
Miles

only fit to die, for the wind was so strong and the sea so wild that the waves
mounted to the skies, knocking the ship about so, that the men were all exhausted, and yet were unable to keep down the water that leaked through our
gaping seams. If we had not had the wind astern we could not have kept afloat
at all. But by God's mercy during the next two days the weather moderated
and we were able to patch up some of the leaks with ox-hides and planks.'
[In view of the next date given by the diarist the two days of moderate weather
must have been the first two of these last three days sailing west, the weather
worsening again on the third day.] 'And so we ran till September 23 when the
wind rose against us and we decided to turn back again and try to reach
Scotland.

'On the 25th we sighted some islands that the pilots said were Scottish and
inhabited by savages'. [Possibly some of the most northerly of the Hebrides.]
'And so we sailed till the 26th to the N.E. in search of land. On that day we

sighted other islands[2] which we tried to avoid so as not to be lost. The weather then got so stormy that our poor repairs were all undone and we had to keep both pumps always going to keep the water down. So we decided to run for the first Scottish land even if we had to run the hulk ashore.

'Later in the afternoon of the 26th we were troubled to see an island to wind-ward of us, for it was getting dark and we feared to be amongst islands in the night.

'We had hoped we were free of them.

'During the night we gave ourselves up for lost, for the seas ran mountains high and the rain fell in torrents. At two in the morning we saw an island right ahead of us,[3] which, as may be supposed, filled us with consternation, after all the tribulation we had passed through. But God in His mercy at that moment sent us a sudden gleam of light through the dark night and so enabled us to avoid the danger.

'Then blackness fell as dense as before.

'Two hours afterwards another island[4] loomed up before us so close that it seemed impossible to weather it. But God came to our aid as usual and sent a more vivid gleam than before.

'It was so bright that I asked whether it was the daylight. So we kept off the island, though much troubled, for we should have been lost if we had not doubled it. This was the island of Cream where we had decided to bring up if we could not reach Scotland, though we did not recognise it until later as we had run farther than we thought. At dawn two hours later we discovered it, and in fear of the heavy sea we tried to get near the island again, but after trying for four hours against wind and tide we found it impossible. The sea kept giving us such dreadful blows that truly our one thought was that our lives were ended, and each one of us reconciled himself to God as well as he could and prepared for the long, long journey that seemed inevitable.

'As to force the hulk any more would only have ended it and our lives the sooner, we determined to cease our efforts. The poor soldiers, too, lost all spirit to work at the pumps. The two companies – 230 men in all and 40 we had taken from the other ship, had pumped incessantly and worked with buckets, but the water still increased till there were thirteen spans of water over the car-lings (as they call them) and all efforts failed to reduce it an inch, so we gave way to despair and each one called upon the Virgin Mary to be our intermediary in so bitter a pass: and we looked towards the land with full eyes and hearts, as the reader may imagine. And God send that he may be able to imagine the small-est part of what it was, for after all there is a great difference between those who suffer and those who look upon suffering from afar off.

'At last when we thought all hope was gone except through God and His holy Mother, Who never fails those who call upon Him – at two o'clock in the afternoon we sighted an island ahead of us. This was Fair Isle, where we arrived

[2] Probably Sula Sgeir, North Rona, Stack Skerry and Sule Skerry.
[3] Probably Papa Westray in Orkney.
[4] Probably North Ronaldsay, which he calls Cream.

at Sunset, much consoled, though we saw we should still have to suffer. But anything was better than drinking salt water.

'We anchored in a sheltered spot we found this day of our great peril, September 27, 1588'.

### When came the Shipwreck?

Here we must interrupt the diarist's narrative to speculate on what happened next, for most tantalisingly he describes neither the disembarkation nor the sinking of the ship; why, one will never know.

It is certain that the ship sank at Stromshellier, on the east coast of the isle. It is a place no-one would choose to put a ship into as it is a narrow opening with no beach and terminating in a cave; but it has a ledge of rock which is the only possible place the men could have got ashore, and the tradition in Fair Isle is that they got ashore on to this ledge off the lower yards of the ship as she struck. Another tradition in the isle, namely, that the Spaniards came in over the land in shining armour so suddenly that the people thought they were a 'heavenly host', supports the idea of a quick scramble up cliffs rather than a stepping ashore from ship's boats as stated long after in 1633 by Robert Menteith, an Orkney laird, in a published description of Orkney and Shetland. He definitely confused Admiral Gomez de Medina with the Duke of Medina Sidonia, so he is not quite reliable.

The diarist describes *El Gran Grifon* as anchoring in a sheltered spot, but his other evidence shows conclusively that she was leaking very badly. Mr Henderson's theory is that an attempt was made to beach the vessel in Swarts Gio, but that the run of the tide through the Sound o da Fless diverted her into Stromshellier. Assuming that this is what happened, is it possible to guess when? The diarist times the ship's arrival at sunset on 27 September, but states (see below) that 'three hundred men of us' landed on 28 September without being able to save any of their provisions. This strongly suggests that the ship remained at anchor through the night of 27–28 September, and that in daylight on the 28th the beaching attempt was made which turned into sudden shipwreck with loss of all provisions, but with no loss of life, as none is mentioned by the diarist. It would seem to be impossible to get nearer the truth than this. It may be added that as the cliffs in the vicinity are fairly high, all this could easily have happened without any of the island's inhabitants being aware of it.

At all events, one thing is certain, these Spaniards now stood on *terra firma* after almost incredible experiences traversing the wild seas between Orkney and Shetland three times on east-west courses and weaving a perilous way through the Orkney Islands in appalling weather, manning the pumps the whole time.

### On Fair Isle

The diarist goes on: 'We found the island peopled by seventeen householders in huts more like hovels than anything else. They are savage people whose usual

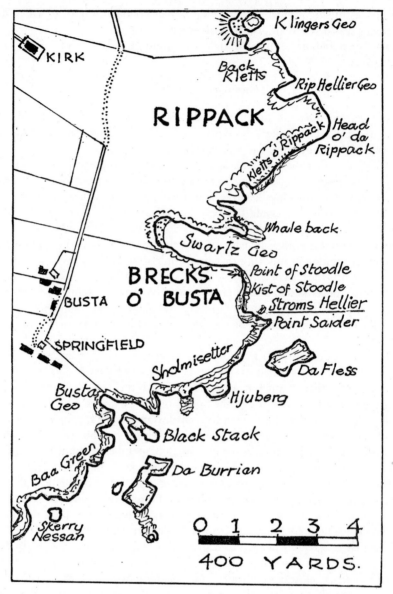

food is fish without bread, except a few Barley meal bannocks cooked over the embers of the fuel they use, which they make or extract from the earth and call turf.

'They have some cattle, quite enough for themselves, for they rarely eat meat. They depend mainly upon the milk and butter from their cows, using their sheeps' wool principally for clothing. They are a very dirty people, neither Christians nor altogether heretics. It is true they confess that the doctrine that once a year is preached to them by people sent from another island nine leagues

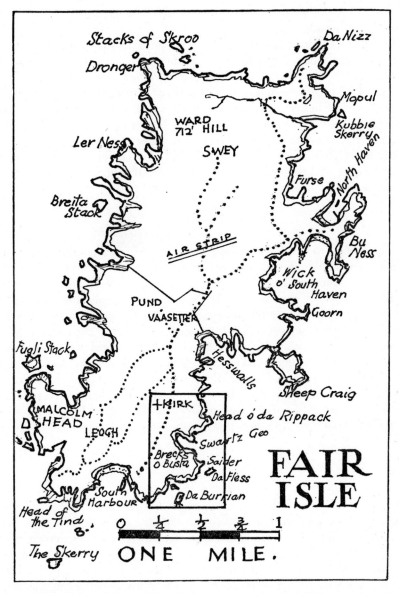

off is not good, but they say they dare not contradict it, which is a pity. Three hundred men of us landed on the island, but could save none of our provisions.

'From that day, September 28 till November 14, we lost fifty of our men, most of them dying of hunger, amongst others the master and mate of the hulk. We had decided to send a messenger to the governor of the next island to beg for some boats to carry us to Scotland to seek rescue, but the weather was so heavy that we could not send until October 27, when the weather was fine and they went.

'They have not yet returned in consequence of the violence of the sea' – and here the diary ends.

It seems clear from this description that the population of Fair Isle at the time was under 200. The sudden addition of another 300 mouths to feed without any of the provisions which *El Gran Grifon* had carried must have put a fearful strain on the island's resources, so that it is not surprising that fifty of the in-comers died of hunger. The payment made to the islanders by the Spaniards according to some accounts could at the time have made no practical difference. (Spanish coins have reputedly been found and given away.)

Mr Bruce states that Spanish grave mounds were visible at a particular spot near the edge of a cliff which became so eroded that about 1908 some bones could be seen protruding.

### The Rescue

The next island to which appeal for help was sent was the mainland of Shetland, and as a result Andrew Umphray of Berrie, near Scalloway, who was tacksman of Fair Isle at the time, sent a vessel which conveyed the Spaniards to Quendale, at the south end of the long island. There Mr Bruce states the men camped while their admiral was hospitably entertained by the laird of Quendale, Malcolm Sinclair, who was also lay-reader and vicar of Dunrossness. While precise dates are not available, the Spaniards are believed to have stayed in Dunrossness between three and four weeks, at the end of which time Umphray conveyed them to Anstruther, for which he was paid 3,000 marks by Gomez de Medina. Mr Bruce disproves the tradition that Umphray conveyed them further to Dunkirk. From Anstruther they actually went to Edinburgh, where a total of about 1200 Spaniards from various shipwrecks eventually gathered.

### In Scotland

The chief description of the ship's company of *El Gran Grifon* in Scotland comes from the Diary, published for the Wodrow Society, of the Rev. James Melville, minister of Anstruther, to whom the magistrates turned for advice on the arrival of the Spaniards in Umphray's ship 'earlie in the morning, be brak of day', and who with the help of an interpreter granted an interview and first broke the news of the destruction of the Armada to Admiral Gomez de Medina, 'a verie reverend man of big stature, and grave and stout countenance, grey-headed and verie humble lyk' who explained his and his men's predicament. Melville made it clear that despite their connection with 'the graitest enemie of Chryst, the Pape of Rome' and the violence done in their country to peaceable Scotsmen, the Spaniards 'sould find na thing amangs us bot Christian pity and marks of mercie and almes leaving to God to work in their harts concerning Relligion as it pleased him'. Medina disclaimed any responsibility for the laws and order of his country's kirk, but asserted that at Calles (Cadiz) he had shown courtesy and favour to 'divers Scotsmen wha knew him . . . and as he supposit, sum of this sam town of Anstruther.' The bailies then granted permission to the Admiral and his officers to go to lodgings for refreshment, which was followed that night by personal hospitality to them in his house by the feudal overlord of Anstruther, who also gave permission to the soldiers to land and 'ly all togidder, to the nomber of threttin score, for the maist part young berdles men, sillie, trauchled and houngered, to the quhilk a day or twa, keall, pattage and fische was giffen'.

This pattern of compassionate treatment was repeated in Edinburgh by everyone concerned, from King James VI and down. The common soldiers and sailors of course fared on the whole least well, but letters from Englishmen in Scotland to England, preserved in the Calendar of State Papers relating to Scotland and Mary, Queen of Scots, Vol. IX, stress the great hospitality accorded to the Spanish officers by the Scottish nobles, one letter going so far as to allege that a plot was hatched for the invasion of England through Scotland. A writer in *Chambers's Journal* for November, 1934, states that King James hired four vessels to convey the Spaniards home and successfully prevailed on Queen Elizabeth to forbid molestation of some who had been driven into an English port by stress of weather.

Admiral Gomez de Medina subsequently proved the consistency of his character by giving warm hospitality at Cadiz to the men off a ship from Anstruther after getting them released from arrest, praising Scotland to his king, inquiring for the laird and minister of the town and his host, and sending 'hame many commendationes', this incident also being described by the Rev. James Melville.

One very interesting fact is that neither in the account given by the diarist aboard *El Gran Grifon* nor in Melville's report of his conversation with Gomez de Medina is there one word about the murder of Spaniards by Fair Islanders. The traditions about this, though very circumstantial, thus fall under suspicion. So much for 1588.

## First Attempts at Diving

The Decreets of the Admiralty Court of Scotland, vol. 35, give details of the financial transactions carried out around 1730 by Captain Jacob Row of London for diving on the wreck of *El Gran Grifon*. As could be expected with a storeship, no treasure was found. Captain Row was diving on the wreck as late as 1740, but one of his men being drowned, he gave up the attempt, and there is no record or tradition of any further attempt till 1970.

## A Question of Jurisdiction

In 1965–9 a company from England carried out successful diving off the Out Skerries, Shetland, on the Dutch East India ship *De Liefde*, wrecked in 1711, and brought up 4,320 coins in one chest. Part of this find was sold by auction in London in 1970 and was reputed to realise some £17,000.

The publicity which this find received, coupled with the complete absence of any control over diving efforts of the kind, so perturbed Mr Henderson, Curator of Shetland County Museum, that he decided, with the complete approval of the Museum Committee, to propose to Shetland County Council that application be made to the Commissioners of Crown Lands that a lease be given to the Council of areas of the sea bed round Shetland where fourteen wrecks of historical significance are known to lie. The Commissioners agreed, and granted the lease for a nominal yearly sum. Under this arrangement, which is unique in Britain, no-one may interfere with the seabed at any of these sites without permission from the Shetland County Council, who in this matter are advised by Mr Henderson. To date permission has been given to dive on five of these wrecks under very strict conditions, the main ones being that due respect be paid to the historical and archaeological aspects of the wreck concerned; and that such sites be properly surveyed and copies of plans be submitted to Shetland County Council at regular intervals during operations. In every case where permission has been given under this arrangement the divers have conscientiously adhered to the conditions laid down.

### Diving on El Gran Grifon

In 1970 permission was given to Mr Colin Martin of Kelso to investigate *El Gran Grifon*. Mr Martin had been second-in-command of a team diving on a Spanish Armada wreck off the coast of Ireland. He and his brother Simon and a friend Mr Christopher Oldfield, were the original team but they were joined in mid-season by a Royal Naval sub-aqua team. The work was at first exploratory but they almost immediately located the ship and against their expectations did so precisely where Fair Isle tradition said she lay at Stromshellier. The work went on from July to September 1970. The main find was a fine bronze loaded gun of demi-saker type, measuring eight feet overall, and weighing about three-quarters of a ton. There were also found part of a much larger bronze gun and a number of iron guns including a couple made of wrought-iron bars hooped together, a medieval type obsolete long before 1588, which illustrates how poorly the hulks were armed. A number of shot including shot for musket and arquebus, some chambers for breech-loading cannon, an iron rudder pintle, six massive lead ingots for casting shot and one four-real coin minted in Toledo completed the finds. All are now in the Shetland County Museum and happily with Government help the Museum has acquired ownership. In the meantime Shetland County Council will not grant permission to anyone else to dive on *El Gran Grifon* so long as Mr Colin Martin is interested.

### A Legal Anomaly

The control arrangement, which was made just in time for the investigation of *El Gran Grifon*, and the actual finds made at that wreck, combine to throw into stark prominence a ridiculous Scottish legal anomaly: any ownerless object of value found on the land is declared Crown property, the finder being suitably rewarded and the object deposited in a museum; but fifty yards below low water springs an ownerless object of value is only retained by the Crown for a year and a day, after which, if no claim is forthcoming, it is sold off by the Customs like any ordinary piece of wreckwood.

T. M. Y. MANSON

# The Political Attitudes of William Drummond of Hawthornden

Recognised as a poet with a derivative style, acknowledged by his contemporaries as a notable historian (but ignored by those moderns who fail to find his work a certain quarry for the nuggets of their own research), known – with a certain amount of amusement – as the inventor of perhaps rather absurd mathematical and mechanical devices, William Drummond of Hawthornden appears little more than a minor figure in the cultural life of early seventeenth century Europe. He was in fact a typical and not untalented representative of the gentleman-scholar of early Stuart times; and his apparently disparate activities, reflected in the books he collected and read, were the closely connected interests of a man with a uniform attitude towards nature and humanity, albeit an essentially conservative one.[1]

It was natural for Drummond, a member of the lesser aristocracy and a man of intelligence, to keep abreast of political events in Scotland, for as we shall see he believed he owed it to his social position to be interested in, if not directly involved in, current affairs of state. He was no practical politician; accordingly, with his bookish nature and his almost hermit-like withdrawal from human society, his involvement took the form of political writing, most of which was done during that major period of crisis in Scottish affairs from 1638 to 1643. The extent of his political influence is difficult to assess. None of his political pamphlets was published in his own lifetime, but it is clear that they circulated to a certain extent among his friends in manuscript copies.[2] In facing the problems of his time Drummond was a not uncritical supporter of the monarchy, a Protestant but not an extreme Presbyterian; he saw a conflict between Covenant and King which he could not easily reconcile for himself until extremist elements had made war on Charles I. It was a dilemma in which other Scots found themselves, such as the covenanted Montrose and Sir James Balfour of Denmilne, one which each ultimately resolved in his own way.

---

[1] Robert H. Macdonald, *The Library of Drummond of Hawthornden* (Edinburgh, 1971), lists the books known or surmised to have been in Drummond's library, and comments on some of the ideas which influenced him.

[2] *The Works of William Drummond of Hawthornden* (Edinburgh, 1711) (hereafter cited as *Works*), saw the first complete publication of his political writings; 'Considerations to the King' and 'An Apologetical Letter' appeared earlier in the 'Memorials of State' appendix in the 1655, 1680, 1681, and 1682 editions of his *History of the Five Jameses*. The original manuscripts (deposited with other Drummond manuscripts by the Society of Antiquaries of Scotland) are in National Library of Scotland MS 2058. Contemporary copies are in NLS Adv. MSS 13.2.5 and 32.4.9.

Drummond already had a formed political attitude before these events took place, and in his political writings expressed this general attitude in relationship to specific events. He did not deliberately expound a political theory as Buchanan or Bodin did, and the nature of his thought must be extracted from his writings. His 'Considerations to the King', dated December 1632,[3] criticises Charles I for his determination to recognise the earl of Menteith and restore him to a revived earldom of Strathearn; he points out that this would be a danger to the crown, the elevation of a possible claimant to the throne who could become a pretext for foreign invasion or a rallying point for insurrection. In 'An Apologetical Letter', dated 2 March 1635 and addressed to an unnamed noble or perhaps to the king himself,[4] he puts forward the argument that when the crown is criticised or 'libelled' by the people, the king's duty is to act in such a way that he maintains his authority. Prosecution is not necessarily the best method because it enhances the significance of the criticism; yet criticism has a legitimate place, for 'the Voice of the People should not be kept up from the ears of a Prince'.[5] According to the nature of the criticism it can be ignored, or carefully considered 'by good reason' and acted upon if necessary. No matter what the complaint, rigorous punishment is the wrong reaction; a good king should act with clemency towards his subjects to maintain his authority and prevent the growth of frustration and rebellion among his people.

Other political works of Drummond include 'A Speech which may be called a Prophecy' addressed on 2 May 1639 to those who supported the National Covenant; and 'Skiamachia', an answer to a declaration made by the Commissioners of the General Assembly in January 1643 as part of the moves leading up to the Solemn League and Covenant with the English Parliamentarians, a move which Drummond very much deprecated.[6] In addition Drummond appears to have written several satirical pieces, 'The Magical Mirror' (1 April 1639), 'The Load-Star', and 'Considerations to the Parliament' (September 1639) in which he 'justifies' the point of view of the Covenanters.[7] But the most important of his works at this time was 'Irene; a Remonstrance for Concord, Amity and Love amongst His Majesty's Subjects', written towards the end of 1638 after the publication on 22 September of a royal declaration to the people of Scotland annulling the Court of High Commission, the Book of Canons and the Five Articles of Perth, and ordering the meeting of a free General Assembly.[8]

This work brings together most of the main features of Drummond's political thinking, and is worth describing in some detail. In Drummond's view Charles I has perfectly fulfilled his obligations as monarch; he has redressed the most important grievances of his Scottish people, he has acted with clemency towards them, and he has with reason and wisdom created a situation whereby the state may be preserved from destruction and society from disintegration.

---

[3] *Works*, p. 129.  [4] *Ibid.*, p. 132.  [5] *Ibid.*, p. 133.
[6] *Ibid.*, pp. 179, 190.  [7] *Ibid.*, pp. 174, 183, 185.
[8] *Ibid.*, p. 163; *Register of the Privy Council of Scotland*, 2nd ser. iii (Edinburgh, 1901), pp. 64–7.

'He not only giveth way to our Zeal, graciously assenting to all our Desires, but condescendeth, yea commandeth, that our own Writ should be current, and imbraced by all his Subjects.' It is now for the other ranks of society to respond in the proper way, to 'run, nay, take wings, with Acclamations, Applauses, lengthned Showts, and bursting Joys to meet him'; for 'It is the Duty of every Man, not only to rest satisfied with this fair Way and Entrance to Peace, Concord and Unanimity, which the Prince most graciously hath yielded unto, but to endeavour and use all possible Means and Industry, that they may be permanent, lasting, and as eternal'.[9]

Acceptance of and obedience to the royal concession is the basis of an effective state, for the people have no right to question their rulers, who have that 'particular Blessing from God, to be instructed in what is most for the Weal of their People, more than the People themselves'. Majority rule leads to anarchy; 'The greater Number, rejecting the Obedience and Yoke of the fewer, would make all Things common, or every Thing their own: Servants should violently over-run their Masters, . . . Children their Parents, . . . the Poor the Rich, and all Civil Order be overturn'd'. Drummond perhaps incautiously points out that 'to League a People, is to make them know their Strength and Power', a fact of which the leaders of the Covenanting movement were well aware, but he qualifies this by asserting that 'a League is an insatiable Monster' enthralling all men, and, without a natural head, leading to internecine divisions and ultimate chaos. Even where, as in the present case, the confederation is for the benefit of the true protestant religion, the subsequent divisions would 'bring Desolation to the Country, and at last, weaken and confound Religion, to the great Contentment and long Expectation of the Church of Rome'.[10] In Drummond's opinion a Roman victory would be to the detriment of both disputing parties.

In the next section of the work Drummond attacks those involved in the movement against the King. They are 'Men full of shameless Hopes' whose actions are hypocritical, seeking their own selfish ends in the name of fallacious principles; 'they make Pretence of the affairs of the Commonwealth', with 'Propositions fair in Appearance, ugly in Effects, sweet to the Taste, loathsom to the Stomach'; and their religious thought is no more than 'the Effects of Atheism'. Since these men include members of the nobility and leaders of the church, they are able to delude the common people. Yet in the long run they cannot win: 'a Prince's Estate deeply rooted by Time and Power, by Reverence and Respect supported, and establish'd by a Succession of many Kings, is not so easily undermin'd', and moreover, 'God, who raised Kings above you, holdeth Himself wrong'd in their Wrongs, and revengeth the Injuries done unto them.' Ultimately no-one will benefit from the situation, the nobility least of all. Those 'who do Falshood to their Superiors, teach Falshood to their Inferiors' will find 'that Stone, which you have thrown at your Princes Heads, may be hurled back again upon your own'.[11]

Drummond is not surprised that some members of the nobility should be involved in insurrection for he can quote many historical examples of this from

---

[9] *Works*, pp. 163–4.          [10] *Ibid*., p. 166.          [11] *Ibid*., pp. 167–8.

the past; but to find men of the church involved, 'the principal *Atlasses* of Peace, the strongest Chains of Union and Concord ... is more than most pitiful'. The 'Holy Chain betwixt Heaven and Earth' has been profaned, and the clergy are not performing their proper duty.[12] He regards the cause of religious dissension as trivial: 'Ye make Divisions for Formalities, Matters not essential to Religion'.[13] The anarchy of civil war should not come from such minor disagreements.

In the final passage Drummond ceases to address the people of Scotland and creates the image of Scotland addressing the King, reviewing difficulties in the past and in the present, and appealing for her people. 'Cure their Sickness by the indulgent Means of Clemency, not by the Severity of Justice'. The people of Scotland 'love that Name of the Liberties of their Country so dear ... that without it they hold their Fortunes lost ... They have also considered, that if your Power shall be in some Things by them restrain'd, and more narrowly limited than was your Predecessors, yet shall you leave your Power and King-dom more lasting and durable to your Successors.'[14] King and People are part of the concord of the state – neither should seek conflict with the other.

From this very brief survey of Drummond's political works it would appear that they contain some inconsistencies. The king is a sovereign and absolute monarch, the vicegerent of God; yet his subjects have the right and power to criticise, with some expectation that their criticism will not be disregarded. The king ought to rule with love and clemency, hearing complaints and acting on them; but even if he does not, the people must obey him in all things. In terms of modern thinking Drummond is confused: at times he writes as though the monarchy was absolute, at others as though he accepted more democratic ideas of monarchic restraint. Overall lies his fear of civil war, of the disruption of the state. A closer analysis of Drummond's opinions, from the accepted commonplace beliefs of his time to the personal arguments he uses, may remove the inconsistencies and will elucidate what was in his mind.

All political thinking must have behind it a consistent view of the nature of the universe and especially of the place of human society within it. There was nothing original about Drummond's conception; he accepted the familiar, commonplace belief of the nature of things taken for granted by the ordinary educated man of his time, 'the idea of cosmic order which was one of the genuine ruling ideas of the age' in Western Europe.[15] Based on Augustinian and Thomist theology modified by renaissance neo-Platonic doctrine, it set up a comprehensive, theocentric, hierarchical system inclusive of all nature, from inanimate objects, plant and animal life, through man, the planets, stars and the angels, to God himself, the controller and creator of all. Each hierarchy was linked together, from the lowest to the highest, to form a series of degrees. This was metaphorically represented as a ladder or a chain, Pope's 'vast chain of being', whereby Man, rising above his earthly imperfections, could strive

[12] *Ibid.*, pp. 169–70.        [13] *Ibid.*, p. 171.        [14] *Ibid.*, p. 173.
[15] E. M. W. Tillyard, *The Elizabethan world picture* (Harmondsworth, 1963), p. 7.

towards heaven; or, in another frequently-used metaphor, the components of the universe embodied a formal cosmic dance to the music of the spheres, each in his own place, yet in continual motion under God's direction.

Clear indications of his belief in this conception of universal order are to be found in Drummond's poetry and in his prose writings.[16] In 'An Hymne of the Fairest Faire' (based on Ronsard's 'Hymne de l'Éternité'),[17] Drummond gives an explicit picture of the universe. God is at the centre of all things, 'Sequestred from this Earth, in purest light' (l.19) where he 'giu'st Lawes, and dost this Word command' (l.26), surrounded by a hierarchy of angels, 'immortall Traines/of Intellectual Pow'rs' (ll.164–5). Below them

> Thy hand-Maide *Nature* thy great Steppes doth trace,
> The Source of second Causes, gold Chaine
> That linkes this Frame, as thou it should ordaine (ll.182–4).

Nature includes the planets,

> . . . those Bodies faire and greate
> Which faint not in their Course nor change their State, . . .
> Times purpled Maskers, then doe them advance,
> As by sweete Musicke in a measur'd Dance (ll.187–8, 193–4).

Drummond is deeply influenced by the conception of world order and within the space of only twelve lines uses all three of the basic metaphors – the 'great Steppes' (or ladder), the 'gold Chaine' and the 'measur'd Dance'. But what concerned Drummond most was the position of Man in this hierarchy. He is above the beasts and inanimate objects through his ability to reason, but, because deficient though not lacking in spirituality, he is below the angels; accordingly he is the central link of the Universe. 'Inferiour things bee in Man more noblie than they exist, superiour thinges more meanely, celestiall thinges fauour him, earthly thinges are vassaled vnto him, hee is the knot and Band of both'.[18] Man, the last created being, comprehends in himself the sum of all creation, the conflicting principles of materialism and spirituality which only his power of reason can resolve; he is, after God, the key to the universe, the Pythagorean microcosm.

Each degree of the cosmic order itself contains a linked hierarchy, the dolphin, the eagle, the lion, the oak, the rose, the diamond each being the leader of its own class, just as God is at the head of all and the emperor is at the head of human society; each political state has its own social hierarchy with its chief magistrate (its king) at the head. It is here that the political consequences of a belief in this consistent view of the universe become clear. Because God is at the head of a universal hierarchy, the lion is the leader of a hierarchy of animals and a king reigns over a hierarchy of people. It is a philosophy of unity, and a

[16] L. E. Kastner, *The poetical works of William Drummond* (Scottish Text Society, Edinburgh, 1913) (hereafter cited as Kastner), is the definitive edition of the poems; it also contains the prose work, 'A Cypresse Grove' and other miscellaneous items.

[17] Kastner, ii, p. 37.

[18] 'Cypresse Grove' (ll. 1015–18), Kastner, ii, p. 98.

situation which exists in one degree must be balanced by a similar situation in all degrees. Argument and discussion is based on the correspondence or analogies between the degrees, and at this time the majority of men thought in this way[19]; even George Buchanan, although he was to give his argument a radical twist unusual for his time, could argue in his *De jure regni apud Scotos* that a monarch is essential to the body politic because a physician is necessary to look after the ills of the human body.[20] Accordingly within this particular philosophic framework, human society and its political structure was natural and pre-ordained. A king ruled as God's vicegerent over the members of his state, members graded in mutually exclusive social classes. Because God imposed natural law on the universe, the king gave law to his people; because the planets followed the paths allocated to them by God, the people were bound to obey the commands of their king.

Clearly the position of the monarch within this cosmic conception of society was a powerful one, and, with insistence on total obedience from the people, could be the basis for a theory of absolute government. James VI and I, his kingship menaced by the thinking of presbyterians, puritans and catholics, extended his own political doctrine to this extent. His *Basilicon Doron* [Macdonald 843] gives a picture of the king as the father of his people, a point developed with others in *The Kings maiesties speach to ... this present parliament ... anno Dom. 1609* [Macdonald 847],[21] where, invoking argument by correspondence to its fullest extent, James proved that kingship is a divine institution with power comparable to that of God, that the absolute obedience of a child to his father is required of his people, and that, because universal order was based on degrees, democratic ideas of equality were unnatural.

Drummond knew these writings of his king well, and acquiesced in them to a certain extent; for him, as for James, kingship is necessary, democracy creates anarchy, and obedience is the key to order. 'Monarchy, for any thing I could learn, by a long continued reading of Books [is], in my Judgment, the best Form of Government';[22] 'Question not the Thrones of Kings, revive not your old Equalities of Nature; Authority is that Chain which linketh you together'.[23] But at the same time he saw that absolute monarchic power can be abused, that some form of limitation on the activities of an individual monarch might be necessary.

Within the framework of the widely held philosophy of divine universal order there was room for non-absolutist political thinking; this, too, was a commonplace of renaissance political thought in Western Europe, and James

---

[19] For argument by correspondence, see W. H. Greenleaf, *Order, empiricism and politics* (Oxford, 1964), pp. 21–6.

[20] George Buchanan, *De jure regni apud Scotos* (Edinburgh, 1579); modern translation by Charles Flinn Arrowood, *Powers of the crown in Scotland* (Austin, Texas, 1949), pp. 50–1.

[21] Books from Drummond's Library are identified by a 'Macdonald' number, referring to the numbered items in Robert H. Macdonald, *op. cit.*

[22] 'A speech ... before the circular tables', *Works*, p. 219.

[23] 'Irene', *ibid.*, p. 169.

VI and I, by extending the doctrine towards absolutism, was the innovator. Briefly the generally accepted attitude asserted that, although the king through his birth is appointed by God to rule and his people owe him obedience, yet, because the people are God's people also, the King has a responsibility towards them and the people themselves have rights which he must not ignore. A good king rules responsibly for the benefit of his people; the bad king or tyrant ignores his people and rules without reference to their welfare. Drummond expresses the idea of the good king clearly. 'The Preservation of Subjects, is the chief and principal Law God and Nature hath imposed on Princes'; the king must regard 'the People . . . as Children, and he their Father, they as a Flock, he their Pastour', and deliberately seek their love. The divine nature of kingship consists fundamentally of the monarch's love for his people, for he cannot otherwise obtain their love and obedience; love 'doth not consist, except by a certain Reflection and reciprocal Being' because 'God loved us before we could love him'.[24]

Accordingly the king must rule with clemency, overlooking the small peccadilloes of the people, acting 'as he would have God Eternal towards him, who, full of Mercy, spareth peopled Cities'.[25] His justice must be mitigated with mercy, he must hear reasonably the complaints of his people and maintain his authority by acting on them, and above all he must make his decisions with the counsel of his advisors. 'It is great Wisdom in a Prince not to reject and disdain them who freely tell him his Duty, and open to him his Misdemeanours to the Commonwealth, and the Surmises and Umbrages of his People and Council for the amending Disorders, and bettering the Form of his Government'.[26]

Drummond accepted this conception of the nature of kingship early in life. In his poem 'Forth Feasting', written for the state visit of James VI to Scotland in 1617, he expressed the sentiment of reciprocal love between a monarch and his people in the line 'No Guard so sure as Loue vnto a Crowne' (l. 246),[27] a line to which James apparently took grave exception at the time, preferring to express the Machiavellian maxim requiring monarchs to inculcate fear in their subjects. Although Drummond possessed *The Prince* in a French translation [Macdonald 1092] he did not allow it to influence his thought. He preferred the doctrine expressed by Innocent Gentillet in his *Discours . . . contre Nicolas Machiavel Florentin* [Macdonald 1055] that the King should be good and humane. And there are other precedents for this political thinking in the works of Jean Bodin, who emphasised the concept of the natural reciprocal responsibility of king and subject, in Erasmus's *Institutio principis Christiani* [Macdonald 486], and in Aristotle's *Politics* which Drummond may have read in Louis LeRoy's French edition [Macdonald 408].[28]

This pedigree shows the orthodoxy of Drummond's ideas in Western

---

[24] 'Irene', *ibid.*, pp. 163–4.    [25] 'Apologetical Letter', *ibid.*, p. 134.
[26] *Ibid.*, p. 133.    [27] Kastner, i, p. 149.
[28] See Robert H. Macdonald, 'A disputed maxim of state in "Forth Feasting"', *Journal of the History of Ideas*, xxxii (1971), p. 295.

European terms, but one should not make the mistake of thinking that Drummond imported them to Scotland as a result of his wide reading in these books. They were already commonplaces of Scottish political thought. George Buchanan, if one again disregards the more radical aspects of the *De jure regni*, emphasises strongly the fundamental nature of the good king using the metaphors of father and children, shepherd and sheep, that Drummond was later to use; he asserts: 'this is the true conception of a king. . . . He is protected by the love his people have for him and not by their fear of his soldiers.'[29] Writing at least a century before, Sir David Lindsay of the Mount expresses in his political verse [Macdonald 1317] the same principles as Drummond: God appoints the king to govern his people on his behalf; he must rule justly and with clemency; and he must seek the guidance of appropriate counsellors.[30] The trail can be traced further, to Sir Gilbert Haye's *Buke of the Governaunce of Princis* of 1456. The king is to use all his abilities to draw to him 'the hertis of thi subjectis and thair curagis', to 'kepe and defende and manetene . . . his subjectis as dois God him selfe', and to 'do na grete thing but counsaile'.[31] Haye's work, a free translation of the 'Liber de secretis secretorum' (attributed erroneously by late medieval scholars to Aristotle, but containing essentially Aristotelian thought) leads us back to the political concepts of the continental writers Drummond read.

This political thinking implies that the good king must seek the counsel of some of his people, and in this the quality of the advice is of importance. The divinely-appointed king cannot of himself do wrong, but because of his human attribute of free-will and the frailty of human nature, he can act wrongly on the advice of evil counsellors. It was normal for a royalist to attribute royal actions of which he disapproved to the influence of the king's false advisors. 'His Ears' Drummond alleges 'are so Often guarded by these Men, that he never hears the Verities . . .'; Balfour of Denmilne in the same vein writes, 'the King is made by thesse Corrupte Counsellers about him . . .' to act in a certain deplored manner.[32] To such writers the difference between good and bad counsel was essentially a moral one; Lindsay's drama personifies this – Verity and Deceit, Good Counsel and Flattery are among the characters who can influence a king.

Drummond undoubtedly regarded the distinction as moral and conceived in terms of absolutes – good and evil were clearly understood ideas to him. He could not imagine the truth, that in the situation of the 1630s and 1640s what was good to one man could be evil to another, any more than he could accept that the king of himself could put into operation a morally 'wrong' policy. In

---

[29] Arrowood, *op. cit.*, pp. 86–7.

[30] Douglas Hamer, *The Works of Sir David Lindsay of the Mount* (Scottish Text Society, Edinburgh, 1931–6). See: 'The Dreme' (ll. 1037–9), i, p. 35; 'The Thrie Estaits' (ll. 1882–4), ii, p. 187; 'Testament of the Papyngo' (ll. 301–3), i, p. 65.

[31] J. H. Stevenson, *Gilbert of the Haye's prose manuscript* (Scottish Text Society, Edinburgh, 1901, 1914), ii, pp. 99, 144, 152.

[32] 'Considerations', *Works*, p. 129; Balfour, 'Memories for the Historey of King Charles his Lyffe and Rainge', NLS Adv. MS 33.2.22, f. 73*v*.

effect he failed to realise that good and evil were become political, not moral, concepts, that they were not absolutes and that they could vary according to the religious or political ideals of the individual expressing them. Drummond throughout his political writings assumed that his readers possessed the same moral outlook as he had, would accept as good what he regarded as good and as evil what he believed to be so. He could communicate only with those who accepted his own premises, he could only harangue, not argue with, his adversaries.

But sixteenth- and seventeenth-century political theorists did believe in absolute moral standards; their real problem was to suggest a method which would ensure that the monarch received only good advice in government. Buchanan was rather vague about this: 'selected persons from all ranks should join with the king in council', the decision reached being 'submitted to the people's judgement'.[33] Lindsay asserts in his later work that the executive should 'do nocht without the conveining Ane Parleament of the estaitis all';[34] but the working out of his drama shows he had little faith in it as a source of good counsel to a monarch, and Rex Humanitas is forced to rely on specialist moral counsellors. In his earlier works he indicates at some times that 'the moste Sapient' counsellors should be chosen without reference to rank or birth, at others that they should be drawn from the nobility – 'Use counsall of thy prudent Lordis trew'; and he deplores 'That prudent Lordis counsall was refusit'.[35] Haye recommends a council of individuals, not necessarily but mainly of the nobility: 'na ches nane to thy counsale . . . for his hie birth bot thare be vertu folowand'.[36]

There was little place for Parliament in Scottish constitutional theory, and Drummond accepted this in his own thought. Admittedly he possessed books such as Richard Hooker's *Laws of Ecclesiastical Policy* [Macdonald 837] which asserted that the [English] monarch was restricted not only by divine and natural law but also by the positive laws of the realm promulgated by a Parliament of which the king was only a part.[37] But, uninfluenced in this respect by English thinking and believing that a Scottish king himself makes law 'which can not erre', he provides no place for Parliament in his own concept of government; he firmly asserts that it is the duty of the nobility to advise and guide a king.

It is because of his firm belief in this natural function of nobility that he attacks so viciously those members of the aristocracy who supported the National Covenant. They are not only traitors to God and to the King but to the whole structure of society, including especially themselves. He appeals to their sense of honour in their family names and titles, and asserts that even the nobility must endure a degree of misery through acceptance of the erroneous deeds of an

[33] Arrowood, *op. cit.*, p. 71.
[34] 'The Thrie Estaits' (ll. 1577–8), Hamer, *op. cit.*, ii, p. 168.
[35] 'Papyngo' (ll. 302–3), Hamer, *op. cit.*, i, p. 65; 'Dreme' (l. 1110), *ibid.*, i, p. 37; 'Papyngo' (l. 454), *ibid.*, i, p. 69.
[36] Stevenson, *op. cit.*, ii, p. 151.
[37] For a brief account of Hooker's political thought see E. W. Talbert, *The problem of order* (Chapel Hill, N.C., 1962), pp. 41–64.

ill-guided king rather than be unfaithful to their class and society: 'Think the just Name of a Traitor, a hard purchase to you and yours, in all Times to come,' and in Histories, for a few Years Date of a miserable Life'. He delivers a warning, almost a prophecy: 'The Climacterick and Period of the Monarchical Governments of *Europe* is not yet come; and when, or if it shall come, ye who are Nobles shall perish with it'.[38] The aristocracy must support the crown with good counsel, loyalty, and obedience. They are the king's natural counsellors, and by their loyalty to the crown they should inculcate habits of obedience among their inferiors. In Drummond's view the nobility performs the key function in maintaining the stability of state and society, and this stability is part of God's order for the universe.

In Drummond's political thinking, an ordered society requires sovereignty to be held by an hereditary monarch; but the monarch can delegate magisterial authority to chosen members of the aristocracy, and can deliberately associate the people with him in the interests of political harmony. But the people have no *right* to this privilege and cannot demand it from the king. Hence the appeal to Charles I at the conclusion of 'Irene' to observe some form of self-limitation. For if the people were to *force* limitation on the king, logically the king's absolute sovereignty would be transferred to or at least shared with them; either would be undesirable within the context of Drummond's conception of unified world order, although he does not himself make this point. There is no dichotomy or confusion in his thinking: the king is absolute, but the wise king governs with a self-restraint which may give the appearance of more democratic processes at work.

The realm governed by Drummond's wise king, loving his people and loved by them, exercising justice with a spirit of clemency, seeking counsel from his nobility and accepting their guidance, would be in a state of stability and peace. But Drummond realised this was an ideal for monarchs to aim at rather than a reflection of fact; for history had taught him that kings could be repressive tyrants, that the people could resist their kings, that factions within the state could bring about civil war. 'No State nor Kingdom hath been' he writes 'which hath not had Insurrections, and been subject to Commotions and Tumults, all Sublunary Things being vassalled to Alterations.'[39] God's universe was imperfect in the area beneath the moon, and this could not be altered; but the pace of the inevitable decay of the world from its past Golden Age could be slowed down by seeking to avert as far as possible the anarchy of civil war and rebellion, the main human factors in the revertive disintegration of the universe into its destined chaos. Contemporary conservative thinkers shared Drummond's fear of civil war even when they did not base it on the same philosophy. Blaise Pascal did not believe in a God-established social order, and the accident of birth was to him an irrational way to choose the highest ranks of society and the governor of a state; yet, because any other more rational way of finding a leader was open to dispute, he feels forced to accept the traditional method by

[38] 'Irene', *Works*, p. 168.     [39] *Ibid.*, p. 164.

heredity: 'Reason cannot do better, for civil war is the greatest of evils'.[40] Thomas Hobbes derived his political thinking from an amalgam of the new mechanistic philosophy with his own psychology of human nature; he asserted (and Drummond would have agreed wholeheartedly with him): 'Take away in any kind of State, the Obedience, (and consequently the Concord of the People,) and they shall not onley not flourish, but in short time be dissolved'.[41]

The problem, given the undesirability of insurrection and civil war, was how to avert them. Mutual understanding of opposing points of view at an early stage would undoubtedly help, and it has been asserted that Drummond put forward principles of toleration.[42] Several passages in his works support such a view. Within God's scheme of universal order there is room for divergence: 'there is no Creature in it, ... that is not composed and existing with some Diversity: ... The Planets have a Motion contrary to the first Moveable; yet is there a perfect Harmony in all this great Frame, and a discording Concord maketh all the Parcels of it delightful'. This discordance within the harmonic whole applies equally to human society. 'Why do we seek to find Men all of one Thought and one Opinion in Formalities and Matters disputable?' Men have the intelligence to think for themselves, and if their thought 'shall be found dissonant and disagreeing from the vulgarly received Opinions or Errors, Why should we by our Fancy and Law of Power banish, prescribe, design or expose them to Slaughter? ... The Consciences of Men neither should nor will be forc'd by the Violence of Iron and Fire...; they are not drawn nor subdued but by Evidence and fair Demonstrations'.[43]

The message of this important passage appears to be that men should tolerate and respect the divergent opinions of others, and not seek to impose on them their own by force. By such means civil war could be possibly averted. In Drummond's time the main source of divergent opinion was religious. He himself was undoubtedly a Protestant, and his abhorrence of Roman Catholicism has already been indicated; yet his view of a God-directed human society demands a single, world-wide Christian religion with an hierarchical administrative system. The true function of clerics in his opinion should be to seek this total Christian union: 'Have we not Millions of Infidels to pursue?' Drummond seeks to revive the medieval ideal of Christendom and the Crusade, for to him this is part of the real truth of religion. 'Compound your Differences', he exhorts the churchman, 'labour to establish Order ... study Unity'.[44] This would be the ideal result of mutual tolerance.

But Drummond finds it difficult to follow his own precepts. In fact he does not truly understand, Protestant though he is, simple Protestant concepts. He believes that, just as the new scientists in their interpretation of the physical world were replacing divine certainty by scepticism and authoritative fact by

---

[40] Blaise Pascal, *Pensées: notes on religion and other subjects*, ed. Louis Lafuma, trans. John Warrington (London, 1960), p. 56 (pensée 208).

[41] Thomas Hobbes, *Leviathan*, ed. W. G. Pogson Smith (Oxford, 1947), p. 261.

[42] David Masson, *Drummond of Hawthornden* (London, 1873), p. 280. 'Drummond ... was indubitably the one eminent representative in Scotland of the idea of Toleration.'

[43] 'Irene', *Works*, pp. 171–2.                    [44] *Ibid.*, pp. 170–1.

opinion, the new churchmen were making havoc of religious truth. 'Those Opinions and Problems . . . are but Centaures Children, the Imaginations and Fancies of your own Brains'; and, having hinted that they are secularly moti- vated, asserts in a typical passage: 'ye have transformed Truth into Rhetorick, by your Commentaries destroyed the Texts . . . Ye have made many Divisions in Religion . . .: Such a Division the unnatural Harlot intended, requiring the living Child to be cut in Two Parts'.[45] There is here no impression of a tolerant mind at work. Although the idea of religious toleration was already advanced in some men's minds, Drummond did not form part of this movement; he could not say with his contemporary Benjamin Winchcote, 'Because I may be mistaken, I must not be dogmatical'.[46] Toleration, if it is not based on total in- difference, requires in a man that quality of mind by which he can be sceptical of his own opinions and recognise the possibility that he himself may be wrong.

Drummond, rather, was an irenicist (as the title of his pamphlet implies); he sought not a true principle of tolerance but a practical means of maintaining peace between divergent religious factions within the state. For him some matters in religion are essential, others not, and agreement is necessary only on essentials. Beyond this point men are entitled to their opinions. For these essentials 'the true Appeal is to that Judge that every Spirit knows', that is, to God himself. Man 'was made that hee might in the Glasse of the World behold the infinite Goodnesse, Power, Magnificence and Glorie of his Maker'.[47] By this neo- Platonic metaphor of the mirror Drummond is indicating that humanity can reach certainty only by striving towards the spirituality of the angels and of God himself. The most extreme of his presbyterian opponents could have agreed with this; but, believing that almost any man might be elected by God as the means of communicating revealed truth to human society, would have under- stood something entirely different from Drummond, to whom communication must come through the proper steps of the universal hierarchy, from 'the Prince, that vital Spirit of the Commonwealth, which giveth Life to so many Millions of Lives, the fairest Image of God upon Earth'.[48] In the mental climate of his time, this appeal to the revelation of God was ambiguous and could not provide the essential agreement. Hence Drummond's irenicism was as impotent as his apparent tolerance.

Drummond had no answer to the problem of an approaching civil war that fitted the realities of the time, for his irenicism leads back to his basic conception of the hierarchical cosmos. 'Every Part of this Universe obeyeth the Supreme Maker GOD; the inferiour Celestial Bodies obey the Superiour; the Earth and Seas obey them', and so through a hierarchy of obedience, which Drummond regards as a model for men in their everyday relations with their fellows. 'Where Laws are not obeyed, there is no Fear; where that is wanting,

---

[45] Ibid.
[46] Quoted in Henry Kamen, The rise of Toleration (London, 1967), p. 180.
[47] 'Irene', Works, p. 172; 'Cypresse Grove' (ll. 1021-23), Kastner, ii, p. 99.
[48] 'Irene', Works, p. 164.

there is no Honour, no Respect is had of Virtue, no Punishment of Vice; and these taken away, nought shall be found but a disorderly Licence to do Evil, a Confusion of every Thing, and a total Ruine of the State'.[49] When disobedience takes charge in civil society, the state will break up in disorder, just as the universe would degenerate into chaos were the natural links of obedience in the great chain to be broken. Good, and thus good government, is the concord of obedience among all men, evil is disobedience which creates

> Discord, that Foe to order, Nurse of Warre,
> By which the noblest things demolisht are.[50]

Men, either in a social group or as individuals, must not seek to disturb the order God has established, and must obey their superiors, especially their kings, even when they appear to make outrageous demands. The tyrannical king must be accepted passively, and the attractions of George Buchanan's theory of lawful tyrannicide shunned as immoral; for only God could give judgement on a king, whose 'Life is a Gouernement and Office ..., of the administration and charge of which ... hee must rander an account, so soone as his Tearme expyreth'.[51] Only God may judge and punish a tyrant.

Drummond's political views can easily be derided by the modern political analyst who cannot accept his method of argument and who sees few signs of the 'advanced' ideas he is generally seeking in his examination of the political writers of the past. It must be accepted that Drummond was a conservative, and that the quality of his thought can only be properly understood within the context of traditional thinking of his own times. In spite of the ideas of Copernicus and Galileo for cosmology, in spite of the sceptical approach of Montaigne, Descartes and Bacon, the majority of intelligent men in the 1630s still accepted the medieval view of the hierarchic universe and would continue in their belief for many decades to come. Within this context Drummond's politics are completely consistent, while Buchanan's, more renowned because of the radical implications grafted on to his essentially traditional view of monarchy, are, seen as they must be in the same context, less consistent. Argument by correspondence within this cosmic philosophy is as logical as other forms of argument; the results are invalid for us today only because we cannot rationally accept the philosophy. Drummond can rightly argue that, because God loves the beings he has created and they in turn love and obey him, a good king must love his people, seeking their love and obedience.

It is this emphasis on love originating in the superior which allows Drummond to develop these apparently inconsistent semi-democratic ideas whereby government decisions must be made with (aristocratic) counsel and responsible criticism must be seriously considered. A king's love for his people insists that he rules with their welfare continuously in view; where this love is insufficiently

---

[49] 'Irene', Works, p. 165.
[50] 'Hymne of the Fairest Fair' (ll. 50–2), Kastner, ii, p. 38.
[51] 'Cypresse Grove' (ll. 1046–51), Kastner, ii, p. 99.

great and the monarch abuses his position in a particular way, the people have a responsibility to draw the matter to his attention.

Drummond explicitly indicates that excessive taxation falls within this category of royal abuse, and feels able himself to point out to his sovereign that 'it is no Property of a good Shepherd to shear often his Flock and ever to milk them'.[52] In the same way a royal action detrimental to the image of monarchy must be criticised as foolhardy; a major obligation of a king is to 'hold . . . dear . . . the Right and Title of his Crown, which concerneth not only himself but his Posterity'.[53] Admittedly, in Drummond's view the people had no lawful means of enforcing a recalcitrant king to act on their criticism, but it is clear that he believed that, should unlawful rebellion or civil war result from the king's failure, the moral blame for the resulting social havoc was to be laid equally on the king. No democrat, he was yet no supporter of royal absolutism.

His attitude to the rebellion through which he lived reflects this position. Charles I was not a completely good king, and his actions certainly called for criticism. But, as the 'Irene' shows, Drummond firmly believed that the king had made sufficient concessions to the Scottish people to regain their confidence, respect, and support; the continuance of revolt was malicious and unjustifiable. Drummond's position hardens after 1640. In 1643 he can state categorically that all insurrections must be crushed: 'A King that doth not punish Rebels, shall never, during his Reign, keep his Subjects in Peace, nor enjoy himself any Quietness'.[54]

In his political writing Drummond is motivated primarily by a desire to preserve monarchy, the God-ordained form of government within the God-centred cosmos. But unlike most royalist writers he depends little on Scriptural quotations for justification of his position; for him the facts of history support his case and he is lavish with historical examples. Accepting the idea of hierarchical society, conceiving human nature as fundamentally unchanging, he believed, as did most other historians of his time, that valid assumptions about the present and future could be made from an examination of the past: 'We may easily conjecture of Things to come, and imagine them by these of the like Nature which have preceded. The Stage of the World is the same still, though in Times the Actors be changed, and come about again'.[55] In common with his contemporaries he accepted unquestioningly the myth of the long line of ancient Scottish kings; addressing James VI, he asserted

> By just Discent Thou from moe Kings dost shine,
> Than many can name Men in all their Line.

And in 1633 when Charles visited Edinburgh, the pageant organised by Drummond displayed 'Fergus the first' accompanied by 'an hundred and seven

[52] 'Apologetical Letter', *Works*, p. 134.
[53] 'Considerations to the King', *Works*, p. 129.
[54] 'Skiamachia', *Works*, p. 204.
[55] 'Considerations to the King', *Works*, p. 129. A more complete examination of Drummond's historical thought and method is in preparation by the present writer.

Scottish Kings, which hee had brought from the Elisian fields'.[56] This concept of Scotland's past enhanced for Drummond the authority of the Scottish monarchy, and he deprecated Buchanan using it to justify his theories of elective kingship and right of rebellion.

Drummond's entire political attitude was based on an abstract conception of the nature of the universe and society which was already beginning to be eroded by the scepticism of some religious thinkers and by the observations of the new scientists. Admittedly the philosophy Drummond accepted remained a potent force long after his death even among scientists; as late as 1667 Thomas Sprat could assert that the function of experimental science was 'to follow all the links of this chain' [of world order] and 'to rank all the *varieties* and *degrees* of things, ... orderly one upon another'.[57] But Drummond was sufficiently perceptive to see that the ideas beginning to come into vogue in his time could not be absorbed into this philosophy; they were totally disruptive of old concepts, and 'leaue the Imagination in a thousand Labyrinthes'.

> Nor can it Blisse you bring,
> Hidde Natures Depthes to know,
> Why Matter changeth, whence each Forme doth spring.[58]

He sought the comfortable total certainty of earlier modes of thought, and feared the doubt created by the observations of sceptical minds. By some process of 'double-think' he could ignore facts before his eyes which did not fit, for example the social mobility already evident in Scotland which weakened his concept of a rigid social hierarchy. What he did see was the disruptive influence on contemporary society of doctrines of equality, and the development of what he regarded as anarchy which, he prophetically indicated, would only be terminated by the dictatorship of 'one who will name himself PROTECTOR of the Liberty of the Kingdom'.[59] He was living impotently in a world disintegrating, near its predestined end; the disruption of religion and the growth of democratic ideas had led to civil war, civil war had ended in the martyrdom of the divinely-instituted monarch.

Disillusioned, sick in body and in heart, Drummond survived the execution of his king by only a few months. Chaos had entered his universe.

T. I. RAE

[56] 'Forth Feasting' (ll. 205–6), Kastner, i, p. 147; 'Entertainment for Charles I', *ibid.*, ii, p. 123.

[57] Thomas Sprat, *History of the Royal Society*, ed. Jackson Cope and Harold Whitmore Jones (London, 1959), p. 110.

[58] 'Cypresse Grove' l. 360, Kastner, ii, p. 78; 'Hymne of True Happiness' (ll. 49–51), *ibid.*, ii, p. 34.

[59] 'Speech which may be called a Prophecy', *Works*, p. 181 (written in May 1639).

# 12

# *Some Aspects of Funerary Monuments in Lowland Scotland*

I am sure the pride of this people never leaves them, but follows them to their long homes (I was about to have said, to the devil), for the meanest man must have a grave-stone full fraught with his own praises (though he was the vilest miscreant on earth) and miserable *memento mori*'s, both in English and Latin, nay Greek too, if they can find a Greek word for a cordinger, the calling he was of, and all this in such miserable Scotch orthography, that 'tis hard to distinguish one language from another.'[1]

With varying degrees of accuracy and geographical range interest in the recording of graveyard monuments in lowland Scotland has a long history which was probably initially stimulated by the publication in 1704 of the first part of Robert Monteith's *Theater of Mortality*. Consisting of inscriptions from Greyfriars and other churchyards in Edinburgh, Monteith's work was apparently so much valued that the Town Council of Edinburgh in September 1704 appointed two of its members to revise the work and to 'cause print the samen upon the Town's expenses'. Encouraged by this move Monteith set out to collect material on a larger scale and after 'eight years of some travel and vast charges and expenses' in gathering the necessary information, he requested the assistance in the Edinburgh *Courant* of December 1712 'desiring all persons who have any valuable epitaphs, or any historical, chronological or moral inscriptions' to forward them to him expressing the hope that 'all generous persons will cheerfully subscribe his proposals in a matter so pious, pleasant, profitable, and national.' To his appeal there responded some eighty-eight men: senators in the College of Justice, writers, advocates, doctors of medicine, schoolmasters, merchants, a shipmaster in Montrose and a periwig maker in Edinburgh. In 1713 the second part of his work was published entitled *An Theater of Mortality: Or a Further Collection of Funeral Inscriptions Over Scotland*. Monteith's work has many merits, the more obvious being that he recorded a considerable number of important inscriptions when they were legible and before extensive weathering had set in, while his near literal translations from Latin are modishly elegant. At the same time one ought to note that apart from his Edinburgh record, his work covers only thirty-three churchyards in Scotland and is concerned solely with epigraphy, this latter feature marking a limitation in approach which was to be perpetuated by such later recorders as Charles Rogers in his *Scottish Monuments and Tombstones* (2 vols., 1872), who while

[1] *Early Travellers in Scotland*, ed. P. Hume Brown, p. 259: 'A Modern Account of Scotland by an English Gentleman', by Thomas Kirke.

admittedly extending the coverage of the survey to some four hundred church-yards, notes only the more diverting and entertaining of the inscriptions.

The north-east of Scotland was well served by Andrew Jervise who published a two-volume work between 1875 and 1879 entitled *Epitaphs and Inscriptions in the North East of Scotland*.[2] Jervise, however, brought a more detailed and comprehensive approach to bear on the subject than is previously evident. His appointment as an Examiner of Registers in Aberdeen, Kincardine, Forfar, Nairn, Elgin and Banff in 1855 gave him the necessary time to concentrate on a given area, while his training as a typographer and ability as an artist gave him the facility to decipher even the most difficult of inscriptions. His work is also supplemented by much valuable genealogical material and includes, apparently for the first time, an awareness of different types of graveyard monuments.

From Jervise's observations and thoroughness one might conceivably have expected at this juncture that immediately subsequent studies would have attempted some sort of classification of the types of monuments possibly based on differing epigraphic styles combined with heraldic devices, mortality emblems and structural details, or even siting. This was not to be the case.[3] Instead, over the next fifty years or so a diversification of techniques dictated by the interest of the individual became discernible.

At the beginning of this present century the *Proceedings of the Society of Antiquaries of Scotland* contained two copious, superbly illustrated articles by D. Christison[4] which highlighted the vigorous pictorial aspects of a large number of monuments in the Scottish lowlands. Christison's line illustrations were of particular value in depicting a wide range of trade implements and quaint variations of mortality symbols, and by his very method of visual exposition, drew attention to the extraordinary richness of sculptural detail which is so characteristic of the area under discussion. Using the format of the gravestone as his main source W. Rae-Macdonald was necessarily compelled to use a similar approach for his article on Heraldry in Elgin and its neighbourhood.[5]

So far it would seem that the general tendency was to record the information and detailing *on* the monument without observing that an emerging pattern of chronological and stylistic change in the actual monuments themselves was evident from the increasing corpus of material by now available.[6] It was not until 1960, when a paper was published by Angus Graham,[7] that we have the first systematic classification of the graveyard monument *per se*. Graham's article was intended to amplify information on graveyard monuments already

---

[2] Jervise also carried out a survey of Fife graveyards which is in manuscript form at the National Museum of Antiquities.

[3] Apart from the more obvious differences Jervise himself makes no attempt at classification but simply refers to a recumbent slab as a 'flat stone', a 'pavement slab' or 'a slab'; cf. *op. cit.*, ii, 223.

[4] *PSAS*, xxxvi (1901–2), 280–457.                [5] *Ibid.*, xxxiv, 344–429.

[6] Sir George Macdonald in his article in *PSAS*, lxx (1935–6), 40–121, which is based on the valuable pioneer work by D. Hay Fleming, classifies monuments but limits his system to three types, failing to distinguish clearly between the recumbent slab and the collapsed table-tomb.                [7] *PSAS*, xciv (1960–1), 211–71.

gathered by the Royal Commission on Ancient Monuments in East Lothian in 1913 whose prime interest had been confined to such monuments as carried heraldic devices or 'possessed some very notable artistic or historical interest' with a limiting date of 1707. Briefly Mr Graham distinguished eleven types, some clearly defined, others showing mutual relationships. They are as follows: early medieval headstones, coped grave covers, Calvary cross-slabs, other medieval grave covers and recumbent slabs, post-Reformation recumbent slabs, wall monuments, post-Reformation headstones, pillars, Reredos monuments, table-tombs, and sarcophagi. In his following discussion Graham expatiates on the characteristic features of the individual monuments with regard to chronology, shape, size, siting, epigraphy, heraldry, trade insignia and local fashions within a compact geographical group. This is a definitive survey of all the greater value because of the wider extent of its application. It requires only slight adaptation or modification to be utilised for any churchyard in the lowlands. Regional variation in numerical densities do, naturally, occur. Older religious centres may, for example, contain a higher proportion of medieval monuments than a burial ground attached to a more recent foundation, but it is nonetheless manifest that this system of classifying monuments has contributed a great deal to a fuller study of them by its careful analysis and statement of types.

From the eleven listed by Graham it is now proposed to select those that merit further discussion as a result of two recent surveys which adhered closely to the system outlined.[8] As a particularly durable example of a pre-Reformation monument the Calvary Cross slab owes its survival *in situ* to the fact that it was constructed, in addition to its commemorative purpose, to be an integral part of the flagging of the church. Normally uniformly rectangular in shape, the flat surface of the stone is incised centrally with the nominal design of the plain shafted latin cross rising from a stepped base and framed by marginal lines within which is cut the Latin inscription in gothic lettering. To relieve the monotonous repetition of parallel lines the terminals of the shaft and cross arms may be variously chiselled or embellished with a fleur-de-lys pattern.[9] A similar desire presumably accounted for the frequent presence of quatrefoils sometimes containing sentiments such as *fratres obsecro orate pro me* or *adjutor meus*. Where the stone commemorates an ecclesiastic it is not uncommon to find the cross flanked by a textus and chalice with the letters IHS at the intersection of the arms. The stepped base of the cross may contain a skull and an assortment of bones or be left blank.

Within the Canon law concept of *honor sepulturae* the privilege of burial inside a church included dead patrons who as founders of, or as representatives of those who had erected the building, were considered to have rights of a personal kind in the structure. This right seems to have had fairly wide interpretation, however, and was extended to include those associated with the

---

[8] *Ibid.*, xcix (1966–7), 211–54.
[9] Revd Charles Lyon, *The Ancient Monuments of St Andrews*, illustrations 1 and 3; Revd James Campbell, *Balmerino and its Abbey*, illustration opposite p. 548.

building on a less elevated social plane. It is interesting to note that a Calvary Cross slab was placed in the south transept of St Andrews Cathedral to an un-named '*vitrarius ac plumbarius hujus almi templi*' and that at Balmerino there is one with the trade emblems of a mason, the trowel, clawed hammer, square and rule cut to either side of the cross. In such cases no significant change is evident in the basic design except that the chalice and textus are replaced by secular emblems. Where a husband and wife are commemorated, as at St Peter's Kirk, Duffus, a sword and pair of shears have been found to flank the cross shaft, but these emblems are not necessarily confined to, or indicative of, a double burial and probably have strong religious connotations in that the sword may symbolise the guardian of the soul *en route* to heaven and the shears as having severed the cord of life. Natural wastage through weathering and other incidental damage has tended to erase inscriptions and destroy details on many of the slabs so that it is not as yet possible to state with any certainty what the time-distribution of the monument is with any confident precision. Nor does it appear that this information will be forthcoming until further regional studies have been carried out. From the few dated examples available a suggested concentration is in the last forty years of the fifteenth century and the first quarter of the sixteenth, but this distribution would have to be revised as, and when monuments are found, and is also subject to the consideration that un-dated, related examples have been assigned to the fourteenth century[10] thus suggesting a longer tradition than is implied here.

By the 1530s, if not slightly earlier, there is a distinct paucity of religious motifs in general on the commemorative recumbent slabs within churches. The Calvary cross suddenly runs out of fashion which, bearing in mind the simplicity and attraction of its linear composition, is not explicable solely in terms of artistic whim; while the garbed figure of the ecclesiastic, a more com-plex incised linear design, but contemporary with the cross slab and similarly situated, also disappears. By the 1540s as at St Bridget's Church, Dalgety[11] a notable change in composition and theme has occurred on the face of the recumbent slab. The cross and the figure of the ecclesiastic are supplanted by a heraldic device and the incised gothic lettering gives way to bold relief Roman capitals. The practice of retaining the epitaph within a marginal band is con-tinued, but the band is sunk and the relief letters, for eminently practical reasons, do not rise proud of the surrounding surface of the stone. In other instances as on the slab to Robert Carnegie of Kinnaird, 1565 (St Athernase's Kirk, Leuchars), the lines are arranged transversely to the longer axis of the slab, and here, quite apart from their outstanding decorative effect and strong sense of pattern, the basis of all good lettering, the letters are so compactly set out that the surface of the stone can be walked on without excessive wear and damage to the inscription. In the 1540 to 1580 period and beyond the inscriptions continued in Latin adhering to the rather stereotyped formula, which at its simplest read HIC IACET HONORABILIS VIR (name) QVI OBIIT (date) AETATIS

---

[10] *RCAM*: Fife, Kinross and Clackmannan, p. 3.
[11] J. R. Walker, *Pre-Reformation Churches in Fifeshire*, Dalgety illustration 4.

SVAE (age). An increasing use of English and Scots is evident at the end of the sixteenth century but the tendency was to translate directly from the Latin to read HEIR LYIS ANE HONORABIL MAN (name) QVHA DIED (date) AND OF HIS AGE (age).

The principles of sound practicability were likewise observed in the execution of the heraldic details. In bas-relief on the slab, or alternatively cut in a sunk panel, the shield is almost invariably either flanked or surmounted by the initials of the deceased and complete the composition in a non-heraldic but visually satisfying sense.

As a part of the flooring the recumbent slab has an added interest in that it continued to mark burials in churches long after Knox had issued his injunctions against this practice. It will be recollected that Knox had stated[12] in the *First Book of Discipline* that '. . . we think it not seemly that the Kirk, appointed for Preaching and Administration of the Sacraments, shall be made a Place of Buryall; but that some secret and convenient Place, lying in the most free Aire, be appointed for that Use . . .' a sentiment apparently shared by Sir James Melvil of Hallhill in 1609 whose composition decorates the wall of Collessie churchyard: 'Defyle not Christ's Kirk with your Carion/A Solemn sait for God's Service prepared/Fro Praier Preaching and Communion/Your Byrial should be in the Kirkyaird . . .' and vehemently developed by the Reverend Mr William Birnie in his work *The Blame of Kirk-Buriall Tending to Perswade Cemiteriall Civilitie*.[13] Ignoring these proscriptions, surviving relatives continued to have the recumbent slabs used and placed in the flooring of the churches until well into the seventeenth century, but one should be careful to note that they commemorated only those of some special social distinction, the local laird, minister, bailie, or their wives, and must not be regarded as monuments of a wide and popular usage.

Unmarked burials in the churchyard were, of course, common at this time, but it is tempting to speculate that the practice of commemorating the dead with a memorial may have more involved social implications than is at first realised. It is noticeable, particularly so in St Andrews where preservation was exercised, and elsewhere where chance prevailed, that a certain type of monument, the table tomb, is used to mark the grave of the bailie, fishing skipper, mason, maltster etc. from the 1630s onwards. In appearance this monument shows strong affinities to the altar tombs and effigy bases of the medieval period, and it may be that its proliferation in the churchyard marks both a conscious desire on the part of certain classes to copy the more ambitious practices of the nobility in the matter of a memorial, and at the same time bears testimony to their prosperity and is a reflection of current economic conditions. For the next hundred years the table tomb was to provide an outlet for the innate sculptural ability of the local stone carver that would have been perhaps inhibited by the

---

[12] *First Book of Discipline*, chap. xiv, section 4.

[13] According to *Nisbet's Heraldry*, appendix, p. 65, Mr William Birnie was presented by James VI on 28 December 1597 to the church of Lanark . . . 'in which parish, because of the several quarrels and feuds amongst the gentlemen, he not only learnedly preached the gospel, but was obliged many times, as he well could, to make use of his sword'.

change to more austere church building patterns in the post-Reformation period. The decorations on these monuments take a wide variety of forms. By virtue of its position it allowed for a bolder and more adventurous development of relief work than would have been possible on the recumbent slab. This includes heraldic devices, scrolls, swags of drapery, fruit, winged cherubs, allegorical figures and the ubiquitous funerary emblems. Extra surfaces for decoration could be provided by using the rectangular end supports, as is done in Moray, or by enriching the pedestals. Many interesting local variations occur. In Fife, East Lothian and Angus, the rectangular slab may feature wide, steeply bevelled sides with hipped gables rising to a narrow central panel, while in Moray the bevelling is less pronounced and is used simply to carry the inscription. The relief work on the slab is subtly contrasted and highlighted by the use of incised Roman capitals and italic scripts, which, in the course of the eighteenth century gave place to minuscule cursive forms no doubt stimulated by the fashionable interest in handwriting. For the social historian and the genealogist the information contained in the inscription can provide a poignant reminder of the high mortality rate, especially amongst younger children. Wishing to extend the scope of his work and acting on the instructions of the buyer, the mason took special care to cut trade emblems and incorporate them into the design of the slab, often in the form of quasi-heraldic devices.

A popular monument for most of the seventeenth and early eighteenth centuries, the table tomb, it has been suggested,[14] was too bulky to survive the increased demands on graveyard space made towards the end of the latter century and thus it was ultimately to be replaced by the headstone which takes up far less room. It is worth drawing attention to the fact that in certain areas[15] the table monument continued in vogue for very much longer and that the dearth of these monuments may be explicable in terms of either removal[16] or regional preference.

The origin and development of the headstone has already been discussed in detail by Angus Graham,[17] and all that is intended here is to draw attention to the figurine carving which achieved a high degree of artistry and drama indicative of a great pool of talent that has not been accorded the full recognition it deserves. Certain themes featuring the body and soul of the departed wrestling with death are popular and are, in all probability, borrowings from similar scenes on the table tombs;[18] others show the Adam and Eve theme, while groups,

---

[14] *PSAS*, xci (1957–8), 5.

[15] St Peter's Kirk, Duffus, Moray. *Circa* eighty table monuments lie to the south of the ruined church.

[16] A large number of collapsed table monuments have been stacked against the church-yard wall at Ceres. In a number of graveyards in Angus, for example at Aberlemno and Inverarity, the same tendency is noticeable.

[17] *PSAS*, xci (1957–8), 1–9.

[18] It is difficult to establish the provenance of the figurine carving in general and its symbolic interpretations in particular. On two bevelled table monuments, however, one in the Howff, Dundee, commemorating the wife of a Thomas Vichtane, 'noter burges', *obiit* 1645 (Lamb's *Guide to Remarkable Monuments in The Howff*, 21), the other in the Prior's House, St Andrews Cathedral (*PSAS*, lxx (1935–6), 81) commemorating one Judith Nairn, wife of John Wemys, merchant, *obiit* 1646, the source of the carving to either side of the cartouches

such as those at Monikie in Angus, depict aspects of industrial activity with the weaver working his loom. In common with the table-tomb a wide selection of trade emblems enrich the facets of the headstone, while both types of monument share similar spiritual admonitions the most common being *memento mori*.

The late eighteenth century saw the impressive and rapid development of a feature peculiar to the headstone, however. At this time modern type founts were in use and the stone-carver was quick to adapt them to his needs. Characteristic of these modern faces were letters with thick downstrokes slender horizontals and delicate serifs, requiring a high standard of control, particularly in spacing where the opportunity of ligaturing was now less acceptable. In using these the mason, with a fine sensitivity to his medium, and achieving an initial balance with earlier vernacular elements, proved equal to the printer in his craft, both in the selection and use of the range of letters that were now available to him and in his ability to elaborate on them to attain more florid, imaginative forms in the course of the nineteenth century.

The wall monuments of the seventeenth and eighteenth centuries are architectural compositions, ambitious in concept and execution, each worthy of its own detailed description so that it is, in fact, idle to attempt a stylistic and structural analysis on a wide regional scale beyond outlining a number of their more common features that might be helpful as a comparative guide. Generally they consist of pedestals, columns, entablature and a pediment, often triangular or ogival, constructed round a central commemorative panel. Renaissance ornamentation abounds but varies in quality, heraldic devices occupy the tympanum and funerary emblems also are incorporated in the design while scrolled trusses may support the superstructure. The columns may be heavily enriched with roped moulding or break out into caryatids. In the majority of cases, although by no means invariably, the inscriptions are incised. In the relationship of their various parts these monuments may adhere closely to architectural orders, while others allow of a freer treatment that borders on a debasement of the classical exemplar. This latter pattern is sometimes evident in remoter country churchyards where one presumes that the mason was working with complex proportional disciplines that he did not fully understand. It has been suggested[19] that the availability of pattern books in the sixteenth and seventeenth centuries by Dieterlin and de Vries may have influenced the design composition of these monuments, but this presupposes a wider distribution of these or similar works than appears likely, and a more practical explanation of their provenance or source of inspiration lies in the sixteenth-century trend in Scottish architecture in general when the established Gothic element in design was being supplanted by the classical impulse that was introduced into Scotland by James V and his

is manifestly a detailed copy of themes illustrated by William Marshall for Francis Quarles' *Emblems, Divine and Moral*. It has been pointed out (*DNB*, XVI, 537) that the forty-five prints in the last three books of this work were borrowed from Hermann Hugo's *Pia Desideria Emblematis, Elegiis et Affectibus SS Patrum Illustrata* (Antwerp, 1624).

[19] K. A. Esdaile, *English Church Monuments, 1510–1840*, 91.

French masons who worked in conjunction with their Scottish counterparts on royal buildings and which in time would conceivably percolate down to the local mason.

It is not proposed to extend this paper beyond the 1850s for thereafter, up until the present day, a period of what amounts to visual illiteracy gradually sets in when the graveyard monument ceases to promote identity or reflect the individuality of either the builder or the deceased and becomes a totally feature-less piece of stone in the regimented matrix of the cemetery. By the twentieth century sepulchral art is dead.

JOHN DI FOLCO

# 13

## *The Swiss and the Covenant*[1]

In the history of the relations between the Church of Scotland and the Swiss Reformed Churches, Zürich is not generally regarded as having played a significant part in the sixteenth or seventeenth centuries. Her connections were much more with England and the returned Marian exiles, while Scotland was always considered to be more closely linked with Geneva, which John Knox extolled as 'the maist perfyt schoole of Chryst that ever was in the erth since the dayis of the Apostillis'.[2] That the Scottish reformers and their successors held Zürich, the mother Church of the Reformed faith, in high regard is amply documented. What is, however, not so readily recognised is the interest taken by the Swiss Churches and the Church of Zürich in particular in Scottish affairs, not just in the second half of the sixteenth century but well into the seventeenth.

The first half of this century has frequently been regarded as one of the most exciting periods of Scottish history – one in which many Scots were acutely concerned that their country was sinking into a mere English province, and consequently it called forth from them a remarkable expression of what had for centuries been one of their most cherished contentions, that the monarch was made for the nation and that he ruled by consent of the people and the law of the land; a period in which religion occupies, as it were, the front line, and provides the immediate cause, and the rallying point for many who were afraid not only for their country but also – and many would have put this first – for the future of their reformed faith. These two, Faith and Fatherland, are linked in the two words which history has given to the document, drawn up when the crisis was felt to be at its height in February 1638 and signed in Greyfriars Church by the high-born and the low-born who together crowded the Church and the churchyard, – the National Covenant.

It is perhaps not surprising that what has appeared to some as 'the offspring of piety and patriotism' has been judged by others as the 'offspring of fanaticism and rebellion'.[3] With the merits and demerits of the Covenanting movement we are not here concerned, but rather with the reaction it provoked, with the interest it aroused among those foreign church leaders who were, in matters of faith, historically most closely linked to Scotland. It has generally been

[1] Inaugural lecture delivered in St Mary's College, University of St Andrews, on 25 January 1972. I am indebted to Dr J. B. Bodmer of the manuscript department of the Zentralbibliothek, Zürich, and to the director of the Staatsarchiv, Zürich, for their generous help during the summer of 1971. In the final preparation of the lecture Mr Cant gave invaluable advice. Dr S. W. Gilley has also read my manuscript and offered helpful criticism.
[2] *The Works of John Knox*, ed. D. Laing (Edinburgh, 1855), iv, 240.
[3] J. Cunningham, *The Church History of Scotland*, 2nd edn (Edinburgh, 1882), i, 529.

believed that the Reformed Churches on the Continent – and this was affirmed by the King in his Large Declaration[4] – were scandalised by the actions of the Scottish Churchmen. Robert Baillie expressed to the minister of the Scots Kirk at Campvere his sorrowful surprise that 'all forraigne divines hitherto hes been silent; they care not for our woes; though popery should swell on Brittaine, it seems they regard it not.'[5]

News of the events of 1638 did not reach Zürich until the spring of the following year, when both parties in Scotland and England were preparing for war – and then in somewhat exaggerated form. The king had enrolled thirty thousand troops including twelve thousand from Ireland (all Roman Catholics) and was bent upon forcing on his own Scottish subjects the 'popish ceremonies' that were already being imposed on the *Ecclesia Anglicana*. The Reformed cantons were deeply alarmed especially for the future of the reformed faith, which seemed to be hanging in the balance. The Continent at that very time had been witnessing the ravages of the Thirty Years' War, and now Great Britain whom they regarded as one of the leading Protestant powers, her Churches united with them in a common faith, seemed to be preparing to consume itself in religious civil war.[6]

The Antistes, or Superintendent, of the Church in Zürich, J. J. Breitinger,[7] was determined to help to prevent what could only be a catastrophe for the reformed faith if King Charles waged war on his Scottish subjects. But what could Zürich and its neighbouring Protestant cantons do? They could write to the archbishop of Canterbury and plead with him to use the great influence which they knew he had with the king to avert the impending disaster. Breitinger, no doubt, seeing in the occasion the opportunity to restore to Zürich something of its former position of renown during the lifetime of Zwingli's distinguished successor, Heinrich Bullinger, drafted the letter and sent it to the Churches of Basel, Bern and Schaffhausen for their approval and support.[8] The Churches of the three cantons eagerly supported Zürich. Theodore

---

[4] *A Large Declaration concerning the Late Tumults . . . by the King* (London, 1639), pp. 74f.; see also Cunningham, *op. cit.*, ii, 529.

[5] On 1 November 1638. *The Letters and Journals of Robert Baillie*, ed. David Laing (Edinburgh, 1841), i, 112.

[6] Zürich, Staatsarchiv, MS E II 369, 211, and Zentralbibliothek, MS B 26, 56, 453. Conrad Wirtz, one of the pastors of Zürich, in a letter of 22 February 1639 wrote: 'Magnae Britanniae Rex, 30,000 peditibus et 5,000 equitibus in Scotiam patriam suam tendit, ceremonias pontificias in ecclesia Anglicana hactenus usurpatas, Scotis suis obrusurus. En expeditionis causam ridiculam et impiam! O! Si tantas vires adversus Ecclesiae et religionis orthodoxae hostes.' (Zentralbibliothek, MS B 36, 27). This information was also passed by J. J. Breitinger, the Antistes, to other Reformed Churches of Switzerland (MS B 124b, 20, 188, MS B 26, 56, 476–8).

[7] J. J. Breitinger (1575–1645) was appointed antistes of the Church of Zürich in 1613. As a young man he had travelled extensively in Germany and the Low Countries and had studied at Herborn, Marburg and Franeker. In 1618 he had been one of the delegates from the Swiss Churches to the Synod of Dort. He does not appear to have visited Britain (*Neue Deutsche Biographie*, ii, 577).

[8] In his covering letter to these churches Breitinger stated that he considered it their duty, as they knew of the zeal and piety of the Scottish Church, to write to the archbishop in an attempt to persuade the King 'ad mitiora consilia . . . et Scoticae gentis innocentia a nobis efflagitare videtur' (Zentralbibliothek, MS B 26, 56, 453–4; MS 124b, 20, 189; Staatsarchiv,

Zwinger, on behalf of Basel, admired Breitinger's prudence in not alluding to the reported causes of the troubles, and applauded his plan of appealing to the archbishop in moderate words even although it was commonly reported and believed that even if he was not the author of the events that had given rise to the deplorable situation he was at least a promoter of them. Zwinger also suggested that the civil authorities and the Genevan and French Churches should be invited to write to the king, as this matter so clearly concerned the entire reformed church, the Communion of the Saints, in which they, in the words of the Creed, professed to believe.[9]

If the letter to Laud[10] had but little hope of impressing him, it nevertheless redounds to the credit of the Swiss pastors, witnessing as it does to their deep concern for the well-being of the evangelical church and the peaceful settlement of its internal affairs. It was despatched from Zürich on 21 March, took three weeks to arrive at Lambeth with another three weeks for the archbishop to reply. If the Swiss had been in doubt about Laud's attitude towards events in Scotland, if they had expected to exercise influence upon him to act as mediator and as pacifier, they were quickly disillusioned. The Scots covenanters are, he declared, first and foremost political rebels against whom the king has justly raised an army. King Charles had made every effort to bring them to a better mind and he will still do everything safe, honourable, and in accordance with the Christian religion and the laws of the land for the sake of peace, and he is ready to bury in oblivion even the most intolerable of their offences.[11]

The Swiss had made a point of not wishing to judge anyone, but Laud invites them to write to those 'conjured' Scots in order to persuade them to obey their king, to point out to them that the royal power *in causis ecclesiasticis* had been exercised by the best kings of Judah, and that armed resistance to the powers ordained by God under pretext of religion was unheard of in the primitive Church. All the reformed Churches should condemn the Scots; in their rebellious audacity the Covenanters surpass even the Jesuits, for they are prepared to do anything against their king under colour of service to God and religion.

---

MS E II 369, 216–18). On 23 August Breitinger wrote that the Swiss churches were compelled to take an interest in what was happening and to try to help because of the examples of their predecessors Zwingli, Bullinger, Calvin, and Martyr (Staatsarchiv, MS E II 404, 77–8).

9 Staatsarchiv, MS E II 369, 216–18. The replies from Bern and Schaffhausen give full approval but without offering significant comment. The reply from Basel, written by Theodore Zwinger, contains the following words about the archbishop, 'non solum nomine suspectus, sed et turbarum istarum haud necessarium, si non Author, saltem Fautor et Promotor perhibetur'.

10 Staatsarchiv, MS E II 369, 200, a contemporary copy is endorsed by Breitinger *21 Martij, 1639*. The letter was known to Robert Baillie. A translation taken from his papers was printed in *The Letters and Journals of Robert Baillie*, ed. Laing, ii, 431ff.

11 The autograph, MS E II 369, 223, dated *April. ult. 1639*, is endorsed in Breitinger's hand *Redditum prid. Calend. Junij 1639*. There are several contemporary copies in MS E II 369, and in Zentralbibliothek, MS A 124b, 20. The letter was printed in *Praestantium ac Eruditorum Virorum Epistolae Ecclesiasticae et Theologicae*, ed. Hartsoeker and Limborch (Amsterdam, 1684), pp. 799ff., and reprinted in *The Works of the Most Reverend Father in God, William Laud*, vi, part 2, pp. 563–6. An English translation from the papers of Robert Baillie was published in *Letters and Journals*, ed. Laing, ii, 433–5.

Especially to be condemned are the ministers, for it was from the pulpit that the minds of the people were most vigorously stirred up against their king. The archbishop himself had spared no effort to bring about a settlement but to no avail. The rebels desire only a peace which no king could grant.

If by this forthright condemnation the Primate had hoped to win sympathy for the royal cause and the ecclesiastical policy with which his own name is so inextricably associated he was indeed mistaken. The vehement acrimony of his reply, whether justified or unjustified, served further to convince some of the leaders in the Reformed Church that Laud bore considerable responsibility for what was taking place. Nevertheless the serious charge of rebellion had been made against the Scots and must be further investigated.

The month of June 1639 was taken up in circulating copies of Laud's letter along with the draft of a letter which Breitinger proposed should be sent to Scotland, and of a reply to Lambeth.[12] Once again, all three cantons supported Zürich's lead. They agreed to convey to the Scottish Church Laud's arguments, in particular that the exercise of royal power in matters ecclesiastical was truly biblical and that resistance to the powers ordained by God was not. In doing so they emphasised that they had no desire to condemn anyone unheard and consequently wished to hear their version of the controversy, for, they write, 'to this very day no one has fully informed us of the true cause of your resort to arms'. They had heard about some difference in rites and ceremonies but the significance of these matters had escaped them. The Swiss pastors entreat their Scottish brethren to render to the king whatever divine and human law granted to those whom God has established and also whatever service can be offered without offence or detriment to conscience.

This letter and the reply to Lambeth do not appear to have reached their destinations.[13] Six months later a second communication was sent to Scotland and was received in March of the following year (1640).[14] Two years had passed since the signing of the Covenant, two years in which both sides had been preparing for war. For a time hostile armies faced each other across the Tweed, but the sword had not been drawn. Two General Assemblies had been held, episcopal government had with the eventual consent of the king's commissioner been declared unlawful in the Kirk but ratification by Parliament had been delayed. Much had been achieved. The Covenanters had been successful in their primary objective, although the king still hoped to restore episcopacy

---

[12] Staatsarchiv, MS E 369, 230–4. In his letter to the neighbouring churches Breitinger notes the extent to which the minds of both parties are inflamed and refers to 'acrimonia illa vehemens qua Scotos, ministros Verbi inprimis, insolentiae rebellionis, conjurationis, armatae resistentiae et inauditae audaciae condemnat asseveranter adeo, ut post se vel Jesuiticam relinquant impietatem'.

[13] The final draft of the letter to the Scottish Church and that to the archbishop are endorsed in Breitinger's hand 24 Junij 1639. The letter to the archbishop had been extensively rewritten as a result of the correspondence. Staatsarchiv, MS E II 369, 232, 235, 236, 242, Zentralbibliothek, MS A 124b, 20.

[14] Staatsarchiv, MS E II 369, 247. No copy of this second letter has been discovered, but from the reply which it called forth from Scotland we can deduce that it was similar to the earlier one.

and it was rumoured that he was again raising an army. Such was the situation when the Swiss Pastors called upon the ministers of the Church to defend themselves.

The task was indeed a delicate one and its presentation required considerable skill. That the challenge was taken seriously is clearly proved not only by the long and carefully constructed letter sent to Zürich in the Church's name,[15] but by the choice of a scholar of high reputation to draft it, a minister who, for much of his earlier career, had supported the royal ecclesiastical policy under both King James and King Charles. Andrew Ramsay (1574–1659) – the author of the reply – was one of the pastors of Edinburgh, and, like so many of the leaders of the Covenanting party, an alumnus of St Andrews University. He had graduated from St Leonard's College in 1589 and had subsequently studied theology in St Mary's College under Andrew Melville.[16] But he actively opposed the liturgical innovations associated with Laud along with Alexander Henderson, and took a prominent part in the events of 1638 and 1639.[17]

His defence arrived in Zürich towards the end of May 1640, two months after it had been written, and is extant in the original autograph and in several contemporary copies. It did much to restore confidence in the Scottish Church and to convince the Swiss of the injustice of Laud's accusations. For those familiar with Scottish ecclesiastical history the letter has little, however, that is new and much that has a familiar ring. The source of all the evils that had ever befallen the nation is the pride, tyranny, and heterodoxy of the Scottish bishops. Ramsay quoted Boece and the Venerable Bede at considerable length in support of his contention that the Church had been successfully ruled for centuries without bishops, that dioceses were, comparatively speaking, of relatively recent development, and that for only five hundred years – which he described as an unbroken night of error – had bishops ruled the Church. At the Reformation they were replaced by a polity in agreement with the word of God which stood until the death of John Knox. Then corruption set in, bishops were

[15] The autograph, MS E II 369, 247, is endorsed by Breitinger, *Reditur 29 Maij 1640*. Several contemporary copies are extant in MS E II and in Zentralbibliothek, MSS A 124b, B 26 and B 28. A contemporary copy is also preserved in the University Library, Basel. The letter was published in 1641 in *Rerum nuper in Regno Scotiae gestarum historia* (Dantisci, [Amsterdam] per Philalethen Eleutherum). 'This work which is usually attributed to William Spang,' Scots minister in Campvere, 'was founded at least upon Baillie's communications to his cousin'. *The Letters and Journals*, ed. Laing, i, 186 n. 7; see also ii, pp. cxii ff.

[16] Ramsay matriculated in St Leonard's College in 1589, was B.A. in 1592 and M.A., as *potens*, in 1593. In 1593–4 he was a student in St Mary's College and again in 1595–6. (I am indebted to Mr R. N. Smart for this information extracted from the University's muniments). He later studied in France. His subsequent career can be traced in the *Register of the Privy Council of Scotland*, David Calderwood, *The History of the Kirk of Scotland*, ed. T. Thomson, Wodrow Society, 1842–9, John Row, *The History of the Kirk of Scotland*, edn. Wodrow Society, 1842, *The Letters and Journals of Robert Baillie*, and *Original Letters relating to the Ecclesiastical Affairs of Scotland*, ed. B. Botfield (Bannatyne Club, 1851). The best biographical notice is in the *Dictionary of National Biography*, vol. 47, pp. 234–7.

[17] *Selections from Wodrow's Biographical Collections*, ed. R. Lippe (New Spalding Club, Aberdeen, 1890), pp. 171f., J. Gordon, *History of Scots Affairs from MDCXXXII to MDCXLI*, ii, 58 (Spalding Club, Aberdeen, 1841); Row, *History*, p. 525; *The Letters and Journals of Robert Baillie*, i, 144ff.; *A Relation of Proceedings concerning the Affairs of the Kirk of Scotland, 1637–1638*, by John, Earl of Rothes, ed. J. Nairne (Bannatyne Club, 1830).

re-introduced and the strength, vigour, and external form of the Church of the Reformation lost. *Hinc omnia in pejus ruere et retro sublapsa referri.* The bishops arrogated to themselves the power of both swords, dominated the Council, prevented the holding of General Assemblies, introduced a book of canons transferring to themselves the entire administrative authority of the Church, and restricting pastors to the administration of the Word and Sacraments. Such was their tyranny and their pride.

What of their heterodoxy? They preach Arminianism, they deny that the pope is the Antichrist, they assert the local presence of Christ in the Sacrament of the Lord's Supper, and some, not the least among them, treat the imputation of Christ's righteousness, on which salvation depends, as a figment of the imagination; they frequently maintain that it would be easy to enter into agreement with the Roman Church with whom they are at one on the fundamentals of the faith. Their heterodoxy has shown itself in liturgical innovation; they have turned the Lord's Table into an altar, placed it at the east end of the Church, protected it by rails, and genuflected to it. They have also sought to impose upon the Church forms of worship replete with idolatrous rites, based on the Anglican Liturgy but with those parts deleted by Martin Bucer restored.[18] This, he writes, is indeed the origin of all you have heard. 'For,' continued Ramsay, 'we were required by royal proclamation to embrace this liturgy which was contrary to our faith and the statutes of our Church, or suffer the accusation of treason. Thus the representatives of the whole nation had counselled together to restore the primitive purity of the Church.'

The prelude to the signing of the Covenant and the holding of the General Assemblies are briefly summarised, and also the subsequent deposition of the bishops and the Assembly's declaration that the episcopal hierarchy had always been harmful to the Scottish Church and was therefore to be abolished. The bishops then fled to the king and assisted by the archbishop of Canterbury persuaded him against his inmost nature to declare war on the Scots as rebels.

It is impossible to maintain that Ramsay gave his Swiss correspondents an unbiased account of these momentous years. Yet this much must be said to his credit: in all his denunciations of episcopacy and the bishops in no way does he stoop to the accusations of moral unworthiness that besmirch the records of the General Assembly of 1638, and of the Presbytery of Edinburgh.[19] Whatever he thought of the charges of excessive drinking, playing of cards, profane language and Sabbath-breaking, he did not consider them worth repeating to add strength to his defence. True, the bishops were primarily responsible for the trouble; they had exceeded the bounds of their spiritual office; they had con-

[18] On the part taken by Martin Bucer in the revision of the Prayer Book see C. Hopf, *Martin Bucer and the English Reformation* (Oxford, 1946).

[19] *Records of the Kirk of Scotland*, ed. A. Peterkin (Edinburgh, 1838); see also *Acts of the General Assembly of the Church of Scotland, 1638–1842*, ed. T. Pitcairn (Edinburgh, 1843), pp. 10ff. For 'the black and fearful catalogue of crimes' alleged before the Presbytery of Edinburgh see *The Large Declaration . . . by the King*, pp. 209–19, and J. Cunningham, *The Church History of Scotland*, ii, pp. 11f., 16ff. Baillie, *Letters and Journals*, i, 155 informs us that at the Glasgow Assembly of 1638 Ramsay was not at first in favour of the summary excommunication of the bishops.

founded the sacred and the secular; they had misused the temporal power to alter in a Romeward direction accepted church practice in worship and in government.

Undoubtedly the events of 1637 had turned Ramsay, after thirty years of support for the modified form of episcopacy introduced by James VI, into an out-and-out opponent of the hierarchy; but neither he nor his fellow Covenanters were political rebels. His letter speaks of the king with due deference throughout; he had been unwillingly urged to action against the Scots at the importunity of the bishops and of the archbishop of Canterbury, who was their staunchest supporter, if not the author of all the innovations. When the two armies met, Ramsay attributed to the king the leading role in the pacification, permitting the General Assembly, in which his commissioner concurred, to condemn the bishops and the principle of ecclesiastical hierarchy. Even when the king had dissolved parliament before ratifying the decisions of the Assembly, and even when it was rumoured that he was again leading an army against them, the bishops were blamed.

The Swiss received the Scottish defence with open arms and thankful hearts, as was virtually assured. In their private correspondence they had not concealed where their sympathies lay[20] and, as copies of Ramsay's letter circulated among them, they not only expressed their conviction that the Scots had vindicated themselves but urged further action on their behalf. Bern recommended that they should encourage the civil magistrates to write to King Charles and at the same time write to the king themselves.[21] Schaffhausen considered that, as Laud was the author of the trouble, they should again address him, even although such action would achieve little or nothing.[22] From Basel, where the cause against the Scots was being championed by a certain Oliver Fleming, a Scot who condemned the ministers of perjury, sedition and rebellion, came further support, but of a more cautious nature.[23] They suggested that any letter to the King should be in general terms, impartial and free from bitterness.

Throughout the summer months the Swiss were drafting and re-drafting letters to the king and the archbishop and discussing how to send them and the language in which they should address the king. (Perhaps knowing the origin of King Charles' wife, they wondered if his French might be better than his Latin!) Meanwhile in Scotland the Covenanters' drums had been beating to arms. By the beginning of August a large army was marching from Edinburgh towards the south and on the 30th they were in possession of Newcastle. The outcome is too well known and need not be rehearsed, suffice it to say that by the end of the year terms of peace had been agreed whereby episcopacy in Scotland was overthrown.

Sometime during the course of these events the Scottish Church leaders

[20] See *supra*, n. 9.
[21] The letters exchanged at this time by Bern and Zürich are very favourable towards the Scots. Staatsarchiv, MS E II 369, 252, 253, 254.
[22] Schaffhausen was also well satisfied with the reply from Scotland. MS E II 369, 258, 259, 260.  [23] MS E II 369, 261, 263–5.

received their last brief communication from Zürich.[24] While bitterly regretting the charges of rebellion against them, from which they had successfully defended themselves, their Swiss brethren earnestly entreated them to remain blameless, so that the entire Christian world might understand that they had never under pretext of religion resisted the ordinance of God, but only that violation of conscience which threatened the very foundations of Orthodoxy.

Thus the Swiss maintained to the end the deep religious concern which had first prompted them to write to the English archbishop. As the issues became more and more entangled in both English and Scottish politics they retired from the scene. It was no longer simply a dispute among churches and between churchmen which might do irreparable harm to the faith, and which fellow churchmen in a neighbouring country with close ties with England and Scotland had to do all in their power to alleviate. A letter from Andrew Ramsay to Breitinger in November 1641 closes the correspondence.[25]

This episode in what today might be called inter-Church relations illustrates in microcosm the province of ecclesiastical history. The church historian, whatever be the period of his study, is primarily concerned with the Christian religion as it has been active in the society of believers and in the society of the wider world. It is not primarily concerned with the lives of the saints and martyrs, with St Ignatius hastening to Rome anxious to meet death in the arena, St Jerome in his cell at Bethlehem, surrounded by his admirers, absorbed in monastic devotion and scholarly labour, Martin Luther wrestling in his study with problems of the divine *justitia*. Of course the church historian is obliged to dwell on the influence of great men and women of faith on the development of the Church. But herein lies a major problem in the writing of its history; the temptation to view the Church in terms of individuals and their achievements, to treat it as biography rather than as the record of its corporate life. As the Christian faith expresses itself in the development of the Church's theology, its worship, and its organisation so these undoubtedly constitute the province of the church historian, but he also has to show the faith of believers active in its struggle to transform the collapsing civilisation of the Graeco-Roman world, in its efforts to build the City of God upon the devastation wrought by the barbarian invasions, in its preaching of the Gospel to all the mission lands, not least the lost societies created by the industrial age. In a word, the province is co-extensive with the spread of the faith.

If this definition be accepted then it follows that the history of the Church can never be studied in isolation, behind national, still less, denominational or strictly ecclesiastical boundaries. Whatever period the student chooses to make

[24] By the beginning of August a reply to the Scottish Church had been drafted (MS E II 369, 266) and one from the civil authorities to the king, of which the final form is dated 6 September 1640 as is the final form of one to Laud (MS E II 369, 269–76; see also MS E II 404, 85, 88, 113).

[25] The autograph sent to Scotland has not apparently survived. A draft is in MS E II 369, 266. The autograph of Ramsay's letter, MS E II 404a, 856–8, is endorsed by Breitinger *Redd. 19 Jan. 1642.* Contemporary copies are in MS E II 369, 293 and Zentralbibliothek, MS B 285, 239.

his own (and no one can hope to become master of a span of 2,000 years), he must bring to his work a whole breadth of outlook and a catholicity of interest. He must not allow his vision to be blurred by theological conviction or political creed. Never must he fail to take into account the riches of contemporary development in the political, social, economic, and artistic realms of human experience.

If such be the nature of the task set before church history, this further point needs clear enunciation. It must be based upon sound, scientifically conducted research. In his inaugural address seventy years ago as regius professor of history in the University of Cambridge, J. B. Bury pointed out that the furtherance of research was the highest duty of the universities.[26] It is, I firmly believe, still so today and I would uphold Bury's contention that the advancement of research in history in all its branches is not a luxury, subsidiary though desirable, but continues to be a pressing need. The advancement of research in ecclesiastical history has, I believe, been among the finest contributions to academic study by my distinguished predecessors in this Chair – men such as A. F. Mitchell and J. H. Baxter. It is a tradition which I trust I may in some part be enabled to uphold.

JAMES K. CAMERON

[26] *An Inaugural Lecture* (Cambridge, 1903), p. 24.

# 14

## The Advocates as Scottish Trade Union Pioneers[1]

'A Trade Union, as we understand the term, is a continuous association of wage-earners for the purpose of maintaining or improving the conditions of their employment.'[2] Sidney and Beatrice Webb provided this definition in 1894, and upon it they founded an account of the origins and development of British trade unionism that is of lasting value. For one thing, their terms of reference enabled them effectively to counter the misleading idea that the mediaeval craft gild provided an analogue of the modern trade union. The gild, as the Webbs showed, 'was assumed to represent, not only all the grades of producers in a particular industry, but also the consumers of the product, and the community at large'.[3] But the influence of the Webbs' discussion of trade union origins was greater even than they would have wished, since for too long it made historians excessively nervous of any investigation of trade union pre-history. Recently however, it has become possible to ask: were there groups in pre-industrial Britain, of lowly social position, whose defence of what little they had took a form in some sense antecedent to modern trade unionism? Edward Thompson, for instance, is now showing us that there were: one seed-bed of the labour movement is the eighteenth-century 'tissue of customary practices, in marketing, milling, baking, which amount to a popular "moral economy", at variance with the assumptions of the rulers'.[4] Another interesting if less crucial question may be posed: were there groups in pre-industrial Britain, of such a privileged social position that it would seem odd to describe them as ancestors of the modern trade unionists, but whose favourable situation enabled them to anticipate modern trade union techniques? My paper is a contribution to this latter enquiry.

The economy of seventeenth-century Scotland was insufficiently developed for wage-earners to have much prospect of forming trade unions with a continuous existence. The earliest Scottish examples mentioned by W. H. Marwick, found among workers in pre-industrial crafts like tailoring, date from the mid-eighteenth century.[5] Evidence of trade union techniques and practices at this period must be sought elsewhere. There is plenty of evidence, from the seven-

---

[1] A version of this paper was read to the Scottish Labour History Society on 28 May 1967. I am grateful to the Society for the discussion on that occasion.

[2] Sidney and Beatrice Webb, *The History of Trade Unionism* (London, 1894), 1.

[3] *Ibid.*, 17.

[4] E. P. Thompson, 'Working Class Culture – The transition to Industrialism', *Bulletin of the Society for the Study of Labour History*, No. 9 (Autumn 1964), 4–5: see also his 'The Moral Economy of the English Crowd in the Eighteenth Century', *Past and Present*, No. 50 (1971), 76–136.

[5] W. H. Marwick, *A Short History of Labour in Scotland* (Edinburgh, 1967), 4–5.

teenth century and earlier, of the robust application of restrictive practices by the craft gilds. An Act of Parliament of 1493 spoke of masons and wrights who sought to 'have thair feis alsweill on the haly dais as for work dais or els they sall nocht laubour nor wirk, and als quhat personis of thame that wald begin ane uther mannis werk and he at his plesur will leif the said werk and than nane of the said craft dar nocht compleit nor fulfill the samin wark . . .'[6]

The 1670s furnish a splendid example of a gild's restrictive practices. David Pringle was surgeon to Heriot's Hospital, through being nearest of kin to the founder. At 9 a.m. on 1 June 1671 the Edinburgh magistrates, as was their annual custom, were to come to Heriot's to hear a sermon. Two hours before, Pringle was, according to his own account, called on to 'poll the childrein's heads that they might appear in better order before the magistrats'. Only one assistant, a boy, was available to Pringle and he sent him to Heriot's, telling him to get help on the way. Unfortunately the boy secured the help of William Wood, a recognised surgeon or barber in the adjacent burgh of Portsburgh, but not in Edinburgh. The deacon of the Edinburgh incorporation of surgeons caused the magistrates to imprison Wood, and then Pringle, for this breach of their rights. The dispute went to the privy council, where the incorporation stated that if Pringle had to perform a rush job on the sixty heads at Heriot's it was the result of his own dilatoriness, and that Pringle himself and not his assistant had employed Wood. Pringle had to sign an acknowledgment of his faults and drop his case before the privy council before the incorporation would restore him to his privileges.[7] Though the Edinburgh surgeons were more like modern barbers than modern surgeons they clearly had many of the aspirations of a modern professional body, and in 1694, they were elevated to the dignity of the 'royal college of surgeons'.

The faculty of advocates, those pleading before the supreme courts, were in the late seventeenth century as capable as any craft gild of vigorous expressions of professional solidarity. It must be admitted that they still lacked many of the rights and attributes of a modern profession, but as J. Irvine Smith suggests,[8] the development of their corporate personality was a continuous process; and the acts of militancy to be described in this paper are part of that process.

Licensed to appear as procurators before the Court of Session in 1532,[9] they were in 1587 admitted to practice in criminal cases.[10] The office of dean of the faculty, first recorded in 1582,[11] gave it cohesion. Entrants to the faculty had to pay a fee, which in the 1680s stood at 500 merks.[12] In 1682 the faculty acquired

[6] The Acts of the Parliaments of Scotland (APS), edd. T. Thomson and C. Innes (Edinburgh, 1814–75), ii, 234, c. 14.

[7] The Register of the Privy Council of Scotland (RPC), edd. J. H. Burton and others (Edinburgh, 1877–), third series, iii, 433–9.

[8] J. Irvine Smith, 'The Transition to the Modern Law, 1532–1660', in An Introduction to Scottish Legal History (Stair Society, 1958: vol. xx), 25–43.

[9] The Acts of Sederunt of the Lords of Council and Session, from . . . May 1532, to January 1553 (AS, Campbell), ed. Lord President Ilay Campbell (Edinburgh, 1811), 5.

[10] APS, iii, 443, c. 16: ibid., iii, 458–61, c. 57.          [11] RPC, iii, 530.

[12] Sir John Lauder of Fountainhall, Historical Notices of Scottish Affairs (Bannatyne Club, 1848), ii, 698.

its library. Since at least 1619 there was normally a comprehensive examination in civil law for entrants to the bar,[13] and in the form it had acquired by the early eighteenth century – private examination, maintaining a thesis before the faculty, and a speech to the judges[14] – this examination gave the faculty a fair degree of control over its own composition.

On the other hand, entrance by a less rigorous and less 'honourable' trial in Scots law was sometimes possible,[15] and indeed until at least the middle of the seventeenth century 'advocates' are named in record sources who do not appear in the official faculty list.[16] Nor did the faculty have the monopoly of places on the bench. Between 1532 and 1608 only one judgeship in three went to practising advocates.[17] Between 1621 and 1646 the proportion was less than one in five. But five of the ten judges appointed in 1649–50 had been advocates, and so were several of the Cromwellian judges, among them one Andrew Ker, who deserves to be remembered for his claim that

> 'many times he had as sweet and as great communion with God when on the bench, and the advocates pleading before him, and the rest, sometimes, as ever he had in secret.'[18]

Just under half the judges appointed in the period 1660–80 had been advocates, or just over half if the extraordinary lords of session, the straight political appointees, are excluded.[19] The advocates were moving towards the position laid down by the Articles of Union,[20] which reserved the office of ordinary lord to advocates, principal clerks of session and writers to the signet, and in practice gave the advocates the monopoly of the bench once the office of extraordinary lord had been abolished in the mid-eighteenth century.

The work of the advocates was regulated by the acts of sederunt framed by the session to govern its own procedure, and in general the seventeenth-century advocates often give the impression of being under the tutelage of the judges. Lord President Spotiswoode (who had not himself been an advocate) sounds in his 1633 address to the advocates, with its peppering of Greek and Latin tags, like a testy and pedantic dominie:[21]

> Have but us that are set over you in that reverence and regard that ye should, and we shall not be much troubled to admonish you of your duty . . . when your clients have ingaged themselves upon your assurance, and are disappointed at last, then you to save your own credit, must lay the blame of all

---

[13] *AS*, Campbell, 75.

[14] *The Acts of Sederunt of the Lords of Council and Session, from the 15th of January 1553, to the 11th of July 1790 (AS, Tait)*, ed. Alexander Tait (Edinburgh, 1790), 181: William Forbes, *A Journal of the Session* (Edinburgh, 1714), p. viii.

[15] Forbes, *Journal*, p. viii: Ae. J. G. Mackay, *Memoir of Sir James Dalrymple, First Viscount Stair* (Edinburgh, 1873), 25, 269–71.

[16] J. Irvine Smith, art. cit.                    [17] *Ibid*.

[18] Robert Wodrow, cited in G. Brunton and D. Haig, *An Historical Account of the Senators of the College of Justice* (Edinburgh, 1832), 347.

[19] My calculations are based on the list in Brunton and Haig, *Senators*.

[20] *APS*, xi, 406–13 (clause xix).

[21] Sir Robert Spotiswoode, *Practicks*, ed. John Spotiswoode (Edinburgh, 1706), pp. vi–vii.

upon the judges ... this doing tends principally to bring us into contempt, yet it indangereth the weal and standing of this House, and if it get way, shall prove a means of the overthrow thereof, which is *theatrum gloriae vestrae et quaestus vestri.*

But this tutelage would not retard the corporate progress of the faculty unless their interests and those of the judges were essentially different. This was not usually the case, and it will be seen that when clashes occurred the hand of the judges was being forced by the government.

If, then, there were bounds to the corporate strength of the faculty, they did not lack the will or confidence to seek to widen these bounds. Their calling required self-confidence of them as individuals, and in return conferred prestige on them as a group. Besides, they belonged largely to the most favoured group in Scottish society as a whole, the men of landed property. Of some ninety entrants admitted to the faculty in the period 1621–40, at least fifty-three were the sons of lairds or became lairds themselves. In the years 1641–60, when the predominance of landed men in Scottish society was more threatened than it ever was again before the nineteenth century,[22] the proportion was nevertheless at least sixty out of ninety-six. For the period 1661–80 it was at least eighty-seven out of one hundred and twenty-nine.[23] In this last period there were also a handful of peers' sons (including three sons of James Dalrymple viscount of Stair), and one peer, George Gordon first earl of Aberdeen, who had an exclusive clientele and who never took fees.[24] Of English lawyers of the period Alan Harding has remarked:

> ... legal training was only a formal episode in a career based on other founda-tions. Those who reached the nobility had often completed by a well-placed marriage what legal talent had but begun generations before – not till after 1660 was legal talent sufficient of itself.[25]

When one considers the career of men like Thomas Hamilton under James VI, Thomas Hope under Charles I, and James Dalrymple later, one is the more impressed by how high the art of advocacy, particularly if applied to the govern-ment's service, could carry a seventeenth century-Scot.

The rights and privileges of landed men were the staple of litigation. There was little notion of judicial impartiality, and the English judges sent by Crom-well were scoffed at as 'a wheen kinless loons'.[26] Judges and advocates thus stood together enmeshed in a system of influence and corruption that too often made the courts merely one theatre for playing out the eternal rivalries among society's most favoured group.

But within that group the advocates were acquiring distinctive corporate

[22] G. Donaldson, *Scotland: James V – James VII* (Edinburgh, 1965), 339–40.

[23] My calculations are based on the list in *The Faculty of Advocates in Scotland*, ed. Sir Francis J. Grant (Scottish Record Society, 1944: vol. 76). Grant's prefatory note explains how he tried to make good the gaps in the books of sederunt, one of which covers 1608–26.

[24] Brunton and Haig, *Senators*, 408.

[25] Alan Harding, *A Social History of English Law* (Harmondsworth, 1966), 207.

[26] Mackay, *Stair*, 62n. says that the remark has been attributed to three different lord presidents – Gilmour, Stair, and the latter's son Hugh.

interests, and on three notable occasions sought to further these interests by taking what we would now describe as strike action. The first occasion was during the Cromwellian regime. Cromwell remodelled the Scottish justiciary, in 1652 replacing the court of session by commissioners for justice, and in 1654 abolishing the baron courts of the lairds.[27] He thus threatened to replace landed influence by a relatively impartial justiciary: 'thair justice exceidit the Scottis in many thinges, as wes reportit'.[28] It was a direct attack on the whole Scottish social order. But the advocates were no more able to resist this than were other landed men, and proceeded to operate within the new judicial machinery. It was only in 1654 that the leading advocates withdrew their labour, and then it was because they were asked to take a tender or oath of allegiance to the Commonwealth and abjuration of royalty.[29] The government did not press the point, and the advocates returned to work. James Dalrymple was one striker whose conduct did him no harm, since in 1657 he became a judge. He had an ingenious explanation of how he could serve on the bench a government whose existence he in theory did not recognise while at the bar:

> He did not become a judge 'without the approbation of the most eminent of our ministers that were then alive, who did wisely and justly distinguish, between the commissions granted by usurpers, which did relate only to the people, and which were no less necessary than if they had prohibit baking or brewing, but by their warrand, and between these which relate to councils for establishing the usurped power, or burdening the people . . .'[30]

This may remind one of the excuses proffered by those who continued to hold office in Nazi-occupied Europe, and sound equally lame to those considering it from a safe distance. The unusual circumstances of the times explain the success of the advocates' first strike. The government could see that the assertion of principle and of professional dignity was a harmless one; and the success of regimes that, like Cromwell's in Scotland, depend on military force, requires that they distinguish level-headedly between those who are real rebels and those who are not.

The court of session and judicial partiality were restored with Charles II. Landed men had learned what the overthrow of monarchy could mean for them, and in power or out of it, it came to be understood that they must have nothing to do with conventicling revolutionaries. With a Lauderdale in power and a Hamilton in opposition, politics began to be the great game of landed men bidding for the spoils of office that it remained throughout the eighteenth century. As Kirkton says: '. . . neither of the sides mentioned the name of religion, either for distress or danger. . . . And this made the lovers of religion to be less concerned for either of the Dukes. . . .'[31] But the very fact that the

[27] Mackay, *Stair*, 58–62: Donaldson, *Scotland, James V – James VII*, 347–8.
[28] John Nicoll, *Diary* (Bannatyne Club, 1836), 104.
[29] Mackay, *Stair*, 61: G. W. T. Omond, *The Lord Advocates of Scotland* (Edinburgh, 1883), i, 159.
[30] *An Apology for Sir James Dalrymple . . . by Himself* (Bannatyne Club, 1825), 8–9.
[31] John Kirkton, *The Secret and True History of the Church of Scotland*, ed. Charles Kirkpatrick Sharpe (Edinburgh, 1817), 342.

game, of which the law was as ever a part, was to be played strictly within the rules of public safety meant that, within these rules, someone like Lauderdale could play it in a boisterous way. When the lawyers staged their second and third strikes, they found that involvement in political opposition did not pay dividends.

In 1669 the king nominated a commission to consider the regulation of the supreme courts in Scotland.[32] There was every justification for this. Judges were accustomed to rig the order in which cases were called, to oblige their friends and surprise their enemies among the litigants. Advocates had a practice analogous to one of which modern working men (if not trade unions as such) have been accused, namely that they filibustered in order to prolong cases from day to day, and then declined to attend without fresh fees. The commission made a preliminary report in March 1670, and after much controversy and a further report, their recommendations were embodied in an Act of Parliament of 1672.[33] Some of the provisions of this act, such as the establishment of the high court of justiciary in its definitive form, were of basic importance. Among the minor provisions was one safeguarding the advocates' professional interests, and was no doubt inserted at their request. While the writers to the signet, representing the solicitors' side of the legal profession, had not engaged in court work, an undefined group of 'agents', who were neither advocates nor advocates' servants, had begun to concern themselves with the litigants' papers. These men were now banned from the courts as being 'of no use but burdensome to the lieges'.[34]

But one regulation aroused the concerted opposition of the advocates: it prescribed their fees, on a scale corresponding to contemporary views of a hierarchical society – £18 from a nobleman, £15 from a knight or baronet, £12 from a gentleman or chief burgess, £9 from any other person. The advocates were so vexed at this curb on their incomes that, according to one of their number Sir George Mackenzie, they 'to render the articles wherein themselves were concerned ridiculous, did exclaim against the whole; and by this practice made the greatest part of them burdens'. . . .[35] Stair, an advocate during the strike of 1654, and now a judge and a member of the reform commission, retained a sense of sympathy with the advocates. He successfully opposed a proposed regulation reviving the division of the profession, found at the beginning of the century, into advocates pleading before the inner and outer houses of the session respectively. He also spoke, albeit unsuccessfully, against the fees regulation. He received the public thanks of the faculty for his efforts.[36]

The judges now sought to impose an oath on advocates and their clients that no more than the regulation fees would be paid. In this the judges were acting on royal instructions.[37] On 8 November 1670 the faculty resolved to refuse the oath.[38] There was only one dissentient, James Foulis, and he had his reward when,

[32] Mackay, *Stair*, 94: Omond, *Lord Advocates*, i, 194–5.
[33] *APS*, viii, 80, c. 16.     [34] Mackay, *Stair*, 98.
[35] Sir George Mackenzie, *Memoirs of the Affairs of Scotland* (Edinburgh, 1818), 213–17.
[36] Forbes, *Journal*, pp. vii, xxxiii–xxxiv.
[37] Mackay, *Stair*, 94.     [38] Omond, *Lord Advocates*, i, 195–6.

during the advocates' strike in 1674, he was raised to the bench as Lord Reidford. The 1670 strike began on 10 November, and lasted about two months. Unfortunately the decisive break in the faculty's solidarity came from its dean, Sir Robert Sinclair. At the end of the year the lord presidency became vacant, and Sinclair expected that the lord advocate Sir John Nisbet would move up, thus leaving his office vacant in turn. In order to become lord advocate Sinclair returned from London, where he had been sitting on the Union commission, and proceeded to take the oath on fees. The strike then collapsed.[39]

Sir John Nisbet did not take the lord presidency, and Lauderdale gave it to Stair; Sinclair's share was the opprobrium of his fellow advocates. As one of them, Sir John Lauder of Fountainhall, says:[40]

> ... its beleived he (Sinclair) would not have bein the coy duck to the rest of the Advocats for their obtempering to the Act of Regulations had he forsein that they would have hudibrased him in the manner they did; hence we said give us all assurance to be Kings Advocat and we shall all take it with the first; and the Lords, when he was plaiding before them in a particular, entreated him to come within the bar and put on his hat, since it was but to make him Advocat with 2 or 3 days antidate.

(The origin of the lord advocate's privilege of pleading with his hat on is obscure, and has probably nothing to do with Sir Thomas Hope's showing a proper disrespect when pleading before his sons on the bench.[41]) It is significant that the judges were as rude about Sinclair's opportunism as were the advocates. This, together with Stair's undoubted sympathy for the advocates on this occasion, suggests that Sir George Mackenzie may be exaggerating when he claims that, as a result of the advocates' exclaiming against the regulations, 'the harmony which us'd to be betwixt Lords and Advocates, was here broke off; the parties injur'd, (as is usual) justifying all that they did, or could do, to repay the injury receiv'd'.[42] When he wrote, Mackenzie was looking back repentantly at his time as a wild advocate and opposition politician.

It was not the judges but the government who outfaced the advocates over the fee regulation. When parliament in 1672 ratified the new regulations, they were 'all voted together, at last, in a very strange and extraordinary manner'.[43] The fee regulation was thus smuggled through with the rest, which would explain why Stair, according to Mackenzie, opposed ratification. Mackenzie himself spoke against the fee regulation, partly in terms that cheerfully allowed for the presence of perjurers among his colleagues:[44]

> And at best, it will be tie such as fear an oath, and enrich such as contemn it; and thus you will seem more careful of the people's money, than of their souls.

---

[39] Omond, *Lord Advocates*, i, 195–6.
[40] *Journal of a Foreign Tour in 1665 and 1666, etc.*, by Sir John Lauder, Lord Fountainhall, ed. Donald Crawford (Scottish History Society, 1900), 214.
[41] Omond, *Lord Advocates*, i, 146.   [42] Mackenzie, *Memoirs*, 216–17.
[43] *Ibid.*, 234.   [44] *Ibid.*, 234–8.

In a revealing part of his speech he turns against the reform commissioners the full force of the advocates' injured professional *amour propre*:

> The proposed regulations 'though they concern the forms of our procedure, and so can only be known to such as have experience, yet were invented and authori'd by noblemen, whose birth and education cannot allow them to understand what was to be introduc'd or abrogated. And since soldiers, salt or coalmasters, would think it imprudence in such as are not bred up in their profession, to prescribe orders for such as serve under it; it is strange why any, save learned lawyers, should adventure upon a task, wherein even reason cannot discover what is fit.'

From the government's point of view it must have told against the advocates that the duke of Hamilton, the centre of strenuous opposition in the parliamentary sessions of 1672–3, was also against the regulations.[45] Lord Chancellor Rothes, himself not the most learned of men, had clashed with Sir John Nisbet and Sir Archibald Primrose during the Union commissioners' time in London, accusing them of walking about on foot despite having a generous expense allowance, and castigating them as 'damned lawyers'.[46] And he wrote to Lauderdale in terms that implied the greatest contempt for those who used the arcana of their profession as a cloak for political opposition:[47]

> The greatest difficulty we have is to order the fees of the advocates. Many of the Commissioners [for reforming the courts] have been advocates themselves, or their sons are, yet they carry pretty fair, for the point is pressed to purpose; and if you hear not we order them and the writers, you may conclude that all we have done is not worth two pears to the poor harassed country.

A government grappling with the religious zealots of the south-west was not prepared to stand any nonsense from its factious but essentially law-abiding opponents among the landed men. The irony of it was that the advocates were a strong enough pressure-group to get their way in the long term, when their tactics were less flamboyant. In 1681 the fee regulation was rescinded.[48]

By early 1674 Lauderdale had met with so much trouble in parliament that he dissolved it, and no other was summoned for seven years. But the opposition had other means of creating a stir, and again the advocates came in handy. The 1674–6 advocates' strike has been fully described by Sir George Mackenzie, but since it was the occasion of his conversion from forceful opposition to support for the court, his account of men and motives must be treated with especial care.[49]

---

[45] *Ibid.*, 234: W. C. Mackenzie, *The Life and Times of John Maitland, Duke of Lauderdale* (London, 1923), esp. 339–40: R. S. Rait, *The Parliaments of Scotland* (Glasgow, 1924), 81–4.
[46] Mackenzie, *Memoirs*, 213.
[47] Rothes to Lauderdale, 17 February 1671, quoted in Mackay, *Stair*, 95.
[48] *APS*, viii, 363, c. 109.
[49] See Mackenzie, *Memoirs*, 267–310, which is quoted extensively below; Andrew Lang, *Sir George Mackenzie* (London, 1909), 114–21, analyses the account given in the *Memoirs*; Mackay, *Stair*, 113–20, provides a balanced discussion.

The affair began with a law-suit between the earls of Callendar and Dunfermline. Callendar's advocates, Sir George Lockhart, Sir Robert Sinclair, Sir John Cunninghame and Sir George Mackenzie, were among the leaders of the bar. When the case reached a stage for which the advocates were apparently not prepared, they advised an appeal to parliament. Callendar was cited for the appeal as a contempt of court, and the advocates then stuck resolutely to the contention that the supposed appeal was really a protest for remeid of law. On the face of it this made better legal sense, since whereas the constitutional theory of the time was clearly opposed to the notion 'that appellation should be normal or frequent', protest to parliament for remeid of law was equally clearly the appropriate remedy for grievances 'produced by the incapacity or the partiality of all officers of the Crown, judicial as well as executive'.[50] But the advocates' second thoughts thus converted a legally dubious point into a politically explosive one.

There is evidence that the government had been manipulating the case through the convenient fact that Lauderdale was an extraordinary lord of session.[51] But Mackenzie admits that the Callendar party's tactics (for which he places the blame on Lockhart) were based on the expedient consideration that 'Dunfermline, as Lauderdale's uncle, would want in Parliament that favour which Callendar might expect, as having married the Duke of Hamilton's daughter'. The subsequent furore had something to do with principles of justice, but the advocates could not have reasonably blamed the government for taking them more seriously as opposition politicians than as constitutional lawyers.

We know Stair's considered opinion on protests for remeid of law, namely that they 'are not in all cases against law, but are sometimes just and necessary, as when the Lords determine without, and beyond their authority and jurisdiction committed to them'.[52] But again he and the judges had in practice no choice but to acquiesce in government actions, even if the government to humble the advocates had to go so far as to outlaw protest for remeid of law.

On 28 February 1674 the judges felt compelled to write to the king about the stand taken by Callendar's advocates.[53] Lauderdale hastened to spell out in person to Charles the consequences, in general as well as in this case in particular, of a fresh summons to parliament: in Mackenzie's words, 'in the Session the King had the sole nomination of all the Judges, whereas the Parliament was not of his election'. The king by a letter of 19 May[54] condemned all appeals to parliament. Any advocates not prepared to disown them were to be disbarred 'from the exercise of any part of their practice as advocates in time coming'. This has an air of finality that is usually assumed to be absent when a modern employer threatens a lock-out, but seventeenth-century governments habitually used strong language that the historian should not take literally.

[50] Rait, *Parliaments*, 474–5.
[51] John Hill Burton, *The History of Scotland* (Edinburgh, 1873–4 edn), vii, 194.
[52] Sir James Dalrymple, Viscount of Stair, *The Institutions of the Law of Scotland* (Edinburgh, 1681), book iv, tit. i, para. lvi.
[53] Mackay, *Stair*, 114.
[54] Printed in Mackenzie, *Memoirs*, 269–72, and in *AS*, Tait, 113–14.

When Lockhart and Cunninghame continued to stand their ground they were disbarred, and about fifty of their colleagues walked out with them. One group under Lockhart retired to Haddington, and the others went with Cunninghame to Linlithgow. Mackenzie, again stressing the sinister influence of Lockhart and the opposition politicians, explains that while 'it might have been reasonably concluded, that this exclusion [of Lockhart and Cunninghame] should have pleas'd the younger advocates whom those seniors overshaded', the majority of the juniors feared 'to offend so eminent men, whom they knew would soon return to their places' and were unduly influenced 'by the lords of the party, and the discontented persons to whom they owed their employments'. . . .

The king wrote again to prompt the judges 'to encourage such advocates as dutifully continued in the exercise of their calling.'[55] These dutiful souls, or 'scabs' as a modern trade unionist would have it, were a source of satisfaction to the authorities as the strike wore on. On 26 January 1675 Stair wrote to Lauderdale:[56]

Ther is abundance of processes before the Session, and all carried through as ordinar, which every day doth mor and mor show how far these gentlemen have mistaken their measures in apprehending they are so necessare as that they would not but get their will if they stuck together.

But in mid-1674 the outed advocates were still seeking to enlarge their struggle. The king favoured the royal burghs also with a letter which was read at their convention on 17 August, and which forbade them to elect to future parliaments persons 'not actual residenters within the burgh commissionating them . . . or such as can gain or lose in any of their concerns'.[57]

This prohibition was based on sound precedents in burgh practice. But on this occasion it was assumed to be aimed especially against burghs who elected lawyers to watch their interests in parliament, and was seen, no doubt correctly, as part of the government's harrassment of opposition elements. The interests of governments and of local communities had long been at variance on this question: in 1372 the election of lawyers as knights of the shire in the English parliament had been forbidden, on the grounds that they presented petitions concerned with their patrons' private interests rather than with the common good.[58] But rather than console themselves with the thought that all such governmental prohibitions were unenforceable, the convention of royal burghs in 1674 decided to answer back. Sir George Mackenzie drew up a reply for them which, he declares, again blaming Lockhart, was altered from 'a discreet and dutiful' to 'a most indiscreet and unpolished paper' before submission. Certainly it led to fines and imprisonment for the provosts of Aberdeen, Glasgow and Jedburgh, an apology by the convention to the king and Lauderdale in January 1675 for the 'impertinent and insolent' reply of 'some turbulent

---

[55] Forbes, *Journal*, p. xix.    [56] Quoted in Mackay, *Stair*, 119.
[57] For this episode see Rait, *Parliaments*, 294–7; Lang, *Mackenzie*, 115; *Records of the Convention of the Royal Burghs of Scotland*, ed. J. D. Marwick (Edinburgh, 1866–90), iii, 639, 644, 649.    [58] Alan Harding, *A Social History of English Law*, 211–12.

persons', and to an act of convention in June that forbade the election of non-residents.

The dispute involving the advocates became gradually intensified. Sir George Mackenzie, not formally associated with the strike at its inception because of illness (and perhaps because of political misgivings), was disbarred on 24 November for failing to give the judges satisfaction on the matter of appeals.[59] The advocates were summoned to petition for readmission before 28 January 1675, or be perpetually disbarred: and on 19 December the privy council forbade their return within twelve miles of the capital in the meantime.[60] Some advocates entered petitions as early as 15 January, and were readmitted.[61] But Lockhart and twenty-nine others submitted an apologia to the privy council instead, which the council declared seditious.[62] Mackenzie was a signatory, but claims he thought that Lockhart had made the address too 'bitter and humorous'. He professes to have signed only out of a sense of solidarity and 'to prevent a rupture at a time when their formal adherence to one another was their only security'.

It was clear that the advocates were now acutely uncomfortable at the publicity their trade union activities had brought them. The address sought to show 'how far they are from combination or factious practices, and how much they will lay aside and abandon their own reason and conviction, as to the lawfulness of protestations for remeid of law' if the 'eminent lawyers' on the bench were to pronounce clearly against them. The word 'combination' had not yet, of course, acquired its sense of 'trade union', and is probably here to be defined as it was in Dr Johnson's *Dictionary* (1755): 'union for some certain purpose; association; league . . . it is now generally used in an ill sense'.

It was now too late for the judges to prevent further embarrassment for the strikers. Lockhart, Cunninghame and Sinclair hurried to London to intercede with the king, and Lord Advocate Nisbet brought an indictment on behalf of the council against those advocates who had not yet submitted.[63] Mackenzie rightly or wrongly became convinced that his eminent colleagues had gone south to let him take whatever punishment was coming. He then urged the other advocates to submit, and by June 1675 secured his own readmission to the bar.[64] The end of the strike was now only a matter of time, and by 25 January 1676 all the advocates, even the three leaders who had gone to London, had submitted.[65]

Mackenzie was now on the road to court favour, and his motives throughout the episode are open to suspicion. But one has to admire the skill with which he sought to persuade the other advocates to end the strike. The stock arguments of corporate professional independence, previously used as a reason for defying the government, were smartly turned on their heads:

> . . . they who by their profession us'd to have others depend upon them, were made daily now the instruments of other mens passions, since they had

[59] Lang, *Mackenzie*, 117.
[60] *Ibid.*; Mackay, *Stair*, 115.
[61] Lang, *Mackenzie*, 119.
[62] *Ibid.*, 117–18; Mackay, *Stair*, 115.
[63] Mackay, *Stair*, 115; Omond, *Lord Advocates*, i, 210.
[64] Lang, *Mackenzie*, 119.
[65] *AS*, Tait, 120–4.

deserted their Prince, his judicatures, and their own employments: nor could there be anything more ridiculous, than to see such as need no faction to support them, become martyrs for any faction, and introduce a necessity upon their successors, of siding in all publick differences, which even the greatest fools shun'd when they could gain nothing, by being engag'd by such of the nobility as had been enemies to their profession, had brought upon them the Regulations ... whereas the Advocates of the former age had retain'd, in much worse times, a neutrality that made all of them necessary to the irreconcilable leaders of both sides.

And so, in the short run, the government had again outfaced the advocates: once again, too, their case was upheld in the long run, though admittedly only after a political revolution. In 1689 the Claim of Right declared 'that it is the right and privilege of the Subjects to protest for Remeed of law to the King and Parliament, against sentences pronounced by the Lords of Session'. . . .[66] One must feel sorry for Stair and the judges, who were caught in the crossfire. Stair was the government's agent, and his claim that he was usually in the country when anything was done against the advocates is as lame as his defence of his conduct in the 1650s.[67] But he was as little able to pursue an effective alternative course of action as he had been then, and his remark about the 1670s, that 'God knows, I had no pleasure in the affairs that were then most agitated in Council',[68] need not be disbelieved.

Stair was ridiculed in several pasquils from supporters of the advocates, not all of them as good-natured as the one comparing the advocates with the boys Stair had once taught at Glasgow University:[69]

> Ill-natured stinkard boys who disobey
> Your regent thus! – Yet for excuse they say,
> Your tupto's and your ergo's are so kittle,
> Your topicks and your ethicks are so fickle,
> Your Ferulas and Taws they are so sair,
> The boys vow that they'll go to school na mair.

But it would probably be true to say that the advocates' third strike, like their second, produced rather a state of general rancour throughout the legal profession than a basic cleavage between bar and bench. The issue, after all, had not been clear-cut. While Sir John Lauder of Fountainhall could say on one occasion that the advocates had been disbarred 'on the accompt we ware unclear to serve under the strict and servile tyes seemed to be imposed on us by the King's letter, discharging any to quarrell the Lords of Session their sentences of injustice' . . .,[70] in 1681 he wrote that 'some think our civil rights and interests as well and safely lodged in the Session as in a Parliament who judge more with a biass and in a hurry, and with less regard to law, than the Lords of Session

---

[66] *APS*, ix, 37–40, c. 28.
[67] Mackay, *Stair*, 118–20: *Apology for Sir James Dalrymple*, 14.
[68] *Ibid.*
[69] *A Book of Scottish Pasquils, 1568–1715*, ed. J. Maidment (Edinburgh, 1868), 221.
[70] Lauder, *Historical Notices*, i, 88.

do'.[71] A bitter pasquil links Stair with those scabs among the advocates who were the real object of hatred for their brethren who had struck:[72]

> But since a Rumple President does sit,
> That rumps at bar should domineer was fit.
> Yet, where the taill is thus in the head's place,
> No doubt the body has a shitten face.

For some time the court of session continued to be exercised over the fact that those advocates who had struck sought to send the scabs to Coventry. The king wrote again on 24 May 1676 to the judges, 'to whom he left the advocates and other members of the college of justice to be ordered and ruled in all things relating to their imployment; and required them to prevent and punish all combinations among advocates, refusing or forbearing to consult, plead or concur with those who continued in the House after the rest made a secession'. ... In accordance with this directive the judges suspended two advocates on 30 June.[73] And on 7 June 1677 an act of sederunt threatened to disbar any other advocate who sent a colleague to Coventry, 'upon the account of personal prejudice, or any other pretence'. ...[74]

The seventeenth-century advocates had their limitations as strikers, in particular lack of solidarity. It might be thought that their second strike had foundered on the ambition of Sir Robert Sinclair, and that their third collapsed through the mutual jealousy of Sir George Mackenzie and Sir George Lockhart. Here a remark by Henry Cockburn may be apposite, made as he sought to explain why the writers to the signet in the early nineteenth century were so zealous for political reform:[75]

> The Faculty of Advocates would not have behaved with such vigour. But we have no pure corporation spirit; and the writers are full of it. Our merit is personal, and we care little for the body. Their professional glory arises from that of their order, and it is the idol.

Perhaps individualism makes for good advocates and bad trade unionists. But many modern strikes, when they have been conducted in unfavourable circumstances, have caused latent personality clashes to come to the surface. Against an implacable government, the second and third advocates' strikes had from the outset little prospect of success. This was the more true in that the characteristic eighteenth-century spoils system of politics was emerging, where, once an opposition had been formed, it was natural for the government to seek to buy the opposition leaders off, and for those leaders to expect it.

I do not suggest that modern Scottish trade unionists learned any lessons from the seventeenth-century advocates. The modern labour movement would be unlikely to conceive of these advocates as forerunners, or to consign them to any pantheon if they did. The faculty of advocates, like all lawyers, have an uneasy relationship with the trade unions. In industrial terms, 'most workers

---

[71] Quoted in Mackay, *Stair*, 116.     [72] *Book of Scottish Pasquils*, 220.
[73] Forbes, *Journal*, p. xx.                    [74] *AS*, Tait, 132–3.
[75] Henry Cockburn, *Memorials of his Time* (Edinburgh, 1909 edn), 419.

want nothing more of the law than that it should leave them alone.'[76] In political terms, one recalls the remark of Jimmie Maxton, when the suggested appointment of Rosslyn Mitchell as lord advocate in the 1924 Labour government proved unacceptable to the advocates, that 'if he continued to have health and strength he would smash the Scottish Faculty'.[77]

If the seventeenth-century advocates based their militancy on a theoretical basis, they must have looked back to the general theory of the *universitas* or corporation that had emerged throughout the mediaeval period, rather than forward to any theory of trade unionism. But no doubt much of their conduct was improvised reaction to circumstances, and lacking a comprehensive basis of articulated theory, just as is much modern trade union activity and much human conduct in general. The seventeenth-century Scottish advocates, privileged individual members of society's most privileged group, could do things that ordinary wage-earners could not do till much later. It is in this sense that I would describe the advocates as trade union pioneers; and I would suggest that to deny that they adumbrated many attitudes and many practices that later trade unionism has made familiar would be unduly pedantic.

JOHN M. SIMPSON

[76] K. W. Wedderburn, *The Worker and the Law* (Harmondsworth, 1965), 9.
[77] *Forward*, 9 February 1924, quoted in R. K. Middlemas, *The Clydesiders* (London, 1965), 141.

# 15

# Educating an Eighteenth-Century Duke

Writing to Adam Smith on 12 April 1759 to congratulate him on the success of the *Theory of Moral Sentiments*, David Hume included some news with a bearing on his friend's future:

> Charles Townsend, who passes for the cleverest Fellow in England, is so taken with the Performance, that he said ... he wou'd put the Duke of Buccleugh under the Authors Care, & woud endeavour to make it worth his while to accept of that Charge. As soon as I heard this, I calld on him twice with a View of talking with him about the Matter, & of convincing him of the Propriety of sending that young Nobleman to Glasgow: For I coud not hope, that he coud offer you any Terms, which woud tempt you to renounce your Professorship: But I missd him. Mr Townsend passes for being a little uncertain in his Resolutions; so perhaps you need not build much on this Sally.[1]

Clever, mercurial of mood, and an epileptic, Townshend dazzled his contemporaries by his speeches in parliament, could work with 'exceeding application' at the public business he loved, and confused almost everyone with his switches of political alignment. Hume's opinion is echoed in a comment of 1762 by a fellow M.P.: 'Charles Townshend, that splendid shuttlecock, veers about him with all these different gales. He laughs at the Ministry at night and assures them in the morning that he is entirely theirs'.[2] Such conduct was indeed a feature of Townshend's career: when in the government he made advances to the opposition, and when in opposition he intrigued to obtain a place. His chronic disloyalty possibly arose from early experiences in a family filled with tension resulting in the separation of the parents in 1741, when he was fifteen. He sided with his father but did not love him, and their uneasy relationship was exacerbated by the son's keen awareness of his financial dependence. The link was broken in 1755 when, not unimpeded by his father, he made a brilliant match: 'Charles Townshend marries the great Dowager Dalkeith: his parts and presumption are prodigious. He wanted nothing but independence to let him loose: I propose great entertainment from him; and now, perhaps, the times will admit it'.[3] Lady Caroline Campbell Scott, eight years his senior, but in possession of a personal estate of £46,000 and a yearly income of £3,000, was the daughter of John, 2nd duke of Argyll, and widow of the heir to the duke-

---

[1] *New Letters of David Hume*, edd. R. Klibansky and E. C. Mossner (Oxford, 1969 reprint), 54.
[2] Sir Lewis Namier and John Brooke, *Charles Townshend* (London, 1964), 75, quoting Richard Rigby to the duke of Bedford.
[3] Namier and Brooke, *op. cit.*, 36, quoting Horace Walpole to Richard Bentley.

dom of Buccleuch. In 1751 her firstborn, Henry, became the third duke on the death of his grandfather, and there were two other children of the first marriage: the Hon. Hew Campbell Scott and Lady Frances Scott. One of Townshend's redeeming traits was his solicitude for the Buccleuch children. Evidence of this in the case of the two boys is presented below, and concerning the girl a contemporary wrote as follows: 'a very clever child, whose humour and playfulness Mr Townshend's good-nature had to encourage and protect against maternal discipline carried too far. He continued to protect and instruct her, and frequently employed her as his amanuensis, as she has frequently told me since; and added, that if he had not died when she was only sixteen, he would have made her a politician.'[4]

So changeable in politics, Townshend persevered with his scheme to enlist Adam Smith's help in educating the duke of Buccleuch. He visited Scotland in the summer of 1759 with Lady Dalkeith and her daughter and went to Glasgow, where Smith was professor of moral philosophy, to make the necessary arrangements for the period five years ahead when the duke would finish at Eton and complete his studies by travelling on the Continent with his tutor. On this visit Townshend cultivated others of the Scottish *literati* and did not neglect politics, for he aspired to the management of Scotland by becoming M.P. for Edinburgh, but his wit and mimicry and 'torrent of colloquial eloquence' aroused no deep response: 'Like a meteor, Charles dazzled for a moment, but the brilliancy soon faded away, and left no very strong impression, so that when he returned to England at the end of two months, he had stayed long enough here'.[5]

Something of Townshend's cast of mind and character, however, is preserved in eleven letters that he wrote to the duke of Buccleuch between 1761 and 1767. Eight of these are printed here as throwing some fresh light on Townshend's career and because they develop a theme of considerable interest: how to fit the duke for a high position in the state by holding before him the classical and renaissance ideal of the aristocrat as the man of letters as well as of affairs.[6] Townshend seeks here to reinforce the teaching of one of the foremost moral philosophers of the age by encouraging Buccleuch to study the polity of France, where he remained with Smith from 1764 to 1766, and English constitutional history during the civil war period. In addition, the duke is encouraged to study the art of expression through application to Demosthenes, Cicero, Tacitus and Quintilian among the Ancients, and Milton, Harrington, Clarendon,

[4] *The Autobiography of Dr Alexander Carlyle of Inveresk, 1722–1805*, ed. J. Hill Burton (Edinburgh, 1910), 413.          [5] Carlyle, *op. cit.*, 409.

[6] H.M. Register House, Edinburgh: S.R.O. GD 224/296/1. The letters not given here are those of 24 February 1761, in which Townshend desires Buccleuch to fit himself for public life; 10 September [1762], concerning the choice of a guardian to conduct the duke's affairs in Scotland – Townshend offers to serve; and one presumably written in 1767, but undated, raising the question of the duke becoming a member of the Order of the Thistle. In the letters presented, contractions are silently expanded, while the original spelling and punctuation are retained except that the opening words of sentences have been capitalised where necessary. The editor's conjectures are placed within square brackets. For convenience, dates of letters and their provenance are placed within angle brackets at the beginning of letters. His Grace the late Duke of Buccleuch kindly gave permission for Charles Townshend's letters to be published in this volume.

Locke, and Conyers Middleton among modern English writers. Notice is taken of the excellence of certain speeches at the trials of Dr Henry Sacheverell (1710) and Bishop Atterbury (1723), and a revealing remark indicates that Townshend in assessing the 'compositions' of the great leaders of the seventeenth century political conflicts could identify himself most closely with the fiery and eloquent Sir John Eliot, whose precipitance and unwillingness to compromise first spurred on and then fatally hampered the parliamentary cause on the eve of the civil war.

Subsidiary themes in the letters are the project of obtaining a commission in the army for the duke's brother and the improvement of Buccleuch's estates. We hear of planting and road-making and work on a river, more ominously of enclosure and eviction and rent-raising. No mention is made of the fact established by modern scrutiny of Townshend's ledger, that he dipped into pay office funds to lend Buccleuch £20,300 to be spent on Adderbury, the duke's estate in Oxfordshire which Townshend occupied.[7]

It is an irony of history that despite the pose of the statesman-mentor adopted in the letters, with their sometimes florid mixture of the charmingly solicitous, the didactic and the unctuous, the fates of writer and recipient were far from what might have been expected. Townshend died in 1767, intriguing to the last with plungers and gamblers, having added considerably to the confusion in British politics which he bewailed so much, and very likely having steered his country towards a disastrous clash with the American colonies. Buccleuch lived a long and steady life until 1812, content to administer his extensive properties, manage Scottish elections, and rally his countrymen in the face of threat from Napoleon, but seek no high office of state. He continued to enjoy the company of men of letters: Smith was welcomed at Dalkeith Palace; the circle that formed the Royal Society of Edinburgh made the duke their first president in 1783; and Walter Scott was his friend. Possibly the classical strain in Buccleuch's education and the example of Adam Smith's retiring nature inclined him to *otium liberale* as preferable by far to the ill-starred Charles Townshend's choice of *municipi negotium*.

IAN ROSS

I

⟨London, 10 April 1764⟩

My very Dear Lord,

As you are now settled at Thoulouse,[8] you will probably be not displeased to hear from a Friend in London; especially from one whose affectionate

---

[7] Sir Lewis Namier and John Brooke, *The History of Parliament* (London, 1964), iii, 546. Such a procedure was not unusual in the eighteenth century: it took until 1782 to separate the accounts of the pay office from the private funds of Henry Fox, Townshend's predecessor as paymaster; see J. Steven Watson, *The Reign of George III, 1760–1815* (Oxford, 1960), 95, n. 1.

[8] Adam Smith joined his pupil in London, January 1764. They arrived in Paris on 13 February and were in Toulouse by 4 March. Toulouse was the second city in France and a

sollicitude follows you wherever you move, and who loves and esteems you truly.

Since you left us, we have had sudden changes in our Parliamentary climate, violent heat & extreme cold alternately and all things in each week. Our debates upon the warrant were eloquent; our number 219 to 208; the Ministry confest the illegality in the House; they grew pale upon the report of the division. They dreamt of more attacks and more divisions, and the Public thought the Field Won. But I know not what private motives operated; the opposition loiter'd upon their success; the ministry resum'd Spirits; and, from that day to this, no union, System or activity has appear'd. As to me, I fought while there was action: since the lethargy has prevailed, I have not been idle in the House, but have endeavour'd to keep myself present to the memory and judgment of others by taking some part in every matter of Finance or commerce which has occurr'd.[9] Upon the whole I have been prepared for all events: had others been more manly, the Cause would have had more success: had They been more united, They would have had more strength, and, as it is, I am glad to have made the trial, as by making it, I have acted according to my opinion, honestly, independently, & therefore wisely. No discernment can foresee the final Event: but as Mr Pitt[10] is reduc'd by illness; Mr Legge[11] on the verge of death; Mr Yorke[12] reluctant to Faction & the Summer arrived, I should suppose *the same* opposition will not be seen in the next year. Lord Bute[13] is in Town; seemingly pleased with Ministry; ever at Court; not abused in the Prints, & in general Chearful.

Lady Dalkeith will send you the common news of the Town, such as unhappy marriages, untimely deaths, and undeserved Preferments, and therefore I pass over these fruitful Subjects. Your road Bill is past, and I hope to execute it to

---

favourite resort of British people: the seat of an archbishopric, a university, a parliament, and modern academies of science and art whose annual *Jeux Floraux* attracted much attention, cf. John Rae, *Life of Adam Smith* (*1895*), intro. by Jacob Viner (New York, 1965 reprint), 174–5.

[9] Townshend was dismissed by Grenville from his office of president of the board of trade in April 1763 and remained nominally in opposition aligned with Newcastle until May 1765 when he became paymaster. An issue before the house of commons in 1764–5 concerned the attempt to muzzle John Wilkes through issuing a general warrant for the arrest of the editors, printers, and publishers of 'a seditious and treasonable paper, entitled *The North Briton*, Number XLV'. In February 1764 Townshend spoke and voted against the government during debates on Wilkes and general warrants, his speech of the 17th, according to Horace Walpole, being 'so fine that *it amazed even from him*'. In August he published anonymously *A Defence of the Minority with regard to General Warrants*, but the pamphlet sold poorly and Townshend blamed the opposition for this. In March he supported the government's view that America ought to contribute to Britain's expenses, and in April he favoured North America having a paper currency. The duty on molasses and the sugar bill also occupied his attention at this time: Namier and Brooke, *Townshend*, 113–22.

[10] William Pitt (1708–78), *cr.* earl of Chatham, 1766; the great leader of the Seven Years War period, whose ill-health and mental imbalance rendered him ineffective in opposition and office after 1761.

[11] Henry Bilson Legge (1708–64), three times chancellor of the exchequer.

[12] Charles Yorke (1722–70), son of Lord Hardwicke; attorney-general during the first prosecution of Wilkes; at odds with Pitt; lord chancellor, 1770.

[13] John Stuart (1713–92), 3rd earl of Bute; George III's tutor and favourite; first lord of the treasury, May 1762, but unequal to the storms of public life, so resigned in April 1763.

your satisfaction.[14] I have bought you for little money a very convenient Adderbury library, of all languages & in all Sciences. The whole purchase, I think, amounts to 30 £ & the collection is both numerous & good.

A thousand thanks to you for remembering the Box, tooth-pick case, and ruffles.

You will make me happy by writing to me. Tell me, if you are pleased where you are? What sort of reading you are employed in? Believe me your future figure & happiness depends upon the use of the few next years and all I wish is to hear you pass them happily & profitably. Remind my Friend of Charles' Tutor: He grows idle, & we wait to hear from Mr Smith.[15]

Farewell, I will write to Mr Smith by the next post, & to your Grace constantly. I am, my Dear Lord, Your Grace's affectionate & faithfull Friend

Charles Townshend

Ap[ril] the 10th. 1764

II

⟨London, 22 April [1765][16]⟩

My Dear Lord,

I have considered the subject upon which you desire my advice with the utmost attention, and I have endeavoured, in forming my opinion, to avoid equally the extremes of indifference and apprehension. Some, in such cases, are too apt to think all caution useless, others too frequently think all confidence dangerous, but I wish to take the middle way, and to treat the subject, you have started, neither as a matter of little moment nor of insurmountable inconvenience.

In the first place then, my Lord, I am to thank you for your great attention, candor & deference to me, for all which I will make you the best return I can, by sincerity, affection and zeal for your interest & personal Honour thro' life.

In the next place I am to acknowledge your extreme respect & confidence in leaving a point, so agreeable to yourself, to my final decision, for which farther instance also of your good opinion I will make the most ample return I can to you, by conforming to your own plan & adding my wishes & advice upon the manner of executing it.

With respect to Tholouse, I consent to your leaving it when you please & for the very reasons which you alledge, but when you settle at Paris, I must entreat you will still think the place of residence only changed, & not your age, nor

[14] When statute labour proved inadequate for maintaining roads at this period, proprietors had recourse to private acts of parliament to obtain powers to construct roads. The one in question was probably on the duke's estates in Scotland: see below, the letter of 16 October 1766.

[15] Presumably Smith had been asked to recommend a tutor for Townshend's elder son, also Charles (b. 1758).

[16] The year is identified by the mention of Hew Scott: on 21 October 1764 Smith wrote to Hume that a servant was to go to Caen to collect Scott to bring him to Toulouse – Rae, *op. cit.*, 182.

your Plan of improvement, nor the propriety of continuing the same Study & the same exercises.[17]

I have already desired Mr Guerchy[18] to signify to the Ministry of France that you are removing to Paris; I have wrote to Lord Hertford;[19] & I will write to Mr Hume. I wish you to fix upon a residence as near the best academy as you can, and at the same time as near to Lord Hertford, that you may take your exercises early, without loss of time, & be as frequently with Lord Hertford as His business & your ages admit. By Mr Hume's assistance, you will have an easy access to men of letters,[20] who, in France, are men of the world, and are therefore the most useful society to you, who must be one, & ought to be the other, of these characters. The conversation of such men will familiarise subjects to you otherwise abstruse; it will give you the fruits, without the labour of application; it will do more, it will lead you to farther application, & insensibly form your mind to a preference of liberal men & a taste for elegant amusements. This habit once obtained, it is, believe me, my Dear Lord, it is a security against every folly, every meanness, nay and every ennui in life.

In your course of study, I shall leave you to Mr Smith, nor interpose farther than to desire you will anatomise the Monarchy of France, view it in it's feudal state; examine the views, measures & effects of Louis the 11th when the Monarchy established itself upon the ruins of the feudal Barons; the commencement of Commerce under Monsr Colbert[21] (for neither Sully nor Richelieu nor

[17] Smith complained to Hume on 5 July 1764 of the dullness of Toulouse, in part arising from Townshend's failure to provide introductions to the notables there, and mentioned that 'to pass away the time' he was writing a book, which we surmise was the *Wealth of Nations*. Matters improved as Smith and his pupils grew more proficient in French and made acquaintances. They left Toulouse in August 1765 for an extensive tour of the south of France, spent October to December in Geneva, and were in Paris by Christmas: Rae, *op. cit.*, 178–94.

[18] Claude-Louis-François de Régnier (1715–67), comte de Guerchy; French ambassador to Britain, 1763–7.

[19] Francis Seymour Conway (1718–94), *cr.* earl of Hertford, 1750; marquis, 1793; ambassador to France, 1763–5. Hume served as his secretary in Paris.

[20] 'Those whose Persons & Conversation I like best,' wrote Hume in December 1763, 'are d'Alembert, Buffon, Marmontel, Diderot, Duclos, Helvetius; and old President Henau[l]t', *Letters of David Hume*, ed. J. Y. T. Greig (Oxford, 1969 reprint), i, 419. For Hume's sake and because of his own reputation, Smith was also welcomed by these men of letters and frequented the salons where they met: in particular those of d'Holbach, Mme Geoffrin, Comtesse de Boufflers, Mlle de Lespinasse, and Mme Necker. Doubtless the duke had his share of attention from this group, also from Smith's fellow students of political economy: Quesnay and Turgot.

[21] Buccleuch may have obtained a more critical view of Colbert (1619–83), Louis XIV's controller-general of finances, from Smith: 'That minister had unfortunately embraced all the prejudices of the mercantile system, in its nature and essence a system of restraint and regulation, and such as could scarce fail to be agreeable to a laborious and plodding man of business, who had been accustomed to regulate the different departments of public offices, and to establish the necessary checks and controuls for confining each to its proper sphere. The industry and commerce of a great country he endeavoured to regulate upon the same model as the departments of a public office; and instead of allowing every man to pursue his own interest his own way, upon the liberal plan of equality, liberty and justice, he bestowed upon certain branches of industry extraordinary privileges, while he laid others under as extraordinary restraints' (*Wealth of Nations*, iv, ch. ix). This rejection of Colbert's system was doctrine among the physiocrats.

Mazarin[22] had the slightest ideas of Commerce) & his regulations, the grounds, & the consequences; the rapid progress of their trade under the neglect of our's during the reign of Charles the 2nd & James the 2nd; it's real state since, and, above all, by this investigation, whence it has happened that this insidious & vast Monarchy, so enormous in it's extent, at the completion, as it should seem, of it's ambitious plan, renowned in arms, formidable in Navy, & flourishing in Commerce, should have been found, in the last minute of decisive trial, a monster in size & Proportion, weak from that very size, and by some secret error in it's condition, the most incapable power by land & sea that modern Times have exhibited. I think I can explain this, but I had rather hear your observations first, & together we shall assist our speculations.

If you go much into mixed company, as I suppose you will, let me warn you against any female attachment. Your rank & fortune will put women of subtle characters upon projects which you should not be the dupe of, for such connexions make a young man both ridiculous & unhappy. Gallantry is one thing; attachment is another; a young man should manifest spirit & decorum even in this part of his character, & preserve his mind entire & free in lesser as well as greater things.

In expence, I would wish you to be proper, rather than magnificent, & such as becomes your rank, restrained by the consideration of your age & situation. I have now opened my whole mind to you. You will not blame the freedom, and you will see now willingly I go with your inclinations, accompanied by my own free advice. I have really no anxiety, but what my love for you creates. My heart is fixed on your success; I must have you active, ambitious, capable; as to your integrity, I know it is a rock which no place, no temptation, no example can shake, & it is this which makes me so earnestly wish to see you fit those stations which such integrity should fill.

Adieu! Tell Mr Scott[23] I mean to write to Him by the next Post. We begin to think of a move in the army for Him, & I am preparing the way for his Seat in Parliament agreeable to your desire.

I write by this very Post to Mr Smith. I must beg you will write often to me. I am, my very Dear Lord, most affectionately

Yours<br>Charles Townshend

London April. 22d.

[22] Sully (1560–1641), minister to Henri IV, actually restored France's finances and encouraged agriculture and manufactures; Richelieu (1585–1642), Louis XIII's minister, depleted the treasury to support an ambitious foreign policy, but he encouraged commercial capitalism and organised companies trading to the Indies and Canada; his successor Mazarin (1602–61) has the poorest record in economic affairs.

[23] The Hon. Hew Campbell Scott (1747–66), younger brother of the duke of Buccleuch.

## III

<Adderbury, 10 June 1765>

My very Dear Lord,

I grew uneasy upon not hearing from you, but your letter soon removed all anxiety, both for your health and your situation, as it assures me you enjoy the one perfectly and are pleased with the other. I have often told you that almost every man's mind, & indeed his Life, takes it's color from His manner of passing & employing the few important years between His leaving school & entering into the world, and I have [therefore] never thought of this part of your Education, without much solicitude. My love for you could not have been more sincere or more hearty, if I had been your Father: my own experience in business convinces me that, in this age, any Person of your rank & fortune may, with tolerable discretion, competent knowledge, & integrity be as great as even this Country can make Him, and therefore I wished to see you placed, with your own approbation, in a forein Country, for some Time, where you might give to the necessary exercises of the body, to the improvement of your mind, and to the amusements of your youth, Their proper & alternate influence. Your letter, with so much sense & such true, natural ease, assures me you are now in that situation, and few things in this world can make me happier than the thought of your being employed as I find you are. Mr Smith, among many other advantages, possesses that of being deeply read in the constitution & laws of your own Country:[24] He is ingenious, without being [over-re]fin'd; He is general, without being too systematical or singular in His notions of our Government, and from Him, you will grow to be a grounded politician in a short course of study. When I say a Politician, I do not use the word in the common acceptance, but rather as a phrase less severe, for that reason more proper to your age, than statesman, tho' the one is the beginning of the other, and they differ chiefly as *this* is the work of study, & *that* the same work finish'd by experience & a course of office. Mr Smith will make you a politician, and time will afterwards, in your example, demonstrate the truth of my opinion. Let me desire you as you are now reading the History of England,[25] to be very attentive

[24] At the end of the period 1748–51 Smith gave public lectures on law in Edinburgh, and on these was based a part of his moral philosophy course at Glasgow: see *Lectures on Justice, Police, Revenue and Arms delivered in the University of Glasgow reported by a Student in 1763*, ed. Edwin Cannan (Oxford, 1896), also the forthcoming *Lectures on Jurisprudence*, edd. R. L. Meek, D. D. Raphael, and P. Stein, in the Glasgow edition of Smith's *Works*. His library contained a number of law books, among them the *Actis of the Realme of Scotland*, 1566, and Sir John Skene's (Latin) edition of the *Regiam Majestatem* and other early Scottish legal sources, 1613. However, on 5 March 1769 he disclaimed to Lord Hailes any specialised knowledge of Scots law: 'I have read law entirely with a view to form some general notion of the great outlines of the plan according to which justice has [been] administered in different ages & nations; & I have entered very little into the detail of Particulars' (MS, Tokyo University).

[25] Possibly David Hume's *History of England, from the Invasion of Julius Caesar to the Revolution in 1688* (1754–62), in view of Smith's estimate of its author as 'by far the most illustrious philosopher and historian of the present age': *Wealth of Nations*, v, ch. i, pt. iii,

to every event & every character in the reign of Charles the first, for, in those times, the rights of the people & the prescriptive claims of the Crown came to issue, and the contest called forth, created, & improved the Talents of men beyond any other period in any History ancient or modern. In the remonstrances of the Parliament and the answers from the Crown you will see almost all the original excellencys & defects of our Constitution eloquently argued & learnedly disscust; and from thence you will by inference form a true Idea of the blessings derived to these kingdoms by the Revolution; when the Frame of our Government was much improved; our natural rights as Men were recognized; our claims as Subjects established, and the liberty of the People placed upon as firm a Basis, as the imperfection of all civil Government, the wickedness of man and the Empire of Chance will ever permit.

Admire, but do not implicitly trust Lord Clarendon.[26] Mark the firmness & the decision tho' you blame the desertion & abhor the Tyranny of Strafford[27] consider the consequences of the indecision & duplicity of the Crown, blindly guided by a woman's passions & prejudices:[28] let the haughty mind of Laud[29] & the preference that pride made him give to the most frivolous tenet or form in Ecclesiastical worship over the most essential constitutional question instruct

---

art. iii. Townshend may have had in mind for special study by the duke the first volume of Hume's *History* to appear, that dealing with the reigns of James I and Charles I. Another boy introduced in the 1760s to the events of Charles I's reign as described by Hume was the duc de Berry, who re-read them as Louis XVI on the eve of his execution: *New Hume Letters*, 75; L. L. Bongie, *David Hume: Prophet of the Counter-Revolution* (Oxford, 1965), 120–2.

[26] Edward Hyde (1609–74), *cr.* earl of Clarendon, 1661; adviser to Charles I and Charles II's chief minister. Smith owned a copy of his *History of the Rebellion and Civil Wars in England* in an edition of 1721, also the *Life of Lord Clarendon by Himself*, 3rd edn, 1761.

[27] Sir Thomas Wentworth (1593–1641), *cr.* earl of Strafford, 1640; 'employed all his councils to support the prerogative, which he had formerly bent all his powers to diminish' according to Hume, e.g., when president of the council of the north using fine and imprisonment by the court of star-chamber to cow the northern gentry; appointed lord-deputy of Ireland, 1632, and then lord-lieutenant, 1640; Charles I's chief adviser from September 1639; vainly urged the king to despotic action, July 1640, in the face of the threat of invasion by the Scottish army; popularly called 'Black Tom Tyrant' from suspicion of advising the use of Irish catholic troops against Scottish and English rebels; attended the Long parliament 1640 on Charles personally guaranteeing his safety, but was impeached and sent to the tower of London; procedure against him by impeachment abandoned, March 1641; bill of attainder passed by commons, 21 April, by lords on 8 May, and assented to by Charles, 10 May; executed on Tower Hill the following day.

[28] Henrietta Maria (1609–69), queen consort of Charles I, youngest daughter of Henri IV and Marie de Medici; favoured catholics and intrigued with the papal court, English courtiers, and Irish and French leaders to aid her husband's cause; generally favoured drastic and unconstitutional action, e.g., the attempted arrest of the five members in the commons, 1642.

[29] William Laud (1573–1645), archbishop of Canterbury from 1633, sought to restore Romanist forms in the church of England; upheld the royal prerogative against the commons; generally credited with inspiring the severity of the court of star-chamber in dealing with the puritans: 'The thorow-paced puritans were distinguishable by the sowrness and austerity of their manners, and by their aversion to all pleasure and society. To inspire them with better humor, both for their own sake and that of the public, was certainly a very laudable intention in the court; but, whether pillories, fines, and prisons, were proper expedients for that purpose, may admit of some question' (Hume, *History*, 'Charles I', ch. iii).

you how to distrust the best talents in spiritual Statesmen, & let the glaring inconsistencys in Clarendon, Falkland,[30] Strafford, Pym,[31] Whitelock[32] and all the leaders of both Parties convince you that man has no safety in acting, but in acting from Himself: to hear others, but not to follow; to connect with them, but not implicitly, & to hold the freedom of your own judgment and the command of your own conduct with firmness, as the first requisite both to real greatness & true satisfaction. I must add I wish you would attend to the compositions[33] also of these times, particularly of Sir J. Elliott;[34] Pym is too studied & His language & matter are too precise; Lord Strafford is eloquent in his Trial; Glanville[35] in His Speech on the Petition of rights, but Sir J. Elliott excells all in the arrangement of his matter, in the force of His expression, and in the simplicity of His Sentiments. I find I am running into a dissertation, & therefore I will check myself, not without telling you, that, if you approve of it & desire me, I will take up the subject again, & write some remarks upon each Reign to this Time.

I am to thank you for your partiality to me in your observations upon the Times. *They* will mend. Administration has made Their own continuance difficult, by disgusting the Public, by leaving the debt unlessened, tho' the

[30] Lucius Cary (?1610–43), 2nd viscount Falkland, opposed Laud and Strafford; upheld episcopacy; served Charles I as secretary of state until the battle of Newbury, when he threw away his life despairing of peace. Hume reckoned that some of the declarations penned by Falkland contained 'the first regular definition of the constitution, according to our ideas of it, that occurs in any English composition; at least any, published by authority': *op. cit.*, ch. vi.

[31] John Pym (1584–1643), parliamentary statesman; active in the impeachments of Buckingham, Strafford, and Laud; one of the five M.P.s whom the king sought to arrest in 1642, an event which precipitated the outbreak of the civil war.

[32] Bulstrode Whitelocke (1605–75), keeper of the great seal; chaired committee which managed the prosecution of Strafford; during the civil war, repeatedly attempted to bring about peace; one of the committee which urged Cromwell to become king; president of the new council of state on the fall of Richard Cromwell. Smith had a copy of his *Memorial of the English Affairs, or an Historical Account of what passed from the beginning of the reign of Charles I to King Charles II's happy Restoration*, 1682.

[33] Among the chief sources for the 'compositions' Townshend had in mind are John Rushforth, *Historical Collections of Private Passages of State . . . Beginning the Sixteenth Year of King James Anno 1618 and Ending the Fifth Year of King Charles 1629*, 8 vols., 1721, and *The Parliamentary or Constitutional History of England . . . (1066–1660)*, 24 vols., 1751–61 (known as the *Old Parliament-History*).

[34] Sir John Eliot (1592–1632), summed up the charges against Buckingham, 1626; insisted on a full acceptance of the petition of right, 1629; imprisoned for conspiracy to resist the king's order to adjourn parliament on 2 March 1629, the occasion when he read out three resolutions against the king's religious policies and the unauthorised imposition of tunnage and poundage, the speaker being held in his chair meantime to prevent an adjournment; died in prison. 'The greatest orator of his generation, he was fiery and impulsive by nature, prone to idealise the commons at the expense of king and lords, and scornful of the daily compromises so essential in political life. . . . On one occasion he had said, "I am confident that, should the lords desert us, we should yet continue flourishing and green"' (Godfrey Davies, *The Early Stuarts, 1603–1660*, Oxford, 1949 reprint, 40). Eliot's attraction for Townshend no doubt lay as much in his defiance of authority and rhetorical skill as in his constitutional position.

[35] Sir John Glanville the younger (1586–1661), lawyer; took leading part in Buckingham's impeachment; speaker of the Short parliament, 1640; tried Northumberland and other peers; removed from office and imprisoned by parliament, 1645–8.

Taxes raised are enormous; by their neglect of forein affairs; by their violence &
Their folly.[36]

Adderbury is in great Beauty. The north side of the House is grown the
Favorite by the last alterations, and every day brings strangers to see the garden.
This flatters me, because I wish to make it pleasing to you, that, upon your
return, you may have a place suitable to you, for your amusement & the
reception of your friends.

Lord Bath is dead.[37] He has left his vast estate to His Brother, with legacies to
a Parson and a comic writer. No notice of those He affected most to express
kindness for, and seemingly pleased with thinking He deceived so many persons.

Lady Dalkeith is well & so are the children. Frances [is] at Margate.

Farewell. Write to me again Soon. I shall overtake this letter with another.

I am my Dear Lord, most affectionately yours

Charles Townshend

Adderbury, June 10. 1765

IV

⟨Adderbury, 23 July 1765⟩

My very Dear Lord,

I can not express to you the infinite pleasure which I received from your last
letter; in which you have given me the most perfect insight into the most
intricate parts of the interior constitution of the civil Government of France.
The precision with which you state, the knowledge with which you discuss,
and the judgment with which you decide upon the operations, defects and
corruptions of the system would do Honour to a writer of any age, and open to
me the most satisfactory contemplation, by suggesting to me what will be the
personal lustre & the public utility of the same Talents & the same mind, when,
from the study of forein States, it shall be exercised in the administration of our
own Country. The age, my Dear Friend, is idle, ignorant, extravagant, &
vain: your own Country is, & will be for some time, in distress, confusion &
danger: these circumstances afford a great theatre for a young man of your
rank, fortune & abilities, and, if you continue your diligence and persevere in
your improvement, you will not only commence, where most men conclude in
knowledge & capacity, but you will find the same pursuits which to others are a
labor, & the same business which to others is a science, an exercise and an

[36] Townshend nominally joined the Grenville–Bedford administration by kissing the
king's hands for the office of paymaster on 24 May 1765, but George III was at odds with his
ministers and by 12 June had asked Cumberland to approach Pitt and Newcastle about
forming a new administration: Namier and Brooke, *Townshend*, 132–3.

[37] Sir William Pulteney (1684–1764), *cr.* earl of Bath, 1742; at first the ally then opponent
of Walpole whose government he helped to bring down; one of the richest men and most
notorious misers of his time. His fortune at his death was reputed to be £1,200,000. A large
part of this afterwards came to Adam Smith's friend William Johnstone, who married the
daughter and heiress of Bath's first cousin. She inherited the Bath estates in 1767, whereupon
her husband took the name of Pulteney and began to exercise considerable parliamentary
patronage.

amusement to yourself. If I may venture to recommend any one part of your present system of application to your particular attention, it should be the forming your language & habit of expression to some model which you shall yourself think suited to your temper & feel you can command readily. It is incredible how much the possession of this easy qualification tends to bring out a young man's ambition as well as His talents, and it is the utmost which an hereditary Senator requires in our Times to establish Him in His own Senate upon the first trial. I have said this to you before, but the more I find you improve the more anxious I become to guard against every thing that can suppress such abilities or conceal their use. May I go one step further, and tell you how much benefit I have found from translating &, still more, from occasionally preparing short speeches upon such incidents in history as have struck me & seemed analogous to events likely to occur in our kingdom. In translating, I would recommend you rather to select part of Orations, than aim at the whole, for in the best of Cicero & even of Demosthenes there are topics so very uninteresting to us that the translation of them naturally fatigues the mind & kills the spirit which it is meant to raise. The second philippic of Demosthenes & even the Ctesiphon is a proof of this; the Milo, the Verres & indeed every oration of the Roman orator confirms it. The critic under whose indoctrination I wish you to form your own idea of Stile is Quinctilian, that is in his 8th & 9th book, & in the translation of Gidoin,[38] which is Quinctilian improved: the works I wish you to read in exercising yourself are the Ctesiphon, even as it is translated by Tourreille,[39] if you have been obliged to drop the greek, some of the most simple passages of the Milo, the Verres, & the whole first Philippic: Sir Clement Wearg's & Mr Harcourt's speeches in Dr Sacheverell's[40] & the Bishop's Trial,[41] with that most excellent of all models for the vast business of a popular

[38] Abbé Nicolas Gedoyn (1667–1744), member of the Académie des Inscriptions, 1711, and Académie Française, 1718; editions of his Quintilien de l'Institution de l'Orateur appeared in 1718 and 1752.

[39] Jacques de Tourreil (1656–1715), member of the Académie des Inscriptions, 1691, and Académie Française, 1692. His Œuvres, 1721, included vol. ii, Philippiques de Démosthène, and vol. iii, Harangues d'Eschine et de Démosthène sur la couronne. English translations of these works appeared in 1702 and 1757 (by Thomas Leland).

[40] In 1709, Dr Henry Sacheverell (1674–1724) published two sermons, 'The Commonwealth of Sin' and 'The Perils of False Brethren', aggressively upholding high church and tory principles. The sermons were declared seditious by the predominantly whig house of commons and the author was impeached in 1710. Burke regarded the speeches for the prosecution as the ablest and most authoritative expression of whig political philosophy and the principles underlying the revolution of 1688 (An Appeal from the New to the Old Whigs, 1791). Sir Simon Harcourt (?1661–1727), later lord chancellor, 1713–14, under Harley and St John, was leading counsel for the defence and made the most of the tory position on obedience to the crown. Sacheverell was found guilty and suspended from preaching for three years, but the trial excited popular support for the tories and helped to bring down the whig government of Godolphin and Somers. See Abbie Turner Scudi, The Sacheverell Affair (New York, 1939) and Geoffrey Holmes, The Trial of Doctor Sacheverell (London, 1973).

[41] Dr Francis Atterbury (1662–1732), bishop of Rochester; erudite friend of Swift, Pope, and Gay; incriminated in a Jacobite plot, 1722; Walpole brought in a bill of pains and penalties against him which passed, May 1723; sentenced to lose all his preferments and be banished perpetually. Sir Clement Wearg (1686–1726), the solicitor-general, distinguished

assembly in so free & factious a kingdom as our's, Serjeant Parker's[42] reply to the whole defence of Sacheverell. For stile, our most correct writers are Doctor Middleton,[43] in his controversial works, Mr Locke, in his Essay,[44] & Harrington in his Preliminarys;[45] Milton's prose should be read in parts to catch the flame, & Lord Clarendon, for the dignity of His Phrase & the perspicacity of His narration. Out of these several manners, make one for yourself; avoid the lavish ornament so vicious in Cicero; reject the frequent interrogatory, too habitual in Demosthenes; shun the obscure brevity & studied contrast of Tacitus, and, having first, by the study of Lowth[46] & a consideration of our best writers, laid the ground of a simple & acurate Stile, cover & adorn it with the tropes of Demosthenes; the amplification of Cicero; the bold moral of Tacitus; and the language which shall result from a careful perusal of the English writers I have named.

I have dwelt so long upon this subject, that I have scarce time left me, to touch upon others, in the first place, I am to justify myself to you for having lately thrice refused the Seals,[47] which I believe I shall easily do, when I tell you, that my Sovereign, at the end of two long audiences, professed himself quite satisfied with my reasons, & gave me leave to decline Them *at this juncture*. It were rash in me to go minutely into this topic by letter, therefore I will only assure you that I have acted, I am sure, from principle, &, I believe, with judgment:

---

himself supporting the bill against Atterbury: *The replies of T. Reeve and C. Wearg in the House of Lords . . . in behalf of the bill to inflict pains and penalties on the late Bishop of Rochester*, 1723.

[42] Sir Thomas Parker (?1666–1732), *cr.* earl of Macclesfield, 1721; lord chief justice, 1710–18; lord chancellor, 1718–25; one of the committee which drew up the articles against Sacheverell and unsparing assailant of the accused at the trial. In 1725 he was himself impeached for selling masterships in chancery and found guilty. Sir Clement Wearg was manager of the house of commons for this trial.

[43] Dr Conyers Middleton (1683–1750), divine; mastered the art of controversy through opposing Bentley's over-vigorous rule at Trinity College, Cambridge; remembered for the stylistic success of his *Life of Cicero*, 1741, and the polemical skill of his *Free Enquiry into the Miraculous Powers which are said to have subsisted in the Christian Church, from the earliest ages*, 1748, which Hume believed had eclipsed his *Essay on Miracles* published in the same year.

[44] John Locke (1632–1704), the 'philosopher' to the eighteenth century as Aristotle was to the middle ages; his *Essay concerning Human Understanding* was first published in 1690, 4th edn, 1700. Smith observed in the 1755 *Edinburgh Review* (ii, 72): 'Mr Hobbes, Mr Lock, and Dr Mandevil, Lord Shaftesbury, Dr Butler, Dr Clarke, and Mr Hutcheson, unlike the French writers, have all of them at least tried to be original, and to make some new contribution to the common stock'. Hume did not consider Locke a model writer: 'As to Sprat, Locke, and even Temple, they knew too little of the rules of art to be esteemed elegant writers. The prose of Bacon, Harrington, and Milton, is altogether stiff and pedantic, though their sense be excellent' (*Of Civil Liberty*, 1741). Swift was Hume's choice as the writer of the 'first polite prose we have'.

[45] James Harrington (1611–77), political theorist; the allusion here is to the preliminary matter of *The Commonwealth of Oceana*, 1656.

[46] Dr Robert Lowth (1710–87), bishop of Oxford then London; published (in Latin) *Lectures on the Sacred Poetry of the Hebrews*, 1753; *A Short Introduction to the English Grammar*, 1762; and a translation of Isaiah, 1778.

[47] Townshend refused three times during 5–9 July 1765 to accept either the office of chancellor of the exchequer or that of secretary of state. He was probably responding to his brother's hostility towards the Duke of Cumberland then charged with replacing the Grenville-Bedford ministry: Namier and Brooke, *Townshend*, 135–7.

meaning in no degree to restrain ambition, unless the regulating it by considerations of honor be called restraint.

I am also to tell you that the estate Here is going to decay, & our enclosure, so material to you hereafter will become impossible, unless some measure be taken. I am now trying to get possession upon payment to the Duchess[48] of a great rentcharge, & I fancy she will be persuaded by the goodness of the bargain. In that case the arrears must be paid to her; and also some heavy repairs she lately made which improve the estate & must of course be shared hereafter by Lady Dalkeith & your Grace. If you are disposed to concur in saving the estate; in immediately making the enclosure; & in improving your situation here, & will empower me to agree with the Duchess & pay her arrears upon the plan of a fair joint expence to Lady Dalkeith & yourself I will obey your commands & undertake to satisfy you most largely in the improvement of everything here. In that case you will be so good as to draw upon Mr Coutts[49] for 400 £, to make your note payable to Mr Kenneth Mackenzie,[50] & to signify to Him that the money is to be paid to Lady Dalkeith at Her demand. I will then settle every thing, & proceed to inclose & retrieve the estate for your future infinite advantage & Lady Dalkeith's. If you should approve of this, you will be so good as to write to me soon & give your orders, because time, with persons of a certain temper, is every thing.

I have a letter from *Tholouse*, to which I will send an answer thro' you by the next post.

My love to Scott. My best respects to Mr Smith. I have made Dr Bernard Provost of Eton.[51]

I am most affectionately

Yours<br>Charles Townshend

Adderbury, J[uly] 23. 1765

V

⟨[London] 30 December 1765⟩

My very Dear Lord,

I take the opportunity of General Vernon's[52] departure, and am glad to write to you by so safe a hand.

You will be pleased to hear how affairs pass in a Country where you have so

---

[48] Jane Warburton (d. 1767), 2nd wife of John, 2nd duke of Argyll. Her death brought Lady Dalkeith and Townshend another fortune worth £4,000 per annum.

[49] James and Thomas Coutts (1735–1822) were bankers in Edinburgh and in the Strand, London.

[50] Perhaps agent or factor for the Buccleuch family.

[51] Dr Edward Barnard (1717–81), headmaster of Eton, 1754, then provost, 1764; connected with the Townshends.

[52] Gen. Charles Vernon (d. 1778): Horace Walpole wrote on 28 April 1766, 'supped at Hôtel de Brancas with Duke of Buccleuch, Lord Fitzwilliam and others. General Vernon came'; *Correspondence*, ed. W. S. Lewis et al., vii, 310.

high an interest & will have so great personal weight, & I am always pleased with the hope of doing anything agreeable or satisfactory to you.

The last sudden change of ministers was entirely occasioned by Their violence in the closet, Their public disrespect to the King in the House of Lords by the exclusion of the Princess Dowager from the possibility of being named Regent, and by several consequential indecencys in the exercise of Their power. It grew to be too strong & too notorious for the Crown to submit without a fatal example; the Duke of Cumberland saw this, interposed, & after offers made to Mr Pitt & to me, which were inadmissible, filled up the offices in the manner you have read.[53] His Royal Highness concluded that the Summer, jealousy, and the usual impatience of ambitious minds would have reconciled either Mr Pitt or myself to the intended plan: perhaps he relied upon having his choice. He certainly wished to separate. In the instant as this view grew desperate, He died.[54] Since that we have had many reports of Mr Pitt's accession to Ministry, but all vague; I have remained upon the same system, and men stand as the Duke left Them.

Mr Conway,[55] tho' a very honest & amiable man, is thought to be unequal to the business of his department, to the difficulties of the hour, and the contests of the house. The Duke of Grafton[56] let the first warm day in the Lords pass him by in silence. Lord Rockingham[57] is new in office, a stranger to his own voice in the Senate, and not of a temperament to bear the fatigues or blows of his station.

In the Commons I have as yet done the business, but I do not mean to labor for others. Let each man have the rank he can fill, and no man, more.

Mr Granville[58] has lost his weight within doors & without, at court & abroad. He is become peevish, obstinate and offensive. The Minority seems very small in each house, and the Government would be without the most distant degree of danger if the Ministry had more confidence from talents or the king were believed to prefer Them in his heart. Their injudicious continuance of Their Predecessors resentment of Lord Bute's family makes this doubted, & this distrust added to the idea of Their insufficiency renders Them weak in general estimation.

[53] The Grenville administration differed from the king in 1765 about the terms of the regency bill, and in July Cumberland prevailed on Rockingham to form a new ministry. Grafton and Conway were secretaries of state, Lord Winchelsea president of the council, William Dowdeswell chancellor of the exchequer, and Newcastle lord privy seal.

[54] William Augustus, duke of Cumberland (1721–65), 3rd son of George II; bloody suppressor of the Jacobite rising of 1745–6; unsuccessful in opening stages of German campaigns of Seven Years War and resigned commands; devoted to the turf and founded Ascot races; died 30 October 1765.

[55] Gen. Henry Seymour Conway (1719–95), secretary of state for the southern department under Rockingham.

[56] Augustus Henry Fitzroy (1735–1811), 3rd duke of Grafton; Conway's opposite number in the northern department.

[57] Charles Watson-Wentworth (1730–82), 2nd marquis of Rockingham, served as first lord of the treasury until the end of July 1766.

[58] George Grenville (1712–70), first lord of the treasury, April 1763 to July 1765: at odds with king over regency bill, with his colleagues over foreign policy, and with the public over general warrants.

You will ask me, in what will this end? It is incertain. Perhaps in Mr Pitt's being Minister & possibly in his union with Lord Temple:[59] it may give me the power directly, it must finally, & I chuse the latter: it can not end in restoring the last Ministry, and the present is not formed for duration.

In the mean time America calls for all our talents, skill, discretion & firmness, but of this more in my next, & and after I have seen the letters by this paquet which will decide every thing.[60]

As to our own matters. I have struggled hard for an inclosure & prevailed. By this I shall turn the road, inclose the meadows; carry the park round the grove and include the Miller's field; make the river broad, visible, & beautifull; extend the paddock walk two miles, and give the place extent, variety, & chearfulness. I hope you will be pleased with having these contests finished before you come to live here; and my chief motive is to express my attention to whatever I fancy interests or accommodates you.

I think it is now time to get Mr Scott a step farther in his profession. Would he chuse to have a company purchased for him, which he might sell again & return into the guards lieutenant, & thereby save some time? If he would, I will obey his commands. My best affection attends him.

General Vernon is a very worthy accomplished man, whom you will be glad to converse with.

My best compliments wait upon Mr Smith. Adieu. I wish to hear from you. I am most affectionately & invariably yours

Charles Townshend

December 30. 1765.


## VI

⟨13 May 1766⟩

My very Dear Lord,

I have lost no time in making my application for Captain Cashell's leave to sell & Mr Scott's permission to purchase; I availed myself also of Lord George Lenox's[61] kind recommendation, but, upon examining the state of the Regiment, Lord Barrington[62] informed me that Captain Cashell had not bought, & that His Majesty had signified by an order in print & circulated that no officer should

---

[59] Richard Temple Grenville (1711–79), succeeded to his mother's title 1752, thereafter Earl Temple; Pitt's brother-in-law but too ambitious to join him in forming a ministry in 1765.

[60] The news from America was of riots and disturbances connected with the attempted enforcement of Grenville's Stamp Act.

[61] Lord George Henry Lennox (1737–1805) went to France in 1765 to serve as secretary of legation while his brother, the 3rd duke of Richmond, was ambassador. The recommendation may have been for a company in the 25th foot (later K.O.S.B.) to which Lennox was attached in 1762 after serving with the 33rd foot and commanding grenadiers in Germany.

[62] William Wildman Barrington (1717–93), 2nd viscount Barrington; secretary at war, 1765–78; held accountable for the poor state of the army during the war of American independence.

sell who had not purchased. This standing regulation has prevented me being able to felicitate your Grace & Mr Scott upon *actual* success, but as the Times are critical, the elements in motion, the strongest general rules of office fragile, and this particular regulation is both unwise & impracticable, I am far from dispairing. I have already been offer'd leave to purchase the first company at sale; I have also been offer'd a company without purchase, but I shall be governed by you & Mr Scott, happy in following your preference & wishing to be disposed of by your joint agreement. So far is certain, in some shape Mr Scott may & shall have a company as soon as He gives me His orders. I could have wished it had been possible in Lord George Lenox's regiment, & perhaps it still may be.

I am desired to thank you for your gift of a miniature picture to Lady Dalkeith, who is very anxious to have you both in that manner. If I may be troublesome, I would affectionately ask a portrait of each in oil colours. I should value it most highly & amuse myself in looking upon the representation of Those whose Honor & happiness are dear to me as my own.

Adderbury is enclosed; the Quaker removed; the estate improved; the roads turned; the river going to be made large & fine; the plantation carried quite around the whole meadows. In short I shall make it beautiful & magnificent. & for whom? For you, whenever you please to tell me you wish it to be your residence. I do not know, if I do not enjoy the labor of improving the more for that very reason.

I have much to say to you about your estate & the plans I have laid for proper improvements. Perhaps I shall be able to show you how to make 20,000, 40,000 per annum with discretion & without severity, but I leave this til I see you, which will be in the beginning of July.

As yet I have avoided the Seals, & I think I shall succeed in my views for meeting you in France. Mr Stanley[63] comes with me.

My best affection attends Mr Scott. Lord Fitzwilliams is extremely admired.[64] We often talk of you. I have a real partiality for Him.

I am, my Dear Lord,
    Your affectionate, faithful friend

                                 Charles Townshend

May, 13th. 1766

## VII

⟨London, 10 June 1766⟩

My Dear Lord,

I have the Favor of your letter, and am very happy to see the anxiety with which you adopt the interest of Mr Scott; every such proof of your mutual affection gives me a new assurance of your mutual satisfaction & union thro'

---

[63] ? Hans Stanley, M.P. (?1720–80): no visit to France at this period by Townshend is recorded.
[64] William Wentworth Fitzwilliam (1748–1833), nephew and heir of Rockingham.

life, than which nothing is more essential to yourselves or more pleasing to Those who love you.

After much solicitation, more than I think the request required, I have obtained a promise that Mr Scott shall very soon have a company. Mr Cashell did not purchase, & therefore will not be allowed to sell: if he retires upon half-pay, it must be by exchange, & halfpay can not be sold by the conditions of the act. I am therefore afraid that it will be difficult to bring Mr Scott into Lord George Lenox's regiment, but I hope, if He has the rank in another, it will be agreeable, tho' less pleasing. I should whisper to you that I mentioned this wish of Lord George's and your's & mine to the new Secretary of State,[65] but he did not at all embrace it, & I can not say that Lord Rockingham has shown the least inclination to help us. Lord Barrington has not even been neutral, & even D'Oiley[66] with all his obligations, is a perfect courtier. I say this that you may remember it; I shall, for ever; I have carried the point by a personal request made to the king, &, had we relied on Ministers or Friends, Mr Scott had been disappointed. I say again to you, remember this, for the hour will come when, if you remember, you may resent. I expected more from Lord Rockingham on your account.

I write in a large company. You will hear again from me by the next post. In the mean time, my love to Mr Scott, & tell him if He will do me the favor of drawing upon me for 3 or 400£ thro' Mr Iday I shall have real pleasure in answering His draft. I suppose such a sum may be of use to a handsome young man in [a] country of gallantry, &, seeing the application, I shall be obliged to answer the payment. My love to Him.

Adieu. Most affectionately yours

Charles Townshend

Grosvenor Square, June 10. 1766


## VIII

⟨London, 16 October 1766⟩

My very dear Lord,

Give me leave to begin my letter with expressing the real happiness which I feel upon your recovery:[67] having suffer'd during your illness the utmost anxiety, which affection & esteem can create in the danger of a friend. It was some consolation in the midst of our solicitude, to receive from all orders of men, from strangers as well as acquaintance, at home & abroad, so universal a testimony

[65] The 3rd duke of Richmond was made secretary of state for the southern department on 23 May 1766.

[66] Christopher D'Oyly (?1719–95), deputy secretary at the war office, 1763–72; M.P., 1774–84; friend of Townshend.

[67] Smith wrote to Townshend on 26 and 27 August 1766 to report that Buccleuch had fallen ill of a fever after a day's hunting at Compiègne. He was treated by Quesnay and members of the French court and other dignitaries expressed their concern: Rae, op. cit., 222–4.

to your conduct & character, and to find you established, as you are, in the judgment & respect of all men who have known or heard of you. I, who have known you from your earlier years, had no doubt of this, but it was a great satisfaction to see my prophecy proved & my opinion become general. You have now nothing to think of, but the care of your health, for you have secured the world, & added the best of characters to the most ample advantage of birth & fortune.

You ask me if I ever sent you a parcel of American papers? They went from hence in June: They were carried by the Duke of Richmond's messenger: Goldicot assured me that He had engaged to deliver them to you, & I had them transcribed for your use. It mortifies me to be told you did not receive them as I had arranged, docketed, & explained them myself. You ask me also what news we have? We have, as usual, a very unsettled state of men & things. Lord Chatham is minister, in the most absolute sense of the word; yet, by being ill & absent, business moves slowly & incertainly. As for me, I obeyed the crown & left a quiet & lucrative office of great rank to come into a scene of hurry and anxiety, with less profit:[68] in this I acted honorably: I find Lord Chatham so incurably jealous of me; so open to idle reports & so reserved that I have little satisfaction in my situation. When He comes to London this ambiguity must have it's settlement, & some final explanation follow.[69] In the mean time I labor, prepare for the Session, & am resigned to the issue.

It is doubted whether the Bedford party will be brought into ministry.[70] Their terms are high, but I should suppose that the necessity will force the union.

Lord Bute's friends seem still distant tho' Mr Mackenzie[71] has his office & Lord Northumberland is a Duke.[72]

I believe some Marquisses will be made, & Lord Townshend will be one of them.[73] I have asked for the Barony of Greenwich for Lady Dalkeith; as yet, the request is undecided; if, after all my sacrifices lately made & my long

[68] Grafton resigned as secretary of state in April 1766 and the Rockingham ministry went to pieces. On 7 July Pitt was called on by the king to form a new administration. Grafton became first lord of the treasury, Conway remained as leader of the house of commons, and Pitt took the privy seal and retired to the house of lords as earl of Chatham. Townshend accepted with bad grace the chancellorship of the exchequer (worth £2,500) and gave up the paymastership (worth £7,000) on 2 August: John Brooke, *The Chatham Administration* (London, 1956), 1–19; Namier and Brooke, *Townshend*, 146–54.

[69] Chatham was at Bath where he went for ever longer periods believing the waters would alleviate his gouty condition. He remained jealous of Townshend and there was no settlement. Townshend went on to frustrate Chatham's hope of reforming the East India Company: Namier and Brooke, *Townshend*, 172.

[70] Followers of John Russell (1710–71), 4th duke of Bedford, among them being Lord Gower, Richard Rigby, and the earl of Sandwich. Rigby wanted to be paymaster and Sandwich had his eyes on the admiralty: Brooke, *The Chatham Administration*, 30–3.

[71] James Stuart Mackenzie (1719–1800), brother of Bute, was minister for Scottish affairs until Grenville forced his dismissal in May 1765. Pitt made him keeper of the privy seal of Scotland in May 1765, but without giving him the power of dispensing Scottish patronage.

[72] Hugh Smithson Percy (1714–86), *cr.* duke of Northumberland, 1766, a follower of Bute.

[73] Charles's elder brother George (1724–1807), 4th viscount Townshend, was not made a marquess until 31 October 1787.

services, this favor, given to others, be denied to me, I shall feel myself slighted & be disposed to act accordingly.[74]

To pass to other matters of more amusement. Adderbury is inclosing & the whole hill opposite to the house is bought & thrown together. The two roads are turned; a piece of water is making in the bottom: Blights groves are in the paddock, & the Quaker can not help moving. It will be the prettiest place in England.

Your road in Scotland is become the most frequented in that country. The woods, waters & pastures are very fine.

I have employed one King, a most sensible man & Steward of Mr Knightley, to survey your estate. He is in rapture, but says it is ill tenanted & under let. Would you have me raise the rents & farm the pastures before you are of age or suspend it for your majority? Perhaps the unpopularity had better fall on me. I can bear that or any thing for your sake. Mr King seems to be of opinion that, by laying out a moderate annual Sum, your rents may be doubled.

I have sent you a fine horse, bred in Derbyshire, the Son [?of] Oronoko by a well bred mare. He is six years old, perfectly sound, & esteemed here a most beautiful horse. I send it because I know such things are valued where you are, especially of this age, breed, beauty & soundness.

I hope to hear Mr Scott is better.[75] I write to him by the next Post, the servant now waiting for this letter.

I hope I have the good fortune of being remembered by you as I deserve to be: I ask no more, & am, with the most unfeigned affection,

My Dear Lord
    Your Grace's most
        devoted & sincere friend

                                    Charles Townshend

Grosvenor Square Oct. 16th, 1766.

[74] Lady Dalkeith was created baroness of Greenwich on 19 August 1767, but the delay in the granting of this favour, which Townshend attributed to Grafton, added to his bad feeling against Chatham's cabinet.

[75] The Hon. Hew Campbell Scott fell ill of a fever in Paris in October 1766 and died on the 19th (S.R.O., GD 1/479/14). Smith and the duke of Buccleuch brought the body back to England, landing at Dover on 1 November.

# 16

# The Administration of the Forfeited Annexed Estates, 1752–1784

From 1752–84 part of Scotland experienced a curious blend of ancient and modern patterns of government. One strand illustrated the age-old method of forfeiture used by kings in dealing with defeated rivals and rebels, the other what we tend to consider a fairly modern concept, state control or nationalisation. It had long been customary for the ruler to take possession of the estates of defeated traitors, but the lands were then most commonly used to reward loyal supporters or their proceeds to line the king's privy purse. After 1715 it had been hoped that the wholesale forfeitures would bring profit to the central government and act as a deterrent to future rebels, but neither of these aims was achieved. Similarly in 1747 the estates of a large number of proven rebels were forfeited. The barons of the exchequer took over the management until legal ownership could be established, creditors satisfied or dissatisfied, and thereafter they hoped to sell the estates at a substantial profit.

However after two major and one minor upheaval in thirty years had originated in the north of Scotland, many besides Duncan Forbes of Culloden believed that one of the first duties of a Scottish statesman was the destruction of the distinctive, or what most lowlanders and English would have preferred to describe as the deplorable features of highland society.[1] The general uncriticised aim of 'civilising' highlanders, in other words making them more like lowlanders and loyal citizens who would no longer disturb the peace of the law-abiding, gave rise to the idea of retaining some of these estates as crown land. It was expected that managed by crown servants they would become models to the surrounding country, while the profits accruing would be devoted to improving the estates themselves and the highlands generally. These areas that were once considered a 'nuisance to the Island'[2] would become hives of industry, trade and manufactures.

An act of parliament expressing these ideas was passed in 1752[3] and thirteen of the forfeited estates were annexed 'unalienably' to the crown.[4] The rents and profits were to be used for 'Civilising the Inhabitants upon the said Estates and other Parts of the Highlands and Islands of Scotland, the promoting

---

[1] G. W. T. Omond, *The Lord Advocates of Scotland* (Edinburgh, 1883), i, 342.

[2] Scottish Record Office, Forfeited Estates Papers, 1745, Reports to the King and Treasury, E723/1, p. 82.

[3] 25 George II, c. 41, henceforth known as 'The Annexing Act'.

[4] In referring to any of these estates I use the spelling adopted in the Scottish Record Office Inventory.

amongst them the Protestant religion, good Government, Industry and Manufactures and the Principles of Duty and Loyalty to his Majesty, his Heirs and Successors and to no other Use or Purpose whatsoever'. A large area of Scotland was involved in the annexation. The estates of Arnprior, Perth, Struan, Lochgarry, Cluny and Lovat are described as forming a chain from six miles north of Stirling to Inverness, interrupted only by Breadalbane's lands, cutting a swathe between thirty and forty miles broad through central Scotland. A short distance north of Inverness the Earl of Cromarty's lands spread across country from the east to the west coast.[5] To the west of this chain were Barrisdale, Kinlochmoidart, Lochiel and Ardsheal. On the east, quite disjoined and so small that its only importance was as a foothold in a strongly Jacobite area, was Francis Farquharson's estate of Monaltry in the parish of Crathie.

Central government negligence was in evidence at once. Under the Annexing Act a commission was to be appointed to manage the estates but for no discoverable reason it was 1755 before this was done, and it was 23 June 1755 before the statutorily constituted board for the Annexed Estates met for the first time, ten years after the Rising. Further delay in the full implementation of the act resulted from the fact that five of the estates *in toto* and two in part did not come under the aegis of the commissioners until 1770. Lochiel, the largest estate in the west, Lochgarry, Callart, Cluny, Ardsheal and parts of Arnprior and Kinlochmoidart held of various subject superiors, the dukes of Atholl, Argyll and Gordon, and John Erskine of Carnock. To overcome any legal let or hindrance to the crown's complete control over the estates James West and Nicholas Hardinge, joint secretaries to the treasury, were appointed in 1755 to compound with the subject superiors claiming the various properties. It was fifteen years before arrangements were made for the Crown to purchase the superiorities. Until 1770 therefore these lands remained under the management of the barons of the exchequer who were responsible for only day-to-day business, rent collection and settlement of debts. Apart from the effect on the individual estates where no long-term improvements could be carried out for twenty-five years, the resources of the Annexed Estates Board were lessened as until then they had no access to the rents of over £1,200.

London control hardly seems necessary when we consider the composition of the board once members were appointed. The first members included such Scottish peers as Archibald duke of Argyll, a 'name on the board' apparently, as he did not appear at even the first meeting; John marquis of Tweeddale, and James earl of Finlater who were well-known for their interest in industry as well as agricultural improvements, being members of the Board of Trustees for Fisheries and Manufactures.[6] The lord president of the Court of Session, the lord chief baron, and the lord justice clerk were all *ex officio* members as was the

[5] National Library of Scotland, Minto Collection EFP 35. I am indebted to Dr T. I. Rae for drawing my attention to the relevant material in this collection.

[6] The Earl of Finlater may have gained vicarious pleasure from this appointment. He had asked for the estates of Lord John Drummond to be given to him in recognition of his services. A. and H. Tayler, *Jacobites of Aberdeenshire and Banffshire in the Forty-Five* (Aberdeen, 1928), 92–3.

commander-in-chief of H.M. forces in Scotland; there were several commissioners of customs but a great preponderance of lawyers. Altogether there were twenty-eight names on the first list recorded in the Register of Commissioners, most of them of proven ability and energy at least in their own pursuits and interests.[7]

Once appointed the board had some necessary initial administrative preparations to make. They had to find an office suitable both for meetings and for storing records; they needed administrative and clerical assistance. A secretary was ready at hand, for at the first meeting a letter was waiting from the duke of Newcastle recommending a Mr Stamp Brooksbank as a 'fit person to be secretary' and suggesting a salary of £500 per annum. As the commissioners were in some doubt about appointing anyone sight unseen, even on the duke's recommendation, and in any case thought the salary too high, no fewer than four members were directed to assist the lord president in preparing an answer to this letter. A secretary was obviously going to be very necessary if the members were to have time for anything else but writing letters in five-part harmony. On the duke's reassurance that he had made all possible inquiries into Mr Brooksbank's character and that both he and his *protégé* were agreeable to the salary of £300 proposed by the Board, Mr Brooksbank was appointed on 14 July 1755. He remained with the board until 1762 when he received another position and was succeeded by Henry Barclay of Collernie. His son, William, followed him in the post and the last secretary served from 1783 to 1784. Two weeks after the secretary's appointment a clerk joined the establishment at £70 per year and provision was made for a second clerk earning £40.

Before a permanent office was found, meetings were held in the hall of the Trustees for Widows' Funds but a solution to the accommodation problem was fairly soon found. A house belonging to the Lovat estates and hence now under the board's management was found to be 'very conveniently situated' in the High Street, Edinburgh 'near the Tron Kirk'. In November 1755 Mr John Adam the architect was instructed to inspect the house with a view to its being used as an office and three months later the Adam brothers sent in a report and plan of the house showing their proposals for altering it. They were less than enthusiastic about this six-roomed flat and their letter remarked that the house was in very indifferent condition so that to put it in proper order and to alter it would require at least £300. They ended: 'At the same time we beg leave to observe that the accommodation would be very much confined and indeed less than such an office ought to have'.[8] Despite this lukewarm comment, it was decided to go ahead as negotiations for other property had been unsuccessful and by 1757 the house had been fitted up by Charles Howison, wright, for £340-2-3$\frac{2}{12}$ reduced to £330-19-3$\frac{2}{12}$ as six mahogany chairs, a chimney grate, 'pocker, tongues and fender' were returned. In 1774 when Major-General Simon Fraser had his family estates restored to him for services rendered to the Hanoverian dynasty he invited the commissioners to continue using his house

[7] SRO, Forfeited Estates Papers, 1745, E722/1.
[8] SRO, Forfeited Estates Papers, 1745, E727/3/5(1).

and to consider it as much at their service as before H.M.'s grant, but that did not stop his agent James Fraser from making a sharp demand for payment for overdue rent after the disannexation of all the estates in 1784. This 'house' or flat was in one of the High Street tenements with a china shop below on the ground floor, and other accommodation on the same stair, part of which was rented by at least one of the board's doorkeepers. It was also quite lavishly decorated, all the rooms being papered, some in pink diamond pattern, some blue-flowered, some in stucco painted paper. Pewter inkstands were provided and the extraordinarily large number of seven and a half dozen purple Dutch pigs. A doorkeeper had to be employed to light and extinguish fires among other duties and one, Alexander Callender, was very quick to see his opportunity for making extra money, whether in asking compensation for the inconvenience and expense he was put to because the office was not large enough to provide him with a room, or in requesting money for mourning clothes on the death of Princess Caroline in 1758 and George III in 1760 'as is given in all other public offices'.

As well as dealing with the minutiae of administration the board almost at once applied themselves to the wider issues. And here they immediately ran into difficulties with the central government, their masters. Despite the duke of Newcastle's promptitude in finding a place for a *protégé* and giving the 'strongest assurance of my utmost assistance' his interest caused little action otherwise. There was nothing so positive as active obstruction that could have been countered, there was just massive indifference. The delay in appointing commissioners was one example, but equally serious was the fact that although from its inception the board faithfully sent biannual reports to their agent in London, Milward Rowe, to forward to the first lord of the treasury and thence to the king, the treasury paid very little attention to these missives and they may or may not have reached the king for there are no records at all of royal approval or disapproval for five years after 1755. This is not because replies have been lost: there were no replies to lose. The reports throughout these years note anxiously that they are waiting comment, list past achievements if any in detail, and suggest future plans but the lack of royal approbation meant that the board and hence the annexed estates were in a state of suspended animation for no major policy could be initiated without this. The estates were carefully and expensively surveyed and the factors wrote very full informative reports but such large schemes as the idea of turning Tarbat House into a linen station similar to the Board of Trustees' establishments at Lochbroom and Lochcarron never got past the blueprint stage. This was a blessing in disguise, as such a plan would have used up the whole surplus of the estates and probably have been as unsuccessful as these others. But this is beside the point when we bear in mind that it could have been a project which would have revolutionised the highland economy, but the board planned in vain. It must be recorded however that in the Minto papers there is an irritated, unsigned and undated 'observation', running to two sides of a large sheet of paper, to the effect that the commissioners had 'sent up no plans, surveys judicial rentals of any estates under their management'. Nor had reports from factors, riding officers or abstracts from these reached the writer. He was prepared to approve such things as schools, bridges, and the manufacture of ashes if these were considered proper, because of the general nature of the provisions, but considered: 'In short no view can be taken . . . or any judgement formed of any plans in respect to the particular circumstances of any of them nor consequently of the plans first mentioned in the report of 1757. . . .'9 Here we see one of the first signs that the central government was not alone in sins of omission.

The commissioners had certainly not been idle since 1755 but their activities had been so restricted by lack of formal royal approval that in 1760, their first report of the year to George II stated that they felt they must stop all proceedings as H.M.'s pleasure had not been communicated to them. Possibly as a result of this the accession of George III brought some action; a new board was appointed, not noticeably different from the old, with a few more eminent 'improvers' like Lord Kames and Lord Gardenstone and official representatives such as the sheriff deputes of Perthshire and Forfarshire. Throughout the life of the board from then on, as need arose through death or as suitable people became available new appointments were made, the second last being that of Henry Dundas in 1783. Thereafter there was some sort of reaction to correspondence from London but all through the period of annexation there were delays and frustrations because of tardy answers from crown and treasury.

No pattern or logic is obvious in what were presumably civil servants' dealing with annexed estates business. Probably eighteenth-century administrative methods generally and a certain disinterest in North Britain specifically combined to ensure that random selection operated. Some ideas were speedily approved or rejected, others sat apparently ignored for years, pigeonholed somewhere in Whitehall. But it must have been extremely frustrating for any of the commissioners who were actively interested in what must have seemed at the outset at least, an exciting, challenging and promising project. Central control of expenditure was also erratically strict and sometimes took the commissioners by surprise. They undoubtedly believed that they would have more freedom of decision than in fact turned out to be the case. In 1762 Lord Milton had been sure that had the sum already allocated to Dr Cullen for his research on cashube ashes been inadequate the board would have been free to allow more.[10] When in fact money was lent to several manufacturers without prior permission the 'dead hand' of the treasury fell flat and clammy and repayment of the money, £2,100, was demanded. The recipients were appalled for the money had been spent on buildings, goods and machinery. It was certainly not liquid. This particular episode illustrates not only the emphasis placed by the central government on absolute control of the disposition of finance but central government delays. The board reported the grants in March 1764, but it was the

9 NLS, Minto EFP 35.

10 Dr William Cullen, 1710–90, was professor of chemistry at Edinburgh University at the time that the commissioners were looking for a native substitute for the imported cashube ashes used in bleaching. He carried out some experiments in Perthshire without being very enthusiastic about the results.

minutes of January 1765 that record the reception of the royal displeasure, a time lag of almost a year.

Sufficiently powerful representation to the treasury was made to enable the entrepreneurs to keep their loans on this occasion but the Edinburgh board was very cautious thereafter. One method of overcoming red tape in smaller matters was to make a request for permission to use a specific amount for very general purpose, for example £900 for three years for the encouragement of the linen industry in 1767, £200 per annum for indenturing and supporting apprentices in 1758, though this of course was not authorised until after 1760. This allowed a little more independence for each year the annual allowance was added to what capital remained and the expenditure subtracted from that. In 1773 £77-4-10 had been spent on the linen industry from the allowance mentioned above, which by this time amounted to £1,804-4-7$\frac{6}{12}$, leaving £1,726-19-9$\frac{6}{12}$ and no detailed account were demanded by the treasury for these sums. It is worth noting that this was largely theoretical finance for there was not necessarily £1,700 available in hard cash. A certain amount of discretion was also exercised in these recurring annual amounts. In 1767 it was reported that the £50 allowed each year since 1763 to set up craftsmen had been used for two years to support a mill in Crieff that made coarse paper.[11] This expenditure could be rationalised but the original idea had been to set up individual crafts-men with a decent house and garden and some necessary tools. Then when the apprenticeship scheme was contracted in some disgust the allowance or £200 was not officially applied to some other purpose; the entries in the Journal read: 'To Henry Barclay for apprentices and incidents' which could cover a multi-plicity of items.[12]

Despite these examples of independence the central government's supervisory powers were sometimes exercised overcarefully, though spasmodically and sometimes tardily, one might go so far as to say most often tardily, sometimes with supreme lack of interest. The commissioners' own organisation in Edin-burgh must be examined, and it has to be admitted that grounds for criticism are so easily found, that one looks for mitigating circumstances. Offices and administrators are sometimes judged by their filing systems but it would be un-wise to condemn the board immediately on this score, though the collection was hardly orderly before the Scottish Records Office recatalogued it about ten years ago, for the papers had been moved and had also been involved in a fire in the exchequer. Against this apologia we must first note that in 1768 one of the clerks, James Morison, was recommended by Lord Elliock for a bonus and commended for the extra work he had had in 'sorting the great confusion in the office accounts'.[13] Secondly, even after Morison's work confusion must have existed in some areas for the following year, the barons of the exchequer threat-ened to take the board to court for omitting to send them records of the money

[11] The commissioners' biannual reports are all contained in SRO, Forfeited Estates Papers, 1745, E723/1–4 in chronological order.
[12] SRO, Forfeited Estates Papers, 1745, Journals and Ledgers, E732/5–9.
[13] SRO, Forfeited Estates Papers, 1745, E721/10, p. 197.

arising from the estates. Now several of the commissioners were also barons so
we can fairly assume that the exchequer court was not over-reacting to the first
occasion on which this had happened. Perhaps the Adam brothers had been right
and the office was not in fact 'what such an office ought to be', however 'conveniently placed' for the lawyers.

However there are other factors which point to a degree of laxity and in-
efficiency and while it would probably be maligning the commissioners to say
they resembled their London masters in indifference it would certainly be true
to say the management of these estates had not first call on their energies. The
first meeting in 1755 attracted a large turn-out of twenty of the twenty-
eight members but board meetings were not infrequently postponed through
lack of a quorum which was only five, and on more than one occasion because
no commissioners at all appeared. In the years 1755–60 there were only monthly
meetings which cannot have expedited business. The clerk wrote to one of the
factors in May 1757: 'I find that the whole business of the Board on Monday
was transacted in one line – Adjourned to Monday 20th June.' That meant two
months delay. He went on: 'Yesterday the standing committee consisted of
Lord Milton and he adjourned himself to the first session in June.' The said
standing committee had been appointed to allow for a certain amount of
specialisation and speedier transaction of business. In March 1760 there was
another adjournment until June but at least the first clerk, John Robertson was
instructed 'in anything of an emergency' to apply to 'any of the commissioners
who might be about town' for directions. In 1760 the new board commissioned
by George III attacked the problem of obtaining a quorum by deciding to hold
meetings at a fixed day and hour each week; with such an arrangement, members could hardly plead previous engagements. Committees were certainly
appointed to look into individual matters though minutes seem to have been
kept only for the major standing committees,[14] but such consistent failure to
attend meetings must surely indicate a less than absorbing interest in the activities
of the board.

One slightly surprising aspect of the administration is that members did not
consider regular visits to the estates as an ineluctable part of their duties. From
the beginning they conceived of the whole administration being carried out on
their part by letters and verbal instructions to officers. In 1755 they immediately
employed surveyors who were given detailed instructions by Lt-Col David
Watson, Deputy Quarter-Master General of H.M. Forces in Scotland. Watson
was eminently suited to this task as it had been he who first suggested to the duke
of Cumberland that the highlands be surveyed and he had had Roy the celebrated map-maker on his staff.[15] Very detailed descriptions of the estates were
obtained as we can see from William Morison's survey of Lochiel in 1772.[16]
A photocopy of Col D. H. Cameron's copy of this survey can be seen in the

[14] SRO, FEP, 1745, E721/3. General and Particular minutes are contained in 27 volumes,
E721/1–27.
[15] *Early Maps of Scotland* (Edinburgh, 1936), 12 and 98.
[16] SRO, RH 2/8/26.

S.R.O. but most of these and any resulting maps seem to have been returned to the reinstated heirs in 1784. On the results of these surveys and on the factors' reports the commissioners proposed to work. They could hardly fail to be aware of the limitations of this approach for, landowners as so many of them were, it is hard to believe that they would have managed their own estates in such a remote fashion. It must be admitted that even Grant of Monymusk did not apparently visit his estate every year but the gardener at Pitfichie, John Middleton, regretted this as his presence would 'goe a greater length for one viwe than 20 precepts will doe',[17] and an obituary on James Ogilvy earl of Finlater and Seafield considered it worth noting that he had 'for many years resided almost constantly on his own estates.'[18] But to abdicate almost entirely from the duties of personal supervision seems irresponsible.

To overcome some of the disadvantages of absentee landlordism the commissioners appointed a riding officer and general inspector as their substitute and consciousness of the defects of this arrangement is shown in a paragraph of instruction to this officer, which significantly was ordered to be struck out and not even minuted. 'You are also to keep in mind that you are appointed for this reason chiefly that the Trustees themselves consist of a number of Lords and Gentlemen who have other Employments, Business or Avocations and can but seldom have opportunity to see with their own eyes what is fit to be done or going forward in several parts in prosecution of the purposes of the said law.'[19] The inspector went out on his tour in the summer, first with a salary of £100 p.a. later of £150, and one guinea a day expenses, to report on conditions generally and on individual schemes which were named in his annual instructions. There was not unanimity among the commissioners about the necessity for this appointment and when Archibald Menzies of Culdares resigned in 1770 on becoming a commissioner of customs but offered to perform his duties gratis the post was left an honorary one until he died in 1780. Unfortunately this hiatus has left us with no more of Menzies' comprehensive reports for that period.

Another means of compensating for the commissioners' absence from the estates was to demand the factors' attendance at the Edinburgh office frequently and expensively. The Struan accounts for example have regular entries of £25 for travelling expenses to Edinburgh. The other side of this coin was the apparent distrust of factors who were on the defensive throughout their tenure of office, however lengthy and satisfactory. In part, this attitude arose from one of the aims of the annexation which was defined by one of the many of those who gave 'Hints of administering the Forfeited Estates in Scotland' as 'demonstrating the lenity and compassion of the government towards the inhabitants' and 'infusing them with a deep conviction of the Goodness of the present Royal Family'.[20] Translated into administrative terms this clashed vigorously with

[17] Monymusk Papers, ed. H. Hamilton (Scottish History Society, 1945), 98.
[18] Scots Magazine, xxxii, 630 (November, 1770).
[19] SRO, FEP, 1745, E726/1, p. 49.
[20] Edinburgh, Advocates' Library MS 19.1.35, ff. 22–4: Hints towards a settlement of the Forfeited Estates in the Highlands of Scotland, anon., 13 December 1752.

efficiency and undermined the position of the board's officers especially the factors, *vis-à-vis* the tenants. Possibly as a result of the preponderance of lawyers on the board, a tenant's complaints about any of the factor's actions immediately set off a series of enquiries, charges, counter-charges, expensive correspondence and visits to Edinburgh, very often inspired by what factors considered the spirit of pure contrariety on the part of the complainants. Menzies on his tours developed a very real sympathy for the factor and in 1767–8 he described what they had to contend with.[21]

Despite their 'great pains' to improve the estates, they had been 'much discouraged from pushing those articles by the licentious dispositions of the tenants', who whenever anything was not entirely to their liking, got an agent to draw up a long paper of complaints and grievances which was laid before the board. Thereupon the factor was ordered to report and 'things are suspended until the factors are further examined and after all tho the tenant is found in the wrong no further notice is taken.' He went on: 'Things are come to such a pass upon these estates that no order of the Board if in the least disagreeable to the tenants can be executed without going through all the different courts.' Note that it was the factors who were 'further examined' not the tenants. Menzies tried to convince the commissioners of the necessity of supporting their authority in the persons of their factors, pointing out the expense of litigation which they could find in their accounts, and he was on a similar tack when he wrote to the secretary from New Tarbat asking him to get the board to defer action on complaints until he returned to Edinburgh 'so preventing the disagreeable situation we have been in for some time past of doing one day and undoing another'.

The factors' duties were heavy and responsible as we can see from the Struan factor's list of only some of the things he had to do in 1759. 'Attend meetings of the Quarter Sessions and of neighbouring Gentlemen and J.P.'s to Concert Measures for the Police of the Country. The personal atendance to every new Work, carrying on in the estate by order of the Board' and here perhaps a touch of bitterness 'even to reparation of a tenant's house, expense of sending money to the Receiver General and other things of that nature'. Added to these extraordinary duties were the ordinary tasks of straightforward management of the estates and on Struan the factor pointed out that this involved expense and 'personal trouble' visiting the 'different corners'.[22] Factors were also directed to assist in recruiting men in 1756 and 1757 for the forces, and another almost incidental duty was accommodating surveyors and other official visitors. James Small had to put up all Dr Cullen's assistants when he was searching for a substitute for cashube ashes by burning ferns and undergrowth. The smell must have been terrible! At one point they did show signs of strain, in the first stages of what Pennant called (with no flattering intent) the Board's 'only utopian' scheme for colonising certain areas with discharged soldiers and sailors. The unfortunate factors were pestered day and night by very dubious characters whom they had to feed, clothe, subsidise and sometimes house until alternative

21 SRO, FEP, 1745, E729/8–10.          22 SRO, FEP, 1745, E721/4, p. 223.

accommodation could be found – or built. A further burden must have been the lack of confidence in their masters' support even when carrying out their orders, as Menzies' strictures show. Of course, the factors were not all faultless; John Campbell of Barcaldine lost his factory of the Perth estate for various reasons, one being that he had accepted 'presents' from tenants which was strictly forbidden. Also he was very lax in sending in accounts, which were over three years in arrears and very inaccurate besides, as he kept no books and the tenants had lost their receipts.

Despite Barcaldine's doubtful reliability it is worth quoting his letter to a neighbouring proprietor for it does illuminate the relationship of the commissioners and factors. He wrote: 'If I was acting for a single person, I would go on with the work (repairing a breach in the banks of the Earn) – and expect his thanks, but I do not know that I might be found fault with if I exceed my order'. On another occasion when Barcaldine asked for instructions and advice he got very little help. The only money being given him for rents was 5/- and 10/- notes from the banks of 'Perth, Dundee, Auchtermuchty, Kirkliston, etc.,' and he wondered if he was at liberty to accept these. Incredibly the first reaction of the commissioners was that they refused to give him any directions. Then one of their number, Mr Drummond, produced the information that the banks of Edinburgh had agreed to give their notes for those of the Bank of Ayr and the three banks of Glasgow and with that information only the factor had to be content.[23]

The pay too was uncertain as salaries were calculated as 5% of the rents which varied annually according to the increase and decrease of grain prices. In 1770 the three longest serving factors were given a considerable increase, £100 p.a. to Captain Forbes of New on Cromarty for 'his great zeal and activity in civilising the Highlands', £100 to James Small and £80 to Henry Butter. They had certainly worked for it but no matter how much energy and ability they expended, lack of authority because of lack of backing from the commissioners handicapped their efforts.

Besides this the commissioners were also dilatory in business. At least one neighbouring proprietor, Lt-Gen Graeme of Gorthie, lost his temper over the delay and what he termed illiberality over a fairly simple excambion,[24] while factors and office staff could be driven to deviousness. One factor, Thomas Keir, suggested to the secretary at one point that as no orders had come concerning a legal process about which the board had been approached about two years before, he should examine the minutes and if nothing had been ordered, he and Keir should just carry on without further reference to the commissioners.[25] This gives more than a hint of flabbiness in administrative methods. Management of the annexed estates was certainly not the board's prime concern, though this may seem an ungracious comment when one considers the volume of correspondence that Lord Kames dealt with. Thomas Pennant was rather appalled at the state in which he found one of the would-be 'new towns'

[23] SRO, FEP, 1745, E721/8, p. 82.     [24] SRO, FEP, 1745, E777/111.

[25] SRO, FEP, 1745, E777/87/25.

of discharged soldiers and remarked charitably of the commissioners that: 'As these gentlemen with rare patriotism discharge their trust without salary, they might not be liable to censure like hireling placemen on every trifling failure'.[26] We need be less apologetic and with hindsight more surprised at the insouciance with which some of the more grandiose plans were formed. Francis Garden lord Gardenstone, for example knew how much time, money and effort were involved in the successful foundation of a village but plans were made in a most haphazard, casual way and left to the factors to carry through. Yet the settlement of sailors alone was estimated at £6,000 and the annual surplus from the estates after management costs and public burdens were subtracted amounted to only about £4,500 in the early years of the annexation.

Nor was time on the side of the commissioners. Though the statutory period of annexation was thirty-two years from the annexing act in 1752 until the disannexation in 1784, long before the latter date attitudes had begun to change towards the highlands and the highlanders as had the ideas, one might say the ideals, behind the annexation. In 1748 it was possible for Baron Edlin to write that he was convinced 'they had better give young Lovat a pension to ten times the value than reinstate him in his Paternal Estate',[27] but in 1774 the same 'young Lovat' was a Major-General in the British army. Without being in possession of these estates he had raised a regiment in defence of the dynasty that beheaded his father, and as a reward for his services was reinstated in his family lands in that year. The highlands that were merely 'a nuisance' twenty-five years earlier were becoming appreciated for their scenic beauty, the inhabitants for their value in the services and for their Gaelic culture, if only in Macpherson's Ossian. The Highland Society's avowed aim in 1784 of encouraging Gaelic culture would have been impossible in 1752.

The commissioners can hardly have felt encouraged in their work after 1774. For only fourteen years of the period of annexation had they been able to take positive steps in carrying out their statutory duties, that is from 1760 when their reports at last received royal acknowledgement; the estates held of subject superiors had been under their control for only four years. A few small firms were thriving with the help of subsidies, but major industrial development was never considered after the deliberate withdrawal of support by the late 1760s from the ridiculously situated linen manufacturing stations set up by the Board of Trustees (When one subsidy granted to the Trustees ended in 1762, they handed over all responsibility for industry in the highland area to the annexed estates board on the ground that their funds were too small to cope adequately in the lowlands.) Minor schemes, minor that is in the expense involved, such as encouraging craftsmanship and settling day labourers, had only modified success; their colonisation plans had gone sadly awry. Agricultural changes were bound to be slow in showing results, but their main aim here was to provide leases and security of tenure, and in 1774, the treasury suggested that no more should be granted. At this point an affronted board dug in its heels and declaring

26 T. Pennant, *Tour of Scotland, 1772* (London, 1776), iii, 91.
27 Adv. MS 19.1.35, f. 26: Letter to the bishop of Salisbury.

that such a policy would be 'fatal to industry' carried on making out leases of up to forty-one years in length to the end of the disannexation. But the treasury mind was plain; Lovat had got back his estates and there was no reason why other heirs of the attainted, many of whom were also loyal and competent army officers, should not soon be similarly rewarded. They would be less grateful if they found their paternal estates encumbered with long leases set at comparatively low rents, enforcing agricultural policies they might not wish to follow.

Despite this flash of defiance from the board the last ten years of the annexation were free of innovations. There were continuing and increasing contributions to the development of communications, notably bridges, harbours and roads, but otherwise no new ideas were promulgated and the old ones just ticked over or were quietly dropped. By 1781 we find the board refusing the prayer of the General Assembly to authorise their agent to carry out the process of a promised new erection of the parish of Ardnamurchan on the grounds that having been 'some time ago discharged from exercising an ordinary act of management', unspecified, they were declining to enter into any matter of great importance 'especially such as tend to entail perpetual burthens upon the Estates under their management'.[28] In 1775 a letter had been written suggesting that the estates should be returned to the old families and the writer, Henry Dundas,[29] was appointed a commissioner in 1783. The writing had been on the wall since 1774 and in 1784 this early experiment of government intervention in regional development came to an end.[30]

There is not space in consideration of this particular aspect of the annexation to attempt a verdict on the effects of the work of the commissioners but the broad question of finance cannot be separated from that of administration. Therein lay the initial, perhaps the greatest, misconception of the whole grand design, that the annexed estates purse would be virtually bottomless. A large surplus was expected once the burden of maintaining proprietors was removed, but it is doubtful if preliminary calculations were made of the cost of centralising the administration or of the possible outlay necessary if the aims of the annexing act were to be adequately carried out. The commissioners very quickly came up against financial problems. Gilbert Elliot of Minto, very troubled at the apparent melting away of resources, repeated the sums from the office in some disbelief. Of £9,000, the surplus available over two years, the Edinburgh office cost £1,200, £1,865 worth of expenditure had already been allowed and plans made that would absorb £5,330 more, a total of £8,098.[31] Later on in 1775 in one of the biannual reports, the board stated that they made no new proposals for expenditure because all their resources were already totally committed, and unlike ordinary proprietors they could not recoup by raising rents for these were statutorily controlled.

[28] SRO, FEP, 1745, E721/11, p. 222.
[29] C. R. Fay, *Adam Smith and the Scotland of his Day* (Cambridge, 1956), 13. Henry Dundas to William Eden, 5 September 1775.
[30] 24 George III, c. 57, 'The Disannexing Act'.        [31] NLS, Minto EFP 35.

The original mistake was the central government's but Lord Kames had to admit that large sums of public money were expended in the highlands and the forfeited estates which had proved 'no better than water spilt on the ground'.[32] Quite large sums were certainly laid out with no apparent reaction from the commissioners or indeed from the treasury to the conspicuous lack of results. The twin faults of bureaucracy, overcentralisation and lack of personal responsibility, can be illustrated time and again in the board's records of the general administration. Of their management of individual estates the final word may come from a speaker in the House of Lords, Lord Sydney, in the debate on the Disannexation Bill. He declared it was easy to distinguish the annexed estates because of the 'bad condition they were in compared to other men's estates and for the almost total neglect of their cultivation. . . .'[33] This was a sad commentary on and a sorry end to a potentially important, influential and dramatic experiment and both the central government and the board for the annexed estates must share the responsibility for its being less than a resounding success.

ANNETTE M. SMITH

[32] J. Ramsay of Ochtertyre, *Scotland and Scotsmen of the Eighteenth Century* (Edinburgh, 1888), i, 198.
[33] *Parliamentary History of England* (London, 1815), xxiv, 1372–3.

# 17

# Coal-Mining in Fife in the Second Half of the Eighteenth Century

Fife: 'The situation of this shire for foreign trade is very favourable, being almost surrounded by the sea, and abounding in harbours of some depth. It has two custom houses at Kirkcaldy and Anstruther: the former extends from Aberdour to Largo inclusive, and the latter from Largo to St Andrews'.[1] Using principally the Customs and Excise records for Kirkcaldy and Anstruther, one extensive set of coal mining records, and an early-nineteenth-century text which examines the coal trade on the Forth, it is hoped to give some indication of the importance, both direct and indirect, of coal to the Fife economy from 1742, the date from which the customs records are available in a complete form, to the end of the century, together with a sketch of mining methods and men.

The importance of coal as a trading commodity for Fife at this time can scarcely be overstated. In the Kirkcaldy customs records from 1743 to 1792, of 3,195 recorded voyages outwards, 2,938 (92%) showed coal as part of the cargo, and with the vast majority, coal was the sole item exported.[2] The Anstruther records in the same period are less dramatic at first glance, the comparable figures being 727 voyages, with 430 (59·1%) in whole, or in part, coal shipments.[3] However, these statistics are somewhat clouded by the fact that coal was not mined commercially in the area to any extent until the establishment of the Newark Coal Company in 1771. Until that time the exports from the ports covered by the Anstruther Custom house had been predominantly agricultural, and it is not surprising that when the coal deposits near Pittenweem were first being explored there was an absence of suitably skilled men. Hence, William

[1] Chalmers, *Caledonia* (Paisley, 1894), vii, 132.
[2] Scottish Record Office, Kirkcaldy Customs Accounts. E504/20/1–12.
[3] Scottish Record Office, Anstruther Customs Accounts. E504/3/1–8.

---

*Author's Note*

(*a*) The Rothes papers were consulted soon after they were lodged with the Kirkcaldy Museum and Art Gallery. The references given are those in use at that time.

(*b*) Several of the references used pertain to a collection of private family papers to which I was, exceptionally, given access. The owner of these papers does not wish to make them generally available, and for this reason has asked that their exact location should not be mentioned. I would, however, be pleased to discuss this source with anyone who writes.

Brown of Throckley was asked, and agreed, to send '2 or 3 men to come that can bore a little and also sink if required'.[4] This inconspicuous beginning should not be taken, however, as a sign that the Newark Company was inconsiderable in organisation or ambition. Some idea of the scale of operations emerges on finding that 'Upwards of 300 men were employed at the mines, and considerable quantities of the mineral were exported to Holland and elsewhere. An impost of one farthing per ton, payable to the town, on the coal, salt and other materials imported and exported by the company was let for a year by roup at £8. 5s. sterling which, without taking into account the tacksman's profit would indicate an import and export of about 8000 tons annually'.[5]

The launching of the Newark Company marked a change in the exporting pattern for the custom house area. From 1743 to 1771, agricultural products accounted for 68·9% of the cargoes exported and coal for 12·9%, all the coal being brought coastwise from various mines on the Forth and subsequently entered in the Anstruther Customs records as part of cargoes for export. But in the period 1772 to 1792, the equivalent figures for agricultural products fell to 13% and those for coal rose steeply to 82·1%. Both the Kirkcaldy and the Anstruther records, therefore, show most clearly that coal was of major importance in the structure of the export trade of Fife, with agricultural products in the east and rough cloth in the west coming poor seconds. This distinct impression of the dominance of coal in the export trade is echoed in the Rev Mr Thomas Fleming's contribution for Kirkcaldy in the Old Statistical Account where he states that 'the greater number (of vessels) is employed in the trade to Holland and the Baltic. To these the only article of export is coals, shipped here, at Dysart, Wemyss and other ports on the Firth.'[6] Robert Bald, a civil engineer at Alloa, writing of the eighteenth-century coal trade, points out that 'in Holland ... the fine splint coals of the river Forth commanded a decided preference, as the Dutch split them into pieces like slates, swept them clean, and laid them up ready for the fire. This arose from their uncommon attention to cleanliness in their houses, for which they are so very remarkable'.[7] But the markets supplied by the Fife collieries were not restricted to those of the meticulous Dutch, as the Customs accounts show.

Taking the three-year periods in the middle of the 1740s, the 1760s and the 1780s, the following are the figures for amounts of coal exported:

|  | Anstruther | Kirkcaldy |
| --- | --- | --- |
|  | tons | tons |
| 1744–6 | 22 | 4,746 |
| 1764–6 | 68 | 12,573 |
| 1784–6 | 4,708 | 22,577 |

[4] Scottish Record Office, Baird of Elie Papers. GD 147, Box 53. Letter included in bundle marked 'Correspondence etc. 1765–69'.
[5] D. Cook, Annals of Pittenweem (Anstruther, 1867), 150.
[6] J. Sinclair, Old Statistical Account, xviii, 25.
[7] R. Bald, A General View of the Coal Trade of Scotland (Edinburgh, 1808), 84.

In the case of the Anstruther area, in the last period when coal was being produced locally, there were two main destinations: Middelburg in Holland with 68·0% of the total and Hamburg with 24·2%. The remainder went to Amsterdam (7·1%) and Copenhagen (0·7%). Compared with the similar figures from the preceding decade, when major coal production began, the Dutch trade increased from 45·4% of the total, to 75·1% while that of Hamburg went up from 14·8% to 24·2%. The Northern European share, however, fell from 34·5% to 0·7%.

The Kirkcaldy customs accounts on the other hand, present a very different picture. The 1774–6 totals are included for the purposes of comparison with those for that period at Anstruther, which were mentioned in the previous paragraph.

|  | Hamburg | Holland | N. Europe |
|---|---|---|---|
| 1,744·6 | 10% | 75% | 15% |
| 1,764·6 | 38% | 30% | 32% |
| 1,774·6 | 59% | 21% | 20% |
| 1,784·6 | 43% | 9% | 48% |

The political and military influences on the smooth flow of goods must be taken into account when examining this pattern of trade, but, that accepted, it is reasonable to assume that the increase in tonnage of coal shipped was the result of an increase in demand. Political effects altered the commercial outlets available at any one time, but the merchants were astute business men who made economic decisions using the same basic principles as their counterparts today, examining various methods of solving their trading problems, 'costing each variation, arriving in the end at the one which will give the desired result at the minimum cost. This method is then the one which will yield the greatest profit (or at worst cause the least loss), so that it will be attractive to a firm which is operating under the incentive of private profit'.[8] The text is modern, but the underlying concept is not. The Anstruther figures give the lie to any thought that there was a general trend away from Holland to the Northern European ports as destinations for Fife coal exports. It would appear that during the period of the war against the Dutch, which began in 1780, alternative outlets were sought, and when peace was restored in 1783, the Kirkcaldy area had reduced its dependence on the Dutch market, while the traders to the east of the Kingdom chose to renew their established links with Holland in general and Middelburg in particular while also keeping up with the new contacts made in Hamburg. The merchants and shipowners came to realise the 'benefits of the steady pounding of a regular beat, where the master and his ship were well known and trusted and could get full cargoes with a minimum of difficulty'.[9]

While it is true that, especially in the early part of the second half of the eighteenth century, 'the seaborne trade in coal was organised by people whose

[8] C. F. Carter, The Science of Wealth (London, 1960), 15.
[9] R. Davis, The Rise of the English Shipping Industry in the 17th and 18th Centuries (London, 1962), 361.

interests and connections were in origin maritime rather than commercial',[10] their trading decisions were taken with commercial factors very much in mind. It did mean, however, that trade was often conducted in a less well-organised manner than it might have been. For example, the master of the vessel would often buy coal on behalf of his owners and sell it on their account on arrival at his destination, in many cases selling from the pierhead to customers who merely chanced to pass. The loss in time was great and the wastage of man-power and capital considerable, with the ship and crew having to await the sale of the coals before setting out with the return cargo. The use of agents in foreign ports grew as the century progressed as did the influence of the pro-fessional merchant who, acting either alone or in company with others to in-crease capital and spread risk, brought his skills to bear in organising both outward and inward voyages, using his knowledge of market conditions abroad and unfilled demands at home. From Holland came linseed, undressed flax and dyestuffs for the linen industry, clover seed for an improving domestic agricultural system; Hamburg provided specialised timber for ship building, oak bark for tanning, ashes for bleaching; the Baltic ports sent timber, unwrought iron and naval stores. These were the trading attractions, and the expenses were defrayed, in part, by the exporting of the one commodity that could command a market in those foreign ports, coal. In addition, it was an excellent ballast, with the advantage over stones and sea water, the other common ballast materials, that it had some value when discharged.

The coal trade overseas, therefore, cannot be viewed in isolation. Part of its value lay in the importance of the goods brought back on return voyages which might provide raw materials for industry, or foodstuffs to alleviate shortages, as in 1782–3. It is doubtful if the coal trade could have survived in other cir-cumstances. The introduction of the steam engine in the early years of the century laid open stocks of coal which had previously been inaccessible. Such seams became practical commercial propositions and the potential supply of coal was so increased that the market was changed from a seller's to a buyer's one, and profits were dealt a severe blow. On the River Forth, the effect was that great coal (as opposed to the smaller pieces, chews and dross) was shipped free on board for 4s. 10d. per ton in 1785, an increase of only 2d. over the figure for 1715, despite a doubling in the costs of labour and materials.[11]

To add to the troubles of the coal exporter, heavy customs duties had to be borne. When the century entered its second half, the export duty stood at 2s. per ton but additional duties laid on coal in 1757 and 1765 raised that figure first to 3s. 4d. and then to 4s. 8d. (These amounts were for British vessels; the corresponding figures for foreign ships were 5s. 8d., 7s. and 8s. 4d.). In 1779 a general surtax of 5% on all existing duties was imposed,[12] followed by a similar increase in 1782.[13] By then, the whole system of duties on coal had become extremely complex, and the various calculations necessary were abolished if 1787 when the existing duties were grouped together in a Consolidated Charge

[10] R. Davis, *op. cit.*, 91.        [11] *A General View of the Coal Trade of Scotland*, 24.
[12] 19 Geo. III, c. 25.              [13] 27 Geo. III, c. 13.

of 5s. 2d. per ton for British ships. In the case of the Fife ports the cost to foreign shipping was of no account for, by that time, this aspect of the trade had been completely obliterated. Where in the past such ships would have taken home a loading of coal, by 1787 it was no longer economically justifiable and alternative cargoes were sought elsewhere.

Foreign trade in coal was, therefore, under considerable pressure by the 1780s with export duties levied which were approximately equal to the cost of the cargo itself. Increased output and increased demand were important but the two could only be economically matched if transport costs could be kept down to a level below the profit margin. Fortunately, the later years of the eighteenth century brought technical advances in shipbuilding, such as improved hull design and more efficient rigging which led to larger ships and an increase in the number of shipping tons serviced by each crew member. In the Kirkcaldy custom house ports the figures of ship numbers, tonnage and men employed[14] show these trends clearly:

|  | Ships | Tons | Men | Average tonnage per ship | Tons serviced per man |
|---|---|---|---|---|---|
| 1760 | 60 | 4,115 | 369 | 68·6 | 11·1 |
| 1772 | 67 | 4,255 | 403 | 63·5 | 10·5 |
| 1782 | 48 | 3,030 | 247 | 63·1 | 12·2 |
| 1792 | 94 | 10,302 | 652 | 109·6 | 15·8 |

Thus, the coal trade overseas was able to grow in the 1780s in response to demand, with the help of larger and more efficiently run ships which cut transport costs, and a gradual increase in price from 4s. 10d. per ton in 1785 to 7s. per ton by the end of the century,[15] though from the outbreak of the French War in 1793 coal exports slumped badly. The merchants' decision to continue the export of coal indicates that some profit was being made for otherwise the outward voyages would have been made in ballast, but it is unlikely that that branch of trading alone produced any mercantile fortunes.

This point introduces the whole question of the profitability of mining for the men most concerned, the coal owners. There is no reason to doubt Robert Bald's statement that 'with respect to the profits of the coal masters, they are said to have been very great about a century ago; but it is certain, that since the introduction of the steam-engine, few or no fortunes have been made in this line in Scotland; indeed, it is commonly asserted, that upon the whole, there has been more loss than gain'.[16] Why then did men engage in an enterprise which produced such meagre returns? In part, the answer is that they were victims of a vicious circle from which they could see no means of escape. The capital investment required in a colliery was great and much of it was in sinking costs, building internal stairways, shoring up workings and the like, and hence not resaleable other than as part of a going concern. So, there was an incentive

[14] Old Statistical Account, xviii, 26.
[15] A General View of the Coal Trade of Scotland, 26.
[16] Bald, op. cit., 25.

to continue working coal mines, even in the face of losses, in the hope that better times lay ahead. Bald estimated that where £20,000 was laid out on a colliery, the owner could not expect more than £4,000 back if the colliery was given up, which encouraged the coalmasters to continue in operation. 'For while a colliery is at work, all the estimated stock is really and absolutely of the full value as it stands; but the instant the concern stops, the stock suffers the full diminution'.[17] Some indication of the extent of the outlay on capital equipment can be gained from the case of the Kirkland colliery at Methil where, in 1738, a machine was erected at a total cost of £17,413 16s. Scots or just over £1,450 Sterling.[18] The loss of £180 2s. 11d. recorded by the colliery five years later in 1743[19] is grim evidence of the financial uncertainty of coal owning, and such returns could not have been encouragements to further investment. However, the economics of the coal industry of the eighteenth century should not be viewed in isolation, but rather in conjunction with those of salt-making which was a natural ancillary industry where supplies of small coal and salt water could be brought together with low transport costs. Salt did not play a significant part in Fife overseas trade at this time, but the demand from the domestic market was greater and more reliable. For Wemyss and Methil the statistics available are somewhat fragmentary but those to hand show annual 'sea sales' of 20,000 bushels of salt or more from each port, with the price rising from 7d. per bushel in 1743 to 2s. per bushel in 1795.[20] An example of the value of the salt industry is given by the accounts for the coal and salt works at Methil and Wemyss in the year to 25 January 1772.[21] With sales set against total charges, which include wages and materials, the figures are as follows:

|              | Loss £ | Profit £ |
|--------------|--------|----------|
| Wemyss Coal  | 214    |          |
| Methil Coal  |        | 249      |
| Wemyss Salt  |        | 82       |
| Methil Salt  |        | 643      |

The owners' financial dependence upon the salt receipts is seen to be even more impressive when one considers that at Wemyss £286, and at Methil £646, of the coal sale amounts were book entries only, being transfers of small coal to the salt pans.

While the profit and loss figures are significant in showing the relative value of the two enterprises at the time, the items included under the heading of 'charges' indicate another aspect of the trade which arose from coal mining. A large range of goods is listed including wood for engine repairs, shoring operations and the like, ropes and plates for the salt pans and the boilers. All these were items which produced a demand for imported raw materials; wood,

[17] Bald, *op. cit.*, 28.
[18] Private Family Papers (P.F.P.), Box C6.
[19] P.F.P. Methil Coal Book (unnumbered).
[20] P.F.P. Methil and Wemyss Salt Books (unnumbered).
[21] P.F.P. Methil and Wemyss Salt Books (unnumbered).

hemp and unwrought iron, creating business for the merchants and employment for the various local manufacturers who turned these imported materials
into the necessary supplies for successful mining. In addition, the wages paid
to the colliers and salters, which were high by the standards of the time, injected
capital into the economy of the district. 'Hewers' earnings were consistently
two or three times as high as farm servants' wages and showed a tendency
(though they varied greatly) to increase from about six shillings a week early
in the century to eight shillings more in the middle, then to twelve or thirteen
shillings around 1770 and fifteen shillings or more around 1790'.[22]

Another aspect of the trade in coal itself was the coal sold and shipped to
other parts of Britain. For most of the period competition from the Northern
English coal fields curtailed this trade severely, but by the end of the century, it
had come to be of considerable consequence, helped in 1793 by Lord Melville
who had 'procured an act, 33d George III. Chap. 69., by which the duty
imposed upon all coals carried beyond the mouth of the Forth was abolished.
Before this period, all coals carried coastwise from Stirling Bridge to Dunbar
upon one side, and to the Redhead on the other side of the Forth, were free of
duty; but the inhabitants north of these limits had a duty to pay of no less than
3s. 8d. per ton, – a sum nearly equal to the prime cost, over and above the freight,
and the risk of a sea voyage'.[23] From 1790 to 1801, the ports of Dysart, Wemyss
and Methil shipped the following amounts of coal:

|  | For Exportation | | Coastwise | | | |
|  | | | To London | | To other British ports[24] | |
|  | tons | cwts | tons | cwts | tons | cwts |
| Dysart | 73,739 | 10 | 184 | 12 | 41,193 | 19 |
| Wemyss | 29,301 | 1 | — | | 30,498 | 4 |
| Methil | 5,514 | 14 | — | | 20,732 | 18 |
|  | 108,556 | 5 | 184 | 12 | 92,425 | 1 |

Hence, the export trade at that time with some 54% of the total, must be
viewed in relation to the 46% sent to other British ports. This rise in the domestic
trade for the mines on the Forth, resulting from the effects of the 1793 Act and
the need to find alternative markets as a result of the trade dislocation caused by
the war against Revolutionary France, meant that the value of coal in helping
to solve the balance of payments problem with the European markets had been
reduced. However, it increased its role as a vital factor in internal industrial
development. It can be argued that this provision of an essential raw material,
making the coal owners feel a part of the progress of the Industrial Revolution,

[22] T. C. Smout, *A History of the Scottish People 1560–1830* (London, 1969), 433.
[23] Bald, *op. cit.*, 103.
[24] P.F.P. Box C 24: 'An Account of the Total Quantity of Coals Shipped from Dysart,
Wemyss and Methil from the Commencement of the Year 1790 to the Commencement of
the Year 1801 . . .'.

was also responsible for continued coal production even though that production gave scant rewards. Rostow points out that 'in terms of human motivation, many of the most profound economic changes are viewed as the consequence of non-economic human motives and aspirations', and goes on to quote, in support of that statement, the dictum of Karl Marx that 'if human nature felt no temptation to take a chance, no satisfaction (profit apart) in constructing a factory, a railway, a mine or a farm, there might not be much investment merely as a result of cold calculation'.[25] While the coal owners in eighteenth-century Fife were essentially business men, with the desire of business men to maximise profits, they could not avoid being influenced by the feelings of an age which believed that the first duty of coal suppliers lay in meeting home demands which would require 'the most vigorous exertions and output of the collieries, and add real and permanent strength to the pillars of the State'.[26] The days of mercantilism had passed, and while knowledge of the extent of the coal resources was limited, it was realised that coal was of more value to Britain as a provider of industrial energy than as a means of minimising a currency outflow.

However, the contribution of the mines on the Forth towards the British march to industrial supremacy could have been much greater but for the use of traditional mining methods which were far from efficient. Adam Smith might well have had the collieries surrounding his boyhood home in mind when he wrote that 'the value of a coal-mine to the proprietor frequently depends as much upon its situation as upon its fertility'.[27] The Fife mines were located over plentiful coal deposits which were easily reachable and of reasonable quality, and were near the sea giving low transport costs. This natural advantage, however, was cancelled out by the use of a mining system which was wasteful in both manpower and output.

At this time, there was 'a strong and deep-rooted prejudice . . . that the coal which is in large masses is of a quality far superior to that which is of a small size' and this idea was held in 'all those towns which are supplied with coals from the river Forth'.[28] Hence, the mine workers endeavoured to keep the coal in large pieces, but at each stage of the process which took the coal from the coal wall to the fireplace, a quantity of small coals or chews, dross and culm was produced, and there were several stages involved. After hewing came transport by bearer to the pit bottom, carriage to the pithead and thence to the coal hill where the colliery's produce was stacked; loading into carts or on to waggons for the journey to the pier head; the loading and discharging of the ships; transporting to and packing into the purchaser's storage space. The wastage in manpower resulting from the need for specialised hewing and careful handling of the great coals was, of necessity, large. Also financial losses occurred with each operation when the blocks of coal were chipped for 'small coals sell at a price

[25] W. W. Rostow, *The Stages of Economic Growth* (Cambridge, 1966), 2.
[26] Bald, *op. cit.*, 108.
[27] Adam Smith, *The Wealth of Nations* (Everyman edition, 1910), i, 153.
[28] Bald, *op. cit.*, 42–3.

far below the great coals, and occasion a dead loss to the shipmaster'. But the final irony came to the 'astonishment of those who have attended to the whole detail of keeping the coal in large masses, to see them violently attacked with every kind of destructive implement . . . all with a view to reduce part of them to chews, which was previously so much avoided, and which could be bought 30 per cent cheaper than the great coal'.[29] Hence we find the Leith company of merchants, Scougall and Ogilvy, on sending an order for a cargo of coal from Wemyss, expressing the hope that 'you will pay attention to give him (Captain Thomas Bridges) of your best splint as they have a great fatigue to go thro'.[30] Some small coal went to the salt pans or was used for lime burning, some met the needs of local industry such as the Pathhead nail makers, and some was used for firing the colliery engines, but any quantity in excess of that required to meet such needs was left below ground as it was not thought to be worth the effort and expense of carrying to the surface.

The estimate by Bald of the amount of coal squandered by the prevailing mining methods on the Forth shows that much wastage occurred, and this wastage is highlighted by the comparison made with the Glasgow system where the worth of chew coal was realised. Both places left pillars of coal to support the workings which accounted for one third of the available total, but in the West the entire remainder was brought out, four fifths being great coals and chews and one fifth dross and culm for the engines. By contrast, the Forth collieries left one fifth below ground, throwing most of the loose coal dross and culm into the waste areas left after the coal had been worked out, and of the rest, eight fifteenths were in the form of the bulky great coal and four fifteenths were chews which were sold at prices thirty per cent below those obtainable for the more popular product. The author's lament that 'our west country friends are better economists in the coal trade, from the wall to the room grate' is sufficient comment.[31]

No examination of the coal industry would be complete without considering the role of the miner, and this is particularly true at a time when the legal position of this large group in the industrial labour force was under regular review. In defence of the coal owner, it seems harsh to say of labour relations in the area that 'possibly the only way Forth coal masters were able to survive was by exploiting their labour to a degree unparalleled elsewhere in the United Kingdom'.[32] Taking examples from either side of the Forth from the Old Statistical Account, we find at Newbattle in Midlothian that 'the colliers can earn in three days as much as may support them very fully through the week; . . . they insist upon making their own terms'[33]; at Pittenweem 'the colliers are all free, stand engaged by the year, and are paid in proportion to the work they respectively perform. A good and laborious collier will earn about 18s. a week'[34]; and at

[29] Bald, *op. cit.*, 50–1.
[30] P.F.P., Box C 10, Letter to Hon. James Wemyss, dated 3 February 1784.
[31] Bald, *op. cit.*, 51–3.
[32] T. C. Smout, *A History of the Scottish People*, 433.
[33] J. Sinclair, *Old Statistical Account*, x, 213.
[34] Sinclair, *op. cit.*, iv, 371.

Newton in the County of Edinburgh 'the business of a collier seems to be a very lucrative one. Each of them may earn 18s or 20s per week ... It is the heavy complaint of all the coal-masters, that a collier will work none, so long as he has any money in his pocket'.[35] The situation, therefore, as the century drew to a close, appeared to be one where the colliers were well paid, and because of this financial security, their possession of unique skills and their limited numbers, they were exploiting their privileged position rather than being exploited by grasping coal owners.

To talk of the Scottish colliers in terms of serfdom, therefore, is misleading for 'If the colliers had been truly slaves there would have been no necessity to pay them more than subsistence wages; and that they were given substantially more than other grades of labour is an indication that it was necessary to overcome by a bribe the natural reluctance of free men to enter an industry which involved so many social disabilities'.[36] Bald, however, being a man involved in mining is clear that the question was not so much one of attracting men to the trade, as of retaining those trained for it. He admits to a few instances in his knowledge of men who had been labourers or mechanics entering collieries doing the various service tasks such as driving mines, sinking pits and making underground roads, but none of these men were willing to become coal hewers despite the doubling of wages involved because of the dangers and the nature of the work which 'requires such constant exertion and twisting of the body that, unless a person have been habituated to it from his earliest years, he cannot submit to the operation'.[37]

Over the period, the miners' legal position was greatly improved by the Emancipation Bill of 1774[38] which proposed a phasing out of servitude, but obliged the individual workers to apply for this benefit through the Sheriff courts. It was not until 6 June 1799 that the Act, introduced by Scotland's Lord Advocate Sir Henry Dundas, was passed.[39] With it went the last vestiges of legal slavery which bound the Scottish colliers and salters. Before 1774, such men had been *ascripti glebae*, excluded from the Scottish Habeas Corpus Act of 1701 and bound along with their families to the colliery or estate where they were employed. However, it would be wrong to conclude, in Fife at least, that before this release from bondage the collier had been treated harshly, or that after 1799 his social position was markedly improved.

There are indications that the owners treated their workmen with consideration and sometimes kindness. As early as 1741, William Hay, factor to the earl of Rothes, made a contract with one Alexander Owen, the son of one of the earl's coal hewers, which was to run for twelve months, and thereafter, Owen was to be 'at liberty to dispose of himself as he pleases'.[40] And during the time of James, fourth earl of Wemyss, i.e. prior to 1756, a William Cairns, sailor of

[35] Sinclair, *op. cit.*, xi, 536.
[36] T. S. Ashton and J. Sykes, *The Coal Industry of the Eighteenth Century* (Manchester, 1964), 78.    [37] Bald, *op. cit.*, 74, 80.
[38] 15 Geo. III, c. 28.    [39] 38 Geo. III, c. 56.
[40] Kirkcaldy Museum and Art Gallery, Rothes Papers, File for 1741, Contract between Alexander Owen and William Hay, dated 25 March 1741.

Campvere, wrote asking for credit for 'ten dozen coals'. The earl showed no exploiting spirit in writing that the man in question was 'Archibald Cairns, Methill coallier's son, and I suppose has elop't from the works. However, as the lad has been long absent, I could not discourage him by refusing his demand'.[41] But at the other extreme of the period, when legal servitude had been abolished, the anticipated inflow of labour to the mines did not occur. On the face of it this was beneficial for the colliers, for it meant that the demand for their services exceeded the supply and the early years of the century saw a steady increase in their wages, reaching a peak at the time of the Napoleonic Wars. Doubtless, the dangerous and unhealthy nature of the work was a contributory factor, but one wonders if enough account is taken of the hostile social attitude towards the trade. In part this had arisen from the inferior legal status of colliers and in part from the fact that 'outsiders regarded mining families as brutish, unpredictable, clannish and dangerous; in Fife in the eighteenth century there was a prejudice against allowing them even to be buried in consecrated ground like ordinary folk'.[42] Such an attitude could not be swept aside merely by an Act of Parliament, and it is not surprising that there was no rush to join their ranks even with the financial advantages such a move offered. In truth, it seems more remarkable that a greater number of men did not choose to leave a life which required them 'to forego the busy haunts of men, and cheerful light of the sun, for the damp, gloomy and dangerous region of a coal-pit.'[43] But the vast majority of coal and salt workers stayed on after 1799. The monetary advantages and the security of belonging to a close-knit social group which was the product of defence mechanisms operating in the face of public disdain, may well have made these men and women hesitant to try a new occupation, and hostile to any incoming recruits with dissimilar backgrounds. From the evidence of the level of wages, the potential bargaining power of labour in short supply and the coal owners' acceptance of short-term contracts of employment, no picture of exploitation emerges. It was clear from the early 1770s that a wind of change was blowing over colliery labour relations, and there is no reason to believe that the coal owners of the Forth did not have the sense and foresight to trim their sails to that wind, realising that a day was coming when experienced colliers would be prized, and there would be no legal sanctions against their seeking employment elsewhere if work conditions proved too harsh. In looking at the dealings between masters and men, it is noticeable that recourse to violent persuasion was only taken when that most fearsome of spectres, the combination, came to the fore. The 1774 Act had included a clause that the servitude of a collier or salter could be extended by two years where such men entered into illegal combinations to seek wage increases, and while this general fear of group action extended to Fife, a softening of attitude can be detected in dealing with combinations as the period progressed. Hence, in 1765, Wemyss colliers were imprisoned and only released on giving a guarantee of future good behaviour

[41] A. S. Cunningham, *Rambles in the Parishes of Scoonie and Wemyss* (Leven, 1905), 146.
[42] Smout, *op. cit.*, 440.
[43] Bald, *op. cit.*, 74.

when they held a meeting which 'took rise from a shameful combination among them to extort a most extravagant price for their work'.[44] In 1783, however, when a new pit was being fitted out to replace another which had been worked out, the manager of the works reported that there was only enough work to justify the employment of two men, and the other colliers 'cald up the two I had in the pit . . . and set the work unless I would employ all'.[45] The only action taken in the face of what would have been considered a shameful combination in 1765, was to use salters to finish the fitting out, and the manager was able to conclude his report by writing 'I understand the colliers will go to work tomorrow'. The combination was still an evil to be fought, but if that fight could be won without direct confrontation then so much the better, for the maintenance of peaceful relations between employers and employed was growing in importance. To embitter the colliers by reprisals held no profit for owners whose reliance on trained men was too great to risk losing their services.

This then was coal mining in Fife in the second half of the eighteenth century. A strange time, when the trade outlets changed, the standing of the workers changed and yet the mining methods themselves remained comparatively static despite the technical and organisational advances elsewhere in society. A hard time, financially for the coal owners and physically for the coal workers; but nevertheless a time when Fife coal had an important part to play in activities ranging from overseas trade to domestic industry and commerce, and its continued production was necessary for the livelihood of not only colliers and salters, but also merchants and craftsmen involved in providing mining supplies. Those concerned with coal production and marketing made mistakes, but without their efforts the beggar's mantle that was Fife would have been less well fringed.

ROBERT DOUGLAS

[44] P.F.P., Box C 37, Memorandum concerning imprisonment and conditional release of Wemyss coaliers, dated 31 July 1765.
[45] P.F.P., Box C 38, Letter from John Kirk to James Wemyss, dated 2 March 1783.

# 18

## Corporate Personality and the Scottish Burgh:
## An Historical Note[1]

The study of corporate personality is the study of those legal rules and concepts by means of which groups of socially related individuals and property devoted to particular purposes may conveniently be subjected to the legal process. These rules and concepts determine, for example, whether the people who are members of an association are treated in litigation and in contracts as a single party, ignoring divergent interests and fluctuations in membership but recognising the continuity of patterns of social behaviour, or are regarded as legally separate; and whether in litigation relating to collective activities only those assets which are devoted to the support of such activities are liable to legal diligence, or whether creditors may seek satisfaction also from the individually-owned property of members. It is also the study of the theories which have grown up around these rules and concepts and which affect their development – for example theories about whether a corporation can commit crimes and delicts, and if so which. The historical study of corporate personality is the study of these rules and concepts as they existed at some point or tract of time in the past, and of the theories which influenced their development.

Sometimes the legal history of corporate institutions has been written as if there has been a gradual but inevitable process of jurisprudential enlightenment. At first, it has been said,[2] a town is 'a mere aggregate of individuals'; slowly it gains a 'quasi-juridical personality'; ultimately it becomes 'a true corporation'. Sometimes studies are concerned mainly with whether the lawyers of a given period accepted the 'Fiction' or the 'Realist' theory of corporations.[3] Neither of these methods will be adopted in this note. The first has been rejected because it assumes that a conceptual ideal can and does exist and that legal development towards it is inevitable, the second because it assumes that the Fiction and Realist theories are still of great interest[4] and must have affected the minds of lawyers of former times. Instead an attempt will be made to consider what rules and

[1] The assistance of Dr Grant Simpson, of the Department of History, Aberdeen University, who read this note in draft and made many helpful suggestions, is gratefully acknowledged. He is not, of course, responsible for any errors it may still contain.

[2] Carr, 'Early Forms of Corporateness', *Select Essays in Anglo-American Legal History*, iii (Boston, 1909), 172.

[3] E.g. Ke Chin Wang, 'The Corporate Entity Concept (or Fiction Theory) in the Year Book Period', *Law Quarterly Review*, 58 (1942), 498–511; 59 (1943), 72–85.

[4] The whole fiction/realist controversy has been shown to be irrelevant by Professor H. L. A. Hart, 'Definition and Theory in Jurisprudence', *Law Quarterly Review*, 70 (1954), 37–60.

concepts existed, and how their development was affected by such factors as the social and economic state of the towns themselves, the sophistication of the legal system and the kinds of problem presented for adjudication, and the juristic influences at work.

The discussion of the corporate personality of Scottish burghs may conveniently be divided into sections relating to four periods corresponding approximately to stages in the development of either legal or burghal institutions. These are:

1. the period between the beginning of the twelfth century and the end of the thirteenth;
2. the period between the beginning of the fourteenth century and the foundation of the College of Justice in 1532;
3. the period between 1532 and the beginning of burghal reform three hundred years later; and
4. the period between 1832 and 1947, the date of the last major Scottish local government statute before the Wheatley Commission.

Of these periods, the second and the third are of most importance, and this note will concentrate upon them, but the first, which saw the granting of the earliest burgh charters, and the last, which saw the burgh reach its final form, will not be forgotten.

## 1. The twelfth and thirteenth centuries

The revival of civilian jurisprudence on the continent of Europe, especially in Bologna, had by the latter part of the twelfth century encouraged the study of problems of corporate personality. The discussion centred on the word *universitas* which in the ordinary speech of classical times had meant 'a whole as contrasted with its parts . . . a group as contrasted with its members',[5] but which Roman jurists had used in a more technical sense as 'a group which has been recognised by the law to be a group and either made capable or recognised to be capable as such of rights and duties'.[6] For example, the Glossator Johannes Bassianus considered the question whether some angry villagers who had together damaged a forest belonging to the archbishop of Ravenna had acted as a *universitas* or as individuals.[7] The subject continued to arouse controversy during the thirteenth century, as indeed it has done intermittently ever since.

However, though the Glossators treated the *Corpus Juris* as universal law, their teachings were not widely received in practice. In Germany, it was not until the establishment of a supreme court for the Empire in 1495 that civilian jurisprudence became dominant.[8] In twelfth- and thirteenth-century England, the law seems to have been indifferent to problems of corporate personality. As Holdsworth remarked, 'Many and various are the forms of community

[5] Duff, *Personality in Roman Private Law* (Cambridge, 1938), 36–7.
[6] Duff, *op. cit.*, 37.
[7] Ullmann, 'The Delictal Responsibility of Mediaeval Corporations', *Law Quarterly Review*, 64 (1948), 80.
[8] Huebner, *A History of German Private Law* (London, 1918), 154.

which existed in the thirteenth century. There are townships and manors, hundreds and counties, franchises of various kinds, and boroughs, and over all is the community of the whole realm. The law and lawyers of this period accept the existence of these communities without speculating as to their nature, and without stopping to arrange them in distinct categories. They seem to regard them as part of the natural order of things . . . Communities and individuals were in their eyes the subjects of legal rules possessed of varied rights and capable of varied forms of wrongdoing.'[9] When the king granted a charter to one of these communities, his act was not understood in the same way as it was later. He did not create a corporation; he granted privileges to a defined class of persons, or made, as it were, special laws for a particular small portion of his kingdom.[10]

The situation in Scotland at this time was similar to that in England. Though there is evidence that by the middle of the thirteenth century Scottish lawyers were already 'habituated to the civilian idiom of legal thinking',[11] and though it is possible that some works of continental jurisprudence may have circulated among them,[12] problems of corporate personality seem to have aroused no interest. The compilers of *Regiam Maiestatem* and the *Leges Quatuor Burgorum* do not tell us whether the townsfolk of St Andrews could be sued in a body for, say, burning the bishop's boats, nor what the consequences of such a suit might be. Perhaps such unruly behaviour by burgesses was unthinkable, or perhaps a bishop had such effective extra-legal (even extra-terrestrial) remedies that the whole problem was academic. More probably it occurred to no-one that the people of one of these small communities could not litigate as a body. In the only case involving a group of burgesses of which there seems to be a legal record[13] as distinct from a passing reference they appear to have complained in a body without any hint of objection. Even when the word *universitas* appears in charters after the end of this period in the reign of David II, it does not seem to have been given a technical meaning. For example, in a grant which begins 'universis sancte matris ecclesie filiis presens scriptum visuris vel audituris . . . Noverit universitas vestra. . . .'[14] the sense of *universitas* is simply 'all' or perhaps 'the whole lot of. . . .'

The purposes of Scottish burgh charters seem very like those of their English counterparts, that is, they are concerned to grant privileges to certain classes of persons and to make special laws for particular parts of the kingdom. For the sake of brevity, one example must suffice. The charter of King William relating to Inverness[15] makes no mention of *universitas* or corporation. Its first concern is to grant economic privileges to the king's burgesses at Inverness.

[9] Holdsworth, *History of English Law*, ii (3rd edn, London, 1923), 401.

[10] Pollock and Maitland, *History of English Law*, i (2nd edn, Cambridge, 1898), 674.

[11] Cooper, 'From David I to Bruce 1124–1329', *An Introduction to Scottish Legal History* (Stair Society, Edinburgh, 1958), 15.

[12] Cooper, *Select Scottish Cases of the Thirteenth Century* (Edinburgh, 1944), p. lviii.

[13] Burgesses of Peebles *v*. Robert Cruik, 1262, *Acts Parl. Scot.*, i, 101.

[14] *Reg. Mag. Sig.*, *1306–1424* (Edinburgh, 1912), 84, p. 24.

[15] *RRS*, ii, 262.

'Sciant Presentes et futuri me omnes Burgenses meos de Invernis quietos Clamasse omni Tempore a Tolneio et omni Consuetudine per totam Terram meam.'

These privileges are fortified by laying an obligation on others not to exact the tolls and customs which otherwise would have been due. Then, by forbidding others to buy and sell in the sheriffdom of Inverness the charter effectively grants a further privilege to the burgesses, giving them also power to extend the privilege to others.

'Prohibeo etiam Ne quis emat aut vendat in Burgo illo aut in vicecomitatu illo extra Burgum aliquam Mercaturam exerceat nisi fuerit Burgensis aut Stalagarius eiusdem Burgi aut per grantum hoc fuerit.'

The final benefit is a grant of land with the power to permit non-burgesses to cultivate it or use it for grazing.

'Dedi etiam et Concessi predictis Burgensibus ad sustentamentum Burgi Terram illam que est extra Burgum que vocatur Burchhaleu ... Ita quod nullus in ea Wannagium faciat aut pasturam habeat nisi per eorum Licentiam ...'

In return the burgesses are said to have agreed to erect and maintain certain defensive works.

'Burgenses vero universi' (the whole lot of the burgesses) 'mihi conventiona-verunt quod cum circa predictum Burgum fossatum fecero ipsi super fossatum totum burgum claudent bono palitio et ... palitium illud sustentabunt et semper bonum et integrum conservabunt.'

The privileges which are granted by this charter are privileges which will be exercised by individuals. The burgesses will not buy and sell in the sheriffdom of Inverness as a body, in a society. Yet however individual the enjoyment of these privileges, their defence is likely to be collective. The burgesses are not a mere legal category, they are a group knit together by strong ties of proximity and economic interest. If one of their number is injured by an infringement of his privileges it affects all. As a later burghal motto expresses it, 'Touch ane, touch a'.

But it is not merely the grant of common privileges that effectively creates or reinforces the association of burgesses. The grant of power to extend those privileges also does this, paradoxically because this is a matter about which there is likely to be disagreement. No doubt there were often occasions when the extension of a privilege was unanimous, but what happened when there were objections? Could the power not then be exercised, 'propter naturalem hominis ad dissentiendum facilitatem'?[16] Such a view would be unlikely to find favour, and hence rules must have been developed for taking decisions by the *maior vel sanior pars*. Such rules, though here acting as a means of interpreting and giving full effect to a royal charter, are essentially rules of an association.

The formation of an association of burgesses was also encouraged through the imposition of obligations on the burgesses. 'All the burgesses have agreed with me', says the king, 'that when I have made a dyke ... they will enclose the

---

[16] The phrase is from Azo, *Summa Codicis*, II, 19, no. 17.

burgh with a sound palisade . . . and will keep it in good and sound repair.'
The language is wide enough to bear the meaning that every single burgess
agreed, though the word 'universi' suggests that they did so together. But these
obligations could only be fulfilled in an organised fashion, and organisation
must be supplied either by the king through his officials or through rules made
by the burgesses for themselves. At first, in all probability, the prepositi or
ballivi appointed by the king saw to it that all the burgesses fulfilled their duties,
but it was not long before these officials were in many burghs appointed by the
burgesses themselves.[17] Then these burghal duties would be exacted by people
acting on behalf of the community, and their performance would seem from
the point of view of the officious mediaeval bystander, to be by the burgesses
acting (to use the civilian phrase) *ut universitas.*

There is one further section of the charter which merits attention in a discussion of corporate personality, and that is the grant of land. The king states
that he has given a certain piece of land 'predictis burgensibus ad sustentamentum
burgi'. The burgesses appear as donees, and have the power to extend their
privileges of using the land for grazing to others. Here again, the exercise of
this privilege and this power cannot in practice be carried on without some
rules, and these rules must, at least in the case of those governing the exercise
of the power, be made by the burgesses themselves.

But in this case there is a problem. The land is to be 'ad sustentamentum
burgi', for the maintenance of the burgh. No doubt it is intended that this includes the support of the burgesses as individuals, but the preservation of the
burgh is paramount. Though to start with there might be no public buildings or
works other than defences, the revenues from this land must not be diverted to
the profit of individual burgesses, even that of all of them, to the detriment of
the burgh as an institution.

During the period now under discussion the conflict over the use of burgh
property – a conflict which one might express as one between the burgh as an
association of burgesses and the burgh as a public institution[18] – did not become
acute. Though the officials administering the king's burghs came to be chosen
by the burgesses,[19] the method of selection was probably not yet corrupted as a
result of tensions within the burgess community. Furthermore, the existing
burgesses probably did not yet control the admission of others to the status of
burgess.[20] Finally, the king exercised supervision over the administration of
burghs through his chamberlain from at least the latter part of the thirteenth
century and probably earlier.[21] The real struggle was yet to come.

It has been suggested above that though charters like that of King William
did not create a corporation, they encouraged the formation of an association
of burgesses, and that there must have been occasion for the burgesses to act
*ut universitas.* It is in this context that the appearance of burgh seals becomes

[17] Dickinson, *Early Records of the Burgh of Aberdeen* (Edinburgh, 1957), pp. lxxx–lxxxi.
[18] For the distinction drawn by civilian jurists between the association and the institution
see Sohm, *Institutes of Roman Law* (3rd edn, Oxford, 1907), 195.
[19] Above, note 16.                    [20] Dickinson, *op. cit.*, p. lii.
[21] Mackenzie, *The Scottish Burghs* (Edinburgh, 1949), 99.

significant. The late Professor Dickinson states that[22] 'Berwick had a common seal as early as 1212 – probably a seal for its court – and, somewhat later, the sale of a toft and tenement in St Andrews was sealed with the vendor's seal "una cum communi sigillo burgensium Sancti Andree . . ." There is a reference to the common seal of Perth in 1219, and, also in the reign of Alexander II, there are references to the common seals of Aberdeen and Elgin.' The seal, he says, clearly 'implied some form of "legal entity"'. It is a pity that this phrase 'some form of legal entity' has been borrowed by an eminent and cautious historian from the opaque usage of some lawyers.[23] To say that a burgh is a 'legal entity' means merely, if it means anything, that the set of rules associated with the English concept of the corporation does not apply to it, but that some analogous set of rules does apply. This does not really help much. We should rather try to describe the rules which did apply, and determine where the uncertainty lies.

The Scottish burgh seals of this period, if those that survive are representative, usually bore a legend referring to a community, or describe themselves as 'common' seals. For example, the earliest seal of the burgh of Perth is 'sigillum communitatis ville Sancti Johannis Baptiste de Perth'.[24] Others describe themselves either as 'sigillum commune burgi de . . .', as in the cases of Ayr[25] and Dingwall,[26] or as 'sigillum commune de . . .' adding the name of the place, as in the cases of Glasgow[27] and Linlithgow,[28] or as 'sigillum commune burgensium de . . .' adding the name of the place, as in the cases of Montrose[29] and Roxburgh.[30] The exception which, so far as its legend is readable, makes no mention of 'communitas' or of the seal being 'common' is Berwick[31] which is simply 'sigillum burgensium . . .'

Since these seals do not seem to have been connected with any specific royal grant, they may perhaps, with their references to the community or to their being 'common', indicate that the burgesses felt a need for something which could be used to show that they acted together as a body, *ut universitas.* The mere use of a single seal without such references was presumably enough to serve such a purpose, as the exception of Berwick suggests, but the normal legends gave the ideas then current fuller expression. But on what occasions were they used, and what was their legal effect? It is clear from the instances mentioned by Dickinson that they were used to authenticate acts in the law done by burgesses in their courts, but they were also used on political occasions.

The common seals of Aberdeen, Perth, Stirling, Edinburgh, Roxburgh and Berwick were affixed to a treaty with France in 1296,[32] and those of Linlithgow[33] and Montrose[34] – and probably also those of Aberdeen, Elgin, Perth, Stirling, Roxburgh, Edinburgh, Jedburgh, Haddington, Peebles and Inverkeithing –

[22] *Op. cit.*, pp. xlix–l.

[23] E.g. in Taff Vale Railway Co. *v.* Amalgamated Society of Railway Servants [1901] *Appeal Cases* 426, per Lord Brampton at 442.

[24] Stevenson and Wood, *Seals,* i, 76.

[25] *Ibid.*, 53.

[26] *Ibid.*, 57.

[27] *Ibid.*, 64.

[28] *Ibid.*, 72.

[29] *Ibid.*, 73.

[30] *Ibid.*, 78.

[31] *Ibid.*, 55.

[32] Dickinson, *op. cit.*, p. li.

[33] Stevenson and Wood, *op. cit.*, 72.

[34] *Ibid.*, 73.

were affixed to fealties recorded in the Ragman Roll in the same year.[35] On this latter occasion the burgesses and communities of these burghs 'of their own free will renounced the league with France and swore fealty' to Edward I, '*tactis sacrosanctis* and kissing the Holy Evangels.' Except in the cases of Elgin and Aberdeen, where no burgesses are named, and except in the case of Perth, which sent seventeen men, all these burghs sent a round dozen burgesses. The recurrence of this number is surely significant. Possibly we have here the twelve sufficient and discreet burgesses referred to in the *Leges Quatuor Burgorum*[36] as required to maintain the laws and true customs of the burgh communities. Certainly a governing body of twelve was then common in England and was later fairly frequent in Scotland, being referred to as the 'doussan'.[37] Perhaps Perth sent extra men so that at least twelve would be available. In any event, it seems likely that it was considered that if twelve of the most important burgesses gave their assent to an act, going through such rituals as might be appropriate such as touching relics or kissing the gospels, and witnessing the affixing of the seal, then an obligation was created and made binding on the whole community.

Just what was considered to constitute failure by a burgh community to fulfil an obligation – particularly an obligation so personal as fealty – or what the legal consequences of such failure were, is not now clear and may not have been certain even then. Probably Edward I would not have been above creating precedents if there were none to follow. In view of the paucity of property devoted to common purposes other than the subsistence of inhabitants, it is likely that obligations to pay money fell directly or indirectly upon the burgesses as individuals; whereas political obligations of the kind created by the Ragman Roll would be broken by failing to keep watch and ward for the acknowledged lord, harbouring his enemies and refusing to welcome and entertain his forces, and would be enforced by cancellation of economic privileges, or grants of land.

If as seems likely contemporaries were not very sure precisely what it meant, legally speaking, to use a common seal, or what the legal consequences of acting *ut universitas* were, this is consonant with the gradual development of corporate personality according to felt need. The very pragmatic approach which seems to run through the Scots law relating to the corporate personality of burghs at this early period will appear from what follows to have continued as long as it retained its distinctness from that of England.

## 2. From the early fourteenth to the early sixteenth century

By the early fourteenth century, the town was already established as a social and economic institution of some importance. On the continent, though the progress of the thirteenth century was not maintained[38] the population of many

---

[35] *Cal. Docs. Scot*, ii (1272–1307), 195, 197, 198.　　[36] *Acts Parl. Scot.*, i, 355.
[37] See Dickinson, *op. cit.*, pp. lxxxiv–vii.
[38] Pirenne, *History of Europe* (London, 1939), 380.

towns did not, in spite of natural and economic disasters, fall back to what it had been during the dark ages. In England during the fourteenth century, 'apart from normal fluctuations of trade and industry and the incidence of plague, many towns seem to have maintained themselves in a state of reasonable, and a few of mounting, prosperity.'[39] and the fifteenth century saw the further expansion of those cities and boroughs engaged in continental or Mediterranean trade.[40] Though Scottish burghs were not populous by English standards,[41] they seem to have been relatively wealthy.[42] So far as the administration of justice was concerned, England was particularly fortunate in the possession of a court system staffed by professional judges and attorneys, but progress was also being made in the rest of Europe, where the civilian jurists now known as the Commentators were fusing the Roman law with Germanic elements and creating 'a body of law which obtained practical force throughout the Western Continent.'[43]

In such circumstances, the corporate personality of towns took on new aspects. The sheer number of burgesses could cause procedural inconvenience, as for example when, in a lawsuit in 1383 involving the city of Göttingen, 278 burghers were obliged to appear before the court.[44] It became even more obvious than it had been previously that the corporation of burgesses could not be regarded merely as a self-governing body, since in fact they were making laws for the whole inhabitants of their town, many of whom were not and never would become members of the corporation. The town, as Lubasz remarks, 'gradually became more "it" than "we"'.[45]

The civilian jurists showed a keen awareness of these problems. For example, that 'juristic giant of the fourteenth century, Bartolus'[46] considered how far a corporation was competent to make binding rules, and argued that 'a distinction must be made between a rule purporting to regulate the affairs of the civil community in general (*statutum pertinens ad causarum decisionem*) and a rule which only purports to regulate the internal affairs of the corporation (*statutum pertinens ad administrationis rerum ipsius universitatis*). Every corporation as such is competent to make rules of the latter kind, but rules of the former kind can only be made by such bodies as possess *jurisdictio*, that is, political authority.'[47] Bartolus also took a stage further the discussion of corporate liability. In law, he argued, 'the corporation represents one person who is notionally something different from the members constituting it.'[48] Though in fact the corporation could not commit offences – 'proprie non potest deliquere'[49] – in law it could be made liable at least for those offences which are the result of failure to carry out obligations, or for acts which individual citizens were incapable of com-

[39] McKisack, *The Fourteenth Century* (Oxford, 1959), 380.
[40] Jacob, *The Fifteenth Century* (Oxford, 1961), 386.
[41] Dickinson, *Scotland from earliest times to 1603* (Edinburgh, 1961), 119, n. 4.
[42] Mackie, *A History of Scotland* (Harmondsworth, 1964), 112–13.
[43] Sohm, *op. cit.*, 147.     [44] Huebner, *op. cit.*, 148.
[45] Lubasz, 'The Corporate Borough in the Common Law of the late Year-Book period', *Law Quarterly Review*, 80 (1964), 230.
[46] Ullmann, *op. cit.*, 85.     [47] Sohm, *op. cit.*, 148.
[48] Ullmann, *op. cit.*, 86.     [49] Ullmann, *op. cit.*, 87.

mitting. In the case of offences which corporations could commit, proceedings should only be brought where there had been a communal resolution arrived at after adequate deliberation or with subsequent approval.[50] Sanctions might be imposed either on the corporation as such, by confiscation of corporate property, or on individual members, or both.[51]

Contemporary English lawyers debate the liability of corporations with as much subtlety as the civilians. In the famous case of the Abbot of Hulme and the Mayor, Sheriffs and Commonalty of Norwich,[52] in which the defence sought to show that a bond executed by the mayor was invalid because, being imprisoned by the Abbot at the time, he was under duress, the pleadings were based on rival conceptions of the corporation. Catesby for the defence argues that 'the imprisonment of the mayor is the imprisonment of the whole corportation, for he who restrains my hand imprisons my whole body'. Pigot for the plaintiff replies that the corporation of mayor, sheriffs and commonalty 'is but a name, cannot be seen, and has no substance. Therefore no tort such as battery can be committed by the corporation . . . nor can anyone commit a corporal tort against it.' In the result, the defence was sustained, and the case played a part in the creation of what Lubasz has called a distinctive 'common law theory of corporations'[53] in which the borough corporation is conceived as 'somehow tripartite, mayor, sheriffs and commonalty each being a "member" of the whole' with the mayor playing a 'crucial, peculiar and distinct role'.

But English law relating to the corporate personality of boroughs is complicated by the fact that the corporation is not simply the mayor, sheriffs and commonalty, it is a set of the most important rights, privileges, powers and immunities required by those administering local government on behalf of the king. This set of powers, gradually determined over two centuries until, by the middle of the fifteenth century, the five 'classic' incidents of incorporation had become crystallised, was reified by English lawyers (as is their habit) so that the incorporation became a legal 'thing' to be granted or withheld by the king like an advowson or an estate in land.[54] Thus the question, in what circumstances does the law consider a group of people to have acted *ut universitas*, is answered by the English lawyer initially 'only if they have been granted the set of powers known as "incorporation" by the king'. The one word 'incorporation' can thus be used to mean two separate though related things, the people who exercise these powers, and the set of powers themselves.

The state of affairs would not have occurred but for the success of the English monarchy in extending its control over local administration and maintaining a strong centralised court system staffed by a professional judiciary. Even in the fourteenth century it is asserted by lawyers that burgesses cannot have a *communitas* – here obviously conceived, if vaguely, as a set of powers – unless this be

[50] Ullmann, *op. cit.*, 90.    [51] Ullmann, *op. cit.*, 89.
[52] Y.B. 21 Edw. IV, Mich. pl. 4.    [53] *Op. cit.*, 243.
[54] Dias, *Jurisprudence* (3rd edn, London, 1970), p. 364. '. . . Certain interests or collections of claims, privileges etc. . . . were conceived of as "things" distinct from the land itself. . . . This made possible the doctrine of 'estates' in land. . . .'

granted to them by the king,[55] and charters begin to refer to the formation or confirmation of the 'communitas'.[56] By the fifteenth century, charters are providing for the erection of a 'corporation' or 'body politic', specifying in detail its name, power to hold property, to have a common seal and to sue and be sued in the corporate name.[57] Litigation involving corporations is becoming highly technical, perhaps needlessly so. As Lubasz says, 'misrecital of the corporate name would invalidate an action' and a new name in a royal grant 'could be said to create a new corporation'.[58] Legal refinements like these are inconceivable unless there is either a permanent school of academic jurists (which existed on the continent but not in England) or an established legal profession and court system.

Thus during this period the rise of the town to economic and social importance was accompanied on the continent and in England by the refinement of laws relating to its corporate personality. The same cannot be said of Scotland. Scottish burgh charters of this period make more frequent reference to the 'community' of the burgh and to the 'heirs and successors' of burgesses, as if the draftsmen wished to emphasise that the privileges granted were to be enjoyed by the holders of a certain status rather than by the particular grantees and their descendants. Possibly also references to the 'community' were meant to indicate that the lands or principles granted were to be administered by those who formally represented the community, that is the 'doussan' or council. The charters make no reference, however, to the king granting that burgesses may have a 'communitas', nor do they mention incorporation. It is in the petitions by craftsmen for formal approval of their societies and for the grant of power to regulate their several crafts,[59] that English styles seem to be influential.

The records of litigation relating to Scottish burghs similarly suggest a lack of legal refinement. There are no subtle debates, so far as one can tell, about the liability of burgh corporations like those in which English lawyers and civilian jurists indulged. In 1488, for example, an action was brought by the Archdean (i.e. archdeacon) of St Andrews against 'William Wauch, provest of Sanctandrois, Andro Kid, Robert Arthure and Thomas Blak bailzeis of the said cite, consale and communite of the samyn . . . for the maisterful outrivin, manuring, ering and sawing of a parte of his lands of Stratirum and the comoun of the samyn and making of dikes thereapone . . .' From the recorded notes of evidence (which the Archdean especially asked to be 'publist') it appears that 'the citineris' of St Andrews had been manuring lands claimed by the pursuer and had made 'dikes and faldis' on it. The Archdean successfully obtained decree against the defenders for twenty pounds, and an order to 'distrenze thaim, thair lands and gudes thairfore'.[60] Though it is not clear from the language of the decree whether payment was to be made in the first instance out of town funds, it is probable that this was so. (In another similar decree, this time against the alder-

[55] Gross, *The Gild Merchant* (Oxford, 1890), ii, 34.
[56] Pollock and Maitland, *op. cit.*, 669.  [57] Jacob, *op. cit.*, 391.
[58] *Op. cit.*, 234.  [59] Mackenzie, *op. cit.*, 118.
[60] *Acts of Lords Auditors*, 117 (17 October 1488); *Acts of Council*, 115 (7 February 1489).

man, bailies and community of Aberdeen, it is specifically stated that the sum
due was 'to be payit of the comoun gude of the said toun'.[61]) Now on what legal
ground could this decree against the provost and bailies of St Andrews be
justified? There is no suggestion that the 'citineris' had acted on any formal
resolution of the burgh council, that they had acted *ut universitas*.[62] The court's
decree seems to have had no firmer foundation than mere 'football jurisprudence'.[63]

Again, the kinds of offence that could be committed by a town do not seem
to be restricted. (I do not wish to suggest that it *is* legally impossible for a corporation to commit certain offences, only that, as has already been indicated,
contemporary lawyers and jurists thought it was). In 1494, the Lords Auditors
interposed their authority to an arbitration agreement between one Walter
Watsone and his wife Ewfame Logain on the one part, and certain burgesses
of Dumbarton 'for thair self and as procurators for the Consale and Communite of the burgh' on the other. The parties agreed to accept the award of a
certain arbiter 'and never to cum in the contrare under the pain of perjure and
infamite and under the pain of 100 pounds Scots to be rasit on the partii brek-
are.'[64] It is clear from the fact that the 'consale and communite' were bound by
their procurators that the burgh as a body was regarded as capable of com-
mitting perjury, an idea which would have aroused great debate among contemporary civilian and English lawyers, but which in Scotland seems to have
been accepted as a matter of course.

The identification of the burgh with its official members implicit in the case
just mentioned, is consistent with the practice of inflicting legal sanctions
personally on the magistrates for failure to fulfil the obligations of the town.
In 1482[65] the provost of St Giles Church brought an action against 'the provest
and bailzeis of the burgh of Edinburgh' for payment of his annual pension which
was described as 'the obligacioune of the said burgh of Edinburgh'. The Lords
Auditors ordered payment to be made by 'the sade provest and bailzeis ...
under the pane of warding of their persons in the blacnes.' The practice of
imprisoning magistrates for the debts of their burghs was accepted in Scotland
as late as the eighteenth century, when it was justified on the ground that this
was a means 'provided by law to oblige the corporation to do justice to the
creditor'[66] and it is possible that the same reasoning may lie behind this earlier
decision.

In the eighteenth century, however, it was vigorously denied[67] that the goods
of the magistrates could be poinded for the satisfaction of the town's debts. In

---

[61] *Acts of Council*, 250 (12 July 1492).

[62] That corporate liability required, for medieval civilian jurists, an act *ut universitas* is
evident from the article by Ullmann cited above.

[63] In 1972 Glasgow Rangers Football Club was penalised by the European football
authorities for incidents at Barcelona in which the team's supporters had shown an excess of
the 'perfervidum ingenium Scottorum'.

[64] *Acts of Lord Auditors*, 185 (28 November 1494).

[65] *Acts of Lord Auditors*, 102 (9 December 1482).

[66] Cumming *v*. Walker, 1742, Morison, *Dictionary of Decisions*, 2501.

[67] Livy *v*. Mudie, 1774, Morison, 2512.

the fifteenth century this is by no means clear. When in 1490[68] the luckless provost of St Giles again sued for his pension, he brought his action against 'the provost and bailzeis of Edinburgh of this instant zere'. The Lords of Council, finding in his favour, gave orders to 'distrenze the said provest and bailzeis their lands and gudes therefor, Reservand to the said provest and bailzeis their accion agane the provest and bailzeis of the zere bipast or any utheris personis . . .' Such an order is difficult to understand except on the assumption that the personal assets of magistrates could be poinded for official debts.

Given the rather slapdash jurisprudence of the Lords Auditors and the Lords of Council exemplified above, it is hardly surprising that such technicalities as misnomer, which created or prolonged much litigation in England at this period, were far from the minds of Scottish litigants and their advisers. Municipal parties are variously designed, even within the record of a single case. Thus the 'provest, bailzeis, consale and community of Striveling'[69] become 'the toune of Striveling', the 'provest bailzeis and consale of Perth' have the 'communite' added,[70] and no one bats an eyelid when the 'alderman, bailzeis and communite of Abirdene' in dispute with the king about their title to the 'forest of Stolkett and Castelhill' produced a charter of Robert I in favour of 'burgensibus nostris et communitati burgi nostri de Abirdene'.[71] English lawyers of the period would not have let that pass unchallenged. The only regularities of designation appearing in the records seem to be, first, that there is no mention of council or community when the magistrates are referred to in their capacity as royal officials charged to do diligence or administer justice, and second, that where reference is made to the summoning of municipal defenders no mention is made of the community. The latter may be explained by the method of citation, which may at this period have been (as it clearly was later[72]) by delivering a copy of the summons to the magistrates and council either at a meeting or to each of them singly and separately. One cannot cite a whole community 'singly and separately'. Alternatively, there may have been a tradition, dating back to the time of the Ragman Roll, that the council represented the community for formal legal purposes. It was still possible, however, even in 1501, to raise an action against the 'indwellaris and inhabintantis (sic) of the toune of Dingvaile'.[73]

Similarly, the legends on burgh seals do not suggest that exactitude in nomenclature was considered important. Jedburgh, for example, is referred to successively as the community of Jeddewurthe, the burgh of Jedburg, and the community of Jedburgh.[74] The first seal of Montrose[75] is 'sigillum commune burgencium de Mumros', the second 'sigillum commune de Munros', the third 'sigillum comune burgi de Muntros'. In English law, it might have been argued that these were the seals of successive and distinct corporations, but there is no

---

[68] *Acts of Council*, 168 (15 January 1490); 170 (18 February 1490).
[69] *Acts of Council*, 406, 408 (29 October 1495).
[70] *Acts of Council*, 314 (24 October 1493).
[71] *Acts of Council*, 331 (19 June 1494); *Acts Parl. Scot.*, i, 118.
[72] Dalrymple *v.* Bertram, 1762, Morison, 752.
[73] *Acta Concilii* (Stair), 27.
[74] Stevenson and Wood, *op. cit.*, 68.          [75] *Ibid.*, 73.

hint of this in Scotland. All this does not suggest that the niceties of citation were of much concern.

Looking at the privileges and powers of Scottish burgesses at this time, it seems on the surface as if they possessed all five 'classic incidents' of the English incorporation – power to sue and liability to be sued as a body (though not by any precise corporate name), power to hold landed property, the privilege of using and the power legally to act by a common seal,[76] perpetual succession (in spite of oddities like actions against magistrates of this instant year') and the power to make by-laws. But it would be a mistake to attribute this to the acceptance of any theory or practice of incorporation. They were liable to be sued in a body, but so (as we have seen) were the mere 'inhabitants and in-dwellars' of any place; they had the power to hold property, but whether that property was corporate or common was not yet settled[77]; they used seals when acting *ut universitas*, but not because of any specific grant of this privilege; they had in a sense perpetual succession, in that their privileges and powers were transmitted automatically and without change from one set of office-bearers and one generation of burgesses to the next, but this was because nobody suggested it should be otherwise; and they had the power to make by-laws, but the acts and statutes approved at the head courts by burghs[78] were made in the same way as in the head courts of baronies. In short, burgesses and magistrates possessed these privileges and powers as a body not so much because they were specifically granted by the king, but because it was convenient to have them. The privileges and powers which in England were united into the legal 'thing' called 'incorporation' and granted out as and when the king thought fit were in Scotland assumed separately as and when necessary. The fact that burghs in fact possessed what in England came to be called the 'incidents of incorporation' made it easier to assimilate them to English borough corporations when the time came, but this should not be allowed to obscure the fact that originally Scots and English corporation laws were very different kettles of fish.

But if the laws of Scotland concerning burgh corporate personality were different from those of England, they were not at this time notably civilian either. We have noted already the case of the Archdean and the Provost and bailies of St Andrews, at the result of which a contemporary civilian jurist[79] would have expressed great surprise. It is also worth noting that the burgesses of Scottish burghs were not regarded in the Bartolist fashion as a corporation possessing *jurisdictio*. They were not, in legislation or litigation, called a corpora-tion at all. Yet what was happening in this period was that a feudal jurisdiction

[76] E.g. in 1478 decree passes against 'the provest, bailzeis and communite of Edinburgh' for 100 marks due 'be the obligacioune under their commoun seele'; *Acts of Council*, 18 (22 October 1478).

[77] Arguably, not until the eighteenth century – see e.g. Robert Fram and Others *v.* Magistrates of Dumbarton, 1786, Morison, 2002; but see Craig, *Jus Feudale* (trans. Clyde, Edinburgh, 1934), 1.15.16.    [78] Dickinson, *op. cit.*, p. lxxxii.

[79] E.g. Philippus Corneus, who denied municipal liability for the lynching of two men by a mob including the senators, councillors and 'quasi totus populus' on the ground, *inter alia*, that there was no proof that a formal resolution of the city council had been taken. See Ullmann, *op. cit.*, 93.

analogous to that of a barony was being captured by an association or perhaps clique of townsfolk[80] or even local landholders.[81] Burgess status, instead of being acquired by the acquisition of a toft within a burgh and the practice of some craft or trade, came to be the result of admission by existing burgesses to their association.[82] And even burgess status was in some burghs not sufficient for attaining a position of influence – membership of the merchant gild was some-times also necessary.[83] The powers over persons and property necessary for the maintenance of burghs slipped into the hands of associations – formal or in-formal – of persons whose interests were not those either of the other inhabitants or of the royal founder of the institution and his successors. Despite attempts to govern the selection of council and magistrates through election clauses in charters[84] and legislation, and despite legislation providing that the 'common gude be observit and keipit to the common proffeit of the town, and to be spendit in commoun and necessare thingis of the burgh'[85] the king's burghs were in effect – though not in the minds of contemporary Scottish lawyers – becoming corporations with jurisdiction over the people of a certain part of the kingdom.

The lack of legal refinement of either an English or civilian kind in the legal conception of the Scottish burgh may be ascribed to the weakness of the royal courts of the period. The Lords of Council and the Lords Auditors were 'an unpaid, part time, lay magistracy masquerading as judges'.[86] Though there were recognised advocates[87] it would have been useless for them to be legally subtle in their pleadings before such tribunals. References to civilian jurists might have been acceptable to the ecclesiastical, but not to the lay members of these courts, and the level of technicality appropriate for the more professionalised English legal system would not have been suitable for transposition to Scotland. Only with the creation at the beginning of our next period of a permanent and professional central supreme court would the corporate personality of Scottish burghs begin to be influenced by foreign legal models.

### 3. 1532 to 1832

The establishment in 1532 of the College of Justice and shortly thereafter of societies of advocates and writers together contributed, as might be expected, to a greater concern for consistency and principle in the administration of justice in Scotland. The common law of England, developed from case to case by law-yers and judges who had not studied law in any philosophic manner, was almost impenetrable by a foreign lawyer not brought up in its practice. The Scots lawyer, therefore turned to the more accessible civil law as expounded by aca-demic jurists. In addition, the texts, reports and even the legends on common

---

[80] Dickinson, op. cit., p. cviii.
[81] This was more serious during the sixteenth and seventeenth centuries. Mackenzie, op. cit., 132–3. See also Lang v. Magistrates of Selkirk, 1748, Morison, 2515 at 2519.
[82] Dickinson, op. cit., p. lii.                [83] Dickinson, op. cit., p. cviii.
[84] Mackenzie, op. cit., p. 122.              [85] Acts Parl. Scot., 1491, c. 19.
[86] Cooper, Selected Papers (Edinburgh, 1957), 227.        [87] Cooper, op. cit., 231.

seals[88] suggest that a certain vogue for classical culture helped in this period to increase the influence of civilian jurisprudence.

It is not therefore surprising that by the end of the sixteenth century, there is evidence of Roman influence even on the corporate personality of burghs, a relatively unimportant aspect of law. Whereas the *Prackticks* of Sir James Balfour, who died in 1579[89] contain no reference to the notion of a corporation, the *Jus Feudale* of Sir Thomas Craig, who passed advocate in 1563 and who had studied under French civilian jurists[90] has clearly accepted it in its civilian form. Discussing 'property belonging to a corporation' Craig states[91]:

> It is dealt with in the same way as property belonging to an individual. An incorporation is regarded as one body – one person in short – alike when it grants and when it receives feudal estate. It gives its consent as a whole to the disposition of the property, the consent being that of the burgh or other corporate body.

Craig's unitary conception of the burgh corporation is quite different from the 'tripartite'[92] conception of the English borough. However, the attempt to Romanise this aspect of Scots law was not without its problems. Craig had to admit that the property of a burgh could not be alienated without the consent of the crown. This could be dismissed as a statutory[93] exception, but burgage feus posed a more difficult subject to mould according to civilian forms. Burgage feus, situated within the liberties of a burgh are, he says[94]:

> the only kind of feus which are completely free from non-entry ... The reason for this is that, while the burgesses hold their feus of the king as their sole superior, their feus (being within the burgh) are held for burghal services only ... For a burgh is an incorporation of the burgesses: it never dies, but dwells for ever in its burghal tenement without heir or successor.

This, however, is clearly unsatisfactory, for the absence of casualties cannot be explained by reference to corporate holding of the land, while it is simultaneously maintained that the King is the 'sole superior' of the burgesses as individuals. In any event, the rules relating to burgage holding were laid down at a time when the law of Scotland cared nothing for corporate theory. The absence of casualties from burgage holdings is almost certainly due not to doctrinal but practical causes.

[88] There seems to have been during this period a certain vogue for Latinising the burgh name on seals, as in *sigillum civitatis Lanercae, Fermiloduni*; *sigillum commune civitatis Elginae, Glasguae, Kirkualensis*; *Insignia urbis Banfiensis*; *Taniae Sigillum Commune*: also for the use of *urbs* as in *sigillum urbis de Cullen*. There is even an instance of *oppidum* as in *sigillum oppidi de Leith*. All these are probably seventeenth-century seals, except that of Leith which may be from the second half of the sixteenth century, and that of Dunfermline, which is probably an eighteenth-century seal. See Stevenson and Wood, *op. cit.*, 70, 60, 63, 64, 70, 54, 81, 56, 71.
[89] Ed. McNeill, i (Edinburgh, 1962).
[90] Irvine Smith, 'The transition to the modern law', *An Introduction to Scottish Legal History* (Stair Society, Edinburgh, 1958), 31.
[91] *Op. cit.*, 1.15.16.      [92] Lubasz, *op. cit.*, 243.
[93] *Acts Parl. Scot.*, 1491, c. 19.      [94] *Op. cit.*, II.19.26.

Stair, writing at the end of the seventeenth century, follows Craig's explanation of the peculiarities of burgage feus. Infeftments in burgage, he says[95]:

> ... are those which are granted to the burghs by the King as the common lands or other rights of the incorporations and that for burghal service in watching and warding within the burghs. These can have no casualties because incorporations die not, and so their lands can never fall in ward or non-entry. These infeftments in burgage are held by the incorporations immediately of the King ... and the particular persons infeft are the King's immediate vassals.

Stair also suggests[96] that the reason why the casualty of liferent escheat does not apply to burgage feus is that 'the fiar is a society and incorporation which dieth not', though this does not prevent denunciation being used 'against the persons administering the same even for that which is due by the incorporation and as they represent it'. This casualty, it should be noted, 'arises by denunciation of the vassal for a criminal cause unrelaxed for a year and a day[97] ...' Stair does not concern himself with whether a corporation can be said to commit a criminal offence – a point which had been widely discussed by civilian jurists and English lawyers – merely noting that denunciation against the administrators is practical because the offence is theirs; '... that being supposed their fault and negligence doth not prejudge the society; as magistrates of burghs ...' There are limits to the reception of Roman law.

Of the other Scottish institutional writers who consider the corporate personality of Scottish burghs, Erskine clearly regards the burgh as a corporation[98] and follows Craig and Stair in maintaining that the burgh itself is the vassal though the burgesses hold immediately of the Crown. Professor G. J. Bell follows Erskine in accepting burghs as corporations[99] but also in his *Principles* lists the incidents of incorporation.[100] His list is not quite the same as that of the great eighteenth-century English jurist Blackstone[101] but it is clear that English influence is now beginning to supplant that of Rome in Scottish corporation theory.

The records of litigation also suggest that Roman law was influential. In 1752, Voet is cited in support of a plea that magistrates named personally in a bond granted by them in their official capacity were personally liable,[102] and in a case in 1748 great play is made of the presumed Roman ancestry of some Scottish municipalities. 'Our Town Council corresponds to their Senate. We have Magistrates and other office bearers as they had, differing only in names.... They had a common good as we have, which was understood to belong not to the particular citizens, but to the politic or corporate body. Our notion is the same, with this addition derived from the feudal law, that this corporate or

---

[95] *Institutions of the Law of Scotland*, 11.3.38.     [96] *Op. cit.*, 11.4.67.
[97] Craigie, *Scottish Law of Conveyancing, Heritable Rights* (2nd edn, Edinburgh, 1891), 102.
[98] 1.4.20.     [99] Para.2174.
[100] *Op. cit.*, para.2178     [101] *Commentaries*, I.475.
[102] Cleland *v*. The present Magistrates of Pittenweem, 1752, Morison, 2511; Voet, *Commentary on the Pandects* (Trans. Gane, Durban, 1955), III.4.

politic body is the vassal, which holds the town, with its common good, of the King as superior. . . .'[103] The idea that the common good belonged not to the citizen, but to the corporation was consistent with civilian opinion[104] as was the notion that the magistrates who acted for the town were in a sense its 'tutors, curators or other administrators'.[105]

But the sharp distinction maintained by some civilians[106] between the corporation and its members does not seem to have been fully accepted in Scotland. When, as sometimes happened[107] a town could not pay its debts, the Court of Session was prepared to ordain the inhabitants (not just the burgesses) to be stented to pay the debt, and to have them cited at the market cross of the burgh for that purpose. It was not infrequent for towns to sue each other in defence of the economic privileges of the burgesses.[108] Though in 1743[109] it was made clear that inhabitants as such were not members of the burgh corporation, the strong feeling of community in the Scottish burgh, fostered perhaps by the fact that it was in a sense a trade protection association for its burgesses, and by the fact that burgh property was still in many places used in common by the inhabitants, may have induced a reluctance to accept too abstract a conception of the corporation.

This feeling for the burgh as a community of people rather than an abstract corporation is also apparent in the language of charters. Though they begin in this period to contain references to incorporation – the earliest mentioned by Weinbaum[110] is a charter of novodamus of 1592 relating to Banff, and the only others before 1660 are one relating to Arbroath in 1599, one relating to Perth in 1600 and one relating to New Galloway in 1630 – this is still the exception rather than the rule. The more usual pattern seems to be that of James VI's charter to Dumbarton[111] of 13 December 1609 the dispositive section of which refers to the 'magistrates, burgesses and inhabitants'. On this occasion, James narrates how faithfully they have served him, 'not only in attending our royal Person in all journeyings and huntings in these parts, specially in the Island of Inchmirrine, and entertaining us, . . . but also by protecting and defending our peaceful leiges of Lennox from the tyranny and cruel oppression of a lawless and wild kind of men dwelling in the neighbouring mountainous parts, not without the great effusion of their blood . . .' and grants lands and money to his well beloved and faithfull servitors, the 'Baillies, Councillors, Burgesses, Inhabitants and Community of the said burgh, and their successors.'

[103] Lang v. Magistrates of Selkirk, 1748, Morison, 2515.
[104] Sohm, op. cit., 191.
[105] McDowal v. Magistrates of Glasgow, 1768, Morison, 2525.
[106] Sohm, op. cit., 190. But see Kaser, Roman Private Law (Tr. Dannenbring) (Durban, 1965), II.17.1, for the view that 'the notion that such forms of organisation may be independent bearers of rights quite apart from their members . . . was substantially developed from earlier beginnings only by the legal science of the nineteenth century.'
[107] Honieman v. Town of Dysart, 1685, Morison, 2510. Dysart in 1691 emphasised its decay and want of trade to the Convention of Royal Burghs; see Mackenzie, op. cit., 153.
[108] E.g. Town of Cupar v. Town of Kinnothy, 1664, Morison, 1905.
[109] Hog, 1743, Morison, 1928.
[110] British Borough Charters, 1307–1660 (Cambridge, 1943), 162, 164, 175, 186.
[111] RMS, 1609–20, 190. Copy in Scottish Record Office, C.S. 235/Innes Mack D/6/5.

A charter of this nature, and the 'personal' notion of the burgh which it expresses, could not but cause problems when it no longer seemed to many of those concerned appropriate for burgesses and inhabitants to make use of burgh property themselves. Burgh lands had been excluded from the scope of legislation facilitating the division of commonties in 1647 and 1695[112] but the eighteenth century saw a number of lawsuits which seem to reflect a division between on the one hand those who, ostensibly at least, wished to obtain for the burgh the maximum revenue to improve its 'police', and on the other those who wished to continue to enjoy their personal privileges. One of these, the case of *Robert Fram and others* v. *the Magistrates of Dumbarton* may serve as an example.[113]

The immediate cause of this dispute was the magistrates' decision to cease requiring the tacksmen of the fishing rights in the river Leven (granted by James VI) to sell a certain amount of fish to the inhabitants at a specially cheap rate. Certain burgesses objected, alleging that under the charter they had a personal right to fish, though it had not been exercised for some time, since 'the practice being found inconvenient for the burgesses by withdrawing their attention from their proper employments, it was agreed betwixt them and the Magistrates for the time that the fishings should be thence furth under the management of the magistrates and council to be set by them for a yearly rent on condition that the . . . whole resident burgesses of the burgh should be furnished with fish at a certain rate of payment'.[114] They argued that though fishings 'may be conveyed to a corporation in such terms as to confine the benefit to the Community . . . without conferring on each single individual any thing which he can possess separately from the Community, yet it may as effectually be conveyed in such terms as to give each individual burgess a benefit independent of the general interest'.[115] The terms of the charter, they said, indicated that 'King James's view was to grant the fishings not to the Corporation alone but to the Burgesses, Community and Inhabitants'[116] to be enjoyed by them individually.

In their defences, the magistrates do not allege that the fishings are the property of the corporation, though their opponents give them the opening to do so. Indeed in their written pleadings they do not use the word 'corporation' at all. They merely claim that, as magistrates, they have the 'right of administration' of the 'common estate or the common funds'[117], and argue that every burgess benefited from the leasing of the fishing because the additional revenue was 'calculated to promote a better police'.[118] Was there any reason why they should not have used a word by then in common use?

It may be significant that the magistrates draw attention to the fact that the pursuers do not appear to wish to include all inhabitants in the category of those privileged to fish in the burgh waters, though the charter refers to inhabitants

112 *APS*, 1647 c.430; 1695 c.36.          113 1786 Morison, 2002.
114 Summons, p.3. In Scottish Record Office, C.S. 235/Innes Mack D/5/6.
115 Memorial for pursuers, pp. 48, 49. C.S. 235/Innes Mack D/6/5.
116 Memorial, p. 52.
117 Memorial for defenders, p. 44. C.S. 235/Innes Mack D/6/5.
118 Memorial for defenders, p. 43.

as well as burgesses. Possibly they feared that if the 'common funds' were regarded simply as the property of the corporation, then since not all inhabitants were members the property might be used for the benefit of too narrow a section of the population. They may have been beginning to think of the burgh in terms, not so much of a corporation of burgesses which had somehow acquired public powers, but as a public institution whose office-bearers were chosen from among the more influential members of the community. If this was indeed the thinking behind the formulation of the case for the magistrates, it foreshadowed the reforms of the nineteenth century.

#### 4. 1832–1947

In the latter part of the eighteenth and early nineteenth centuries the burghs and their economic privileges had become 'increasingly out of step with the new commercial aims and developments'.[119] There was no longer a place for them as corporations of burgesses exercising public powers but concerned mainly to prevent encroachments on the trading rights of their members; they had to become public institutions, units of local government.

This was achieved by a series of enactments which began with the reform of the electoral franchise in 1832.[120] In that year the £10 householder in thirteen non-royal burghs as well as in the royal burghs obtained the vote in Parliamentary elections, and reform of the method of electing councillors for parliamentary[121] and royal[122] burghs followed immediately. Power to adopt a system of burgh police for the administration of what were then considered the most essential services was given to inhabitants of royal burghs and burghs of barony[123] and in 1846 the exclusive trading rights of burgesses were formally removed.[124] Police powers were given in 1847 and 1850 to parliamentary burghs and 'populous places' and for a time the administration of local affairs was divided in some places between police commissioners and town bailies and councillors, but consolidation was achieved by statutes in 1892 and 1900.[125]

The burgh was by now quite a different kind of body from what it had been prior to the nineteenth century. The strong element of association, fostered by the economic privileges of the burgesses, had been swept away, and the privilege of participating in the election of councillors had been extended to most adult inhabitants, The burgh was now a public institution, administering local affairs in accordance with laws laid down by Parliament through councillors approved by a wide electorate. Yet juristic statements about the burgh did not

---

[119] Mackenzie, op. cit., 144.
[120] Representation of the People (Scotland) Act 1832 (2 & 3 Will. 4, c. 65).
[121] Parliamentary Burghs (Scotland) Act 1833 (3 & 4 Will. 4, c. 77).
[122] Royal Burghs (Scotland) Act 1833 (3 & 4 Will. 4, c. 76).
[123] Burghs & Police (Scotland) Act 1833 (3 & 4 Will. 4, c. 46).
[124] Burgh Trading Act 1846 (9 & 10 Vict., c. 17).
[125] Burgh Police (Scotland) Act 1892 (55 & 56 Vict., c. 55); Town Councils (Scotland) Act 1900 (63 & 64 Vict., c. 49).

reflect these changes. William Bell's *Dictionary and Digest of the Law of Scotland* defined a royal burgh as 'a corporation consists of the magistrates and burgesses of the territory erected into a burgh.'[126] This may be compared with Erskine's definition which regards the 'inhabitants of a determinate tract of ground' as members of the corporation.[127]

If we may regard the 'members' of a burgh corporation as those who, as a body, exercise the privileges and powers granted by the law to the corporation, the latter part of William Bell's definition is nonsense, as the burgesses have, as such, nothing to do with these things; and if the 'members' are those for whose benefit the office-bearers act and who choose those office-bearers, it is still nonsense. In effect, Bell's definition, which is repeated in the *Encyclopaedia of the Laws of Scotland*,[128] is a correction of Erskine which would have been appropriate to the unreformed Scottish burgh, but which is quite inappropriate to the reformed institution.

The provisions of the Town Councils (Scotland) Act 1900 which can be regarded as the basis of the corporate personality of the twentieth-century Scottish burgh, in spite of its reconstitution in 1929 and 1947, do not refer to membership at all. 'A town council', it is stated, 'shall be elected for every burgh under the provisions of this Acts and shall be designated by the corporate name of 'the provost, magistrates and councillors' of the burgh, and the common seal shall be adhibited under their authority and subject to their directions. The town council of a police burgh shall be a body corporate with a common seal'.[129] Other sections provide for suit by and against the town council and for the mode of authentication of deeds, and for the vesting of property in the council. Though the tripartite name of burgh corporations has almost certainly nothing to do with the traditional three parts of the common-law English municipal corporation[130] and probably reflects rather the former Scottish method of citation,[131] the conception of the burgh corporation which lies behind these provisions is fundamentally English. The notion of incorporation as a grant carrying the classic 'incidents' has ousted the notion of a corporation as an association of people. Though for some purposes the English notion is inappropriate, for local government – the purpose for which it was originally formulated – it is perfectly suitable. On this occasion Scots lawyers need not be resentful over the consequences of English influence.

R. L. C. HUNTER

[126] 7th edn (Edinburgh, 1890), 140.
[128] Vol. ii (Edinburgh, 1932), para. 1112.
[130] Lubasz, *op. cit.*, 143.
[131] Dalrymple *v.* Bertram, 1762, Morison, 752.

[127] *Op. cit.*, I.4.20.
[129] Section 5.

# 19

# Lexicography and Historical Interpretation

Words are the visible or audible vehicles of human thought, they are labels that signpost every highway and byway of culture and experience. Without them, the transmission of all that makes up our concepts of history and civilisation would be quite impossible. There could not be the kind of communication on which depends so much of the stability of our existence as individuals within our social and administrative groupings, though it must, of course, be remembered that language is itself a social construct.

Words are essentially symbols, without the concrete qualities of material objects, but involving concepts and connotations that differ in some minute degree from person to person, depending on his background and range of knowledge. Much of the fascination of words and language lies in this infinite variety, and in their reflection of the origins, personality, and thought-processes of a speaker.

With the written word, the personal dimension is much less. Whether a written text constitutes literature, with many subtle forms of expression and several levels of comprehension, or whether it is merely a list, as in a testamentary inventory, there is always a need for interpretation, which increases the further back the text goes in time. For such interpretation, since no one is omniscient, we must have dictionaries as primary working tools.

Scotland is better off for dictionaries than almost any other country in the world, and indeed much of the inspiration and activity that has gone into making the lexical record of the English language as a whole has been due to Scotsmen. The great *Oxford English Dictionary* was begun in 1901, under the editorship of Sir James Murray, 'arguably the greatest lexicographer the world has known' and completed under another Scot, Sir William Craigie, 'at least of comparable stature and of an equally prodigious capacity for work' (Aitken 1972, 34–5). As a dictionary of English it naturally includes Scots and can itself serve as a general dictionary of Scots. In this it supersedes the material in the pioneering *Etymological Dictionary of the Scottish Language* published in two volumes by the Secession minister Dr John Jamieson in 1808 and 1825, though this Dictionary may still be the one best known and in widest use, as I have observed amongst friends involved in education, and as A. J. Aitken has noted in relation to some recent historical writing (Aitken 1964, 129).

During the nineteenth century, knowledge of language progressed rapidly into a well organised science, a fact reflected in the philological quality and etymological trustworthiness of the *Oxford English Dictionary* and Joseph Wright's *English Dialect Dictionary* of 1905, itself a considerable mine of information on Scottish dialectal material, with the additional virtue of showing its extensions into England and into Ulster. As a dictionary of modern Scots, Wright 'is in almost every way superior to Jamieson', and along with the *Oxford*, multiplies 'by about four the coverage of Scottish sources which Jamieson – was able to achieve' (Aitken 1964, 130).

The further development of Scottish lexicography was very much due to William Craigie, whose inspiration led to both of the great dictionaries currently under compilation, the *Scottish National Dictionary* and *A Dictionary of the Older Scottish Tongue*, of which the first published parts appeared in 1931. These are two of a series of large historical dictionaries that Craigie envisaged for the main periods in the history of English and Scots (Craigie 1931, 6–11).

*A Dictionary of the Older Scottish Tongue* deals with Older Scots from the twelfth century till about the year 1700, the period, that is, when Scots was a national language, used for literature and all legal and official business. The *Scottish National Dictionary* covers the period from 1700 to the present day, after standard English had taken over in many respects from the old standard Scots. It therefore records Scots as the language chiefly of 'a group of mainly working-class and rural regional dialects, and also of course as the vehicle of a considerable vernacular literature' (Aitken 1964, 129). Between them they draw on over 8,000 printed volumes as well as on hundreds of manuscript sources and question-naire answers relating to current terms and usages. Perhaps only one who has worked on such an undertaking (as I did for four years, as Senior Assistant Editor of *The Scottish National Dictionary*) can fully appreciate the range and extent of the coverage of Scottish sources of all kinds and at all levels. They include, for example, 'volumes of various characters and dates, such as Dictionaries and Glossaries; 'Kailyard' novels; Poetry, specially of the minor bards; Humorous Readings; Dialect Stories in Newspapers and Magazines; books on Coinage, Agriculture, Social and Domestic Life, Manners and Customs, Memoirs, Games, Travels, as well as of Scots Law, History, and old Theology' (Warrack (1911) 1930, p. *v*). Their immensely dense network of extraction from almost everything in print and much of what is in manuscript gives them their special value as tools for historical interpretation.

This also follows naturally from their aims and methods of presentation. The linguistic aspect is implicit in lexicography and most of the published articles that discuss dictionary work have a linguistic emphasis, but dictionaries of the kind and on the scale of those referred to here have a unique value not only as an aid but also as a guide to all kinds of historical research.

First comes the stage of data collection, usually achieved with the help of a team of readers who over a period often of many years, go through the corpus of sources and excerpt from them the relevant words, each with a quotation illustrative of its use. These are transferred to slips of paper, and then comes the work of sorting, which 'may be regarded as the sum of three processes – alphabetic or "approximate" sorting, "lemmatization" or the grouping of orthographically and morphologically related variants under a single head-word (thus the quotations for *ran* and *running* would be grouped below those for *run*), and the separation of homographs (thus the quotations for *lead* (the verb) would be grouped separately from those for *lead* (the noun))' (Aitken 1971, 7). Though the rate of collection and in part sorting can be speeded up by the photocopier and guillotine, and lately also by the electronic computer (for the possibilities and limitations of which see Aitken 1971), there is as yet no means of speeding up the final process when the editors 'subdivide the quotations for each lemma by "sense" (in effect by common context), excogitate definitions for each sense and select for printing those quotations which best illustrate the word's formal, semantic and grammatical histories and the distributions of each form and sense in time, space and genre' (Aitken 1971, 8–9). This, called by Aitken the 'heart of the lexicographical process', involves analysis and selection of a human intellectual variety to which computers cannot now and may never be able to attain. It is at this point too that the final selection of quotations to illustrate points of syntax, semantics etc., is made and if they are also chosen to highlight appropriate historical and cultural phenomena, then the dictionary becomes far more than just a source for the meanings of words.

For example, a count made in the course of a review of three parts of the *Older Scottish Dictionary*, covering the entries from Law to Lyv(e) tennandry, produced 'the following numbers of entries to, *inter alia*, these subjects: agricultural implements, 10; apprenticeship, 3; arms and armour, 16; boats, 12; buildings and parts of buildings, 30; clothes and cloth, 70; crafts, 20; fishing, 18; folklore, 24; food, 10; furnishings, 7; games, 5; harness, 5; harvest and treatment of grain, 21; hunting and fowling, 6; land use, 33; mills, 9; mining, 8; numismatics, 16; peat, 4; rope making, 6; servants, 14; stock, 29; transport, 9.' In addition, the entries for the important words *law* and *lord* provide perhaps 'the fullest treatments given to these subjects in the dictionaries of any country' (Fenton 1966, 198). The historian wishing to originate or expand a subject of research can use such a ready-to-hand tool in a variety of ways which can be co-ordinated to fill out the story.

First, the dictionaries provide a *chronological* dimension. Because of their dense coverage of sources, it is now possible to accept that the earliest date of occurrence of a particular phenomenon given in the *Older Scottish Dictionary* is probably as close as it will easily be possible to get for the vast majority of subjects (including place names and place name elements). The latest dates may also be ascertainable within the time-span of the *Older Scottish Dictionary* or may run on into the *Scottish National Dictionary* period. A provisional bracketing in time can be quickly obtained in this way, with the further possibility that the etymology will extend the chronological depth and may indicate a possible direction of origin.

Second, they provide a *spatial* dimension, which depends on the localisation of words and the phenomena to which they refer. During the period of Scots as the standard language the evidence for localisation is, relatively speaking, slight, though it occurs in relation to land-use terms such as the Gaelic *davach* (north-east Scotland), and the Northumbrian *husband-land* (south-east Scotland). As has been pointed out, 'in this matter of geographical distribution the

*Scottish National Dictionary* especially is a powerful tool, since for every single word it provides a clear indication of the area the word or its use or pronunciation occupy' (Aitken 1964, 135–6). This is further helped by the absorption into the *Scottish National Dictionary* of all existing local word lists and glossaries.

It scarcely needs emphasising that these two elements, time and space, form the interpretational groundwork of all historical research. By a careful use of the two great Scottish dictionaries, eventually also in conjunction with the *Oxford* and the *English Dialect Dictionary*, something rather more than a mere skeletal outline of a particular subject can be obtained, for in addition to the chronological and geographical distributions, it is usually possible to pinpoint what is likely to be the most useful methodological approach, with regard to ethnic origins and stratification, centres of innovation and lines of diffusion, patterns of obsolescence, and the like. Indeed, for the later periods where sketch-book and other types of popular literature, including the press, have been drawn on, it is also possible to get something of what may be called a psychological dimension, since the illustrative quotations frequently reflect in an interestingly unsophisticated fashion the attitudes and prejudices of the individual writers, which as often as not are conditioned by contemporary events and thinking with a social and political emphasis. The more ephemeral types of literature can be remarkably sensitive *Zeitgeist* indicators, and carry their own brand of perfectly valid historical interpretation.

Neither the *Scottish National* nor the *Older Scottish Dictionary* is as yet complete and this may have an inhibiting effect on their use. Their value even in their incomplete state is so considerable, that to say so almost appears to be pointing the obvious. Some years ago it was noted that 'the dictionaries are indeed already being used as detailed source-books in this sort of way by one or two scholars whom we know of – students, namely, of agricultural history, of rural crafts, of mediaeval arms and armour, and of old weights and measures – but they could, and doubtless ultimately will, be similarly used for many other purposes' (Aitken 1964, 138). This is only common sense, but it can well stand re-iteration.

The Gaelic side has not been as well served, lexicographically speaking, but it is a matter of satisfaction to note that work towards a *Historical Dictionary of Scottish Gaelic* was begun in 1966 under the sponsorship of Glasgow University. Its aim 'is to present the Gaelic vocabulary in a way that will illustrate the range and development of its usage over the centuries, and the collection of material will consequently involve the exhaustive examination of the documentary sources of all periods, as well as the collection of dialect vocabulary both in Scotland and Nova Scotia' (MacDonald 1968, 185). It has in addition to the normal editorial staff a full-time field-collector using subject-questionnaires and a tape-recorder, because of the urgency of recording the living speech while there is yet time. This is a formidable task, to which there can be no quick and easy end. For the time being, the history and culture of the Gaelic-speaking areas is best served by Edward Dwelly's *Illustrated Gaelic-English Dictionary*, containing 'every Gaelic word and meaning given in all previously published Dictionaries, and a great number never in print before'. Though it gives no etymologies or illustrative quotations, nevertheless sources are often given, so that localisation is possible, and the background notes and diagrams with named parts give it considerable interpretational value. It is far from being a complete record of Gaelic, but can be supplemented by Rev Fr Allan Macdonald's *Gaelic Words and Expressions from South Uist and Eriskay* and Volume VI (Indexes) of Alexander Carmichael's *Carmina Gadelica* (Edinburgh and London 1971), as well as short glossaries that have appeared, for example, in the *Transactions of the Gaelic Society of Inverness*. What there is is useful and useable, but it will be some time before Gaelic lexicography can provide research data comparable in linguistic and historical range to that of the Scottish 'period' dictionaries.

In order to exemplify some of the interpretational points raised in this brief review, an example that includes both Scottish and Gaelic terminology is given from an as yet unpublished study of corn-drying kilns which seeks to co-ordinate the evidence of archaeology, existing structures, documentary sources, and terminology. Only the linguistic data, however, are examined here in any detail.

It must also be observed that, though it is not possible to exemplify every aspect of the interpretational uses of dictionaries with a single example, the one chosen nevertheless illustrates a range of points, such as the ease of access to the relevant parts of early and later records, the possibility of quickly assembling comparative data for within and without the country, and of constructing sequences in time and space to show diffusion due partly to climatic circumstances but primarily to the movement of peoples and their culture.

In Scotland there are two basic types of corn-drying kilns (leaving aside from

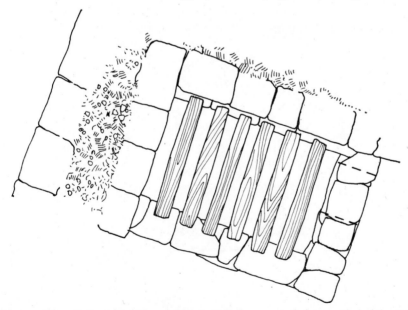

FIGURE 1. Plan of a four-sided kiln, or *sinnie*, built in the corner of a barn, with the kiln-sticks in position. The fire-hole is marked by broken lines.

the discussion the large kilns associated with meal-mills and commercial or semi-commercial meal production). The smaller type, known in Shetland as a *sinnie*, is characterised by a *four-sided* form (Fig. 1). Its main survival area is Shetland, but its distribution must originally have been wider, for one was found in the corner of a barn of late thirteenth-century date during the excavations of the Viking settlement at Freswick in Caithness (Fig. 2), and it may be relevant

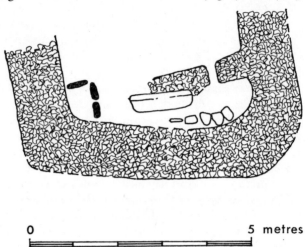

0                                                    5 metres

FIGURE 2. A four-sided structure, probably a corn-drying kiln, at the end of a barn in the Viking settlement at Freswick in Caithness, dating *c.* 1270 or earlier. After Curle, 1939.

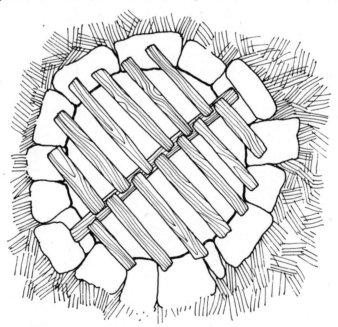

FIGURE 3. Plan of the bowl of a circular kiln, with a central beam to support the kiln-sticks.

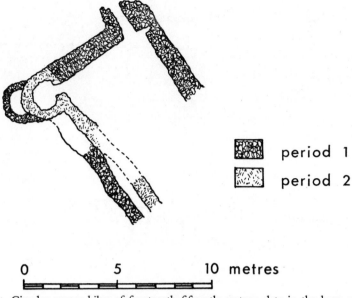

period 1

period 2

0       5       10 metres

FIGURE 4. Circular corner kilns of fourteenth–fifteenth century date in the barn of the medieval farm at Jarlshof, Shetland. The original kiln was replaced by another at a later building period. After Hamilton, 1956.

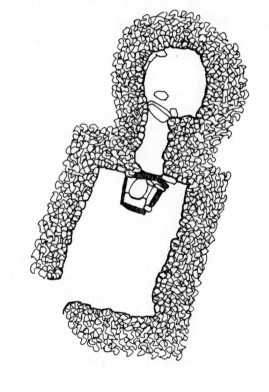

0       5 metres

FIGURE 5. A kiln-barn and kiln with a straight flue, from the farm of Gröf i Öræfum in Iceland, overwhelmed by a volcanic eruption in 1362. After Gestsson, 1959.

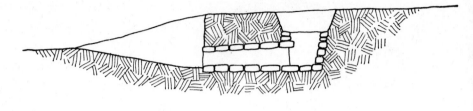

0                    5                    10 metres

FIGURE 6. A circular kiln from Muirkirk, Ayrshire, with its straight flue and round bowl
built into a hill-side. After Fairbairn, 1927.

that the drying-kilns of the Faroe Islands, though much larger in scale, are also
four-sided in form (see Williamson 1948, 207). The Shetland kilns were little
more than two feet high, and ranged from four to six feet long by three to four
feet wide. In one side was an opening, little more than a foot square, where the
fire of hard, dry peat was lit, and through which the heat travelled. The drying
floor itself consisted of cross bars of wood laid in a grid, and these in turn were
covered by a layer of straw, drawn out straight and set at right angles to the
run of the cross bars.

The second type is the *circular* kiln (Fig. 3), characterised by a round, bowl-
shaped drying chamber, into which the heat is carried through a flue. The drying
floor is again of wood and straw, and usually has a main central beam running
from front to back for central support to the wooden spars. Such kilns are normally built at the ends of kiln barns, or they may be free-standing structures
backing into a hillside. The longish flue may be straight, or curved.

Archaeological dating evidence has been found in both Shetland and Iceland.
In Shetland, the medieval farmhouse at Jarlshof had a circular kiln that pro-
truded like a corner-turret from the barn wall. It has been dated to the fourteenth-
fifteenth century (Hamilton 1956, 191). At Gröf i Öræfum in south-east
Iceland a circular kiln with a straight flue formed part of a small, free-standing
kiln barn. It and the farm to which it belonged had been destroyed by a volcanic
eruption in A.D. 1362, according to the tephrochronological evidence (Gestsson
1959, 32–36).

## The Complete Kiln

The general name for a drying kiln of any type is *kill* in Lowland Scots, and in Gaelic *aith, àth, àmh* (South Uist), *sòrn* (Uist).

*Kill* or kiln is from Old English *cyln, cylene*, ultimately from Latin *culina*. According to the *Oxford English Dictionary*, the word is 'outside of English known only in Scandinavia, O.N. *kylna* (Norw. *kjølne*, Sw. *kölna*, Da. *kølle*), probably adopted from English (as Welsh *cilin, cil* certainly are). In ME. the final *-n* became silent (in most districts), hence the frequent spelling *kill* in place of the etymological *kiln*'.

Gaelic *aith* with its variants corresponds to Irish *áith*, a word of unknown etymology which 'for linguistic reasons must be much older in Ireland than the fifth century A.D.' (Gailey 1970, 69).

Of particular interest is the word *sòrn*, applied in Gaelic not only to the kiln itself, but also to the fireplace, the flue, and the kiln platform. *Sorn* also occurs in Irish as 'a kiln, a furnace, an oven, chimney or flue of a furnace' (Dinneen 1927, s.v.), and is used in the sense of a kiln fireplace, *sorn na hatha*, in a fifteenth-century life of St Finian of Clonard (Gailey 1970, 64). *Sorn* originates in the Latin *furnus*, an oven, bake-house, and on the evidence of the *a / o* affection sound-change in stressed syllables, goes back at least as far as the second half of the fifth century (Jackson 1953, 132, 143). It does not follow that the Irish (and perhaps also Gaelic) word, at this early date, necessarily referred to a corn-drying kiln. Indeed, in current or recent Gaelic, *sòrn* may be used for a hearth or for the fireplace of an oven, as well as for several parts of the kiln.

Outside the Celtic language area, variants of the term are known in Shetland, Caithness, Norway, the Faroe Islands and Iceland.

The Shetland forms are *sonn, soin* (Jakobsen 1928, s.v.), and the diminutive *sinnie*. Of those, there are no documentary records earlier than the late nineteenth century. The Caithness *sornie*, 'the flue or hot air channel leading from the fire-place to the underside of the drying platform of a kiln, and, by extension, the fireplace itself' is a diminutive form directly based on the Gaelic.

In West Norway (Sogn) the name *þorn*, applied in a probate inventory dated 1314 to a building, is represented in modern Norwegian by *tonn, torn*, in the sense of a floor of wooden spars on which malt was dried (Ropeid 1957, 279). Some writers have associated this with another West Norwegian name, *sonn*, from Tröndelag, but it is more likely to belong to the group of words like *tarre, terre*, applied to drying. It is generally accepted that *sonn* is a borrowing from Irish (or Gaelic) *sorn*, probably in the Viking period (Ropeid 1957, 279; Talve 1960, 279). It is suggested in the *Scottish National Dictionary* that in Shet-land, *sinnie* is a derivative diminutive form of the Norwegian dialectal *sonn*.

In the Faroe Islands, the form is *sodnur*. This is undoubtedly from *sorn*, for the *-rn-* combination is generally pronounced *-dn-* in Faroese (Lockwood 1955, 20). In the late eighteenth century, *sodnur* was glossed as 'a room in the kiln-house separated off by a wall, roofed with laths and straw, on which the ears are dried with fire', and there were also the combinations *sodnhús*, kiln-house, *sodnkjeer*, a separate room in a house where corn is dried, and *sodnspølur*, the laths of the drying floor (Matras 1966, I. 795).

In view of the Celtic origin of *sodnur*, it is of interest to note that built structures for drying grain are said not to have been common or particularly early in the Faroes (Rasmussen 1955, 147–8). The earliest recorded reference to a kiln is in 1669. According to Tarnovius, (in translation) 'when harvesting time comes, they cut the corn (bere) with a knife, and carry it to the house on their back. Afterwards they do not thresh the corn, but pluck all the ears from the straw and lay them on a kiln to dry. When the ears are dried, they take round stones and laying them on their knee, beat out the corn from the ears, and then sift it to clean it' (Hamre 1950, 55). However, the name used by Tarnovius was his native Danish 'kiølne' rather than the Faroese equivalent.

The Icelandic equivalent is *sofnhús*, with its drying area, the *sofn*, roofed with spars, *sofnraftar* or *sofnspelir* on which straw was spread. Such kilns were in use in Iceland for drying a kind of rye until the 1890s, and have been recorded from the second half of the eighteenth century. A small rectangular building excavated at the farm of Bergþórsvoll, which probably belonged to Njál who died in 1011, has been tentatively identified as a drying house (Talve 1960, 368). The circular kiln dated to 1362, from Gröf i Öræfum, is however, of a different type.

### The Parts of the Kiln

(1) The fireplace. The complete kiln was sometimes called the *killogie* in Scots, but usually this name was reserved for the fireplace of the kiln or for the covered space or porch in front of it, depending, probably, on the size of the kiln. It is first recorded in the sixteenth century, and was used over much of Lowland Scotland.

In the Northern Isles of Scotland the kiln fireplace is called the *kiln huggie* or -*hoggie*, with a Fair Isle and Dunrossness variant, *kiln sluggie*, used both of the fireplace and of the flue that carried the heat under the drying floor.

The form *logie* stretches across from the Lothians to Galloway and into Ulster, with its aphetic variant *ogie* more closely restricted to south-west Scotland.

In Orkney and Shetland (including Fair Isle), *ingle* is also used for the fireplace.

Gaelic has a number of terms: *sòrn* again, as well as *aingeal* (South Uist), *bialaisg* (South Uist), *ceal(l)ach*, *coileach-gròid*, and *fadadh*.

The etymology of *killogie* is uncertain, but appears to be a formation based on *kill* plus the suffix -*ogie* or -*logie*. The *Scottish National Dictionary* suggests Gaelic *logan*, *lagan*, the diminitive of *lag*, a hollow, pit, cavity, as the origin of *logie*, and this seems reasonable in view of the fact that kilns were frequently built into a hill-side, in which a hollow had to be dug to accommodate the bowl of the kiln (Fig. 6). This also fits the earlier quotations in the *Dictionary of the Older Scottish Tongue*, some of which suggest that the *killogie* was the lower portion of the kiln, below the drying floor.

Regarding *kiln sluggie*, the *Scottish National Dictionary*'s suggestion that the second element is probably originally an adaptation of Norwegian *slok*, 'the channel which brings water to a mill, *sloka*, a channelled hollow, but assimilated in form and meaning to *Logie*', remains uncertain.

*Ingle* in the sense of a kiln fireplace seems to be confined to the Northern Isles, Banffshire, and, in the Gaelic form *aingeal*, to Uist (and probably adjacent areas). In Dwelly, *aingeal* is glossed merely as 'fire', 'light', and in Old Scots 'ingill' was found in this sense by about 1500. It is associated with kilns as a verb in Old Scots in the general sense of lighting the kiln fires. Thus in the *Glasgow Charters* for 1605 a man was accused of profaning the Sabbath by 'ingilling of killis', another was accused in the *Dundonald Parish Records* for 1607 'of Sonday wark by setting ingill to his malt in Hilhous kill', and a third, in the *Falkirk Parish Records* for 1650, was 'delaited . . . for haveing ingle at his kilne . . . in the tyme of sermone.' Only in the areas specified, however, is 'ingle' used for the kiln fireplace. In Orkney, in the manuscript diary of a Sanday farmer, the word was used as a verb, for on 3 December 1765 he spoke of grain 'all which was Ingled for seed and was of clean Otts 57 barrels'.

(2) The flue. The flue may be short and straight in the case of four-sided kilns, and small kilns with circular bowls (e.g. in Fair Isle), or it may be long and curving as an extra precaution against fire. Lowland Scots has no specific name for this element, except for the Gaelic derived *sornie* of Caithness. The Gaelic names are *cealach* (Benbecula), *leum-srad*, *sòrn* once again, and *sor(r)ag* (South Uist). *Leum-srad* is purely descriptive, from *leum*, to jump, and *srad*, a spark. The other names are all also attached to the fireplace or the bowl, and the real status of the flue as a separate element deserving independent nomenclature is in some doubt.

(3) The lintel or baffle over the fire-place. In the four-sided *sinnie*, the name for the lintel or baffle over the fire-place is the *kilpinsten*, a word for which there are many variant forms in Shetland: *kelpinsten*, *kjolpin-*, *kilper-*, *kelper-*, *hjelpin-*, *hjalpin-*, *hjolpin-*, *hjelper-*, *hjilper-*, *hjolkin-*, *jalpin-*, *jalpersten*, and *chylpin-stane*. It is defined in the *Scottish National Dictionary* as 'a flat stone placed at the top of the mouth of a kiln, above the fire, and projecting into the kiln space so as to shield the drying floor of wood and straw from the flames, and to catch any corn that trickles through.' It also deflected from the fire the dried grain that was pushed and prodded by hand through the straw bed, to be collected later from the clean clay or paved floor of the kiln (as was done, for example, in Papa Stour (oral information, 1964), and also in Iceland (quoted in Talve 1960, 368)). The range of variant forms, involving palatalisation of the first element and subsequent interchange of *ky-* and *hj-*, is evidence that the word *kiln* and very likely its derivative *kelpinsten* were in use early enough in the Northern Isles, before the late fifteenth century, to participate in sound-changes that characterise Norse-derived dialects and languages. There is, however, nothing particularly Norse about the word itself, which probably comes from *kiln* + *pend*, an arched or covered-in passage or entry + *stane*, a stone.

(4) The bowl or hot-air chamber. No special name has been noted for the

hot-air chamber of the four-sided kiln. The bowl of the circular kiln may stop at the level of the drying floor, like half an egg sunk in a platform of stone, or it may continue above platform level to complete the egg-shape, with a smoke opening at the apex. The recorded terms appear to refer to the part that underlies the drying floor.

The Lowland Scots names are *kiln mathie*, from Aberdeenshire, and *kiln-pot*, from Galloway (as well as Ulster and Northern England). Gaelic has *comhan*, *sor(r)ag* or *surrag* (Benbecula, South Uist), and *sùil* (ib.). Here, *sùil* is a figurative extension of the common word for eye.

There are also in Gaelic a number of names for associated parts. The back of the kiln is *druim sùirn* (South Uist) and the rim of the bowl, *sòrn na h-àmhadh* (ib.). According to one gloss, 'the part round the bowl immediately above the fireplace' is *a' mheilisg*. Possibly this refers to a lintel similar to the *kilpinsten*. The flat kiln platform into which the bowl was sunk was also called *sòrn* in Benbecula and South Uist.

Only two Scots terms have been noted, both from Orkney. There, the sloping sides of the drying chamber are called *tramins* (North Ronaldsay), and the ledge round the chamber that acted as a support for the spars of the drying floor was the *hemlins*.

*Hemlins* can also apply to the beams of the drying floor. According to the *Scottish National Dictionary* it is a derivative of *hemmel*, a shed and open communicating court for housing cattle, a square rack on posts in a cattle court for holding fodder. This in turn is said to be a metathetic form of *helm*, in the general sense of a covering, and a comparison is made with Norwegian dialectal *hjelm*, the straw covering of a rick, a slated roof. Since *hemmel* is confined to Northern England and Southern Scotland, the possibility arises that *hemlins* may result from metathesis in Orkney of a Norn word analogous to Norwegian *hjelm* or may be related to the Swedish dialectal *hammel*, a little bar or beam. At any rate, it is obviously in this general area of semantics that the sense belongs.

*Tramins* is a derivative of Lowland Scots *tram*, a beam, bar, prop, pillar, supporter. As used in North Ronaldsay, it is applied to the sides of the hot-air chamber of a type of large rectangular kiln that is a nineteenth-century innovation built on the analogy of the kilns attached to commercial mills. Most parishes in Orkney had such combined mills and kilns by or shortly after 1850, and this in turn had an effect on the form of farm kilns, many of which remained in use to dry the malt for home-brewed ale until within the last three decades.

(5) The drying floor. The chief variations in drying floors lay in their shape and size. The smaller ones were simply made of cross-spars laid parallel to each other from front to back, the larger ones had to have one or more main beams to give central support.

Such a main beam has several names. In Orkney it was the *kilnace* or *kiln-laece*, described as 'a strong beam . . . about four inches square, . . . fixed across the opening at such height, as that sticks laid with one end resting on the beam and the other end resting on the projecting stone-work, formed a perfectly level floor' (Frith 1920, 19). The second element, -ace, is from Norwegian ås, Old Norse áss, a pole or rafter. The phonological development of the vowel is as in Mainland Scots, so that the word must be reasonably old.

The Shetland equivalent is kiln-simmer, used in Dunrossness where bigger kilns with circular bowls of 'Orkney' type are to be found. The second element, simmer was in widespread use in Scotland, in this sense going back at least to 1462 when the Peebles Burgh Records mention 'a aktre tyll be a summer tyl the kyll' (DOST s.v. Kill). This is a specific Scottish use of the obsolete English summer, Middle English somer, a beam or joist, from Old French somier. It is curious that in using this term Shetland matches Mainland Scotland rather than Orkney. Yet is is almost beyond doubt that the larger kilns of South Shetland must have originated from the Orkney islands, long renowned for their grain production. It is likely, therefore, that the term kilnace had not come into use in Orkney before the kiln type was adopted in Shetland, as it had been by the fourteenth century (Hamilton 1956, 191).

Other terms are kiln kebbar, kill-rammek or -remmek, kiln-stick(le), and kill-tree. Kebbar is a form of Old Scots caber, a pole, rafter, Gaelic cabar, id. Rammek is a Shetland name, a diminutive form of rem, 'a fisherman's taboo word for an oar, an oar blade'. No doubt part of a worn oar frequently served as part of the drying floor (as observed, for example, in North Ronaldsay). The etymology is uncertain, but appears to belong to the group of words that includes Norwegian dialectal and Old Norse reim, a strap or band, Swedish dialectal räimu, a narrow board, Low German remme, a strake in a boat, and reme, a punting pole or tiller.

In Gaelic, the main beam was the damh-sùirn, druim-sùirn (Benbecula, South Uist), maide-sùirn (ibid.). laom-chrann, simisd (Wester Ross) and sticil mhòr (ibid.). These are for the most part descriptive terms. Laom-chrann is a specific sense of a more general word for a rafter or beam, and sticil mhòr, the 'big stick' or 'stickle', parallels the Lowland Scots name.

The cross spars of the drying floor are called kill-ribs or kiln-sticks, the former term going back at least to 1675 when it was recorded for Stirling (DOST s.v. Kiln(e)).

Gaelic is again fertile in terms: ciùthlein (Benbecula, South Uist), ciù(tha)ilean (South Uist), cuiligean, fiodhrach-tarsuing, slinnteach, stic(ean) (Mid Perthshire), sticlean beaga, stiligean. Of these, fiodhrach-tarsuing means only 'cross timbers', and is also applied to boats, slinnteach is defined by Dwelly as 'house-tiles, quantity of house-tiles', and must be used in relation to kilns in a restricted sense, and the Mid Perthshire stic(ean) is a borrowing from Lowland Scots 'stick'.

The straw bed on which the grain was spread is the kiln-beddin, the kill-gloy, the kill-strae, the kiln-straik or -strike. All of these are purely descriptive, and both gloy and straik refer to drawn straw.

The Gaelic names are brat, sreathainn, straothag, and traghaid. Brat, a general term with the sense of 'covering', is also used for a horse-hair cover laid over the drying-floor rimbers, and in this sense (and in its extension to straw) is likely to be fairly recent. It is known, for example, that about the 1830s 'a covering made of hair, and called "brat", was introduced into the island of Luing; and it is believed that it was introduced into Luing as early as into any other part of Argyllshire, (Macinnes 1893–4, 213–4). *Sreathainn* is a word having the basic sense of rows, regular lines, and is therefore equivalent to *gloy* and *straik*. The number of words that incorporate the sense of drawing out the straw shows well enough how important it was to get a firmly made bed of straw with all the pieces of chaff and broken straw removed to minimise the fire risk.

The lexical data is by no means exhausted, as a glance at the entry for *Kill* in the *Scottish National Dictionary* will show. It would be possible, for example, by using terms such as *kill-breist*, 'the arch over the entrace to a kiln', *kill door*, 'the steps up to the entrance to a kiln', *kill-ee*, 'the open space in front of a kiln fireplace', *kiln-heugh*, idem, to get a good deal of technical information on the form, size and structural detail of Lowland Scottish kilns, and other terms can throw light on the work-organisation of the kiln, and on superstitions and customs connected with it. It is not, however, the purpose of this exercise to be exhaustive, but to exemplify some of the ways in which lexicography can be used for historical interpretation.

It can be seen that in Lowland Scotland small-scale kilns of the types under discussion disappeared earlier than in the Highlands and Islands, and correspondingly greater dependence must be laid on the linguistic data for their elucidation. Some Gaelic influence is evident in the Scots terminology, in words like *ingle*, the second elements of *kill kebbar* and *killogie*, and *sinnie*, but there is little doubt that, for the most part, they developed specific senses in relation to kilns only after the Gaelic words had become part of the general Scots vocabulary. They do not suggest west to east influence. On the other hand, the *sticil mhòr* of Wester Ross and *stic(ean)* of Mid Perthshire show incipient east to west movement, but only in relation to kiln elements that were standard in all areas.

Much more important for the early history of the subject and as a clue to ethnic movement and the diffusion of elements of material culture is the spread of a term such as *sòrn* far beyond the bounds of the country. This Celtic word, of Latin origin, phonologically naturalised in pre-Viking times, has been adopted as the name for a corn-drying kiln in Western Norway, the Faroes, and Iceland, and it is hard to avoid suspecting that the adoption of the name went with the adoption of the material object, and that this is part of the contribution of the Celtic West to the North Sea and Atlantic cultural area. The fourteenth century Icelandic kiln exists in this instance to support the theory suggested by the linguistic data. At the same time, few or no terms are demonstrably directly Norse in origin.

Numerous problems have also been raised in the course of this study, for example, in relation to the differences in terminology between Orkney and Shetland. This must again adumbrate a historical situation, which remains to be further investigated through other methods of approach. Equally, the wealth of Gaelic terms is itself a problem, which only the completion of the eagerly awaited historical Gaelic dictionary will help to resolve.

In using dictionaries, it is necessary to remember always that just as a conclusion is never better than its premise, so is a definition never better than the data on which it is based. No one is infallible, and though a reasoned guess based on inadequate evidence may often be better than none at all, it nevertheless remains a guess. There are many occasions, known to no one better than to lexicographers themselves, when certainty is impossible. At the same time, it will often be necessary to seek for non-linguistic means of establishing more closely what a particular term really covers at a particular period. Dictionaries must always be used critically, but if this is done, the chronological and spatial dimensions of some aspect of the human social or cultural fabric will readily appear from dictionary entries, given that the sources have been adequate, and can be set in comparative relationship with data from the dictionaries of other areas and other countries.

The historical skeleton thus obtained can be mounted and its joints provisionally strung together, and the flesh can be filled in through non-linguistic methods of investigation. Words and language occupy with right a main position in historical research, for by their means the accumulation and transmission of knowledge is made possible, and without them each generation would be faced with the new creation of a great part of its social fabric. The record of this most essential of all man-made tools is in the dictionaries, as a ready-made index to historical change and a means of historical interpretation. There is no doubt in my mind that training in the use of dictionaries should be a normal and standard feature of training in the methodology of historical research.

*Acknowledgment*

I am indebted to Miss Helen Jackson for drawing the diagrams.

ALEXANDER FENTON

# References

Aitken, A. J., 'Completing the Record of Scots', in *Scottish Studies*, viii, pt. 2 (1964).

Aitken, A. J., 'Historical Dictionaries and the Computer', in R. A. Wisbey, ed., *The Computer in Literary and Linguistic Research* (C.U.P., 1971).

Aitken, A. J., 'The Present State of Scottish Language Studies', in *Scottish Literary News*, ii, nos. 2 and 3 (March, 1972).

Campbell, J. L. (ed.), *Gaelic Words and Expressions from South Uist and Eriskay, collected by Rev. Fr. Allan McDonald of Eriskay* (1859–1905) (Dublin Institute for Advanced Studies, 1958).

Craigie, W., 'New Dictionary Schemes presented to the Philological Society, 4th April 1919', in *Transactions of the Philological Society*, 1925–30 (London, 1931).

Craigie, W. A. and Aitken, A. J., *A Dictionary of the Older Scottish Tongue from the Twelfth Century to the end of the Seventeenth* (Chicago and Oxford, 1931–).

Curle, A. O., 'A Viking Settlement at Freswick, Caithness', in *Proceedings of the Society of Antiquaries of Scotland*, lxxviii (1939).

Dinneen, P. S., *An Irish–English Dictionary*. Dublin, 1927.

Dwelly, E., *The Illustrated Gaelic–English Dictionary*. Glasgow, 1901–11 (5th edn, 1949).

Fairbairn, A., 'Notes on Excavations of prehistoric and later Sites at Muirkirk', in *Proceedings of the Society of Antiquaries of Scotland*, lxi (1927).

Fenton, A. Review of *A Dictionary of the Older Scottish Tongue*, Parts XIX–XXI, 1961–4, in *Scottish Studies*, x, pt. 2 (1966).

Firth, J., *Reminiscences of an Orkney Parish* (Stromness, 1920).

Gailey, A., 'Irish Corn-Drying Kilns', in *Studies in Folklife Presented to Emyr Estyn Evans* (*Ulster Folklife*, xv–xvi, 1970).

Gestsson, G., Gröf i Öræfum, in *Árbok hins Islenska Fornleifafélags*, 1959.

Grant, W. and Murison, D., *The Scottish National Dictionary, designed partly on regional lines and partly on historical principles, and containing all the Scottish words known to be in use or to have been in use since c. 1700* (Edinburgh, 1931–).

Hamilton, J. R. C., *Excavations at Jarlshof, Shetland* (Edinburgh, 1956).

Hamre, H., *Ferøers Beskrifvelser*, af Thomas Tarnovius, in *Færoensia*, ii (1950).

Jackson, K. H., *Language and History in Early Britain* (Edinburgh, 1953).

Jakobsen, J., *An Etymological Dictionary of the Norse Language in Shetland* (London and Copenhagen, 1928).

Jamieson, J., *Etymological Dictionary of the Scottish Language* (1802, 1825).

Lockwood, W. B., 'An Introduction to Modern Faroese', in *Færoensia*, iv (1955).

Macdonald, D., 'Some Rare Gaelic Words and Phrases', in *Transactions of the Gaelic Society of Inverness*, xxxvii (1934).

Macdonald, K. D., 'The Gaelic Language, Its Study and Development', in Thomson, D. S. and Grimble, I., edd, *The Future of the Highlands* (London, 1968).

Macinnes, D., 'Notes on Gaelic Technical Terms', in *Transactions of the Gaelic Society of Inverness*, xix (1893–4).

Matheson, A., ed., *Carmina Gadelica*, vol. vi: Indices (Edinburgh and London, 1971).

Matras, Chr., ed., *Dictionarium Færoense. Færøsk-dansk-latinsk ordbog*, af J. C. Svabo in *Færoensia*, vii (1966).

Murray, J. A. H., Bradley, H., Craigie, W. A., Onions, C. T., *A New English Dictionary on Historical Principles* (Oxford, 1888–1933: re-issued 1933 as *The Oxford English Dictionary*).

Rasmussen, H., Korntørring og Tærskning på Færøerne, in *Kuml* (1955).

Ropeid, A., s.v. Brygging, in *Kulturhistorisk Lexikon för Nordisk Medeltid*, ii (1957), 279.

Talve, I., s.v. Kölna, in *Kulturhistorisk Lexikon för Nordisk Medeltid*, x (1965).

Warrack, A., *A Scots Dialect Dictionary* (London, 1911, reprint, 1930).

Whitaker, I., 'Two Hebridean Corn-kilns', in *Gwerin*, i, pt. 4 (1957), 161–70.

Williamson, K., *The Atlantic Islands* (London, 1948).

Wright, J., *The English Dialect Dictionary being the Complete Vocabulary of all dialect words still in use, or known to have been in use during the last two hundred years* (London, 1898–1905).

# 20

# Bibliography of the Works of Ronald Gordon Cant

1938  The future of St Andrews, what preservation means. *Scots Magazine*, N.S. xxix (1938), 339–47.

The University and the preservation of St Andrews. *Alumnus Chronicle* [of St Andrews University], No. 23 (1938), 6–11.

Review: *Shrines and Homes of Scotland* by Sir John Stirling-Maxwell. London, 1937. *Quarterly Illustrated of the Royal Incorporation of Architects in Scotland*, No. 31 (1938), 29–31.

1939  The University a hundred years ago. With T. M. Knox. *Alumnus Chronicle* [of St Andrews University], No. 25 (1939), 7–12.

1941  The Making of the Nation. *Britain and its people*. 1. Oliver & Boyd.

1942  Scottish History: A General Review. *Scotland and its people*, ed. J. N. Wright and N. S. Snodgrass, 1. Oliver & Boyd.

1943  Old St Andrews: The Handbook of the St Andrews Preservation Trust (ed.). St Andrews Preservation Trust Limited. (Re-printed 1944)

1944  Old St Andrews (ed.). 2nd edition.

1945  Old St Andrews (ed.). 3rd edition.

Scottish 'Paper Universities'. *The Scots Magazine*, N.S. xliii (1945), 415–23; N.S. xliv (1945), 39–48.

1946  The University of St Andrews: A Short History. Oliver & Boyd.

Georgian and Early Victorian St Andrews: An Illustrated Survey. St Andrews Preservation Trust Limited.

Old Elgin: A Description of Old Buildings, Illustrated with Photographs and a map. With Ian G. Lindsay. Oliver & Boyd.

The St Andrews University Theses 1579–1747: a bibliographical introduction. *Edinburgh Bibliographical Society Transactions*, ii (1946), 105–50; 263–72.

1947  Old Glasgow: A Description of Old Buildings, Illustrated with Photographs, Plans and a Map. With Ian G. Lindsay. Oliver & Boyd.

Old St Andrews (ed.). 4th edition.

The University portraits. *Alumnus Chronicle* [of St Andrews University], No. 28 (1947), 13–17

1948   Old Moray: A Description of Old Buildings, Illustrated with Photographs, Two Plans, and a Map. Oliver & Boyd.

Old Stirling: A Description of Old Buildings, Illustrated with Photographs, Plans, and Diagrams. With Ian G. Lindsay. Oliver & Boyd.

The North of Fife: its natural beauty and historic interest. *Rothmill Quarterly*, xx (1948), 6–9.

The Kirk and College of St Leonard. *Alumnus Chronicle* [of St Andrews University], No. 30 (1948), 19–25.

Review: *The Founding of Marischal College* by G. D. Henderson (Aberdeen University Studies, No. 123), Aberdeen, 1947. *English Historical Review*, lxiii (1948), 403.

1949   Cathedral life in medieval Scotland, with special reference to the Cathedral Kirk and Chanonry of Brechin. *Book of the Society of Friends of Brechin Cathedral* No. 2 (1949), 4–7.

Review: *Art in Scotland* by Ian Finlay. London, 1948; *Vision of Scotland* by G. S. Fraser. London, 1948. *The Architectural Review*, cvi (1949), 333–4.

1950   The College of St Salvator: Its Foundation and Development, Including a Selection of Documents. (St Andrews University Publications, xlvii). Oliver & Boyd.

John Major *and* Men of Affairs. In *Veterum Laudes* ed. J. B. Salmond. (St Andrews University Publications, xlviii), Chapter III, 21–31, *and* Chapter X, 188–205.

The History of the Mace. In *The Mace of the School of Medicine of the University of St Andrews* (ed. J. B. Salmond), 5–7. St Andrews University.

The Five Hundredth Anniversary of the Foundation of St Salvator's College. *Alumnus Chronicle* [of St Andrews University], No. 33 (1950), 18–22.

Review: *William Kelly: a tribute offered by the University of Aberdeen.* ed. W. D. Simpson. (Aberdeen University Studies, 125), Aberdeen, 1949. *Scottish Historical Review*, xxix (1950), 117–18.

1951   St Andrews: Its Character and Tradition (ed.) St Andrews Preservation Trust Limited.

1952   Moray in Scottish History. Elgin Society.

The constitution of the University in the early eighteenth century *and* The buildings of St Leonard's College in the early eighteenth century. In *Two students at St Andrews, 1711–1716*, by W. C. Dickinson. (St Andrews University Publications, L), Appendix III, pp. lxviii–lxxii, *and* Appendix IV, pp. lxxiii–lxxvi.

Reconsecration of St Leonard's Chapel. *The Scotsman*, 5 Nov., 1952, 10.

1953    The Churches of St Leonard at St Andrews. With W. L. Coulthard. *Church Service Society Annual*, xxiii (1953), 18–21.

Review: *Illustrated guide to ancient monuments in the ownership or guardianship of the Ministry of Works, Volume VI: Scotland* by V. G. Childe and W. D. Simpson, Edinburgh, 1952. *Scottish Historical Review*, xxxii (1953), 173–4.

1954    OLD ELGIN. Revised and enlarged edition.

OLD DUNKELD – [Appeal pamphlet]. National Trust for Scotland.

1955    ST LEONARD'S CHAPEL, ST ANDREWS: THE KIRK AND COLLEGE OF ST LEONARD: A SHORT ACCOUNT OF THE BUILDING AND ITS HISTORY. Council of the United College.

OLD ST ANDREWS (ed.) 5th edition.

Review: *The University of Glasgow, 1451–1951: a short history* by J. D. Mackie, Glasgow, 1954. *College Courant* [of Glasgow University] No. 14, (1955), 64–6.

1956    ST ANDREWS UNIVERSITY CALENDAR. Revised and re-edited, with R. C. Johnson.

History and constitution of the University. In *St Andrews University Calendar*, 1956–57, 81–120. [and subsequent issues.]

1958    ST LEONARD'S CHAPEL, ST ANDREWS. 2nd edition. (Re-printed 1962 and 1967.)

Review: *King's College, Aberdeen*, by F. C. Eeles. (Aberdeen University Studies, No. 136), Aberdeen, 1956. *Scottish Historical Review*, xxxvii (1958), 163–5.

1959    HISTORIC CRAIL AND ITS PRESERVATION. Crail Preservation Society.

1960    Review: *A History of the Scottish Reformation*, by J. D. Mackie. Edinburgh 1960. *Library Review*, xvii (1959–60), 530.

1962    THE EAST NEUK OF FIFE AND ITS PRESERVATION: an illustrated survey of its burghs and countryside. East Neuk of Fife Preservation Society.

Academic dress [of the University of St Andrews]. *St Andrews University. An historical exhibition*, 30–33.

1963    ST ANDREWS PRESERVATION TRUST: A SURVEY OF ITS WORK DURING TWENTY-FIVE YEARS. St Andrews Preservation Trust Limited.

1965    CENTRAL AND NORTH FIFE: an illustrated survey of its landscape and architecture. Central and North Fife Preservation Society.

Moray in Scottish History. In *The Third Statistical Account of Scotland: The Counties of Moray and Nairn* (ed. H. Hamilton), Chapter II, 49–55.

St Andrews street names, I. *St Andrews Preservation Trust Annual Report and Yearbook for 1964*, xxvii (1965), 12–14.

Review: *Historical Essays 1600–1750, presented to David Ogg*, ed. H. E. Bell and R. L. Ollard. London, 1963. *Scottish Historical Review*, xliv (1965), 161–4.

Review: *The fusion of 1860. A record of the centenary celebrations and a history of the United University of Aberdeen. 1860–1960.* (Aberdeen University Studies, 146.), Edinburgh, 1963. *Scottish Historical Review*, xliv (1965), 187.

1966    St Andrews street names, II. *St Andrews Preservation Trust Annual Report and Yearbook for 1965*, xxviii (1966), 12–14.

Review: *Scotland: James V – James VII. The Edinburgh History of Scotland*, vol. iii, by Gordon Donaldson. Edinburgh, 1965. *Scottish Historical Review*, xlv (1966), 207–10.

1967    HISTORIC CRAIL: AN ILLUSTRATED SURVEY OF THE HISTORY AND ARCHITECTURE OF THE ROYAL BURGH AND PARISH. Crail Preservation Society.

St Andrews: The Handbook of the St Andrews Preservation Trust to the City and its Buildings. St Andrews Preservation Trust Limited.

The Scottish Universities and Scottish society in the eighteenth century. *Studies on Voltaire and the Eighteenth Century.* lviii (1967), 1953–66.

St Andrews architects, I. *St Andrews Preservation Trust Annual Report and Yearbook for 1966.* xxix (1967), 12–17.

1968    THE EAST NEUK OF FIFE: AN ILLUSTRATED SURVEY OF ITS BURGHS AND COUNTRYSIDE. Revised and enlarged edition.

ST ANDREWS PRESERVATION TRUST: A SURVEY OF ITS WORK DURING THIRTY YEARS. St Andrews Preservation Trust Limited.

Historical development of the Tayside Region in the Middle Ages. In *Dundee and District* ed. S. J. Jones, 153–61.

St Andrews architects, II. *St Andrews Preservation Trust Annual Report and Yearbook for 1967*, xxx (1968), 12–17.

Obituary: Emeritus Professor W. L. Lorimer. *Alumnus Chronicle* [of St Andrews University], No. 59 (1968), 4–5.

1969    The West Port of St Andrews. *St Andrews Preservation Trust Annual Report and Yearbook for 1968*, xxxi (1969), 12–16.

1970    THE UNIVERSITY OF ST ANDREWS: A SHORT HISTORY. New and revised edition. (St Andrews University Publications, No. lix). Scottish Academic Press.

ST LEONARD'S CHAPEL, ST ANDREWS. 3rd edition. (Re-printed 1973).

The Scottish Universities in the seventeenth century. *The P. J. Anderson Memorial Lecture, 1969. Aberdeen University Review*, xliii (1970), 223–33.

The restoration of Holy Trinity Church, St Andrews, 1907–1909. *St Andrews Preservation Trust Annual Report and Yearbook for 1969*, xxxii (1970), 12–16.

Professor Baxter. *Alumnus Chronicle* [of St Andrews University], No. 61 (1970), 13–14.

Review: *Mary, Queen of Scots* by Antonia Fraser. London, 1969. *Scottish Historical Review*, xlix (1970), 203–4.

Review: *The Historic Architecture of Scotland* by J. G. Dunbar. London, 1966. *Scottish Studies*, xiv (1970), 198–9.

1971    St Salvator's Chapel, St Andrews, The College and Collegiate Kirk of St Salvator: A Short Account of the Building and its History. St Andrews University.

St Andrews: The Handbook of the St andrews Preservation Trust to the City and its Buildings. Revised edition.

The development of the burgh of St Andrews in the Middle Ages. *St Andrews Preservation Trust Annual Report and Yearbook for 1970*, xxxiii (1971), 12–16.

1972    The church in Orkney and Shetland and its relations with Norway and Scotland in the Middle Ages. *Northern Scotland*, i (1972), 1–18.

Shetland Buildings of the Middle Ages. *The New Shetlander*, No. 100 (1972), 30–2.

The Blackfriars and Greyfriars of St Andrews. *St Andrews Preservation Trust Annual Report and Yearbook for 1971*, xxxiv (1972), 12–16.

Review: *The Man behind Macbeth and other studies* by Sir James Fergusson of Kilkerran, London, 1969. *Scottish Historical Review*, li (1972), 75–6.

1973    The archbishopric of St Andrews: a quincentennial retrospect. *St Andrews Preservation Trust Annual Report and Yearbook for 1972*, xxxv (1973), 12–17.

Obituary: Professor James Houston Baxter. *Alumnus Chronicle* [of St Andrews University], No. 64 (1973), 69–70.

*In the press:*
Medieval Churches and Chapels of Shetland. Lerwick.

Academic Dress and Ceremonial of the University of St Andrews, St Andrews.

DUGALD MACARTHUR.

# Donors and Subscribers

R. J. Adam
J. W. L. Adams
Miss Helen Alexander
J. C. L. Anderson
Janet F. S. Anderson (Mrs Butler)
Mrs Marjorie O. Anderson
J. A. K. Angus
John McNicoll Archer
Mrs Caroline E. V. Armstrong
Dr Marinell Ash
Vivian J. W. Auster
Andrew Bain
Miss Cecilia L. G. Baird
Miss M. M. Baird
John Bannerman
G. W. S. Barrow
Miss E. R. Barty
David W. Bayne
William Beattie
Mrs Frances Bennie
Ernest Best
Kristian Bjerknes
Mrs M. Black
Matthew Black
Sheila E. Blair (Mrs Weaver)
Miss Janka Blatt
Alan M. Boase
W. B. Borthwick
Ronald W. Brash
E. V. K. Brill
Mrs Anne Brocklehurst
Robert Brodie
N. P. Brooks
Mrs Jennifer M. Brown
Miss M. P. Brown
J. W. Buchanan and Mrs Buchanan
Mrs Julia M. Buckroyd
J. M. Buist
D. R. R. Burt
Lionel Butler
Mrs M. S. J. Byrde
Miss Penelope Byrde

James K. Cameron and Mrs Cameron
Ian Campbell
William I. P. Campbell
R. H. Carnie
Miss Florence Carstairs
Gordon Christie and Mrs Christie
Miss S. Aylwin Clark
Mrs E. Ritchie Clark
A. H. LeQ. Clayton
Dr Isobel J. Cochrane
G. A. Collie
D. C. Cook
Roy J. A. Cook and Mrs Cook
A. R. Cooper
B. G. Cooper
E. T. Copson
Charles S. Coventry
Ian B. Cowan
Miss Brenda J. Cowper
The Earl of Crawford
R. M. M. Crawford and Mrs Crawford
Michael Crichton Stuart
T. W. Cubitt and Mrs Cubitt
Miss Anna F. Cunningham
Alexander Cuthbert
Miss Ruth D'Arcy Thompson
R. A. McL. Davidson
James C. Davie
Janet B. S. Davie (Mrs Robinson)
Gerald E. Dempsey
Rona Denny (Mrs Korycinska)
David D. Dick
Edgar P. Dickie and Mrs Dickie
David Dickinson and Mrs Dickinson
John di Folco
G. M. Dilworth
Brian G. H. Ditcham
Ian G. Docherty
Ronald P. Doig
Sister Dominic Savio
Gordon Donaldson
Robert Donaldson

D. P. Dorward and Mrs Dorward
R. Douglas
K. J. Dover
H. I. Drever
D. I. Duff
J. G. Dunbar
Miss Nan V. Dunbar
A. A. M. Duncan
Mrs Muriel Duncan
Mrs Annie I. Dunlop
S. T. Dunstan and Mrs Dunstan
John Durkan
Albert Edwards
A. S. Eggo
Miss K. M. Fairweather
A. F. Falconer
Miss Catherine C. Falconer
Ian G. S. Ferrier
D. M. Finlayson
Gerard Follon
D. A. R. Forrester
W. R. Forrester
Kenneth C. Fraser
A. R. B. Fuller
Robert S. Fyall
Dr Janet Helen Garrow
N. Gash
Clarke Geddes
Douglas J. Gifford
John M. Gilbert
Sheridan Gilley
L. Goddard
Arthur D. Gollifer
Hugh Gordon
Mrs F. M. Grace
Mrs Beryl Graham
Douglas Grant
George Gray
Miss J. Gray
J. Grimond and Mrs Grimond
Miss Margaret L. S. Grubb
Miss F. Doreen Gullen
J. C. Hall
Miss Lisbeth R. Hall
Mrs Agnes M. Halliday
Miss M. Hamilton
E. S. Harrison
Vernon J. Harward and Mrs Harward

Denys Hay
Mrs R. M. Hedderwick
A. Bruce Henderson and Mrs Henderson
Hamish Henderson
T. A. Henderson
Mrs Louise Hood
D. R. A. Hotchkis
J. M. Howie
R. L. C. Hunter
Maximo Huzarewicz
D. Jack and Mrs Jack
W. Murray Jack
A. A. Jackson
Miss Dorothy J. Jackson
Joan Jamieson (Mrs Horsley)
Miss Jessie D. Kay
Miss Ann A. Kaye
A. A. Kean
T. W. Kean
A. Kennedy
Miss C. D. M. Ketelbey
Miss Ann J. Kettle
I. G. Kidd
James Kidd
Miss A. A. Kidston
Miss M. H. Kidston
Russell Kirk
Thomas Kirkwood
Sir T. M. Knox
R. P. W. Kup
Edward P. Kyle
Eileen M. Laing (Mrs Young)
Dr Margaret E. R. Lang
Mrs Alison Langiert
John Law
Ian R. Lawson
Mrs M. S. S. Lawson
Miss M. Ann Ledwith
Maurice Lee Jr
Professor M. Dominica Legge
Bruce Lenman
Dr Magdalene Linton
Herbert M. Lord and Mrs Lord
Hew Lorimer
R. C. Lorimer
Andrew Lothian
Ian C. Low
K. G. Lowe

S. G. E. Lythe
D. MacArthur
Miss J. S. A. Macaulay
D. M. McCall and Mrs McCall
Anne T. MacDonald (Mrs Murley)
Miss Florence Macdonald
Mrs M. A. Macdonald
Mrs Agnes C. Macdonald
J. A. Macdonald
Stuart McDowall
Mrs Gordon L. MacEwen
Colin R. G. MacFarlane
Leslie J. Macfarlane
Miss M. McGraw
Allan I. MacInnes
Dr K. M. MacIver
Miss R. J. MacKechnie
Mrs Agnes W. McKenzie
Norman McLean
Mrs Marjorie D. C. MacNab
Peter G. B. McNeill
Archibald C. MacPherson
Miss F. E. M. Macpherson
Miss Jean McPherson
David McRoberts
Mrs D. MacWatt
Dr Rosalind K. Marshall
Stuart Maxwell
R. S. May
B. Mayo
T. C. Mendenhall
Mrs J. C. G. Mercer
Miss M. F. Michie
F. S. Miles
David Mill
Mrs J. W. Miller
Dr Doreen J. Milne
Miss Isobel M. Milne
A. G. Mitchell
Mrs R. M. Mitchison
Mrs Marie Louise Moffett
Mrs B. Moir
Miss Jessie L. Moir
Miss P. S. M. Mugliston
R. W. Munro and Mrs Munro
Athol L. Murray
Peter J. Murray
L. Nash

Miss Mary P. Nicol
W. F. H. Nicolaisen
Mrs I. M. Nicoll
David Niven
Miss J. S. Oliver
Miss M. E. Osman
D. D. R. Owen
William Park
L. C. Parke
Alexander B. Paterson
J. H. Paterson
Elspeth S. Paton (Mrs Grant)
David Pattullo
Miss Nan Pattullo
Mrs D. M. C. Paulin
W. C. G. Peterkin and Mrs Peterkin
William S. Pickard
Willis Pickard
Mrs Joan Pipe
H. Burton Pirie and Mrs Pirie
Miss Eleanor M. Playfair
J. M. Playfair
John Prebble
G. L. Pride
J. Linda Proom (Mrs Drury)
James Emery Pryde
R. W. B. Purvis and Mrs Purvis
Thomas I. Rae
W. E. K. Rankin
Mrs I. Read
Miss Betty G. R. Reid
Mrs Shirley Richardson
Miss A. M. Robertson
Alex G. Robertson
Miss E. B. S. Robertson
Mrs M. Robertson
Iain M. Rose
Angus Ross
Ian Ross
D. F. O. Russell
Mrs J. M. Russell
Dr Margaret H. B. Sanderson
A. A. B. Scott
Alfred G. Scott
J. L. H. Scott
M. G. Scott
W. W. Scott
Miss M. C. Scott Moncrieff

Miss N. L. Scrymgeour
Geoffrey Seed
Henry R. Sefton
W. D. H. Sellar
Duncan Shaw
Grant G. Simpson
John M. Simpson
Miss Mary E. Skeldon
B. C. Skinner
Mrs H. R. Skinner
R. N. Smart and Mrs Smart
A. Smith and Mrs Smith
C. P. C. Smith
David B. Smith
Miss Ella M. Smith
Martin S. Smith
Richard N. W. Smith
Catherine M. Snell (Mrs Fraser)
George A. Spater
Miss Dorothy J. Steele
Dr Ettie S. Steele
John Steer
Geoffrey Stell
Hugh L. M. Stewart
James C. Stewart
Archibald S. Strachan
Adam Rennie
J. Sullivan
Miss Margaret Tait
Margaret Tainsh (Mrs Maggs)
Mrs Mary G. Templeton
J. Thompson
Arthur Thomson
John M. Todd
Mrs Elizabeth P. Torrie
Miss Jean R. Trimmer
Mrs Christian J. Tudhope
Bruce M. Tulloch and Mrs Tulloch (Jill Gourlay)

Mrs R. J. Tweedie
Mrs Jean B. Tynte
R. M. Urquhart
Graeme Verden-Anderson
N. M. L. Walker and Mrs Walker
Miss Lorna E. M. Walker
R. Walmsley
D. E. R. Watt
Bruce Webster
A. G. Wernham
N. R. Whitty
James A. Whyte
I. D. Willock
Mrs Peter B. Willis
Mrs E. C. Willsher
R. McL. Wilson
Donald J. Withrington
Roy Wood
L. J. Woodward
Victor L. Worsfold
Christopher Wright
Mrs Mary N. Wright
Peter A. H. Wyatt
Douglas Young
Miss Margaret D. Young

Dunblane Cathedral Museum
Glasgow City Archives
Glasgow University Library
Kirkcaldy Technical College Library
Pennsylvania University Library
Massachusetts University Library
Riksantikvaren, Oslo
Royal and Ancient Golf Club
Smith College, Nielson Library
St Andrews University Library
St Andrews University Student Union
Stirling University Library